Political Justice in the USSR:
Dissent and Repression
in Lithuania, 1969–1987

Thomas A. Oleszczuk

EAST EUROPEAN MONOGRAPHS, BOULDER
DISTRIBUTED BY COLUMBIA UNIVERSITY PRESS, NEW YORK

1988

EAST EUROPEAN MONOGRAPHS, NO. CCXLVII

Copyright © 1988 by Thomas Oleszczuk
ISBN 0-88033-144-5
Library of Congress Catalog Card Number 88-80382

Printed in the United States of America

In Memory of Michael Gelfand

Contents

Preface

Politics centers on change. Those desiring it struggle to accomplish it; those wishing stability, oppose them. Communism is no different. Only the forms, rates, and mechanisms of change are unfamiliar to Westerners. The Soviet Union in the last three years has seen more change than in the previous twenty-five. The transformations are rooted in political conflict, personal ambition, and systemic/structural imperatives.

For the past decade and a half, I have studied the processes of change under communism. Liberalization in Yugoslavia and dissent in Eastern Europe have particularly been my concerns. From this work, I drew the conclusion that the Soviet Union plays both limiting and catalytic roles in its sphere of influence. It was also clear that state mechanisms are used to control opponents. This led me to the analysis of the state apparatus in the Soviet Union.

This book emerged from a pilot study for a larger empirical project on Soviet repression. The fruit of that project has begun to ripen, with articles appearing on arrests and foreign trade, and on regime treatment of artists (with TC Smith and MJ Wyszomirski). Further work will involve analysis of psychiatric abuse, nationalities, and other topics in a book we are developing.

This book also has more practical significance. I am convinced that the repressive operations of the USSR are important for the Soviet future, and for ours. Many actions of a state against its citizenry now violate international law. The issue of human rights is covered by increasing numbers of covenants in ever more specific detail. As world citizens, our interests now expand to include those of countries far away and unclear to us. It is in this spirit that I present this work.

Among those many who played a role in the creation of this book, there are a few whom I would like specifically to thank, with the understanding that I alone am responsible for errors of interpretation. I would like to acknowledge my intellectual debt to Dr. Peter R. Reddaway, Director of the Kennan Institute, the Smithsonian Institution; and Dr. Rudolf L. Tokes, Department of Political Science,

University of Connecticut, for the concepts and awareness of the need for systematic information on dissent and repression.

My graduate professors at the University of Wisconsin taught me the need for data and the appropriate degree of the statistical analysis thereof. Even some of them may quibble with the absence of highly technical statistical tests of signficance in the body of the text of this book, but I preferred to look to "substantive" significance, and to avoid cluttering up further a work already full of numbers with such tests. (For those who are interested, the overwhelming majority of the tables are "significant" at very high levels, $p = .001$ or better, most of the rest at the "normal" $p = .05$.)

Important access to library archives and emigres was provided by Ms. Ginte Damusis and Father Casimir Pugavicius, of the Lithuanian Information Center (Brooklyn, New York); Mrs. Margarita Samatas, the Lithuanian National Foundation (formerly VLIKo Lithuanian Information Service, ELTA; Washington, DC); Mr. A. Bagdonas, the Society for the Publication of the Chronicles of the Catholic Church in Lithuania, Inc. (Chicago); the Reverends Michael Bourdeaux and Michael Rowe, Keston College (Kent, England); and Ms. Barbara Futterman, Freedom House (New York City), whose enthusiastic help with data and networking went beyond the call of duty.

Research aid was provide by Ms. Cyndi Beaver and Mr. Neal Knudsen, who collected data from Keston College archives during a summer trip to England and who were otherwise quite helpful with clerical tasks. The staff at the Rutgers University Hill Computer Center were necessary guides through the circles of computing fire-and-brimstone, and the Rutgers University Research Council provided limited funds for computer work, xeroxing, and office supplies.

Reading and editing the manuscript itself were cheerfully done by Drs. C. Richard Lehne (Rutgers University), TC Smith (Mankato State University), and Robert Sharlet (Union College/Columbia University). The work is a far better piece thanks to their efforts.

For *not* asking when the book would be done over the years, I would like to thank my family and friends. Finally, for reading the work many times, for making stimulating and mostly pertinent criticisms and suggestions, and for staying around through it all despite various disasters, I am eternally endebted to my wife, Jo Lorraine Sotheran.

T. O.
New Brunswick, New Jersey
May 1988

1

Law and Politics
in the Soviet Union

"The state is the coldest of all cold monsters."
—*Nietzsche*[1]

" . . . legality will continue to be not only a matter of crucial importance
in everyday Soviet life, but also a master key to Soviet politics."
—*Harold Berman*[2]

In the winter of 1981, an elderly priest was walking in downtown
Vilnius when several men sudddenly pushed him in front of an
oncoming truck. Despite the witnesses who saw the attack and public
outrage among parishioners and non-parishioners, no one was ever
arrested for the crime.[3] A year earlier, the police had entered the
apartment of a young woman, found several pages and carbons of
an unauthorized religious newsletter near her typewriter, and arrested
her. Based on this evidence, she was sentenced to one and a half
years of corrective labor in a Siberian labor camp.[4] Official com-
mentators claim that the Soviet judicial system provides full protection
for citizen rights and the prompt removal of criminals from society,
but these two incidents demonstrate that the system does not always
perform as claimed. Reports smuggled out to the West indicate that
the rights of dissenters are not fully protected and that crimes against
them frequently go unpunished.

This book is a study of the legal treatment of dissidents in Lithuania,
where those incidents occurred. Soviet treatment of dissidents is usually
depicted as dull-witted and unchanging, but this analysis of political
and religious dissent demonstrates that reality is more complex. In
the post-war period, the Soviet judicial system has differentiated
among types of dissent and matched well-defined institutional responses to differing patterns of conduct. The courts and the secret
police have been used to stop the rise of mass movements, undermine

1

potential opposition to Soviet Communist Party, and preempt any
challenge to the Soviet state, but strategies and tactics have shifted
over the years as new political leaders have emerged and new political
problems gained prominence.

Most Western studies of dissent and repression focus on "elite"
dissidents and rely for their evidence on samizdat, the "self-published"
accounts of dissenters. The emphasis on well-known cases, such as
Solzhenitsyn, Sakharov, and Medvedev, has distracted attention from
broader patterns of repression and created a Western impression that
Soviet dissent is a Moscow-based, intellectual movement.[5]The rare
empirical studies of dissent do provide a fuller portrait of dissent,[6]
but these studies tend to neglect the historical, institutional, and social
dynamics of dissent and repression.

These problems are specifically addressed by the recent literature
on "social history"—not previously considered relevant for the study
of dissent and repression—in which the ordinary lives of common
people are the center of attention.[7] The problems with the addition
of information on less well-known aspects of the lives of relatively
unknown people include trivialization through numbers, underem-
phasis on leadership, blindness to systemic causation and forces of
social change and stability; and at times, de facto overgeneralization
to all places and times from single case studies.

This study attempts to avoid all these problems by viewing dissent
and repression, not as individual tragedies (which, of course, they
are) but as parts of the understandable, but complicated reality of
Soviet politics. This work incorporates both elite and mass "data,"
combines the perspectives of two models of Soviet law, and emphasizes
systemic interpretations of social events. It views citizen experience
with the legal system not as idiosyncratic events but as a product of
the evolving relationship between the state and the forces of dissent.

Theme and Plan

Dissent in Lithuania has been remarkably resilient in the post-war
years, and campaigns of repression have achieved only temporary,
limited success. Instead of quieting the disturbances, political use of
the courts has "educated" dissidents in the ways of the state and
aggravated the situation which the regime was seeking to contain. In
the next chapter, we analyze the institutional, historical, and legal
context of Lithuania which has given rise to this pattern of dissent
and repression. The important features of the socio-political environment are examined, the performance of the local components of the
centralized bureaucracy is appraised, and the significance of the history

of social, cultural, and political resistance to Russian influence is assessed.

Following that, the focus narrows from the systemic to the individual, and the population directly affected by repressive policies is described. The analysis demonstrates that dissidents are typically male, Roman Catholic Lithuanians of varying ages who are motivated by varying bases of discontent. We then proceed to follow the "career" of the political prisoner by identifying, first, in Chapter 4, the major actors and stages in the judicial process which select dissidents for further action, and by analyzing, in Chapter 5, the patterns of repression that actually appear. We find that the regime targets nationalists and "hybrid" dissidents, including students, intellectuals, and white collar workers, and that it "filters out" nearly all the priests, most of the females, many of the religious dissidents, and some of the higher status occupations.

In Chapter 6 we explore the conduct of trials and the determinants of sentencing. This chapter appraises the influence of socio-demographic features, type of dissent, and actual "criminal" behavior and it reveals a close relationship between formal charges and final punishment meted out to the dissident. The chapter reveals that cases which involve charges of "especially dangerous crimes against the state" are marked by an astonishing degree of "legality" in sentencing.

In Chapter 7, we demonstrate that historical changes in sentencing are *not* related more closely to changes in political leadership during the Brezhnev era. Instead, we find that the development of the social movement of dissent itself is a primary historical element in the amelioration of sentences and an increasing "tolerance" of dissident behavior. In Chapter 8, we discuss the changes in dissent and repression since the death of Brezhnev. We note the big changes under General Secretary Gorbachev, both in policy and in the struggle in Lithuania. In last chapter we return to the general issues of law and politics in the Soviet Union with some discussion of the future relationships of dissidents and their regime foes.

The Soviet system is not simple, despite the elegant presentations of Carl Friedrich and Zbigniew Brzezinski, David Lane, and others. Soviet law certainly needs more elaboration. Our examination of the operations of legal institutions in cases of political and religious dissent in a Soviet republic demonstrates that political leaders do attempt to control opposition by manipulating the court system, but it also indicates that the leaders must act within a series of constraints. The dissidents themselves possess some resources and the leaders must take care to avoid too great reaction to any particular act of repression. In addition, the judiciary in the Soviet system has many functions, and the importance of these functions leads political leaders to adhere to the sentencing standards of the criminal code.

When the regime seeks to intensify the punishment of dissidents, its respect for sentencing standards leads the regime to alter the charges made against the accused, to add new articles to the criminal codes, or to avoid the courts through "medicalization"—the use of psychiatric detention—but these tactics, in turn, often lead dissidents to increase the activities which the regime had originally sought to quell. Indeed, the process of dissent and repression in the Soviet Union may be seen as a series of "dialectics" involving feedback loops, unintended consequences, and non-obvious limitations, and our analysis ultimately pictures the Soviet regime as far less arbitrary, and certainly less omnipotent, even vis-a-vis its own citizens, than it is often portrayed.

Guiding Concepts

This study of dissent and repression is guided by two models and five concepts that are commonly used to analyze Soviet politics and law. The structural functionalist model aids our analysis by identifying the courts and the police as conceptually distinct institutions of government and by depicting them as agencies which help sustain the overarching structure of the state.

The courts and police have several specific functions. First, they laud and legitimize contemporary Soviet life and instruct Soviet citizens that the state should receive their support. Second, these institutions assist ordinary government administration by punishing non-cooperation and non-compliance with official rules and regulations. Third, the courts resolve interpersonal conflicts and settle inter-factory disputes over economic issues. Finally, the judicial system discourages public support for unusual political views by removing potential leaders to camps and by separating leaders from followers.[8]

This model of Soviet law focuses on the operating routines and the organizational details of legal institutions. It describes the institutions, examines their immediate effects on the world around them, and appraises their overall contribution to the functioning of society. It integrates a micro-level analysis of the activities of legal functionaries with a macro-level appraisal of the structures and processes of the society. The assumptions of structural functional analysis have been elaborated and criticized at length. The model assumes that a social system is internally coherent and that it needs only the performance of certain functions to persist into the future. It also presumes that the social importance of major institutions is based on their contributions to a specified set of activities. This perspective on Soviet law illuminates the forms and "benefits" of legal institutions, but unfortunately it ignores other crucial dimensions of social life. It fails to recognize the dynamics of change embedded in social conflict and the imbalances of power, and, most importantly, it neglects the ways in which the activities of both society and state may shape the activities of the legal system. In contrast, the second model highlights these factors.

The "political process" model views law and legal actors as characters in an ongoing conflict over "who gets what." It focusses on legal decisions made by leadership and functionaries, and it emphasizes dramatic events, differing personalities, and the passage of new laws and policies. Conflicts among leaders, mass-elite conflict, the use of law to protect political positions, and the consequences of political activities for the substance and practice of Soviet law are this model's central concerns.

The political process model makes different assumptions from the structural functional model. Here the law is seen as both the result and the instrument of conflict among leaders. Legal institutions are viewed as tools in the elite struggle among patronage machines within the Soviet party-state apparatus, and they are portrayed as weapons by leaders against those who may or actually do pose challenges to them. The model regards legal institutions as elements of the politics of a country and not as objective, socially neutral structures immune from political pressures. It assumes that legal institutions, like all other institutions in modern systems, are influenced by the various structures of power that exist in a society.[9]

The political process model assumes that the courts and police are important not only for their societal functions, but because they affect the daily lives of ordinary citizens. This model analyses the actual patterns of judicial and police behavior, and it appraises the impact of these institutions on the activities of specific groups and individuals.[10]

This study combines elements of each model. It examines the actual patterns of action and reaction in Lithuania, and it analyses their implications for the legitimacy of the state, the dynamics of social control, and potential support for dissident viewpoints. This study also employs analytical concepts that have made significant contributions to our knowledge of Soviet politics. While these concepts do not contain all knowledge or wisdom on a topic, each has shed some light on some aspect of reality.[11]

First, "totalitarianism" points to coercion, ideology, and a concern to preempt opposition. Second, "bureaucracy" highlights the proliferation of organizational structure, the growth of rules and regulations, the increased specialization of task, and the centrality of struggles among bureaucratic units for scarce resources. Third, the idea of "imperialism" indicates the importance in each situation of the domination of non-Russian peoples by Russians in positions of power. Next, "oligarchy" emphasizes the dispersion of power among the ruling elite and the role that oligarchical conflict plays in mobilizing support within the ruling establishment and possibly beyond. Finally, "industrialization" denotes the possible dependence of a modern economic system on highly trained technocrats, and it suggests that their position might give this group some influence over both policy implementation and policy formation. We will discuss these models in Chapter 9, where we analyze the prospects for the future.

The approach taken in this book combines both the major models of Soviet law *and* elements of each of these concepts of Soviet politics, to yield our notion of the "expanded criminal justice process."[12] The judicial process in political cases is seen as occurring within a complicated socio-political environment, an environment that changes as dissent develops and leadership changes. That environment conditions the activities of those institutions in two ways. It provides opportunities for action by stimulating laws and directives from the leadership about "deviant behavior" and by producing "deviance" in the society at large (including the elite itself). In addition, the environment conditions costs and benefits for certain kinds of actions— again by those in judicial institutions and in the society outside them. Those costs include the penalty of laws and of informal harrassment (and so on), while the benefits include avoidance of such costs as well as possible promotion and even psychological uplift from obedience to authority.

This expanded criminal justice model is commonly found in behavioral studies of Western, and especially the American courts and police,[13] but is rarely encountered in the analysis of the Soviet judicial system. Indeed, it is in the interest of the first steps in comparative analysis of political justice that this book is so structured. It will provide information and a perspective on the courts not found among most Western studies, especially in the area of differential "legality" of sentencing and the linkages of judicial behavior to national leadership changes.

Yet, it is also an intended cross-fertilization of a particularly interesting field of research unknown to most Soviet area specialists. This is especially the case given our use of the concept of "social movement" in analyzing the affected population in Chapter 3. This concept implies some diversity among those who "belong," but suggests that the degree of organization, the kinds of symbols used to mobilize followers, and the distribution of resources among parts of the movement are important subjects for study. This concept thus implies extending the "who gets what and how" of political process to the dissidents themselves, a connection infrequently and incompletely made by Western specialists on Soviet dissent.

In addition, the melding of the differing approaches and concepts allows us to pose fundamental questions about the nature of Soviet law and its place in the Soviet system. For example, we will be able to ask the question (in the last chapter) of the role of constraints on leaders in Soviet politics. Do legal regulations in some sense form a *fabric* of normative bonds on arbitariness? This locates the entire study in the formulation of the now-classic study of Soviet law by Harold Berman,[14] who devoted many pages to distinguishing the concepts of law, laws, justice, and legal institutions.

It might serve us well to repeat in summary form Berman's definitional boundaries. Laws are the products of institutions and form the basis of activity in most modern societies. However, merely because something has been approved by an institution, or more precisely by the leadership in control of that institution, does not mean that such legal prescriptions are part of the accepted norms within any particular country. Indeed, in American political culture, it is a common theme that opposition to a law on substantive grounds is often converted into opposition on the procedural basis that a particular enactment is not part of *the* law because it is "unconstitutional." Although such has not been the case in the Soviet Union, nonetheless, "the law" may be seen to be violated by the behavior of legal agents, as in the post-Stalinist denunciation of the "cult of personality."

In addition, both the law and laws are distinct from the courts and their activities, for the courts can be seen as part of the "judicial apparatus" including the procuracy which is responsible for the correct operations of the courts and the KGB that in turn checks on the political competence and loyalty of both (among other institutions). In turn, the judicial apparatus is part of the overarching structure of government institutions that play a role in the proclamation of regulations and policies, as well as their implementation. That structure is commonly called "the state" and includes economic planners and those others specializing in violence, the "coercive apparatus" (army, police, and intelligence agencies).

This study moves from social context inward to the courts, and then upward toward the state's leadership. However, the analysis will not focus on the meta-political questions of "the law," "natural right," and "justice" in the more general and philosophical sense.

Instead, the underlying question must be to what degree the particular provisions of "the laws" constrain the behavior of masses engaged in political and religious activities unapproved by the elite, and of the institutions of "justice" that are used in dealing with them. The constraints are not assumed: they are demonstrated in the patterns of actions, in the Soviet legal system at work. Yet the existence of any such constraints does change our perception of the Soviet state as an unfettered dictatorship. It raises the possibility of the "rule of law," as well as the possibility of massive unrest if any trends in that direction are suddenly reversed. Thus, this book is about Soviet laws, political criminals, the use of the courts as an instrument of public policy. It is also, ultimately, about the nature of power—as well as law—in a contemporary bureaucratic state.

Notes

1. *Thus Spoke Zarathustra*, translated by R.J. Hollingdale (Baltimore: Penguin Books, 1961), p. 75.

2. Harold J. Berman, "Introduction," in *Soviet Criminal Law and Procedure: The RSFSR Codes*, translated by Harold J. Berman and James W. Spindler (Cambridge, Mass.: Harvard University Press, 1972), p. 89.

3. For more on the death of Father Bronius Laurinavicius, see *Chronicle of the Catholic Church in Lithuania* (hereafter, CCCL), 50: 8–12. For more information about this periodical, cf. the Appendix, below.

4. Ona Vitkauskaite was tried in April 1980, along with Genovaite Navickaite, under similar circumstances. See CCCL, 43: 9–10; 46; *ELTA*, 254: 4; 257: 8–9; 263: 3, 6–7; *Chronicle of Current Events* (Moscow: samizdat), 56:139; and *Chronicle of Human Rights in the USSR* (New York: Khronika Press), 40: 7. Two similar cases occurred in 1973 (Vladas Lapienis) and 1974 (Nijole Sadunaite).

5. For example, even Joshua Rubenstein, *Soviet Dissidents* (Boston: Beacon, 1980).

6. One of the few scholars doing empirical work on this topic is David Kowalewski. See his articles in *Journal of Politics* (no. 42, 1980, *Journal of Baltic Studies* (no. 4, 1979), *Catholic Historical Review* (no. 4, 1981), etc.

7. The following discussion is taken from Michael Kammen, ed., *The Past Before Us* (Ithaca: Cornell University Press, 1980), especially J. Morgan Kousser, "Quantitative Social-Scientific History" (pp. 433–456) and Peter N. Stearns, "Toward a Wider Vision" (pp. 205–230).

8. Among the many works on this subject see Harold J. Berman, *Justice in the USSR* (Cambridge, Mass: Harvard University Press, 1963); Merle Fainsod, *Smolensk Under Soviet Rule* (New York: Vintage, 1958), pp. 197–185; George Ginsburgs, "Soviet International Trade Contracts and the Execution of Foreign

Commercial Arbitral Awards," A.K.R. Kiralfy, "Soviet Labor Law Reform Since the Death of Stalin," and Peter H. Juviler, "Criminal Law and Social Control," all in *Contemporary Soviet Law*, ed. Donald D. Barry, William E. Butler, and George Ginsburgs (The Hague: Martinus Nijhoff, 1974), pp. 195–212, 158–174, and 17–54, respectively; Walter Connor, *Deviance in Soviet Society* (New York: Columbia University Press, 1972).

9. Cf. Robert Conquest, *Justice and the Legal System in the USSR* (New York: Praeger, 1968); Zhores Medvedev, *Let History Judge*, pp. 388–394; Robert Sharlet, "The Communist Party and the Administration of Justice in the USSR," in *Soviet Law After Stalin: Soviet Institutions and the Adminstration of the Law*, ed. Donald B. Barry and others (Germantown, Maryland: Sijthoff and Noordhoff, 1979), pp 362–380; F.J.M. Feldbrugge, "Law and Political Dissent in the Soviet Union," in *Contemporary Soviet Law*, pp. 55–68; Fainsod, e.g., pp. 180–185; Robert Sharlet, "Constitutional Implementation and the Juridicization of the Soviet System," in *Soviet Politics in the Brezhnev Era*, ed. Donald R. Kelley (New York: Praeger, 1980), pp. 200–234; Peter H. Juviler, *Revolutionary Law and Order* (New York: Free Press, 1976), chapter 4; Berman, *Justice in the USSR*, pp. 69–96.

10. This is not to deny the usefulness of studies of legal principles. These works about the underlying axioms of legal codes are of interest in the comparative analysis of human rights protections, for example, by indicating the range of formal descriptions of such rights and by enumerating the kinds of mechanisms implied by the fundamental principles. However, the current work focusses on behavior, rather than norms per se.

11. The following listing of theoretical concepts is borrowed from John S. Reshetar, Jr., *The Soviet Polity*, (New York: Harper, Row: 1978), pp. 336–361.

12. This follows usage related to the expansion involved in "expanded reproduction," "expanded plena," and other common phenomena in socialist systems.

13. Among the numerous texts on the empirical study of crime and the courts, see Sue Titus Reid, *Crime and Criminology* (New York: Holt, Rinehart and Winston, 1982), for example.

14. Berman, *Justice in the USSR.*

2
The Case of Lithuania:
The Socio-Political Context

The Soviet Union is a multi-national, multi-ethnic state occupying parts of two continents. This study focuses on one small republic on the far western edge of the country: Lithuania. While Lithuania possesses a unique configuration of historical, political, and social characteristics, many of the features that condition its processes of dissent and repression occur elsewhere in the USSR. Thus, Lithuania in a sense represents many of the important aspects of the contemporary condition of dissidents which are also found in various other Soviet republics.

Nationalism, Religion, and the Soviet Union

To see the Soviet Union as a nation of Russians is an error of oversimplification. In 1980 barely one half of the 270 million inhabitants of the Union of Soviet Socialist Republics were Russian. The other ethnic groups span a great diversity of languages, religions, cultural heritages, and histories.

The diversity of population itself aggravates several problems. First, there is military security. Most non-Russians live in strategic borderlands adjacent to European and Asian states along which military and political threats have come to the Soviet state, and to its Czarist predecessor. Active non-Russian collaborators welcomed and cooperated with external invaders in both world wars.[1] This problem of loyalty is exacerbated by the common bonds of many ethnic groups to peoples outside the Soviet Union. In Czechoslovakia in 1968, for example, it proved necessary to rotate European Soviet troops out and bring in Asian Soviet troops, a maneuver to some degree being reversed in Afghanistan.

In addition, ethnic diversity exacerbates economic difficulties.[2] The Asiatic non-Russians have much higher birth rates than the European

Soviets, including Russians. This means that they form increasingly the labor pool from which economic growth must be drawn. Yet the Soviet Moslems especially are more rooted in their national areas, less likely to abandon family and village for city life, and are simply less mobile at the same time that the more highly productive European labor pool is more stagnant.

This presents a serious dilemma to the leadership: highly productive but aging European workers are not being replaced in highly productive but aging European factories, while less productive, younger, and rapidly growing Central Asian populations require more social expenditure and rapidly increasing numbers of new jobs. What can be done? The transfer of capital to Central Asia—to use Asian labor in situ—will drain more productive plants of funds needed for modernization, while the transfer of labor to European plants will most likely require massive coercion and end up producing *two* alienated labor forces—Asians who do not wish to be where they are and Europeans who view the culturally different Asians as a threat to their communities.

This economic dilemma is intensified because the economy is imbedded in a global system where there are major political-military competitors, whose power is amplified by high technology. Thus, maintaining economic growth and the full utilization of all resources are necessities for the Soviet Union.

More important, ethnicity presents a political problem of major structural proportions. Nationalism for both Russians and non-Russians alike has not evaporated differences in economic condition may make ethnic conflict the solvent destroying the bonds of the Soviet system. There already have been frequent reports over the last twenty years, even in the censored Soviet press, of secret nationalist groups proliferating among many nationalities: Russian, Ukrainian, Tatar, Baltic, Caucasian, and Jewish. Members of these groups have hijacked airplanes, bombed subways, rioted in republic capitals, and developed extensive illegal networks of communication. Moreover, from time to time there are denunciations and purges of nationalism within the ruling establishment, whether directly or under the guise of "localism" or "corruption." Most strikingly, under Gorbachev many Kazakhs, Armenians, and Azeris have rioted on ethnic grounds.

The distinctiveness of ethnic groups persists despite some tendencies to linguistic and cultural assimilation. In part, the strength of religious feeling—which often reinforces nationalist separateness—provides a long-term base for anti-Russian (or pro-Russian) nationalist sentiments. In part, it is symptomatic of the societal differences in the material position of each group. A major economic downturn, or increasing disparity in the distribution of goods and services might fuel the sparks of ethnic discontent into major challenges to the status quo, as the case of Solidarity in Poland shows.

Thus, it is not surprising that some analysts have viewed the Soviet system as an unstable empire. For example, Helene d'Encausse suggests that the Soviet Union is a state dominated by Russians but potentially explosive because of the rise of non-Russian nationalism "on the periphery." The dominance of Russians in political institutions at the center is reflected in economic disparities, social discrimination, political cultural chauvinism, and repressive policies.[3]

On the other hand, Seweryn Bialer sees the Soviet state as an empire in equilibrium: the "deepest challenge to the legitimacy of the regime" is, for him, successfully dealt with through a variety of policies, including promotion of regional economic development, selective recruitment of minority nationalities into the apparatuses of the border republics, and the limited symbolic recognition of the separateness of the non-Russian nationalities are the instruments of that success.[4]

This ethnic feature of the environment is clearly important to Lithuanian dissent and repression. As we shall see, the history of pre-war independent Lithuania and the post-war Soviet republic is one of anti-Russian political movements. This ethnic distinctiveness is reinforced by religious difference—Lithuanian Roman Catholicism in opposition to Russian Orthodox Christianity—as well as the operations of the repressive apparatus itself.

Then, we will analyze how the Soviet leadership has addressed the problems of nationalism, religion, and dissent. We will describe ideological attacks, dating from Lenin, on ethnic separatism and religion; the major laws of the criminal code to deal specifically with such phenomena; and the centralized institutional arrangements, in part designed to *undermine* the long-term efficacy of nationalist and religious sentiments while at the same time controlling the immediate possibility of their affecting the political system, including the party itself.

The Heritage of Lithuania as a State

Lithuania occupies a modest land area about the size of the state of South Carolina on the coast of the Baltic Sea. The land is not rich—indeed, amber and peat are the two major natural resources. Even today, it is somewhat economically backward: it is among the least industrialized, least urbanized of the European Soviet Republics.

The territory is occupied mostly (80%) by over two million Lithuanians. They speak a language unrelated to either the Slavic or Germanic languages of the peoples of the surrounding area. (It and Latvian belong to their own separate linguistic family, the Baltic.) Their writing is in the Latin script, like that of its neighbor Poland, with whom they also share Roman Catholicism. They, thus, have more in common with their much more numerous Polish brethren than with the dominant Russians, with their Cyrillic alphabet and Russian Orthodox Church.

This commonality with Poland is rooted in the several-century-long union of Poland and Lithuania. In the early Middle Ages (12th to 14th centuries) Lithuania had had its own "state"—to the degree that any of the political organizations of the time could be called "states." Then, the ruling houses of Lithuania and Poland united, and after two centuries this monarchical consolidation led to the unification of the two kingdoms. In this period, Lithuanian nobility became "Poles" in language, culture, and religion. However, for Lithuania, in contrast to Poland, the demise of the Polish-Lithuanian state in 1795 did not produce an ethnic fragmentation. Lithuanians were all brought into the Czarist Empire, and as a consequence, the emotive appeal for Poles of national *unification* was not to be found among Lithuanians.

It was only in the midst of the disorder of the First World War that Lithuanians succeeded, like other non-Russian peoples, in breaking away from the Russian Empire. A small committee of Lithuanian intellectuals, clerics, and businessmen proclaimed their independence and set up a new government. The new state in 1918 was threatened by the new "internationalism" of the Russian successor-state, created under the Lenin-Trotsky leadership. In October 1918, the newly organized Communist Party of Lithuania called for revolution and the establishment of "Soviet power." However, the attempted Bolshevik overthrow of the new "bourgeois" state of Lithuania was only briefly successful: it was defeated militarily in mid–1919. The attempted revolution did little but confirm the anti-Russian and anti-Communist bias of the educated, wealthier leadership of the new republic.[5]

As the other new states of Europe born in the collapse of empires in that period, the Lithuanian political system was originally a multi-party parliamentary democracy, although a conservative, pro-clericalist one. As time went on, it followed a trajectory similar to that of many other European democracies: it fell victim to the economic pressures of the Depression, and to the fear of Communism that accompanied the economic crisis throughout Europe. In 1926, the democracy became an authoritarian dictatorship with only a few trappings of its previous self: there were parties, even some of the strongest of the democratic period, but there were restrictions on political activity and the police and courts proceeded in much the same fashion as their counterparts in Poland, Rumania, and Yugoslavia.

An essential difference between the Lithuanian dictatorship and most of the others of Eastern Europe was its *triple*-opposition to the "colossus" of the East: the Lithuanian government was anti-Russian, pro-Roman Catholic,[6] and anti-Communist. The first and second were rooted in the rise of Lithuanian nationalism in the latter half of the 19th century, and the last was a clear product of the attempted revolution and the activities of the Comintern. The dictatorship was acceptable to the population at least in part because of the interplay of these factors and the obvious threat posed by the USSR. In addition, it legitimated and promoted such orientations during its years in power.

For the Lithuanian government of the interwar period and for much of the population, the threat was, pure and simple, "imperialism," i.e., reincorporation. By 1922 the states of the Ukraine, Byelorussia, Georgia, Turkestan, Azerbaidjan and Armenia were returned to the central direction of the leadership of the Soviet state, despite public commitments to respect their independence, including treaties of friendship and cooperation and diplomatic recognition. There were objective bases for the fear of Lithuanians that Soviet forces, given the opportunity, would move to annex their territory in toto.

The loss of independence became a reality in 1939, when a deal was made between Stalin and Hitler. The Nazi-Soviet Pact originally allocated Lithuania (along with much of Poland) to Germany, but the rapidity of the German military's advances led to a renegotiation. Soviet interests in Poland were traded for Lithuania. Immediately, Stalin pressured the Lithuanian leaders to accept Soviet "protection," Soviet troops stationed inside their borders (on October 10th). Within a short eight months, after those troops provided the political leverage for Stalin to insist on pro-Soviet promotions in the Lithuanian government, the anti-Communist elite was paralyzed by numerous arrests. An entirely docile Diet thus voted in July 1940 for the state's "admission" to the Union of Soviet Socialist Republics.

Ironically, only when the *German* invasion took place did the anti-Communist opposition organized for guerrilla warfare. At that point, the anti-Communist nationalists grouped into small armed bands, began a long campaign to harrass the occupiers, first Nazi, then Soviet.[7] This type of nationalist resistance was characteristic of several of the non-Russian groups along the European border: one major example is the Ukrainians. Of course, this suggests that the strength of non-Russian nationalism is not peculiar to Lithuania. The reinforcement of these social, cultural, and ethnic features was not unique to Lithuania. In Georgia, Armenia, and the Ukraine, religion, nationalism, and politics have interacted for decades. However, the survival of an independent Lithuanian state during the interwar period produced an especially strong amalgam of the ties, that fed immediate and long-term post-war resistance.

After the German armies began their retreat from the USSR, the Lithuanian Partisans tried to establish bases of operations against the Red Armies. However, with the return in 1944 of Soviet troops after combat victories over the Axis, these partisans had poor strategic prospects. Nonetheless, they held out until 1952, despite the "aid" provided by Western intelligence agencies. Several dozen guerrillas were airdropped behind Soviet lines by the West, but each one was easily captured, if only because the British secret service was penetrated at high levels by a series of Soviet agents.[8]

With the surrender of the last guerrillas in 1952,[9] the "Lithuanian state" once again became a part of the Soviet Union. Its structure paralleled that of the RSFSR (see below) and the Communist Party occupied all significant positions of responsibility in society and polity. A period of political calm, economic growth, and modernization followed. The Lithuanian Soviet Republic in 1953 became a political "backwater" of the Soviet Union.

Yet, in 1970–1971 on-going petition and underground publishing activity began among thousands of Lithuanians. This activity was at first clearly limited to religious matters, but rapidly expanded to national concerns, including questions of industrial development, Russian migration, pollution, and the destruction of national-cultural sites and resources.

Such dissent included at least the 129,000 people who signed a petition in 1977 for the return of the Klaipeda Cathedral from its use as a municipal auditorium. Also, there were thousands who, after soccer matches, rioted against the Russianization of the republic, and many individuals raised traditional, pre-Soviet flags during the outlawed traditional day of independence. Finally, there were the unknown numbers involved in the writing, reproduction, and distribution of literally dozens of underground publications spanning religious, nationalist, and human rights themes. Truly, in the 1970s there was a massive amount of dissent in Lithuania. (We shall have more to say about the dissident "movement" of Lithuania in Chapters 3 and 7.)

Party Policy Statements
on Nationalities and Religion

The Bolsheviks were concerned with problems of nationalities from the earliest years. Lenin himself felt that the struggles of repressed ethnic groups within the Czarist Empire, like those of their counterparts in other capitalist imperialist states, could easily be used to overthrow the bourgeoisie.[10] In addition, he felt that the success of the new socialist state in part depended on the respect for national feelings of non-Russian peoples. He even opposed Stalin's plan to absorb new states directly into the Russian Republic, perferring instead a "union" of republics.[11] This was a distinction without a difference in practical terms.

Nonetheless, Lenin was wary of nationalism, identifying it with the old culture of capitalism. Thus, "bourgeois nationalism" was opposed to "proletarian internationalism."[12] To try to break away from the Union of Soviet Socialist Republics was "counterrevolution."[13] However, overall, Lenin suggested "it is better to overdo rather than underdo the concessions and leniency towards the national minorities" in the Soviet state.[14]

Stalin's contribution was the concept of "national in form, socialist in content." His argument was that non-Russian nationalism was fulfilled in a revolutionary way only within the USSR. Independence outside the union would allow domination by European imperialists and would thus be only a thin mask for colonial status.[15] Nationalism within the USSR was supposedly manifested in the "flowering" of ethnic cultural events and artifacts, without separate political ideas for each group. Of course, Russian nationalism even in the pre-war period became, in practice, increasingly a base for popular legitimacy in Russian areas.[16]

In the post-Stalinist period, the latest twist is the simultaneous flowering and "growing together" of nationalities.[17] As more theatrical plays and concerts were held, each nation would appreciate its common ties to the others, and each would increasingly use a common tongue (naturally Russian) for communication. This socio-cultural development was supposedly rooted in the sociological development of a new demographic entity, "the Soviet people(s)." As the material base of economic development was firmly established throughout the USSR, differences among peoples and among classes would disappear, and with them the differences in everyday life that feed the traditions of separateness.[18]

Moreover, the party continues to have as a duty the creation of a new type of person, a post-capitalist personality with all sorts of good features—among them was the absence of ethnic malice, and sense of unity with all other "toilers" of the USSR and around the world. The "new Soviet man" was to be without nationalist feeling, except for a pride in the new multi-ethnic polity.[19]

In practice, Soviet policy has involved both concessions to and pressures on the non-Russian ethnic populations. There are separate republics with their own constitutions, government structures, and official languages; formally separate party organizations, with some attempt to recruit non-Russians into positions of responsibility; and economic investment patterns to promote development in each republic.[20] However, the process of all-union national integration can be seen in the "Russification" and "Russianization" of non-Russian areas: use of Russian language is promoted in the schools, technical books and journals are considerably less numerous than Russian language ones, and in some republics at least there have been net inflows of Russians that are shifting the demographic balance, at least in the major cities.[21]

Thus, Lithuanian nationalism, especially when tied to anti-Russian sentiments, was interpreted as counter-revolutionary and anti-Soviet, if only because of the express rejection of Russian language and culture. It is not at all surprising that party officials tried time and again to paint nationalist dissidents this way.[22] What is so unexpected is the short-sighted attempt to connect them to the anti-Soviet partisans and the Western democracies, especially the US. For example, in 1978, an entire book of invective against Lithuanian-speaking Roman Catholic clergy in the West was published in Vilnius under the name of *Hatredmongers: Anti-Soviet Activity of the Lithuanian Clerical Emigres.*[23] Such a putative relation would only solidify the support of large numbers of older people, at least, who had been supporters of the Partisans and held positive attitudes toward the West.[24]

The ambiguity on nationalism was paralleled by one on religion, although ultimately the balance was set against it. Lenin followed Marx in denouncing religion as the bourgeois ideology of oppression in that it counselled obedience and offered reward in the afterlife.[25] However, he recognized that at least some religions under some conditions could be revolutionary and could aid in the destruction of capitalism.[26] It was thus clear that Russian Orthodoxy had to be deracinated from Russian life, given the close ties of church and state. On the other hand, some collectivist forms of worship, like Protestant fundamentalism, were to be tolerated for the time being, while the general fight against religious belief proceeded unhindered.[27]

The basis of official atheism was simply that religion was only myth and superstition, in contrast to what should exist under socialism, namely science. Thus, anti-religious tracts were treated as necessary truth, while observance of religious rites was behavior suitable only for illiterate and backward peasants. Moreover, the regime started early to propagandize science as an alternative to religion, under the banner of "scientific atheism." This continues to this day as the *Znanie* society supposedly expounds the scientific worldview among the general population, but in practice engages in systematic anti-religious campaigns.[28]

This broad-spectrum attack coexisted with official declarations about the freedom of religion. The Stalin constitution of 1936 guaranteed not only worshippers the right to worship, but also priests the right to vote and hold office.[29] (These were paper provisions.) The official line is that religion is an outmoded form of thought that is gradually withering away as the material advances of socialism are producing more enlightened people.[30]

The placidity of this position was upset only when religion took on anti-Soviet, especially nationalist overtones. Thus, the Roman Catholicism of most Lithuanians was seen as potentially dangerous. At least certain of some of the activists among dissidents were denounced as "reactionary" and politically "naive."

Finally, the development of official views of dissent has also showed some variations. Since the seizure of power by the Bolsheviks, opposition to party policy and leadership has been ideologically suspect. Lenin tolerated it better within the upper ranks: witness his acceptance of Kamenev and Zinoviev, after their initial opposition to seizing power in the October Revolution. However, he was especially distrustful of undirected mass activity, so-called "spontaneity"—which he felt too easily diverted energies and led the workers to accept wily bourgeois propaganda.

Stalin solidified the temporary restrictions on factional activity in the party established in 1921 with Lenin's blessing. One hallmark of Stalin's conception of "socialism in one country" was the evil effects of "capitalist encirclement" on party members and masses alike: both were tempted into anti-Soviet conspiracy. Stalin denied the legitimacy of any opposition to his leadership and to the "leading role" of the party. Naturally, in practice the latter was tempered by Stalin's use of his personal secretariat and the secret police. By the time of his death, Stalin had even proclaimed certain forms of "internationalism" to be anti-Soviet; namely, "rootless cosmopolitanism" that ignored party directives in art and culture.

In the post-Stalinist period, Soviet leaders tried to combine some reform of the worst repressions (the worst oppression was blamed almost entirely on Stalin personally in the phrase "cult of personality") with denunciation of opposition, while opposition was explicitly denounced as anti-Soviet and "criminal."

Soviet leaders assert that all citizens have rights and freedoms. The assertion generally ignores the flood of restrictive and punitive regulations, as well as the practice of the KGB, courts, etc. It is asserted that Soviet dissent does not really exist as a natural phenomenon. It is a form of crime, and as such is either the result of hostile bourgeois propaganda or of mental illness. In either case, those who oppose are seen as requiring incarceration of some sort for behavior that is contrary to law. The violation of legal proscriptions is what triggers arrest and conviction, or psychiatric internment, according to this third official position on dissent.

Soviet Laws on Dissent

Given the ideological predispositions to view nationalism and religion as abnormal activity, it is not surprising that there are laws based on these interpretations. Thus, many articles of the criminal code of the republic of Lithuania (which by design parallels that of the Russian Soviet Federated Socialist Republic) can be and are used against dissidents.[31] The major ones that exist in all the republican codes of the Soviet Union fall into three categories.

First are the "especially dangerous crimes against the state." These include articles 64–70 of the RSFSR Criminal Code.[32] Perhaps the two most significant of this group are 64 and 70. Article 64 is the treason clause. It indicates that "an act intentionally committed by a citizen of the USSR to the detriment of the state independence, the territorial inviolability, or the military might of the USSR" is one type of "especially dangerous crime against the state."[33] More specifically, "'going over to the enemy, espionage, transmission of a state or military secret to a foreign state, . . . [or] rendering aid to a foreign state in carrying on hostile activity against the USSR, or a conspiracy for the purpose of seizing power" can be punishable by death or up to fifteen years imprisonment and five years in "exile" in remote regions of the USSR.

How can dissent be "treasonous"? Soviet authorities interpret the transfer of information about the economy or secret administrative decrees as endangering the security of the Soviet state. Thus they can and do indict dissidents who write about poor economic conditions in Lithuania, unpublicized rules governing religious affairs, or about

Major Laws against Dissent

Category	RSFSR Article No.	LCC No.	Summary
Especially dangerous crimes against the state	64*	62	Treason
	70	68	Anti-Soviet agitation and propaganda
Daniel-Sinyavsky laws	190.1	199.1	Slander of the state
	190.2	199.2	Flag crime
	190.3	199.3	Group civil dis- obedience
Anti-religious laws	142	143	Separation of church and state
	227	144	Violation of rights of non-believers

*The treason provision (Article 58) of the previous Criminal Code, superceded in 1960, was similar in content but prescribed harsher penalties.

trials of dissidents themselves. Indeed, top KGB officials have publicly linked dissent, treason, and danger to the Soviet state. For example, then chairman of the Committee for State Security, Vitaly Fedorchuk, reported to the Supreme Soviet in November 1982 that

> Today our class enemy is—more vigorously and on a more massive scale than ever before—conducting espionage against our country, practicing ideological subversion, and striving to damage the Soviet economy.[34]

Article 70 is somewhat less onerous in that it does not prescribe the death penalty under any circumstances for "anti-Soviet agitation and propaganda." However, 10 years' incarceration and 5 years in "exile" is possible if the court finds that the defendant has engaged in "agitation or propaganda carried on for the purpose of subverting or weakening the Soviet regime or of committing . . . especially dangerous crimes against the state, or the circulation of slanderous fabrications which defame the Soviet state and social system." Indeed, even "preparation or keeping . . . literature of such content" is equated to the actual dissemination of such hostile propaganda. This is a clever rule against dissidents' writing or exchanging criticisms of the system: a grave infraction of the security of the social order of the Soviet system.[35]

Second is the series of laws adopted in the wake of the Daniel-Sinyavsky trials [36] of 1966. They were adopted in the aftermath of massive intellectual discontent when two writers were tried for disseminating anti-Soviet propaganda, short pieces of fiction. These new articles—190.1 to 190.3—allow the regime to apply somewhat more lenient punishment, namely three years' imprisonment, for similar offenses. The most important is Article 190.1. It prohibits "the systematic circulation in oral form of fabrications known to be false which defame the Soviet state and social system" as well as preparation or circulations of "written, printed, or any other forms of works of such content."[37]

Of course, *any* material chosen by the KGB can be interpreted as "anti-Soviet," including Marxist analyses of the Soviet system and romantic poetry alluding to heroes of the past or to the existence of the soul and afterlife.[38] Although not a response to any particular Lithuanian situation, these articles were used to jail numerous Lithuanian dissidents.

The last group of laws used against the dissidents is related to the practice of religion. Two are markedly more important than the others: Articles 142 and 227. Article 142 prohibits the "violation of the separation of church and state and of school and church." In practice, this means that no one except parents can give religious instruction to minors, or even bring youngsters in religious gatherings. Moreover, a soccer match in which a priest plays is considered a religious meeting. The grounds are that education is solely the province of "state" and religious groups and clerics do not have a warrant to teach the young anything.[39] The article allows for up to three years' incarceration for repeat offenders.

In addition, adults who are non-believers are "protected" from activities based on religious beliefs by Article 227, "violation of the rights of non-believers." This article has been used to condemn the singing of hymns as the violation of the privacy of non-believers who might be walking along the street outside the church, and public funeral processions as the violation of the rights of non-believers to unhindered access to public thoroughfares.[40] The article prescribes a term of up to three years.

Chapter 6 will examine the actual use of these articles of the criminal code. For now, we will examine the institutions involved in the formulation and use of these laws against the dissidents.

The Institutional Framework of Soviet Lithuania

The major reality of Soviet life throughout the USSR is the dominance of the Communist Party. That institution has tried to reconcile its rejection of spontaneity with a pragmatic accommodation of ethnic diversity. Its structure is that of a centrally directed, hierarchic set of bureaucracies divided into republic parties for the major ethnic groups.[41] Lithuania has its "own" Communist Party, with a Congress, Central Committee, Secretaries, Politburo, and lower levels organized like other republic parties. Each lower level of the Lithuanian hierarchy reports to and is responsible to the next higher one. Each level varies in its degree of differentiation, with higher levels possessing complex administrative structures in the Secretariat. However, this does not mean that Lithuania's party is autonomous. These bodies routinely endorse the decisions made by higher levels of the All-Union party soon after they are propounded. In addition, there is some overlap in personnel in leadership bodies; for example, the First Secretary is always a member of the CPSU Central Committee, and thus subject to the constraints of those bodies. Finally, the internal structure and operations that allow the party to dominate government bodies also allow for great central control of republic parties.

The party tries to fulfill its role as the "leading force" in Soviet society by monitoring and attempting to direct all the social, political, and economic institutions. That is accomplished by bureaucratic means that penetrate the fabric of the other organizations. Not only may party members appeal outside the institution to the party on what is perceived as undesirable behavior, but this process of promotion is coordinated in great detail by the party through the system of lists of persons and posts of responsibility that the party maintains. This system is called "nomenklatura" and can supplement the other levers of power such as the courts.[42]

The specialization of task at the republic and regional levels is so extensive that there exist experts within the party who devote their time to cultural affairs, ideological questions, and so on. It is not surprising that this specialization exists, but it must be remembered that this is an important mechanism by which the *center* controls the periphery. Thus, the top party posts in Lithuania are on the nomenklatura lists in Moscow, and occasional supervisory visits from Moscow specialists keep the local leaders in line.

It should be pointed out, however, that the leaders in Moscow have tried to accommodate, at least symbolically, the persistence of ethnic identification. A type of nationalization" has occurred in that all leadership posts in the Lithuanian party have become increasingly

Lithuanian in ethnic composition. The original leadership was overwhelmingly Russian because of the fashion of incorporation into the USSR as discussed above; but over the years there were promotions of Lithuanians and re-assignments of Russians with the result being "Lithuanianization."[43] This physical change in elite membership might become more important because of the *possibility* of sympathy at some level of individuals of the same ethnic group, especially in opposition to an "out-group." There were reports that this was the basis for the ouster of Pyotr Shelest from the first secretaryship in the Ukraine: "lenience" toward dissidents and an increasing Ukrainian orientation in his speeches. Nonetheless, there are no signs of such an alliance in Lithuania.

The same structural features pervade Lithuanian governmental institutions. They too are patterned after the Russian Soviet Federated Socialist Republic, have centralist direction, are controlled in part by personnel promotions of nomenklatura, and have become increasingly Lithuanian in ethnicity.[44] However, there are some points of difference: first, there are some significant institutions with direct lines from locality to the center. For example, the procuracy, courts, and KGB all function as district offices of the Moscow headquarters.[45] Of course, other ministries with republic headquarters are also ultimately responsible to Moscow, but they have republic apparatuses that may at least slow down implementation or provide localized input into planning. The coercive apparatuses are of such importance that they are to be shielded from any possibility of the slightest "republican" pressures.

Second, there appears to be a far greater differentiation within governmental units for specific problems. There exists a particular agency for religion—Committee for Religious Affairs—that monitors and tries to direct organized religion, including the Roman Catholic Church. Its commissioner has his own staff to follow affairs of each denomination and to pressure the clergy and followers of recalcitrant groups.[46] Also, within the KGB at least one "main directorate" was established in 1969 to deal with dissent. Within it are several departments specializing in non-Russian nationalities, Jews, and samizdat.[47] The existence of a special department for Balts and other ethnic groups indicates a great concern by the central authorities about dissent in Lithuania.

Third, there is some fragmentary evidence that governmental institutions especially are pushed by general as well as specific directives from above. That is, there are some reports that the courts, the prosecutors' offices, and the KGB all have detailed statistical reports to compile periodically. Such summaries of their activities play a role in individual careers, as well as the inter- and intra-bureaucratic conflicts over resources. Thus, it is likely that dissidents are at least occasionally brought in for interrogation or worse simply to "pad the figures." More abstract notions of "severity" and "order"—bureaucratized as quotas—most likely complement more individualized orders on specific dissidents.[48]

Thus, the party has tried to deflate some of the centrifugal pressures by a limited accommodation in organization of itself and the state. However, the party does not wish to unleash destabilizing forces. Consequently, the state is controlled by the party. However, the highest levels of the party in Moscow control lower levels of both hierarchies, including the republic party leadership.

An Overview of Post-War
Lithuanian Dissent and Repression

There have been two major periods of "dissent" in Lithuania. The most dramatic and violent was the 1941–1952 period of armed resistance, described above. However, the Stalinist techniques of military maneuver, mass arrests and exile, and direct anti-clerical violence (including murders of priests and members of the hierarchy in churches) eliminated the leaders of this opposition, and thus rendered it ineffective.

In the middle 1950s, there was some isolated dissent, sparked by the denunciation of Stalin at the 20th Party Congress and the liberalization occurring in Hungary and Poland. In 1956, there were students and intellectuals who felt that official "de-Stalinization" meant an opening to more democratic values, but these dissidents were isolated and readily dealt with. Only with the 1959 promise of a new cathedral in Klaipeda and the subsequent reneging on its opening—after the voluntary collection of materials and labor by believers—did priests lead their parishes in protests, with jail terms the only result.[49]

However, the second major period of dissent really began in 1970, when the government arrested and tried two popular priests. Then activity took a quantum leap forward and the dissident movement started to emerge. We will discuss the *parts* of this movement at some length in Chapter 3, and the dynamics of its struggle with the regime, in Chapter 7. For now it will suffice to describe its content and extent.

Catholic activists started their own "illegal" journal, copied from the Moscow-based *Chronicles of Current Events*.[50] Their periodical— *Chronicles of the Catholic Church in Lithuania*—was intended to publicize the unjust actions of the government (and Communist party) and served to unite disparate groups around the country. This unification, rooted in the common indignation at the plight of their coreligionists and fellow countrymen, as well as in the cooperation required to produce and disseminate their journal, yielded ever greater activity and ever more widespread actions, such as massive petitions on the old question of the Klaipeda Cathedral and the anti-religious tone of the media.[51] Perhaps even more important, the rise of Catholic agitation was accompanied by the blossoming of the *samizdat* publishing "industry" and the diversification of oppositional demands. Non-religious, or partially religious documents appeared in the 1970s and some clearly nationalist acts—including street demonstrations and riots—were signs that other dissident elements became encouraged by the survival of the *Chronicles*.

It must be noted that the timing of religious dissent among other religious groups in the Soviet Union varies from this somewhat. Two groups of Moslems, the Crimean Tatars and the Meskhetians, started to dissent when they were physically deported from their ethnic homelands in 1944. The Uniates in the Ukraine also began their dissident religious activities in the late 1940s. The Pentecostalists began in 1947, the Baptists in 1961, and the Seven Day Adventists as early as 1924. Others seem to have begun somewhat later: the Russian Orthodox in the early 1960s, Jews and Buddhists in the 1960s, Georgian Orthodox in the 1970s, and Armenian Gregorians in the late 1970s.[52]

Other republics had some degree of samizdat, clear signs of nationalist dissent, and even (infrequently) linkage of religious to nationalist discontent. Estonians, Ukrainians, Armenians, Georgians, and Jews have produced a great deal of protest and on many occasions, nationalist demands accompanying those relating to the practice of religion or the absence of spiritual values.[53] The links among dissidents in various republics were institutionalized by the establishment of the Helsinki Watch Groups in Lithuania, the Ukraine, Armenia, and Georgia, as well as the first in Moscow. (We will discuss this group in Lithuania in Chapter 3.)

How did the regime respond to such dissent? In Chapters 4 through 7, we will analyze the state's specific responses to dissent, but a brief answer to this question is in order here. As noted, during the Stalin period, massive and arbitrary terror was the prime weapon, as hundreds of thousands were summarily tried and sent to Siberia in the early years of incorporation, and as military units took the field against the anti-Soviet partisans.

The Khrushchev period was more complex. There were occasional trials, and an anti-religious campaign from 1959 to 1963 during which the city government confiscated the Klaipeda Cathedral. At the same time, however, liberalization at the all-union level involved changes in the criminal code, some penalties becoming lighter.

With the replacement of Nikita Sergeyevich by Leonid Ilich Brezhnev and his colleagues, the regime attempted a more differentiated policy. Psychiatric detention, intimidation through interrogation, and mindless bureaucratism (in response to complaint)[54] were combined with selective use of the courts. This more sophisticated policy included the introduction of yet more new laws to provide further options to deal with dissidents within the court system. The details of exactly how the regime responded, which options were taken with whom, will be analyzed in Chapters 4 through 7.

Conclusion

Nationalism and religious belief are important problems for the Soviet Union, and are especially salient for Lithuania. The regime has tried to reconcile its insistence on centralized control with the continuing strength of ethnic and religious feelings. It has incorporated ethnic distinctiveness into its party and state structures, and it has granted some ideological concessions in the struggle to defeat "bourgeois ideology." However, it has continued to face difficulties in Lithuania.

National sentiment is rooted in the social, economic, and historical distinctiveness of Lithuania and Lithuanians. Roman Catholicism separates Lithuanians from almost all other Soviet peoples, especially Russians, and reinforces ethnic distinctiveness.

The major question is to what degree these factors affect dissent and repression. We will see in Chapter 3 that nationalism and religion are important components of the dissident movement, and that regime responses lead to specific grievances by dissidents from many social strata. In Chapter 4 we will find that the institutional patterns are critical to understanding the stages of the process of repression in Lithuania, as elsewhere.

The institutional and ideological ambivalences and ambiguities on nationalism and religion, despite rejection of dissent, imply conflicting directions in policy. Who is to be arrested when and with what result is not automatic; neither is the mutual feedback of dissent and regime repression. The actual patterns of repression in Lithuania are examined in Chapters 5 through 8.

Notes

1. Of course, Russians too have fought against the regime during these wars, but *Russian* nationalism has been used during World War II to mobilize the majority of Russians, whereas this did not guarantee any significant support among the strategically important nationalities on the border.

2. The following discussion on the political and economic implications of demographic patterns is taken from Murray Feshbach, "The Soviet Union: Population Trends and Dilemmas," *Population Bulletin*, vol. 37, no. 3 (Population Reference Bureau, Inc., Washington, D.C., 1982); Warren W. Eason, "Demographic Trends and Soviet Foreign Policy: The Underlying Imperative of the Labor Supply," in *The Domestic Context of Soviet Foreign Policy*, ed. Seweryn Bialer (Boulder: Westview, 1981), pp. 203–226; Morris Bornstein, "Soviet Economic Growth and Foreign Policy," in Bialer, pp. 240–242; and Helene Carrere D'Encausse, *Decline of an Empire: The Soviet Socialist Republics in Revolt* (New York: Harper Colophon, 1981).

3. D'Encausse, ibid.

4. Seweryn Bialer, *Stalin's Successors: Leadership, Stability, and Change in the Soviet Union* (Cambridge: Cambridge University Press, 1980), chapter 10, especially p. 207. Cf. his *The Soviet Paradox* (New York: Random House, 1987), Chapter 2.

5. V. Stanley Vardys, *The Catholic Church, Dissent and Nationality in Soviet Lithuania* (New York: East Europe Quarterly Press, 1978). Cf. Antanas Snieckus, *Soviet Lithuania on the Road of Prosperity* (Moscow: Progress Publishers, 1974), pp. 16–24.

6. The connection of nationalism to Catholicism (which would later be reinforced within the dissident movement) was not as strong in the interwar period as it might have been. The time for the development of such a tie was relatively short: only a few decades after emergence from clear Polish clerical influence. Also, Church figures in politics opposed secularization on such questions as official records, education, financial aid, etc.; they were usually pitted against "leftist" reformers. Moreover, territorial disputes with Poland divided the Catholic Church from right-wing nationalists. Finally, the right-wingers who led a successful coup in 1926 led a strong political campaign against the political role of the church, until the 1938 coalition government appeared. Vardys, *The Catholic Church*, chapter 3.

7. Thomas Remeikis, *Opposition to Soviet Rule in Lithuania, 1945–1980* (Chicago: Institute of Lithuanian Studies, 1980), chapter 2, has considerable material on the Partisan struggle. See also, V. Stanley Vardys, "Lithuania's Catholic Movement Reappraised," *Survey* 25 (3)(1980), p. 52, fn. 12 for other sources on the guerrilla war.

8. V. Stanley Vardys, ed., *Lithuania under the Soviets* (New York: 1965); cf. Remeikis, pp. 48–52.

9. At least four Partisans went deeply underground and were only tracked down and arrested in the mid–1960s and the 1970s. They include Ceslovas Stasitis who was uncovered in 1965 after becoming chairman of the executive

committee of a village soviet (i.e., the leading non-party official of the village; see ELTA 87: 67; 252: 8; and CCE 46: 158), Antanas Dziaugis (tried with Stasaitis, had been working in Riga, Latvia), Merkunas (arrested in 1969—see CCE, 51: 79), and Boleslovas Lizunas (who had for 34 years hidden under the name of Boleslavas Karaliunas until his arrest in 1979—see *USSR News Brief*, 1980, no. 6, item 6:12; CCE, 57: 83; ELTA, 250: 9). All were convicted of treason and given 15 years imprisonment.

10. See the following in Robert C. Tucker, ed., *The Lenin Anthology* (New York: W.W. Norton, 1975): "Communism and the East: Theses on the National and Colonial Questions," pp. 619–625, particlularly p. 621; "The Right of Nations to Self-Determination," pp. 153–180, especially pp. 162–165; and "Imperialism," pp. 268–269.

11. "The Question of Nationalities or 'Autonomisation,'" in Tucker, pp. 719–724.

12. "Two Cultures in Every National Culture," in Tucker, pp. 654–658, especially p. 655.

13. Interestingly, even in 1913 Lenin opposed the separation of the Ukraine from Russia as a "betrayal of socialism." "Two Cultures," p. 657.

14. "The Question," p. 723.

15. About "Georgia, Armenia, Poland, Finland, and so forth," J.V. Stalin said: "the border regions of Russia . . . are inevitably doomed to imperialist bondage without the political, military, and organizational support of more developed Central [Bolshevik] Russia." "The Policy of the Soviet Government on the National Question in Russia," in *Marxism and the National Question* (New York: International Publishers, 1942), pp. 76–85, pp. 76–77. Cf. also, "Thesis on the Immediate Tasks of the Party in Connection with the National Question," in the same volume, p. 91, pp. 86–87; and *Foundations of Leninism* (Peking: Foreign Language Press, 1976), pp. 67–78, especially 76–77.

16. Robert McNeal, *The Bolsheviks* (Englewood Cliffs: Prentice-Hall, 1966).

17. See the 1961 Party Program, and V.G. Afanasyev, *Foundations of Scientific Communism* (Moscow: Progress Publishers, 1972). See also Zvi Gitelman, "Are Nations Merging in the USSR?", *Problems of Communism* (32) (5) (September-October 1983): 35–47, for a discussion of both the current ideological positions and some results on Soviet attitudes derived from a project on Soviet emigres from the post–1970 period.

18. G.E. Glezerman, *Classes and Nations* (Moscow: Progress Publishers, 1979), chapters 4, 6–9.

19. Cf. 1961 Party Program; David Lane, *Politics and Society in the USSR* (New York: New York University Press, 1978); Afanasyev, pp. 220, 247–249.

20. D'Encausse, pp. 27–33, 121–164; Bialer, chapter 10.

21. D'Encausse, pp. 70, pp. 165–189. Also, Alex Inkeles, *Social Change in Soviet Russia* (New York: Simon and Schuster, 1968), chapter 13.

22. For example, see ELTA.

23. Written by Jonas Anicas, and published by Mintis, it directly mentions the posited ties in the footnote on p. 16.

24. A similar propaganda mistake is that of the Nazi radio broadcasts denouncing the little-known Charles DeGaulle as the handmaiden of the British.

25. Blakeley has pointed out that Lenin was even more "violent" and less "rational" in his anti-religious position than Marx and Engels. See Thomas J. Blakeley, "Scientific Atheism: An Introduction," *Studies in Soviet Thought* 4(4) (December 1964): 279. (His footnote 4 lists the 6 major works by Lenin on religion).

26. Unfortunately this is missed by many analysts of Lenin's thought, like Blakeley, "Scientific Atheism," and J. M. Bochenski, "Marxism-Leninism and Religion" in *Religion and Atheism in the U.S.S.R. and Eastern Europe*, ed. Bohdan R. Bociurkiw and John W. Strong (Toronto: University of Toronto Press, 1975), pp. 1–17. This is particularly curious because of later Leninist turn to "the East", even the "Moslem East." (The latter phrase is from one of the earlier expressions of the shift of revolutionary optimism to the less developed countries of Asia—Lenin's "Interview with Mohammad Wali-Khan, Ambassador Extraordinary of Afghanistan, October 14, 1919," *Collected Works*, vol. 42, p. 146 [Moscow: Progress Publishers, 1969].) For a good monograph on the limits of this shift, see Alexandre A. Bennigsen and S. Enders Wimbush, *Muslim National Communism in the Soviet Union: A Revolutionary Strategy for the Colonial World* (Chicago: University of Chicago Press, 1979).

27. Lane, pp. 464–465.

28. Vardys, *The Catholic Church*, chapter 5.

29. This constitution was evaluated as one of the most "liberal" even by many Western legal specialists.

30. This is parallel to the argument on "bourgeois ideology" in general.

31. Cronid Lubarsky enumerates over two dozen. *List of Political Prisoners in the USSR* (Bruxelles: Cahiers du Samizdat, 1983), pp. 9–12.

32. Lubarsky gives the equivalents on pp. 11–12. These are articles 62 through 68 of the Lithuanian Criminal Code. For purposes of simplicity we will hereafter use the Russian Criminal Code equivalents, for they are far more commonly known in the West.

33. The wording of each article used in the text is taken from *Soviet Criminal Law and Procedure*, translated by Harold J. Berman and James W. Spindler (Cambridge: Harvard University Press, 1972), pp. 152–154, 180–181, 169, 192.

34. *Current Digest of the Soviet Press*, 5 January 1983, p. 18.

35. See, for example, Amnesty International, *Prisoners of Conscience in the USSR* (New York: Amnesty International, 1980). Cf. Berman, et al.

36. They had written several short stories about a fictional future society with some similarities to the Soviet Union, and had sent them outside the country to be published under pseudonyms. Eventually, both emigrated to the West.

37. Article 190.2 criminalizes protests using or abusing the Red flag or the emblem of the USSR or any of its component republics. Article 190.3 makes group civil disobedience—whether in the form of strikes or unofficial

meetings—illegal by prescribing punishment for either organizing or partic-ipating in any disobedience of the orders of authorities.

38. Examples can be found in the cases of Tamonis and others. Cf. issues of the underground periodicals *Ausra, Pastoge,* and *Tiesos Kielas.* For more discussion of these and other journals, see Remeikis, pp. 123–170; Vardys, "Lithuania's Catholic Movement Reappraised," pp. 65–73; and "The Underground Periodicals in Lithuania," *ELTA* (261) (1981): 9–13; and Appendix.

39. Lithuanian Article 143. Cf. Amnesty International, pp. 35–37, for further examples.

40. Lithuanian Article 144. Cf. various issues of CCCL; Amnesty International, pp. 37–39.

41. See Ronald J. Hill and Peter Frank, *The Soviet Communist Party* (London: George Allen and Unwin, 1981), chapter 3. The exception is that the Russian Republic has no republic party organization per se.

42. Cf. Hill and Frank, pp. 86–87; Bohdan Harasymiw, "Nomenklatura," in *Canadian Journal of Political Science* (2) (1979): 493–512.

43. See Remeikis, *Opposition to Soviet Rule,* chapter 3.

44. Ibid.

45. Of course, one could make too much of this, for all government and party institutions do have strong ties to the center. But these particular ones are explicitly tied to higher levels without the facade of "dual responsibility" to republic or lower authorities.

46. There is no good systematic analysis of this institution, unfortunately.

47. Brian Fremantle, *KGB: Inside the World's Largest Intelligence Network* (New York: Holt, Rinehart and Winston, 1984), pp. 48–54.

48. See Chapter 4 for more ön judicial institutions and practices.

49. Vardys, "Lithuania's Catholic Movement Reappraised," pp. 55–56; *The Catholic Church,* pp. 126–49.

50. This has been translated into English in two forms. First, the initial seven issues have been published in book form by the Society for the Chronicles of the Catholic Church in Lithuania. Second, every few months, the Lithuanian-American Roman Catholic Priests' League (Brooklyn, New York) translates and distributes the latest issue of this journal. For a quick overview of its history, orientation, and coverage, see Tomas Venclova, "The Chronicle of the Lithuanian Catholic Church," *Chronicle of Human Rights in the USSR* 30 (1978): 36–40.

51. This is discussed in Vardys, *The Catholic Church.*

52. Michael Bourdeaux and Michael Rowe, *May One Believe—In Russia?* (London: Darton, Longman and Todd, 1980); Christel Lane, *Christian Religion in the Soviet Union: A Sociological Study* (Albany: State University of New York Press, 1978); Barbara Wolfe Jancar, "Religious Dissent in the Soviet Union," in Rudolf L. Tokes, ed. *Dissent in the USSR* (Baltimore: Johns Hopkins University Press, 1975), pp. 191–230.

53. In addition to the sources mentioned in the above note, see for example, Rubinstein on Soviet Jews, and George W. Simmonds, ed., *Nationalism in the USSR and East Europe in the Era of Brezhnev* (Detroit: University of Detroit

Press, 1977) on several groups including Ukrainians, Byelorussians, Balts, Caucasians, Central Asians, Jews, and Moldavians.

54. Frederic Barghoorn, "The Post-Khrushchev Campaign to Suppress Dissent: Perspectives, Strategies, and Techniques of Repression," in Tokes, pp. 35–95.

3

The Dissidents

Given the vast panoply of regime weapons arrayed against the dissidents—institutional, ideological, coercive—it is something of a surprise that *anyone* acts to express dissatisfaction with official policies, personnel, or programs. Yet a great deal of dissent is to be found in the Lithuanian Republic. In this chapter, the features of who, what, and why of dissent are analysed. They form the dynamic part of the environment of political repression, for it is the process of dissent that produces likely candidates for political justice, even they it resist that justice.

We find that although most dissidents are male and Roman Catholic, dissidents are drawn from diverse social groups, with differing resources and locales. The dissidents are of varying ages, not merely pre-war anti-Communists. The three most numerous groups are priests, students, and intellectuals. Finally, we discover that dissidents from all groups have differing bases of discontent, symbols of resistance, and types of organization. The religious dissident is most common, with nationalist dissidents a close second. The most theoretically significant group drawing on nationalists is the "hybrid" dissident, whose discontent spans two or more such groups and whose links to them help unify the dissidents into a social movement.

Lithuanian Dissent as a "Social Movement"

Dissent in the Soviet Union is a complicated social phenomenon that too often has been oversimplified in the West. As a form of "collective protest" against either basic or specific aspects of Soviet politics and society, dissent must be conceptualized as closely and mutually related to the Soviet state and its policies. As such, the phenomenon involves not merely isolated individuals who dissent, but individuals whose actions are related to others' acts, whose grievances are not idiosyncratic, and who derive from various parts

33

of the social structure. Thus, "dissidents" may be seen as discontented people who protest out of collective concern. Our concept of "dissent" must not restrict a priori the phenomenon to one or two parts of the social structure or to a certain type of issue, but also must leave open the nature of the connections among dissidents and their collective resources in their interactions with the government.

This conceptualization of dissent as collective in form and rooted in several parts of the social structure is something of a departure from standard formulations. Dissent has been most commonly presented by Western analysts as the overt, basic criticism of the systematic underpinnings of Soviet life. For example, one typical definition of dissident is "someone who disagrees in some measure with the ideological, political, economic, or moral foundation that every society rests on."[1] This concentration on the most basic, systemic criticisms has the effect of excluding less self-consciously "ideological" differences with the regime from the category of "dissent."[2] Since dissident criticism is thus supposedly concerned with basic values and with universalist demands, instead of with specific and particularist grievances, "dissent" becomes too often equated with "human rights activism."[3]

In addition, many analysts assume that this basic criticism is found only in some parts of the social structure. The basic criticism of societal values is implicitly possible *only* for articulate people— intellectuals. Thus, the social base of dissent is seen as restricted to one relatively small part of the social structure, the highly educated.[4]

In this type of conceptualization, dissent is in effect reduced to intellectuals protesting over human rights violations. Yet this reduction ignores two vital factors: the empirical complexity of Soviet dissent, and the active role of the state in defining dissent.

Limiting dissent to intellectual human rights activists is inappropriate to Soviet reality. As Tokes says, "contemporary Soviet dissent is an extremely complex, multifaceted, and often contradictory phenomenon."[5] Frequently even the analysts who make this reduction recognize the existence of "separate movements" or "mass discontent," sometimes conceding some connection of dissidents to these others.[6] Using the term "mainstream dissent" for the intellectuals-human rights activists itself implies that others are not "mainstream," but on the "fringe"; those most often mentioned in this context are the religious and nationalist dissidents.[7] Thus, there are those who are not human rights activists, and not intellectuals, who do dissent in the Soviet Union, but who may remain largely unexamined.

A second, more basic problem with the reductionism is that it ignores the role of the state and the interactive nature of dissent.

People may oppose the government, but this does not automatically make dissidents of them: it is the government that determines who are dissidents: "as far as the authorities are concerned, dissent is whatever they choose to label as such."[8] What this means is that there may be policy-specific, not fundamental, opposition *outside* the apparatus that is nonetheless unacceptable to the regime and is labelled as such. (On the other hand, it is also possible that there may be value-based opposition *within* the regime that does not become "dissent"; it is accepted, or at least tolerated, if articulated in the properly "esoteric" fashion by individuals and groups with enough power and legitimacy.) Thus, the authorities draw the line less on the basis of *what* is said, than on the basis of how and by whom:[9] this may not respect what Western analysts have defined as the conceptual boundaries of "dissent."

This role of the state does not end with labelling and official ostracism. Indeed, the phenomenon of dissent is not episodic and isolated. It continues, when the government in some fashion treats the dissidents as illegitimate pariahs of the social order, which in turns intensifies the dissidents' behavior and produces new dissidents. This is, of course, the "dialectic of repression and dissent."[10]

While the state plays a major role in defining and thus *creating* dissent, the outcome of dissent is conditioned by the resources available to both sides. The interaction of state and dissident is conditioned by the relative balance of resources, a balance heavily weighted in favor of the government. The resources available to dissidents are less obvious, although several Western analysts have commented on how the intensity of repression of a *particular* individual dissident depends, among other things, on his political, legal, and economic situations, such as international concern, a skilled and dedicated defense attorney, or a sensitive job.[11] What is needed, however, is an appreciation of the resources of the dissident that transcends an individual level of analysis, for social resources are often available to both sides of the interaction. This appreciation, however, must specify the differential distribution of social resources among different kinds of dissidents, for not all individuals are equally well placed in the social structure or well connected to various social networks.[12] Thus, resources as well as governmental actions are important to understanding dissent. However, attention to social resources should not result in our assuming levels of cohesion and organization that may need to be demonstrated.

Tokes uses the concept of "political reform movement" to analyze dissent[13] but it falls short by assuming too much. The concept "political reform movement" implies a high degree of organizational cohesiveness, policy uniformity, commonality of mobilizing symbols, and consistent, effective leadership, aspects of political dynamics that are problematic in reality. In addition, we shall see that there is some evidence of divergence among the three types of dissidents on these dimensions.

There is another, more useful concept for us: the "social movement,"[14] sometimes defined as "a deliberate collective endeavor to promote change."[15] A social movement, thus, is a group of persons with a common set of values who attempt to bring about change. This means, according to Tilly's "mobilization model" of collective protest,[16] that 1) common experiences and interests produce 2) shared disadvantages or grievances which lead to *collective* or joint action, within 3) a context of some degree of unity—common identity of participants and underlying unifying structure. (A coherent and elaborate institutional structure is not required, although there needs to be some social and attitudinal connectedness, some "linkage" of the disparate groups and individuals into something more than an amorphous mass.) Moreover, the collective action is conditioned by 4) the resources available to those who act, and 5) the costs of their acts, as reflected in the governmental repression that may follow.

Thus, with the concept of "social movement" there are no a priori limits on the composition or aims of the participants, and no assumptions of any uniformity of the specific political goals of various parts of the movement. This allows us to investigate the phenomenon along the lines of recent studies of the Russian Revolution, analyzed not solely from the perspective of the organized leadership, but also from that of the social bases of various less cohesive groups and classes that participated at different times.[17] In addition, there is no assumption of any degree of organization, of any particular balance of resources vis-a-vis the government (or, indeed, among each other). By conceiving of dissent less in terms of its specific content and more as a form of collective action, we can go beyond the extant literature's focus on limited content (human rights) and certain actors (intellectuals), and include otherwise omitted dissidents, as well as examine the form of dissent (in terms of organization and activity), as a resource for dissidents.

The concept of social movement, with Tilly's analytical adumbration, produces important questions of social phenomena of discontent: who are the participants, what are their grievances and resources, to what degree are a common identity and unifying structure present, what are the acts of protest, and what is the government's response? In this and subsequent chapters we will ask these questions.

In general, we will suggest that dissent in Lithuania comprises an emerging social movement. Although there are several grounds for dissent, there seems to be a *shared* national identity (Lithuanian) with many different grounds for dissent (religion, culture, individual rights) distributed among many different groups (including nearly all social strata). We will see some common values among Lithuanian dissidents, something approaching a "contra-culture" with its own history, literature, heroes, and symbols.[18]

Dissidents frequently, but not always, act collectively to try to bring about change on nationalist, religious, and human rights issues, using the symbolic, material, and social resources available to different groups of dissidents. So far, the dissidents do have a limited degree of unity, based on "networking": communications and coordination are facilitated by the rise of a critical type of "hybrid" dissident, a person who participates in several kinds of dissent. However, as yet no more comprehensive "structure" or organization has arisen.

In sum, the concept of dissent as "social movement" allows us not only to go beyond intellectuals and human rights activists, but also pushes us to examine the resources and grievances of nationalists and religious dissidents, of priests and white collar workers. It impels us to look for commonalities and linkages among them. Finally, it will eventually help us understand how the regime responds in different ways to different kinds of dissidents, including targeting and intensified repression of the strategic parts of the "social movement," the hybrids. However, it is first necessary to discuss the empirical base of the data to be analyzed.

The Sources

The empirical data used in this study are derived from several different kinds of sources on repression in Lithuania. They include 1) specialized (on Lithuanian affairs) samizdat, 2) general samizdat, 3) emigre organizations, 4) human rights organizations (with a particular interest in the Soviet Union), and 5) nationally renowned newspapers. (For more detailed description of each source and an analysis of the problems of bias in them, see Appendix.) The major sources are as follows:

1. The specialized samizdat—*Chronicles of the Catholic Church in Lithuania* (hereafter, CCCL; in Lithuanian, *Lietuvos Kataliku Baznycios Kronika*), issues 1–49.
2. The more generalized samizdat—*Chronicles of Current Events* (hereafter, CCE; in Russian, *Khronika Tekushchikh Sobitii*), issues 1–58.

3. Emigre sources—*ELTA* (published by the Lithuanian National Foundation), issues 1–124 and 161–275; and the archives of the Lithuanian Information Center (Brooklyn, NY)
4. Human rights organizations—Keston College lists of prisoners of conscience, 1977, 1979, and 1981; *USSR News Briefs* (hereafter, Vesti; in Russian *Vesti iz SSSR;* Munich-based, run by Cronid Lubarsky), numbers 1/1978 through 12/1981, and Lubarsky's lists based on these issues, for 1978, 1980, and 1981; and *Chronicles of Human Rights in the USSR* (hereafter, CHR; Khronika Press, New York), issues 1–41.
5. International newspapers—the *New York Times*, from January 1, 1968, through December 31, 1981 (hereafter, NYT; called "the best single available source" for data on both international and domestic conflicts in foreign countries).[19]

Events: Collection of the Data and the "Universe"

From each of the sources, information was collected on several kinds of events and characteristics related to each individual: dissident acts like petitions, demonstrations, possession of samizdat material; repressive acts like interrogations, arrests, trials, and non-trial psychiatric detention; and social features like nationality, religion, gender, occupational group, place of residence, year of birth, and so on. Generally, there was little difficulty in coding because each event type is clearly indicated in the sources, although many of the social characteristics were totally undescribed. For example, "Z was arrested on DATE1 and convicted on DATE2 under article Y, and was given 1.5 years in corrective labor camps," is a common type of event description.

Data collection resulted in a file of individual cases of repression.[20] From this file of 842 individuals, with 1362 dated events from 1941 to 1981, is derived a file of 594 cases of dissent and repression in the 1969–1981 period. This latter file is used for the analysis that follows. Most of the individuals had reports on them from several differing sources, although individual events might be derived from only one. Those reports that were overwhelmingly contradicted by more numerous, more detailed, or later reports were discounted and eliminated altogether.

There are at least two reasons why this composite file can be believed to be a reflection of the underlying, unknown real population of repressed dissidents. First, the makeup of the total file does not diverge from what one would expect from a dissident movement that is national in scope: as we shall see later in this chapter, there are some social features of dissidents that are not "representative" of the general population, but in such areas as occupation, residence, gender, and the like, the patterns are consistent in general with a nationally rooted phenomenon, not of an isolated set of individuals.

Second, there occurred a diminishing of returns in the research process that suggests the possibility of ever smaller numbers of yet-unknown cases coming to light in "new" sources. After CCCL and CCE were consulted a full 684 individuals were recorded. Indeed, by the time the last two sources, NYT and CHR, were examined, no new individuals were added (although a few details of already-known events and some previously unreported events involving known individuals were added).

However, it is still ultimately necessary to make a strong caveat about the generalizations to be made below. The data are the best available. It is impossible to use public opinion surveys of samples to delineate the rates of participation in differing dissident activities and to estimate the differing numbers and social characteristics of the population of dissidents. The data gathered is from samizdat and Western emigre sources. There may be major cases that do not emerge in those sources because of pecularities of the cases' location (isolated villages and the like), but that is only likely to delay the reportage, for if one examines the reportage, events in the most insignificant villages and towns *are* noted although sometimes months after the fact. Major cases are most certainly included in the data here.

Nonetheless, it was not possible, because of the unavailability of information, to create a data-file including all the individuals who did dissent on a one-time or infrequent basis in mass petitions (like the series signed by over 100,000 Catholics in the 1970s, demanding the return of the confiscated Klaipeda Cathedral into church hands); or the street riots after soccer matches in the 1970s (in which possibly as many as 2,000 on each occasion marched and chanted, but of whom only five are known by name because of subsequent criminal repression). Thus, the data-set reveals an important view of the most consistent and prominent dissidents, but does not extensively cover the "occasional" or "inconsistent" dissident who takes advantage of a community-based mass action to express discontent at little personal cost.[21]

A word is necessary here about the variables used in the analysis: almost all the values were determined by direct reference in samizdat or other sources. Social group into many categories came from specific descriptions of a dissident's occupation or title (such as Father, Professor, etc.). Residence similarly was found in direct mention in samizdat (with the more obscure towns allotted to their districts according to the officialmap edited by M.P. Lapkina and L.N. Soboleva, published in Moscow by the Geodetic and Cartographic Agency of the Ministry of Internal Affairs in 1976). Ethnicity is simply assigned on the basis of first and last name, or by specific reference for non-Lithuanians. Age is derived from year of birth if given in the sources. Arrest, trial, interrogation, detention, and dissident act dates are as reported (with year, month, and day, if available or at least year if possible); similarly, article of the criminal code and length of sentence are as reported.

Religion was somewhat more difficult: although one might presume that the vast bulk of Lithuanians are Roman Catholic, in individual cases one might be wrong. Thus, membership was not assumed but allocated on such evidence as existed about it, for example, direct reference, religious title, or information about activity (such as dissident religious actions, or religious materials reported confiscated by police during searches, etc.). Similarly, type of dissident could only be determined by the kinds of evidence mentioned above.

Who are the Dissidents?
Socio-demographic features

The Lithuanian dissidents are predominantly male, Roman Catholic, and from various status positions in the society. These features are shown in Table 1 on the general data-set of 594 individuals.

Social group

The dissidents of Lithuania come from several different groups in the social structure. They form an unlikely combination of traditional anti-Communists and educated modernizers, and are rooted in different grounds.

The most dominant social category is *Roman Catholic priests* (nearly one third). Clearly the "national religious dissident movement"[22] is organized in part at least around the lower levels of the Roman Catholic Church: the increased pressure on the practice of Catholicism in the early 1960s was a prime factor in producing dissent. Petition drives to object to such pressures as the confiscation of property and buildings, bureaucratic harassment of priests and local lay religious leaders, and campaigns to humilate young believers in the schools were organized at the parish and diocesan levels, and soon (in 1972) the petitions were joined by on-going samizdat "publications"—especially the *Chronicle of the Catholic Church in Lithuania*, which has

Table 1
Social and demographic characteristics

Feature		Dissidents# Per cent	General population* Per cent
Sex	(N=594)		
male	(428)	72.1	46.9
female	(166)	27.9	53.1
Residence	(N=372)		
Vilnius	(115)	30.9	11.9
Kaunas	(121)	32.5	9.8
Ethnicity	(N=589)		
Lithuanian	(583)	98.9	80.1
Russian	(4)	0.7	8.6
Other	(2)	0.3	12.3
Occupation/Social group			
	(N=362)		
Worker	(43)	11.9	54.0 of workforce
Peasant	(4)	1.1	26.2
White Collar			
	(39)	10.8	together (13.4)&
Intelligentsia			
	(60)	16.6	24.9 (0.5)
Student	(103)	28.5	0.9 (5.1)
Priest	(107)	29.6	--- (0.0005)
Other	(6)	1.7	29.9
Religion	(N=363)		
Roman Catholic			
	(349)	96.1	(50.0-85.0)
Jehovah's			
Witness	(10)	2.8	--
Jewish	(3)	0.8	0.8
Adventist	(2)	0.6	--

#Percentages of those with any information on the feature.
*Data on general population from 1970 Census; Murray Feshbach, "The Soviet Union: Population Trends and Dilemmas," Population Bulletin, 37 (3)(1982): Table 3, p. 16.
&Occupation figures in parentheses are as follows: 1)students (number on stipends and the percentage of the entire population in secondary and higher institutions of education--the last figures taken from The USSR in Figures for 1980 [Moscow: Finansy/Statistika, 1981], pp. 202 and 10), 2) white collar and intelligentsia subtotals (those possessing higher and middle level education, and highest education, respectively), 3) priests (not included as a separate category in the census reports, but they number 770, according to Vardys), 4) Roman Catholics (official estimates, discussed in Vardys).

always run reports in the latter half of each issue from the varied parishes and church territories.

The dramatic role of the clergy in the petition drives can be seen in their increasing willingness to focus attention on *their* position as local religious leaders, by signing and publicizing, as groups of priests, petitions to authorities in samizdat. For example, several articles of the draft constitution (namely, articles 52 and 53) were one source

Table 2

Average Age by Social Group

Group	Age*	(N)
Workers	25.3	19
Peasants	42.1	3
White collar	31.1	16
Intelligentsia	40.7	20
Students	18.3	24
Priests	44.9	87
Other	37.0	1
Unknown	33.4	51
All dissidents	37.5	220

----
        *Age calculated at first event in data-set: dissident act, arrest, interrogation, etc.

of one complaint in 1977. There were 7 petitions, 4 of which were signed exclusively by over 400 of the 750-plus priests in the country[23] Another example is the petition drive over the introduction of new, more restrictive regulations on religious activity in 1978: after the initial Christmas Day 1978 petition of the Catholic Committee for the Defense of the Rights of Believers (mostly clerical in composition), there were 8 petitions totalling 522 priests' signatures (3 of every 4 priests in the republic).[24]

This is not to say that only priests were involved in the petition drives. As early as 1972, there was a series of interrogations of women in several parishes about the massive Appeal to the UN about repression of religion in the republic. Also in the controversy over the new constitution, there were at least three petitions of parishioners, which more than 1755 signed.[25] However, it does seem fair to say that clerics were a pool of leadership, as examples and as activists, in the 1970s.[26]

There are several inherent sources for the recruitment of priests into dissident activity. The "clerical" dissidents, of course, have an education (seminary training), that inculcates humanistic values in spiritual forms, values that may conflict with the technocratic, atheistic, and anti-individualist attitudes of the regime. Moreover, these individuals will have some understanding of the incongruity of religion and Marxist-Leninist doctrine and practice, if only from their day-to-day experiences. Finally, one must add that these men are generally older than the rest (see Table 2). They often are of the World War I generation, and can remember the various historical events that feed anti-Soviet nationalism as well as religious dissent.

Also, for historical reasons the role of priests in the dissident movement should come as no surprise. Even during Czarist times, the clergy provided a route of social mobility for ambitious young men who did not wish to leave their homeland. The czar's policy was in essence to force nationalist young men who wished some higher education and some higher status than peasant or worker to go into the seminary: those with secular higher education were required to leave Lithuania because the czarist government feared the rise of an alienated nationalist (secular) intelligentsia. Thus, the real leaders of villages and small towns across the country were the parish priests.[27]

Moreover, according to Vardys, there exists in Lithuania a specific tradition of clerical resistance to the USSR. The leaders of the Catholic Church were in the interwar period among the most fearful of Bolshevik influence/subversion. At the time of the first incorporation of Lithuania into the Soviet Union (1940), at least 25 of the 1500 people actively opposing the Soviets and arrested by the secret police were priests. In the second incorporation (1944–1945) the secularization and repression of the Church led to a series of dissident activities from petitions by the bishops on down the hierarchy. This in turn led to mass arrests in 1945 of one-third of the clergy, including three of the four bishops. It must be admitted, however, that only a few Catholic priests were active in the anti-Soviet partisan warfare in the 1944–1952 period: only one was captured with arms in his possession, although several others were openly sympathetic and frequently provided religious rites for the partisans.[28]

However, nearly half of the dissidents are in the second and third most numerous categories, *students* (slightly fewer than the priests) and *intellectuals* (about 17%). The student and intellectual participants are to be understood in part by the alienated condition of intellectuals everywhere, in part by the particular exposure to the incongruity between official values and real behavior seen most clearly in its complicated details by those in education, who have some recourse to libraries with historical materials.

It has been argued by several social scientists that intellectuals are natural reservoirs of dissidents or even revolutionaries. They maintain that it is inherent in the social position of intellectuals for them to develop oppositional or dissident ideas, no matter the social system. Nettl, for example, sees intellectuals as engaging in the activity of argument, in the rearrangement of ideas, with particular prediliction to find problems in the social and political environment. This activity does not automatically produce dissent—a passive recognition of "paradox" can also result—but there is nonetheless discussion and development of "potentially actionable ideas" which can become the basis for dissident activity.[29] In addition, Shils suggests that the production of ideas is the function of the intellectual in modern society, a production that can make them *either* revolutionaries or agents of legitimation for the existing institutions.[30] A third, somewhat more cynical version of this notion is that of Gouldner: he sees intellectuals as those who reject authority of established ideas, who are critical and "emancipatory" believers in rationality, but who nonetheless seek power of their own in the name of other forces, depending on the prevailing winds of political conflict and often on both sides of such conflict.[31]

For Soviet-specific reasons also, intellectuals, either as autonomous and independent adults or as students, can be expected to be a recruiting ground for active dissidents. Several authors have made the argument that the stratum of "intelligentsia" is historically one that has produced individuals and groups discontented with the regime. Konrad and Szelenyi of Hungary suggest that the intellectuals of Eastern Europe (including Czarist Russia) were bifurcated into those who were absorbed into the ruling class-bureaucracy of the absolutist states of Eastern Europe and those who were revolutionaries, desiring to overturn the decadent and anti-modern system, only to replace the old elite with their own—the party.[32]

In Shatz' view, under czarism the rise of an educated stratum was inevitably associated with the development of discontent among the sons of the nobility—the major component—because the existing system did not conform to the expectations of good government derived from Western political philosophy. That discontent, he maintained, continues to this day, as the dissident movement in Moscow and Leningrad.[33] Finally, Cox has indicated that a self-interested, insecure intelligentsia opposed the political elite in the post-Stalinist period because of several conflicts with that elite. He sees a structural conflict between the intelligentsia's "partial interest" and the overall social interests represented by the elite (cf. Gouldner, above), as well as a series of issues rooted in the prior insecurity and restriction of the intellectuals. Among the latter issues are the questions of police terror, political centralization, censorship, economic rigidities, and minimal contacts with Western culture.[34]

Indeed, even some Soviet dissidents of international reknown state that the major social base of dissent is the intellectuals. For example, Roy Medvedev says that circles of intellectuals are the main type of dissident. Of course, he goes on to grant that certain national and religious groups (presumably including Lithuanians and Catholics) also dissent, but his position is clear. These other groups play only bit parts, while intellectuals are on center-stage.[35]

That means that the phenomenon of dissent is not limited to intellectuals and religious leaders. It is of some interest that in the Lithuanian case there are some *lower status groups*, such as workers

Table 3
Kaunas and Vilnius Dissidents

City	Intellectual		Student		Priest		White Collar		Worker		Average Age*
	%	(N)	%	(N)	%	(N)	%	(N)	%	(N)	Years
Kaunas	21.9	(16)	37.0	(27)	2.7	(2)	17.6	(13)	19.2	(14	29.3
Vilnius	35.7	(30)	33.3	(28)	4.8	(4)	19.0	(16)	7.1	(6)	29.1

*See note to Table 2 above. N for age base=34 and 47, respectively. There was one Kaunas case that fell into the "other" category.

and white-collar employees (nurses and clerks, for example). Of course, their numbers are not great, in a relative sense. Only 43 and 39 dissidents (including both men and women) out of the sample were identifiably from these two social groups. However, they represent over 22% of the dissidents whose occupation was known.[36]

It is difficult to ascertain the true peasant involvement in the social movement. Only 4 cases were of this occupational category, but there are many missing cases, many of which could easily be peasants whose status would be "unmemorable" in the lives of the dissidents in rural areas. Also, the extensiveness of samizdat reportage throughout the republic, including the most rural areas, would suggest some peasant support, as would the massive petition drives of the 1970s.

Thus, one can say that while the dissidents were overwhelmingly, those with higher education and/or with a special position (priest) in the communities of the country, dissent is by no means as restricted to these groups as some analyses have suggested. The specific recruitment from these groups is logical, but does not refute the likelihood that dissent is a nation-wide activity, for the less educated are present also.

Geography

Where do these dissidents come from? Is dissent an artifact of life in urban university centers? In fact dissident is only partially concentrated geographically. The two major university towns (Kaunas and Vilnius) together account for about 20% of the population generally (Kaunas 9.8% and Vilnius 11.9% according to the 1970 Census), and produce over half the dissidents (32.5% and 30.9% respectively).[37]

Are the dissidents in those cities in fact mostly university intellectuals of one kind or another? Table 3 suggests that this is the case. Over one-half of the dissidents known to be from each city are either students or intellectuals. The proportion of priests is negligible in comparison to the overall dissident group (thus the average age is seven years younger). On the other hand, the percentages of white collar (for both cities) and blue collar workers (for Kaunas) are considerably higher. The implication is that the activities of the intellectuals and students may well encourage the lower-status dis-contents into dissident activity, while the relative absence of priests does not have debilitating effects because of the alternate source of leadership.

On the other hand, it is a fact that over nine-tenths of the 47 districts and special areas of the republic have some dissidents in the overall file. (Only three districts are completely absent.) The dispersion of dissent over this broad of territory cannot be seen except as a consequence of truly national activity. Moreover, these data suggest that there are two major bases of institutional resources for dissidents—the church and the higher educational institutions—each of which operates in separate geo-political conditions. The former is stronger in smaller towns and villages, where local priests have solid backing by the local community, and the latter is stronger in the two main cities, where they have some resources in the size and concentration of higher education.

Religion

As might be expected, an overwhelming majority of the dissidents are Roman Catholic. Estimates in the Western and Soviet literatures on the extent of Catholicism among the general population does range from 50% to over 85%, but the lower boundary is still the majority.[38]

Of course, it is difficult to identify religion from many accounts of dissident activities and regime responses (nearly half of the data-set contains missing information on this point), but through analysis of the contents of dissident acts and of their own documents, it is possible to determine that 95.5% were Catholic.

The Roman Catholic participation rate is understandable for several reasons. First, most of the population is Catholic. Second, one group of dissidents is clerics—almost by definition and certainly here in fact, Roman Catholic. Third, as elaborated later, the parish structure has continued and provides some degree of organization in which dissent can flourish. Finally, the historical ties of religion to nationalism mentioned in chapter 2 continue in the current connections of na-tionalist and religious dissent—which we will discuss shortly.

Less than 3 per cent were Jehovah's Witnesses, and less than one percent were Jewish. This finding is somewhat disproportionate to the general population, but it is obvious that the smaller religious groups are weakened by their smaller numbers and that it is rare for

Table 4

Birth Cohorts of Dissidents

Birth years	Percent of Total	Number	Rate per year
1873-1899	2.4	6	0.2
1900-1913	18.2	46	3.3
1914-1917	9.1	23	5.8
1918-1939	28.5	72	3.3
1940-1945	8.3	21	3.5
1946-1953	11.9	30	3.8
1954-1964	17.0	43	3.9
1965-1968	4.9	12	3.0
Total	100.0	253	2.6

them to become actively involved in much dissent because of their social isolation and vulnerability. The Witnesses, as elsewhere in the world, are marked by their willingness to risk social and legal consequences by intense proselytizing.[39]

Age

How old are the dissidents? We have mentioned ages in the specific contexts of priests and students, as well as residence in the two largest urban areas. A more general overview of this factor is appropriate.

The age range is from 11 to 76, with the average being 36.1. The birth cohorts go back to 1873 and up to 1968. Dissent is not a phenomenon of young men alone, although they may be major participants. What is remarkable about the age distribution is: 1) the concentration in the interwar generation, and 2) the steady recruitment in the postwar period, despite major changes in the system. As Table 4 shows, nearly a third of the dissidents were born in the pre-Soviet republic of Lithuania, and about a tenth of the dissidents were born in each of the major Soviet periods: World War II, late Stalinism, and Khrushchev's dominance. On a per annum basis, there is a peaking of recruitment for the First World War generation, and a brief decline, and then a steady recovery afterwards. Given the young ages of the last, post-Khrushchevite cohort (from 11 years old up), the comparability of its rate to the Khrushchevite generation is impressive.

What does this mean for the Soviet authorities? That dissent will not die out along with the pre-Soviet generation. It has revived and will continue to be a problem for decades to come.

Ethnicity

Although last name is not an infallible indicator of nationality because it does not reveal the mother's nationality, nonetheless the low intermarriage rate in Lithuania (7%)[40] allows us to draw some tentative conclusions. Simply put, only two non-Lithuanian groups are active in Lithuanian dissent. Jews (a nationality by official Soviet policy) are not numerous in dissent, and are becoming much less numerous in the Lithuanian republic's population throughout the 1970s because of emigration. Russian dissidents are usually those, like Sergei Kovalev, who were brought to trial in Vilnius on the grounds of a putative connection to the Lithuanian samizdat network. These two groups are nearly non-existent: almost all the Lithuanian dissent is Lithuanian by background.

Sex

Two-thirds of the dissidents are male, not surprising given what we know of political behavior—and anti-regime behavior in particular—from other political systems. Most rebels—as well as establishment politicians—are men. However, this gender distribution is also to be expected from the occupations of people who are dissidents. One group of dissidents is formally exclusively male (priests), while the others are probably predominantly male for logical reasons.

It seems that the general pattern of sexist hindrances makes more upwardly mobile females (intellectuals and students) somewhat more reluctant to participate, for fear of losing too much. It is notable that their lower status sisters, having less to lose, do participate considerably more. The students and intellectuals are even more female than the overall dissident population (33.9% and 32% v. 20.3%), but still far less than the over one-half proportion of the general population. The greatest proportion of women is to be found among the lower status manual and white collar workers (39% and 35.6%, respectively). Also, the female dissidents are young compared to the males: 30.3 years old (n=19) v. 36.6 (n=202).

Who Dissents?: Content of Discontent

The real fabric of dissent may be lost if the preceding demographic information is the sole focus of attention. Dissidents are varied in background, yet at the same time some patterns are clear: clergy, intellectuals, students, males, residences in the two major cities do predominate. In addition, it is obvious that some of the basis of their discontent is rooted in history and social position.

However, a more complete understanding of the phenomenon of dissent, and its significance for the Soviet regime itself, must come from a closer consideration of the content of dissent. More important than history or social position is the dimension of motivation. Even some Marxists with a great respect for "objective conditions" treat social reality as contingent on "consciousness" or "subjective conditions." Thus, one must ask the question, what are the areas of discontent indicated by the dissidents themselves?

In the last 40 years of dissident activity, several areas of discontent have emerged. Complaints focus on the pressures on ethnic identity, on the constraints on religious practice, and on the absence of many features of individual liberty and protection from arbitrary power. Other criticisms are far less frequent, and do not form a coherent set of patterns: violation of Marx's promises, prohibitions on romantic poetry, bossy superiors, etc.

Each of the three major kinds of dissent involves, as we shall see, numerous criticisms of the Soviet system, varied types of activity and a degree of organization. Our typology itself is based on information about the dissident's activities, from reports of his actions, the content of petitions signed by him and others, and the materials taken from him in searches by militia and secret police. However, although each type draws from differently from several social groups (which implies some localized resonance of appeal), there is an indication of an underlying unity of discontent: a large hybridized group. Indeed, the entire phenomenon of dissent is far more unified than at first is apparent, and thus the Lithuanian dissidents, despite their demographic differences, ought to be conceived of as a diverse but interconnected movement.

Religious Discontent

As may be seen in Table 5 (below), the most prevalent type of dissent is religious: it is the largest single "pure" category (over one quarter—159 individuals of the 559 that can be identified by type). In addition, religion forms one component of the largest "mixed" category—religious plus one or more other types. That type numbers about an eighth of the entire sample (74 people). Thus, a total of 41.5% of all dissidents have a religious basis for their discontent.

This is not at all surprising. Given the restrictive laws, anti-religious ideology, and the pervasiveness of Catholicism among the general population, it would be unusual if religion were not a ground for dissent. The closing of churches, the ridicule of religious youth in the schools, the bureaucratic harrassment of religious congregations by local and republic authorities are all general grievances to be noted. In addition, there are frequent petitions and demonstrations in support of priests who were punished by authorities for giving religious instruction to children, administering rites illegally, and other religious activities.[41] Moreover, there are numerous restrictions on such activity, from the limitations on the geographic scope of rites given by the individual priest, through the complete prohibition of church social welfare or youth activity, to the legal status of "non-person" in the courts when it comes to the ability to file suit, etc.[42] Finally, there are dissidents who support priests and lay people who have been caught up in the coercive apparatus for such actions as possession, distribution, or production of illegal publications, or more open human rights activities.

The religious form of dissent has the power of several highly emotive symbols. One activity that has mobilized thousands has been processions carrying the Cross (a reenactment of one of the key aspects of Christianity). Other activities include wearing, possessing, and putting up crosses; holding masses and other rites. The churches themselves (if damaged or demolished) are potent socio-religious symbols for religious dissidents, as well as the "innocence" of youth (harmed by Soviet atheist norms) and "Christian morality" (especially in the campaign against alcoholism).[43]

Perhaps the most dramatic forms of religious dissent focus on the symbols with major material consequence: the administrative exile of Bishop Steponavicius that precluded his fulfilling his duties, the illegal seizure of the newly built Cathedral of Our Lady in Klaipeda and its conversion to a municipal auditorium, the trials of Fathers Seskevicius, Zdebskis, and Bubnys in 1970 and 1971 (and of Tamkevicius and Svarinskas in 1983). Nonetheless, it is remarkable how massive the petition drives for substantive changes have been, including return of the Klaipeda Cathedral (over 168,000), end to restrictions on religion (petitions to the UN, Brezhnev, and others in 1972–1973, each about 16,000 signatures), and most recently protests against the arrest and sentencing of two priests (over 123,000 in 1983).[44]

The religious dissidents are relatively well organized. After all, there is the overall structure of the church in Lithuania: parishes are to be found throughout the country, and most have their own local priest. These priests, who are the alternate symbol of moral authority, are in turn connected to one another through the diocesan structures, if not the personnel at the central offices of the church (who are closely supervised, and sometimes directly selected by the Republic Commission on Religious Affairs). Also, there is a seminary that continues to operate, in which informal ties among young priests are formed, although the numbers of young men admitted to the seminary are artificially limited, with those refused admission including many devout individuals.[45]

However, the degree of illegal organization paralleling and supplementing the formal legal structure is amazing. Occasionally, in samizdat there are self-descriptions of this parallel structure, with its religious and organizational activity outside the "normal" mechanisms of supervision and control. This parallel structure is known as the "church of the catacombs,"[46] referring to earlier groups of underground Christians. Thus, in response to the limitations on the seminary, there have been cases of underground ordinations, which implies the possibility of an underground seminary. In addition, there are occasional references, usually in charges by police investigators, to underground convents.[47] This too would be an understandable development given the post-war abolition of the religious orders and the confiscation of their properties. Here the point is that there may be a set of religious training institutions in which devout Catholics can and do obtain more intense religious instruction and perform religious tasks. Some of the individuals involved in this kind of underground activity go further, into some other forms of public religious dissent.

Among the other forms are several on-going underground periodicals, including the *Chronicles of the Catholic Church in Lithuania, Sorrowing Christ, God and Country, The Path of Truth,* and others, that keep the general population informed of the latest dissident actions and governmental countermeasures throughout the republic. The journals include some specifically oriented to priests and religious young men (*The Path of Truth,* appearing beginning in January 1977), and some oriented to theological problems. Clearly, these as well as the *Chronicles* are likely to involve those in the church of the catacombs.[48]

Finally, there are several groups that operate to maintain organizational ties among priests and faithful outside the official parish structures. Among the most important is the "Friends of the Eucharist" Society, established in 1969, to promote greater devotion and activism among young adults especially, most notably during periodic ritual celebrations of carrying the Cross, praying at historically important religious sites, etc.[49] In addition, one must add the open organization of the religious created to publicize the repression of Catholics: the Catholic Committee for the Defense of the Rights of Believers.[50] Its continuing existence is due in no small measure to the commitment of a series of activist priests, who have taken on a great responsibility, for the openness of the committee and its work renders it vulnerable to the same coercive pressures applied to the more secular human rights groups, like the Helsinki Watch Group.

Table 5

Type of Dissent by Content:
Percentage of Dissidents in Each Category

Type	"Pure"	Mixed	Total
Religious	28.3%	13.2%	41.5%
	(158)	(74)	(232)
Nationalist	18.2	11.8	30.0
	(102)	(66)	(167)
Human rights	1.1	12.5	13.6
	(6)	(70)	(76)
Other*	6.4	0.9	7.6
	(36)	(5)	(41)
All Hybrids	----	----	15.7
			(88)

Nationalism

Discontent rooted in attachment to and a sense of the distinctiveness of the nation is significant too, coming in a second place numerically. One-sixth were nationalist alone, and another one-tenth of the dissidents were nationalist in some combination with other forms. Thus a total of 30.0% of all dissidents had some nationalist sentiment. (See Table 5.)

The content of nationalist grievances concerns the sense of injustice to the ethnic group of Lithuanians, in a great variety of areas, including language, history, literature, environmental pollution, and political independence. Among the specific concerns expressed are the Russification of communication (especially for Lithuanians outside the republic), the demolition or neglect of Lithuanian historical shrines, the absence of genuine historical analysis of the Lithuanian experience, the question of the Nazi-Soviet pact of 1939, and the neglect of Lithuanian interests resulting in increasing industrial pollution and a distortion of its own literature.[51] It should be noted that strong ingredients in much of this ethnic identity are anti-Russian sentiment (expressed sometimes as simply as shouts of "Russians Go Home"), anti-Communism (although there have been some explicit divergences here), and demand for retribution for the coercive apparatus' victims—especially unreleased Partisans.

It has been argued with some cogency that there are several subvarieties of nationalist dissent. Vardys suggests that among younger intellectuals of 1960s one can find three: autonomist, national Communist, and liberal-democratic-socialist-Catholic.[52] Remeikis also sees three types: Catholic Nationalism, Liberal Nationalism and liberal-socialist.[53]

There are problems with such typologizing: for example, the two schema are not the same, and it is difficult to judge which, if either, would be more appropriate. Also, the commonalities of nationalist discontent are marked. There do not appear to be major gulfs on the issues, for there are cross-references, and there seems to be no clear activity differentiated by kind of nationalism. Indeed, both Vardys and Remeikis have difficulties applying their own categories.[54]

Another sign of cohesiveness of nationalist dissent is the prevalence of the same symbols: the traditional flag (illegal after admission to the USSR), the traditional national anthem, the old holiday of independence (February 16th), the June days of Soviet occupation, the historical shrines (especially graves of nationalist poets and non-communist leaders), and even sports competitions in which Russian teams are defeated (even by other Baltic teams!).[55] One must add that the dissident movement itself has produced nationalist symbols. One young man, who committed self-immolation in front of the building wherein the request for admission to the USSR was voted forty years before, posthumously became a figure representing the Lithuanian people as well as the idealism of the young despite decades of political socialization.[56]

This symbol of a young man dying for his country personifies a marked difference in the activities of the nationalist, as opposed to the other two types of dissent: nationalist actions tend to be more dramatic, violent, and politicized. These actions include spontaneous riots, hijackings, escapes, self-immolations, and conspiratorial groups, as well as the more common production of samizdat and petitions.[57]

However, it should also be noted that the nationalists have also engaged in more overt forms of cooperation with national groups other than the religious dissidents: namely, the Baltic Declaration of August 1979. This was a joint protest of 45 dissidents from the three Baltic nationalities (Lithuanian, Latvian, Estonian), on the 40th anniversary of the Molotov-von Ribbentrop Agreement that allowed the Soviet Union to occupy the Baltic states. The petition demanded that the pact be declared null and void, and that the political independence of the three states be restored. About three quarters of the signers were prominent Lithuanian dissidents, and included 4 priests.

The predominant form of organization for nationalist dissent is the conspiratorial group. There are several mentioned in samizdat (see above), but little is known about them. Indeed, it has been suggested by some that a number are "phantom" bodies with names "created" by a handful of dissidents for their manifestos. Such a group is the

Free Communist Party of Lithuania. Nonetheless, a samizdat *network* does exist: many journals have appeared (and many continue) for several issues, despite efforts of the regime to eliminate them: for example, *The Dawn, Archive of Culture, Herald of Freedom, The National Path, The Knight.*[58] An important point here is that these publications are far less numerous than religious journals.

Human Rights

The third category—human rights—accounted for only slightly more than one-eighth of the dissidents (13.6%). Indeed, it was more often found combined with other forms of dissent: only one percent of the dissidents (six cases) were solely human rights activists.

The human rights type of dissent has, at its base, a universalist perspective. The grievances about the violation of fundamental rights due individuals and peoples are not "exclusivist" in that human rights advocates accept the obligation to take up *all* causes of injustice. This universality is visible in a perusal of the subjects of statements by the major human rights group of Lithuania, the Lithuanian Helsinki Watch Group: banishment of bishops, restrictions on religion, arrests, persecution of Estonians, reunification of families with West, discrimination against Volga Germans in Lithuania, persecution of Russian Baptists, political prisoners, psychiatric abuse, the 1939 pact mentioned above, persecution in Czechoslovakia, the Soviet invasion of Afghanistan, the banishment of Sakharov, arrests and slanders of its own members.[59]

Of course, this is not to say that the other types of dissent are totally "exclusive": we have noted above the cooperation of Balts in the August 1979 Declaration against the Nazi-Soviet Pact, for example. However, the basis of dissent for these others is the substance of injustice per se, not the violation of *rights,* including rights of legality protected by constitution and international law. Indeed, those who call themselves human rights activists make the attempt to extend their activities, as far as possible, to include those with differing ethnic, religious, and even political perspectives.

It is difficult to suggest any specific symbols for this type of dissent. Only the documents enumerating such rights, like the UN Declaration of the Rights of Man, and the Final Act of the Helsinki Conference on Cooperation and Security in Europe, are of transcendent importance to these dissidents, yet they can scarcely be thought of as symbols. Perhaps this is the reason so few individuals have been recruited to this type of dissent: symbols to mobilize the masses or to inspire great numbers of new recruits are simply not present.

This type of dissident engages in both conventional actions, such as the signing of petitions, and in somewhat irregular behavior for the contemporary Soviet Union, namely, the creation of independent groups. Indeed, it is on this score that human rights dissidents differ most clearly from others: their prediliction for public organization. The major example is the Lithuanian Helsinki Watch Group. Established on 25 November 1976, it was connected to the monitors of other republics. The members made public announcements of their membership and issued all sorts of public statements about human rights in the Soviet Union, as noted above.

A related group, modelled on the Russian Orthodox experience with the Christian Committee for the Defense of the Rights of Believers (established in November 1976), is the Catholic Committee for the Defense of the Rights of Believers (founded two years later). It too is public in membership and issues statements, but generally speaking it specializes in the human rights of Catholics in Lithuania.

One ought to notice the occasional concern by different kinds of dissidents for others, a kind of spillover effect. This suggests a greater degree of association than what one might otherwise suspect. Indeed, it raises the question of the possibility of dissidents possessing several grounds of discontent, of being a "hybrid" of two or more types.

The Hybrid Dissidents: a Linkage of Types

A hitherto unknown feature of Lithuanian dissent is the proportion of dissidents in the "hybrid" category—14.4% (see Table 5). Thus, to a sizeable part of the "dissident movement," the varied problems of the Lithuanian SSR seem to intertwine. The net effect is the merging of the several streams of dissent in the physical persons of about one sixth of the dissidents. Such an integration provides instantaneous connection of the differing kinds of discontent to each other, while preserving some degree of separation for the development of discussion of specialized issues. Thus, the marble cake mixture of Lithuanian dissent, with some parts being of diverse content, while others are mixed together, can be easily seen as an advantage in the long-term development of a dissident movement.

The general scholarly description of Lithuanian dissent is of several separate groups that have some but limited interaction. Vardys and Remeikis imply by their typologizing of dissent and of the differentiation within nationalist, religious, and other types of discontent, that the types are distinct from one another.[60] However, a closer look at the dissidents will reveal a group of people who mediate among the differing types.

Table 6

Recruitment by Age and Gender
into Different Types of Dissent

Type	Age in Years		Males	
		(N)		(Total N)
Religious	40.5	(78)	71.5%	(158)
(hybrids)	34.0	(40)	75.7	(74)
Nationalist	32.9	(44)	86.9	(104)
(hybrids)	29.4	(30)	79.0	(62)
Human rights	23.3	(4)	50.0	(18)
(hybrids)	34.6	(38)	75.9	(58)
All Hybrids	32.6	(48)	75.0	(88)
All dissidents	37.6	(273)	72.9	(594)

Table 7

Recruitment by Social Group
into Different Types of Dissent

Type	Occupation											
	Workers		Peasants		White Collar		Intell.		Students		Priests	
	%	(N)	%	(N)	%	(N)	%	(N)	%	(N)	%	(N)
Religious	6.7	(7)	1.0	(1)	2.9	(3)	5.8	(6)	9.6	(10)	72.9	(73)
(hybrids)	15.1	(8)	––	(0)	20.8	(11)	15.1	(8)	11.3	(6)	34.0	(18)
Nationalist	20.5	(9)	4.5	(2)	6.8	(3)	13.6	(6)	51.8	(25)	4.5	(2)
(hybrids)	20.5	(9)	––	(0)	20.5	(9)	18.2	(8)	20.5	(7)	20.5	(9)
Human rights	14.3	(1)	––	(0)	14.3	(1)	42.9	(3)	14.3	(1)	14.3	(1)
(hybrids)	11.4	(5)	––	(0)	20.5	(9)	22.7	(10)	15.9	(7)	29.6	(13)
All Hybrid	15.9	(9)	––	(0)	22.2	(14)	17.5	(11)	12.7	(8)	28.6	(18)
Total	11.9	(43)	1.1	(4)	10.8	(39)	16.6	(60)	28.5	(103)	29.6	(107)

Vardys suggests explicitly that the "Catholic movement" is "allied though *not merged* with the nationalist Lithuanian underground.[61] There is something to this picture: there *are* distinct groups of religious, nationalist, and human rights dissidents. Yet, this image of isolated components of a dissident movement only occasionally interacting is deceptive. The high rate of "hybidization" (about one sixth) indicates that, to many dissidents, the differing types are closely related in reality (or simply aspects of the same set of problems).

One important, previously neglected aspect of this hybridization is common bases of recruitment. It must be carefully noted that our conclusions in this area can only be tentative, because of the small numbers in some of the categories. Thus, Tables 6 and 7 suggest that the hybrid group draws from all social sectors, and that it is more "representative" of them than of any of the three major types. Some selective recruitment among the pure types may be moderated in the hybridization of that basis of discontent. For example, the religious types are dominated by priests (nearly three-quarters), and average in age nearly 41 years old. Religious hybrids are far less likely to be priests (less than a third), far more likely to be white collar, intellectual, or worker (15–20% each), and six years younger. The entire category of hybrids, moreover, is even less likely than religious hybrids to be priests (29%), slightly more likely to be each of the other categories (by a few percentage points each), and a year and a half younger.

Thus, the hybrids seem to draw from the major social base of *each* of the types. Indeed, the same "connecting effect" can be found empirically in the data on the other major types of dissent, with one small exception. "Pure" human rights dissidents seem to be older than the human rights hybrid dissident, and more likely to be female. However, there are only 18 human rights pure types, and only 4 with age data.

The significance of these facts is simple: hybrid dissidents are probably not as likely to be seen either as spokesmen for narrower social groups or as different from those groups (because there are hybrids of similar background for each group). This commonality makes possible the increasing articulation of common positions and the coordination of future dissident activities.

Related to this general reinforcement of activities by dissidents of differing types is the personal connection, sometimes in the "union" of the differing types within the same person. This type of connection means that communications among the differing types of dissidents are more rapid, and the possible coordination of positions more easy, than if the streams require mediators. One recent case, that of Skuodis, clearly demonstrates this linkage.

Vytautas Skuodis (a.k.a. Scott), a former university professor of geology, did not come to the attention of dissidents or authorities until a year after Petkus' trial. Skuodis, nonetheless, concentrated a great amount of activity into a short period of time—necessarily because of the likelihood that he would soon follow Petkus. In the summer of 1979 he signed the protest on the Nazi-Soviet Pact of 1939. For this action his apartment was twice searched and typewriters, tape recorder, several issues of nationalist samizdat including *Ausra*, and his own manuscripts were taken. One manuscript was a 300–400 page book entitled *Spiritual Genocide in Lithuania*, which must have displeased the authorities greatly. Despite this, he added to his own file at KGB headquarters by joining the Helsinki Watch Group, as well as the Catholic Committee for Defense of the Rights of Believers.

The time between joining these groups and joining their earlier members in camp was even shorter than for Petkus, if only because of Skuodis' public position in Vilnius at the University. He was arrested, tried, and convicted in 1980 for anti-Soviet agitation and propaganda and given, as a first sentence, seven years in camp plus five years exile.[62]

Hybridization as Radicalization: Career Paths

In the example of Skuodis, we have an individual who gradually moved beyond one basis of dissent to add others, until finally he dissented on the grounds of all three of the major types. This represents a "radicalization" of dissent. The hybrids thus are catalysts in the increased sharing of values and coordination among dissidents that are part of the process of the unification of divergent groups into one social movement. Thus, the hybrids play a critical *strategic* role in the struggle of dissidents against the regime. There is yet another, perhaps more threatening aspect to the rise of this group: the radicalization of dissent.

To be radical is to reject the existing social order. To be "radicalized" is to reject more and more of that order. In Lithuania in the contemporary period, one such path of an increasing rejection involves the addition of nationalist and human rights concerns to those of religion, for example. One would reject first the aspects of the political system that constrain religious belief and practice; then national discrimination or Russification; finally, an appreciation of general human rights violations beyond one's own nationality and religion would develop. Indeed, this path, or variants thereof, is found in the histories of the dissidents.

The analysis of such "career paths" with the existing data is not easy, and cannot be pursued too far. The information is limited and the classification of type of dissent is, after all, frequently based on hints in the reportage of items confiscated during searches, of questioning during interrogation, and the like. Also, the number of hybrids is not large (88), so that detailed statistical breakdown to ascertain the differences of background, age, activity, and other variables would produce little more than a great number of "empty cells" (where the number of individuals in parts of tables is zero). Nonetheless, one can examine the transition from one type to another in general terms, especially by the original type of dissent. (Future research into the question of the details of biographic development awaits the emigration,

Table 8
Transformation of Dissident Type

Original Categories of Hybrids	N	changing	Second step	Third step	"Final" type*
Religion	20	all	3	2	2
Nationalism	32	all	2	1	1
Both	13	3	21	14	24
Human Rights	0	0	2	3	3
HR and Relig.	5	1	18	16	20
HR and Nat.	2	0	3	3	5
All three	3	0	6	16	19
Other	1	all	0	0	0

*This includes those who did not change from an initial hybrid category.

Chart 1
Religious-Based Hybridization

Religious (20) ——> Religious-Human Rights (11)

Religious-Nationalists (5)

(1)

Nationalists (2)

(1)

Triple Hybrids--Religious-Human Rights-Nationalists (1)

as yet unforeseen, of larger numbers of non-Jewish Lithuanians, for in-depth interviewing.)

Table 8 demonstrates that it is rare for a dissident to change by straightforward substitution of one pure type for another (only 6 of the total end up any of the three pure categories). On the other hand, several varieties of hybrids show marked increase: religious-nationalist, religious-human rights, nationalist-human rights (to some extent), and religious-nationalist-human rights (a "triple-hybrid"). The "triple-hybrid" type, especially, shows great growth from 3 to 19.

A closer examination of the paths is even more revealing.[63] We discover that some forms of hybrids arise more easily out of religion, and that such religious-originated hybrids are more "resistant" to further hybridization, in contrast to nationalist-originated dissent. Chart 1 shows that the bulk of the religious dissidents who are radicalized add human rights concerns and stay there. A smaller number add nationalist concerns, and stay; and a small fraction substitutes nationalist dissent (one of two then returns to religious dissent with the addition of both nationalist and human rights). In other words, religious dissent is a source for radicalization to both religious-human

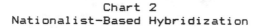

Chart 2
Nationalist—Based Hybridization

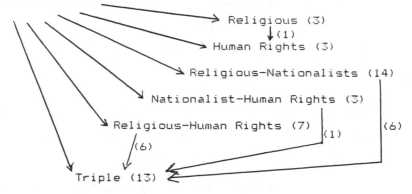

rights and religious-nationalist categories, but little for any other category or combination.

Chart 2 demonstrates, on the other hand, that nationalism is more volatile. It often leads to a displacement of simple nationalist concerns by religious-plus categories, with the religious-nationalist category, of course, being the largest. However, that hybrid type is itself volatile, as nearly half then become "triple-hybrids," also recruited from religious-human rights and nationalist-human rights hybrids to a lesser extent. It is to be noted that these paths contribute to the vast majority of the triple hybrids: only 3 of the 16 who go through three stages do not come from the nationalist type originally.

This volatility of nationalism may lead the regime to move more quickly and more severely against nationalist dissidents than against others. We would expect to see both a targeting of nationalist dissidents and harsher sentences given to those who are tried. Indeed, we will notice these patterns in later chapters.

Conclusion

Thus, we have seen the diversity of the dissidents: priests, intellectuals, students, religious dissidents, nationalists, and human rights supporters are all represented. Each group has somewhat different locales and resources, issues and symbols, types of organization. The diversity is, nonetheless, only half the story. These various groups have been able to form a social movement of nationwide proportions. Otherwise diverse groups share common experiences and identity as Lithuanians. Frequently one group's grievances are articulated by others. Most often this is done by human rights dissidents, acting on general principles, but sometimes it is done by individuals—the hybrids—who belong to more than one category.

However, we should not overestimate the developmental stage of the emerging social movement. The degree of organization and the closeness of the linkages of the various types of dissent do vary. As we have seen, the religious dissidents are particularly well organized, both above and below ground, but the nationalists do not seem organized beyond small-group conspiracies. Some inter-group linkages are built in, as in the Helsinki Watch Group and the Catholic Committee for the Defense of the Rights of Believers. Other linkages are more episodic, as in occasional reportage of nationalist dissent in religious samizdat, or vice versa. Moreover, dissident activity is to a considerable extent not a collective endeavor: individuals write complaints and petitions by themselves, small groups have little visible contact with others. This "individualism" is a sign that the social movement has not yet become a dominant force for some of its own members.

That the movement should be as pervasive and as strong as it is, is a tribute to the efforts of activist dissidents and a reflection of the failure of the repressive campaigns of the regime. In the next several chapters we will examine the way in which the authorities have tried to use the courts to deal with the challenge of the dissidents, especially by concentrating judicial attention on hybrids (the most strategically important part of the movement) and nationalists (the major breeding ground for hybrids).

The significance of the hybridization process, radicalization, is the rooted in the problem presented to the regime. There is implied a real possibility of political challenge developing, if the hybrid radicals increase in number and develop an effective network of communications to lead the "pure" types in varied oppositional activities. Thus, it is not surprising what the response of the regime is: the differentiated use of judicial apparatus.

Notes

1. Italics added. Although this specific quote is from the Soviet dissident Roy Medvedev—*On Soviet Dissent* (New York: Columbia University Press, 1980), p. 1—it has many somewhat less concise equivalents in the works of Westerners. See, for example, Frederick C. Barghoorn, "Political Dissent," in *The Soviet Union: Looking to the 1980s*, ed. Robert Wesson (Stanford: Hoover Institution Press, 1980), p. 152.

2. Also, "opposition" rooted in the personal struggle for power within the Communist Party. Cf., Barghoorn's "Factional, Sectoral, and Subversive

Opposition in Soviet Politics," in *Regimes and Oppositions*, ed. Robert A. Dahl (New Haven: Yale University Press, 1973), pp. 27–87; and H. Gordon Skilling's "integral," "fundamental," "factional," and "specific" oppositions, in his "Opposition in Communist East Europe," ibid., pp. 92–94.

3. David Kowalewski, "The Human Rights Movement Under Brezhnev," in *Soviet Politics in the Brezhnev Era*, ed. Donald R. Kelley (New York: Praeger, 1980), and Ludmilla Alexeyeva, "The Human Rights Movement in the USSR," *Survey* 23(4) (Autumn 1977–1978): 76, do recognize the existence of particularist demands, but they both subsume them into the "human rights movement."

4. Medvedev; Peter Reddaway, "Soviet Policy towards Dissent Since Khrushchev," RFE-RL Report, no. 297/80 (21 August 1980), p.62; Joshua Rubenstein, *Soviet Dissidents: Their Struggle for Human Rights* (Boston: Beacon Press, 1980); Marshall S. Shatz, *Soviet Dissent in Historical Perspective* (New York: Cambridge University Press, 1980). Some exceptions to this delimitation are Tokes; Alexeyeva; David Kowalewski, "National Rights Protest in the Brezhnev Era," *Ethnic and Racial Studies*, 4 (2) (April 1981): 175–188.

5. Rudolf Tokes, "Varieties of Soviet Dissent: An Overview," in *Dissent in the USSR: Politics, Ideology, and People* (Baltimore: Johns Hopkins University Press, 1975), p. 30.

6. Shatz, p. 178; Medvedev, p. 8.

7. Reddaway, p. 62, Sharlet, p. 112; Bohdan R. Bociurkiw, "Political Dissent in the Soviet Union," *Studies in Comparative Communism* 3(2) (1970): 75; Ghita Ionescu, *The Politics of the European Communist States* (London: Weidenfeld and Nicolson, 1967), p. 179. However, the second author does go considerably beyond this in a later article as we shall see below.

8. Barghoorn, p. 158.

9. It is because of this that A. Y. Shtromas' original expansion of the term dissent—to embrace all "deviant" behavior and the entire population—was conclusively rejected in the debate in *Studies in Comparative Communism* 12 (2–3) (Summer-Autumn 1979): 212–276. (Shtromas' article is "Dissent and Political Change in the Soviet Union," pp. 212–244.) The regime simply does not label its entire citizenry as "dissident."

10. Robert Sharlet, "Dissent and Repression in the Soviet Union and Eastern Europe," *International Journal* 23 (4) (Autumn 1978): 763–795; Alexeyeva, pp. 72–73; and others.

11. Reddaway, "The Development of Dissent in the Soviet Union," in *The Soviet Empire: Expansion and Detente*, ed. William E. Griffith (Lexington, Mass.: DC Heath, 1976), p. 80; Howard L. Biddulph, "Protest Strategies of the Soviet Intellectual Opposition," in Tokes, p. 96–115; cf. Kowalewski, "The Protest Uses of Symbolic Politics in the USSR," *Journal of Politics* 42 (1980): 439–460; Barbara Wolfe Jancar, "Religious Dissent in the Soviet Union," in Tokes, pp.228–229.

12. Most Western analysts and Soviets would reject the idea that well-placed *party factions* are dissident, and many would exclude the articulation of policy alternatives in professional journals from dissent as well. This exclusion of factional leaders and followers is reasonable if one considers the

difference between them and the "ordinary" dissident. The faction's activity of opposition is within the accepted "rules of the game," and it has political resources with which to defend its legitimacy within policy-making institutions, whereas dissidents are not engaging in "acceptable" opposition and cannot defend their position. (The "sectoral opposition" type is here similar to the factional.) We will discuss both factionalism and sectoral/interest group activity more in Chapter 7.

13. R.L. Tokes, "Dissent: The Politics for Change in the USSR," in *Soviet Politics and Society in the 1970s*, ed. Henry W. Morton and Rudolf L. Tokes (New York: Free Press, 1974), p. 10.

14. A good discussion of the term may be found in Charles Tilly, *From Mobilization to Revolution* (Reading, Mass.: Addison-Wesley, 1978), pp. 8–10, 39–43. Although Tilly prefers the more general terms "collective action" or "collective protest," his analysis of organization, mobilization, opportunity, and activity is readily applicable to the specific subcategory "social movement."

15. Paul Wilkinson, *Social Movement* (London: Pall Mall, 1971), p.27, as cited in Charles Tilly, *From Mobilization to Revolution* (Reading, Mass.: Addison-Wesley, 1978), p. 39.

16. Tilly, pp. 54–55.

17. Ronald Grigor Suny, "Toward a Social History of the October Revolution," *American Historical Review* 88 (1983): 31–52.

18. See Sharlet, "Growing Soviet Dissidence," *Current History* (October 1980): 96. Cf. also Tokes, "Varieties," p. 19.

19. Joseph M. Scolnick, Jr., "An Appraisal of Studies of the Linkage between Domestic and International Conflict," *Comparative Poltical Studies* 6 (4) (1974): 491.

20. There is a second file, on mass dissident activities, derived from the sources. This we will use in Chapter 7.

21. This has implications for the social composition of dissent. We will see below how several social groups make different contributions to the dissident movement.

22. V. Stanley Vardys, *The Catholic Church, Dissent, and Nationality in Soviet Lithuania* (Boulder: East European Quarterly Press, 1978), chapter 10.

23. One in July 1977 to Brezhnev signed by 149 priests of the Vilnius Archdiocese and 70 of the Vilkaviskis Diocese; one to the First Secretary of the Communist Party of Lithuania in September 1977 signed by 120 priests and the Bishop of the Panevezys Diocese; and two in April 1978, to the Presidium of the Supreme Soviet of the Republic of Lithunian, signed by 58 priests of the Kaunas Archdiocese and 20 of the Telsiai Diocese—cf. CCCL, 30: 9–14; CCCL, 33: 3–9; ELTA, 228: 8–9; ELTA, 235: 9–11. Vardys, p. 199, says that in 1974 there were 772 priests.

24. Cf. CCCL, 38: 4–25; ELTA, 243: 10–14; ELTA, 245: 7–8. See also Vardys, "Lithuania's Catholic Movement Reappraised," *Survey* (25) (3) (Summer 1980): pp. 59–60.

25. Cf. CCCL, 33: 9–10; ELTA, 235: 10–11.

26. Vardys, *The Catholic Church*, chapter 10; cf. numerous issues of CCCL.

27. Vardys, *The Catholic Church,* ; cf. Frederick Engels, *The Peasant War in Germany 1525* (New York: International Publishers, 1966).

28. Vardys, *The Catholic Church,* ch.3–4, p. 51, pp. 74–77, p. 70. Priests do not always and automatically oppose Soviet authorities. There were and continue to be some priests who cooperate fairly closely with Soviet authorities. Foreign Minister Reinys—who would become Archbishop—negotiated a treaty with the Soviet Union in 1926 (Vardys, op. cit., p. 20). But more significantly there were a total of three clerical "informants" in the 1940–1941 period—actually a trivial percentage of the total, but existing nonetheless. Also, several of the religious teachers who were fired in the aftermath of incorporation were rehired as instructors in non-religious subjects. Finally, the hierarchy accepted a restricted "mission" even as it resisted some encroachments on religious practice.

29. J.P. Nettl, "Ideas, Intellectuals, and Structures of Dissent," in Philip Rieff, ed., *On Intellectuals: Theoretical Studies, Case Studies* (Garden City, New York: Doubleday, 1969), expecially pp. 65–67, 80–81. Cf. Peter Raina, *Political Opposition in Poland: 1954–1977* (London: Poets and Painters Press, 1980), pp. 17–20.

30. Edward Shils, "The Intellectuals and the Powers," in Rieff, *On Intellectuals,* esp. pp. 33–43; Shils, "The Intellectuals and the Powers: Some Perspectives for Comparative Analysis," *Comparative Studies in Society and History* 1 (1) (October 1958): 5–22.

31. "Prologue to a Theory of Revolutionary Intellectuals," *Telos,* 26 (Winter 1975–76): 3–36.

32. *Intellectuals on the Road to Class Power* (New York: Harcourt, Brace, Jovanovic, 1979).

33. Marshall S. Shatz, *Soviet Dissent in Historical Perspective* (New York: Cambridge University Press, 1980), mentions non-Russians and non-intellectuals only as "victims of oppression and injustice" whom are the *objects* of attention of "dissidents" on pp. 168–176.

34. There is an element of circularity to his analysis for he at the same time argues that the restriction on the KGB in the 1950s was in the party leadership's interests as well, and that the economic problems were part of the source of the intellectual dissidents' political protection from extinction. Ed Cox, "The Politics of the Dissenting Intellectuals," *Critique* (1975) 5: 5–34.

35. *On Soviet Dissent* (New York: Columbia University Press, 1980), pp. 1–14 and 118, esp. p. 6.

36. It is curious to note that this rate for workers exceeds the figure of 6% given by Alexeyeva for participation in the Galanskov-Ginzburg letter campaign of 1968.Ludmilla Alexeyeva, "Worker Participation in the Dissident Movement, *Chronicle of Human Rights in the USSR* (39)(July-September 1980): 52–53. This may suggest a greater worker involvement in the Lithuanian movement than elsewhere in the USSR, or only a difference of data-collection technique. Alexeyeva also rightly points out (p. 54) that "the tens of thousands of signatures on the protests against harassment of believers that have been

issued by the Lithuanian Catholics could not have come from the Lithuanian intelligentsia alone." Thus, the caveat noted above, must be kept in mind. The "occasional" dissident who signs such items on a one-time or infrequent basis is likely to be non-intelligentsia, if only on grounds of numbers.

37. Part of this proportion might be a reporting problem: particularly small villages and towns may be less readily remembered by samizdat "reporters" during the time between oral communication and write-up in samizdat reports within the samizdat network. Alternatively, these smaller and lesser known places may be subsumed into larger district or diocesan units for ease of reference of readers.

38. Because of the small numbers it is difficult to analyze the non-Catholics at any depth. The only major sex difference of note, , is for the Jehovah's Witnesses, of whom slightly more are female than Roman Catholics are, namely, 28.6% v. 23.3%.

39. Vardys, *The Catholic Church*, pp. 212–215. There is no information on the occupational background of the Witnesses, and the number of the other non-Catholic groups is too small for meaningful comparison.

40. Wesley A. Fisher, "Ethnic Consciousness and intermarriage: Correlates of Endogamy among the Major Soviet Nationalities," *Soviet Studies* (29)(3)(1977): 398, as cited in Thomas Remeikis, *Opposition to Soviet Rule in Lithuania, 1945–1980* (Chicago: Institute of LIthuanian Studies, 1980), Table 2, p. 27.

41. The Zalioji Church was turned into a mill in 1979 (CCCL, 38:47), and a chapel elsewhere was physically demolished at about the same time (CCCL, 42: 36–37). Ridicule of students is a frequent topic reported in the section "In the Soviet School" in many issues of CCCL (e.g., 11: 5–14, 49: 67–69). Harassment is also frequently reported in the section "News From the Dioceses" (e.g., 49: 62–67). Punishment for educating children, and similar offenses, will be discussed in the next chapter. Finally, vandalism to churches and violence done to religious people are unfortunately increasing subjects of CCCL reports and petitions by believers: for example, twenty-five incidents from 1977 through 1980 are enumerated in CCCL, 48: 47–49, in a complaint by the Priests' Senate of the Diocese of Telsiai to the Procurator of the USSR.

42. Vardys, *The Catholic Church*, , pp. 89–107; Vardys, "Lithuania's Catholic Movement Reappraised," pp. 53–54; Michael Bourdeaux and Michael Rowe, *May One Believe—In Russia?: Violations of Religious Liberty in the Soviet Union* (London: Darton, Longman and Todd, 1980), pp. 1–18, 73–90.

43. See many issues of CCCL.

44. See CCCL, and press release by Lithuanian Information Center, Brooklyn, New York, 27 February 1984.

45. For one list of refused applicants, see CCCL, 45: 17–18. For the founding date of the underground seminary, see CCCL, 42:5–6, where the first student Father Jaugelis is discussed. A list of five such unofficially ordained priests is included in CCCL 48: 36. (The KGB attempted to counter this by allowing an ex-seminarian to say mass, despite a morals charge. This was intended to discredit the underground seminary. See CCCL, 33: 18–21; 37: 20.)

46. See "Life of Catholics in Lithuania and the Soviet Union at the Election of Pope John Paul 2," CCCL, 36: 7–28.

47. This is a frequent accusation: see the case of Elena Sulinauskaite, CCCL, 8: 26; CCE, 30: 106, for example. For a dissident mention of such convents, see CCCL, 9: 371.

48. Cf. "The Underground Periodicals in Lithuania," ELTA 261 (February 1981): 9–13, as well as *Violations of Human Rights in Soviet Lithuania*. Note, by the way, that there are some infrequent occasions when religious samizdat will articulate support of nationalists per se. See the editorial of CCCL in favor of the Baltic Declaration against the Molotov-von Ribbentrop Pact, CCCL, 40: 6.

49. On the "Friends of the Eucharist" Society see CCCL, 39: 30–32. For the ritual of carrying the cross to Jurgaiciai Hill (since 1904), see CCCL, 48: 16 (and 8: 27–33 and 12: 30–31 for details of the April 1973 procession). For more on the July rosary devotions at Zemaiciu Kalvarija, see CCCL 45: 34–35. Finally for a description of the procession to Siluva, see CCCL 40: 51–54. Several dissidents were tried and convicted for organizing this procession illegally (see, for example, CCCL 48:5–16) and in 1981 it was stopped by the imposition of a health quarantine (CCCL 49: 6–16).

50. See the initial announcement of goals and members in CCCL, 36: 3–7. Its subsequent documents are reprinted or summarized in many issures of CCCL: e.g., 42: 19–22; 44: 28–30.

51. See, for example, Remeikis, pp. 152–170, and documents he translated from samizdat and the Western ethnic press, pp. 275–482.

52. Vardys, *The Catholic Church*, ch. 12; also, "The Problem of Nationality: Modernization and Baltic Nationalism," *Problems of Communism*, 24 (September-October 1975): 45–46.

53. Remeikis, *Opposition*, pp. 123–170. Examples of the three types are: 1) the samizdat journal *Ausra* in which national consciousness and moral strength are emphasized and Roman Catholicism is portrayed as necessary to the nation's survival; 2)ethnographic clubs, the *New Bell* (a planned journal that was preempted in 1974 by five arrested), *Varpas* [The Bell—the organ of the Lithuanian National Revolutionary Liberation Front which supposedly included Human Rights Committee, the Lithuanian National Revolutionary Council, the Lithuanian Freedom Fighters Movement, and the Free Communist Party of Lithuania], *Laisves Sauklys* [Herald of Freedom in 1976–7]; 3) journal *Perspektyvos* which, from its beginning in 1978, emphasized independence and nationalism and criticized Russian dissidents. Note that he does not demonstrate that the ethnographic clubs have any political content whatsoever, much less that of Liberal Nationalism.

54. Vardys presents no real analysis of interrelations there, or in his article. The rest of the chapter lumps them together back to same causes (Kudirka, cultural policy after 1965 attacking culture, Baltic linguist's death, public criticism of youth—especially of borrowings from West, and death of Palach in 1969 and its subsequent reflections in the Soviet Union, including Kalanta in 1972). Remeikis is unclear in his usage of his third category, which is

lumped in with liberal nationalists as "secular nationalists." In addition, this last is subsequently called "nationalist Communist" in that it "certainly articulated their viewpoint," of secession from the SU). And this new term "national communism" is in turn conflated with the National People's Front as "nationalist left" although the NPF's espousal of secession proceeded from a Maoist analysis of Soviet imperialism and was tied to the goal of an independent People's Republic similar to the People's Republic of China since 1974.

55. Remeikis, documents on pp. 275–482.

56. This is the case of Romas Kalanta, whose story is told in several places. See for example Remeikis, pp. 292–299.

57. A particularly interesting form of nationalist dissent, with some counterpart in the religious form, is the public singing of nationalist songs, including the old national anthem. This is not violent, but has been associated with more violent outbursts, as in 1972. Remeikis, p. 276.

58. According to ELTA, "The Underground Periodicals," this also includes *Perspektyvos* and first four issues of *Varpas*.

59. "The Lithuanian Helsinki Group: Chronology and Documents, November 1976-July 1981", ELTA 268 (September 1981): 11–14.

60. One ought not be too critical of Vardys at this point. He does at one point suggest "there exists between the religious and national dissent much overlapping and even convergence, but *not* general identification" ("Lithuania's Catholic Movement Reappraised," p. 63, emphasis added). Unfortunately, this omits the general human rights group and is contradicted by his repeated attempts to distinguish the two kinds of dissent.

61. Vardys, "Lithuania's Catholic Movement Reappraised," p. 51. However, in 1975, he did suggest the "merging of religious and nationalist dissent" in the form of the samizdat journal *The Chronicles of the Catholic Church in Lithuania*. "Problem of Nationality," p. 47. Vardys also points out that some items of samizdat also picture the Lithuanian dissenters as belonging to distinct "wings." His own account, however, directly shows the interrelatedness: " . . . of the currently known samizdat periodicals possibly only one, *Varpas*, started in 1977, is not Catholic-church oriented," and he notes that Lithuanian dissidents themselves see all types as unified into a diverse movement. Vardys, "Lithuania's Catholic Movement Reappraised," pp. 65 and 72. Remeikis' discussion of the substance of disagreement of differing groups of dissidents also suggests conscious interaction, with conscious differentiation. He presents a good case that nationalist and liberal-democratic dissidents read each other's works and those of the religious dissidents. He maintains that all three have significant differences on several points, especially on the importance of free religious expression of Catholics in relation to national self-identity and the struggle for change. Remeikis, pp. 160–164. Cf. Vardys, "Lithuania's Catholic Movement Reappraised," pp. 69–72.

62. See CCCL 41, 42, 46; CCE 55:33, 56:153–154; ELTA 249:3, 251:4,7, 256:11–12, 263:3,11–15; CHR 40:8–9; LIC files; KC 80, 81; *USSR News Briefs* 1980, nos. 4.37, 1.10, 1981, no. 3.1.

63. Five other cases for which we have biographical information show generally idiosyncratic development. Three are religious-nationalists, who become triple hybrids. One is a religious-human rights dissident, who then becomes a religious-nationalist. The fifth is a literary dissident, who then becomes a religious-nationalist, and finally ends up a nationalist-human rights dissident.

4

The Judicial Process: Politicization

"When the people found out that the priest had been arrested, they came to the Procurator's Office and demanded the release of the priest . . . From the Procurator's Office the believers marched off to see the Party secretary, who, however, refused to see them."[1]

The dissidents who challenge the regime do not go unscathed. This chapter examines the formal steps in the judicial process used by the regime as a major instrument of social control over them, to restrict, punish, and preempt their activities.

The various stages from initiation of the case through execution of judgment involve several institutional actors making decisions about the "political" suspect/defendant/convict. Formally, the most important is the procurator, who supervises every step and can abort or appeal any prosecution. However, in practice his role does not protect the rights and interests of dissidents. The Communist Party and KGB, through various mechanisms, prevail on procurators to "avoid trouble" in dissident cases. In addition, increasingly an alternate route to incarceration of a different kind has been used. This route—the psychiatric internment—involves less procuratorial participation. Thus, the judicial process is politicized in the cases of dissidents, in Lithuania as elsewhere in the Soviet Union, despite formal protections and an institution (the procurator) to uphold them.

Stages in the Soviet Judicial Process

According to Soviet law, there are five major steps through which an individual travels before he or she emerges from the judicial process; these steps are illustrated by the figure below. Each of these steps involves somewhat differing sets of actors and differing decisions about the individual and his actions.[2]

Figure 1
Legal Process and Participants

Stage	Decision	Major Actor(s)	Others
1. Initiation of case	To proceed	Procurator, Militia, KGB	Anyone
2. Preliminary Investigation	Interrogation Detention Indictment	Militia investigator, KGB, Procurator	Court
3. Trial	Preliminary Determination Guilt or innocence Sentencing	Court judges	Procurator, Defense counsel Public
4. Cassation (appeal)	Upholding, Vacating, Remanding, or Amending	Procurator, Higher court	
5. Execution of judgment	Which camp	MVD	Procurator

Initiation of case

A case may be begun against a suspect after an action suggesting that a crime has been committed.[3] These actions are the surrender and confession of the criminal; the "direct discovery" by police, judges, and other agents of the court system; and reports from outside what is normally considered the court system. This latter category includes citizens (via letters and "declarations"), trade union officials, Komsomolists, non-volunteer policemen ("people's militia"), even newspaper reports or letters to the editor. Also, reports by "comrades' courts" and "druzhinniki" and enterprise personnel and official inspectors of fire, safety, and other conditions are legally acceptable.[4]

The receipt of a report begins the first stage: the first decision to be made by the recipient (judge, policeman, etc.) of such reports or "discovery" is whether a criminal case is to be started, either by him or by another agency. Supposedly, this decision must be made within three days. If a case is begun, the procurator makes his first incursion into the process: he verifies the grounds and supervises the process to preserve the rights of the potential defendant. There exist statutory constraints on *opening* of the next stage, the preliminary investigation. The following conditions should lead to end of the case: no crime committed, no corpus delecti, an amnesty covering the event, an underaged "suspect."[5] (A third, minor possibility is referral to a different judicial agency.)

At this first stage, preventive detention can occur, but also only under certain specified conditions. These include: a) the unestablished identity of the suspicious individual, b) the lack of permanent residence by the suspicious individual, c) attempted escape, or d) certain circumstances of a possible offense that can lead to incarceration. In this last category, interestingly, only three possibilities can lead to preventive detention: if the person was caught red-handed, if there are eyewitnesses clearly identifying the person, or if evidence is found on the person or in his apartment.[6] Here again, the procurator is important: any such arrest must be approved by him or the court.[7] Of course, there are other measures available to authorities to prevent further crime; for dissidents, the main one is the solicitation of a written promise by the person under suspicion not to engage in specific activities.

Preliminary Investigation

The second step is the preliminary investigation, usually by police investigators, and again supervised by the prosecutor (more properly, by the special investigatory office of the procurator).[8] Significantly, some crimes, namely, "especially dangerous crimes against the state" and "anti-Soviet agitation and propaganda," are the concurrent investigatory province of both the procurator and the KGB.[9] For the category of especially dangerous crimes, the republic procurator and the KGB have specially designated interrogator/investigators. The procurator's, at least, has a high official rank, "Justice Counsellor."[10]

In practice, the KGB has a far wider field of operations in the realm of Lithuanian dissidents than is suggested by "especially dangerous crimes against the state." The special KGB departments for nationalities (number 6) and for samizdat (number 9) have a great deal of investigative work to do,[11] in addition to uncovering samizdat, and interrogating and arresting those involved in its production and dissemination. Recall that complaints and reports from a wide variety of sources are sufficient grounds for investigation. First, KGB personnel conduct inquiries, and occasionally recruit informants, in many institutions: schools, religious bodies (including church choirs and the seminary), cultural clubs, even homes for the aged.[12] Because of recruitment and the "nomenklatura" system, the KGB directly monitors activity in many places, even (it seems) the Council on Religious Affairs in Vilnius.[13]

In less politicized, more "common" crimes, the regular police (MVD militia) is most likely to be the major partner of the procurator during the investigation. Of course, for Lithuanian dissidents, there is almost always at least some slight degree of KGB participation, although for the most part the degree is more than slight.[14] The cases of MVD inquiry mentioned in samizdat are almost always characterized by a great degree of secret police cooperation, from stake-outs of religious processions, to interrogations, to use of psychiatric hospitals.[15]

No matter which agencies are involved, the preliminary inquiry is supposed to determine if a crime has been committed and by whom. However, conclusiveness is not required: a vague standard of "sufficient" evidence that some crime may have been committed is formally the basis for judgment by the investigators. Indeed, the code of criminal procedure expressly rejects binding "precedence" in the acceptance of evidence: article 71 states that "no evidence shall have a previously established force for the court, the procurator, investigator, or person conducting the inquiry."[16] Note that this differs markedly from American criminal law, in which higher courts determine the acceptability of *modes* of procuring evidence, and enforce this acceptability on lower courts and police by throwing out judgments based on "illegal" evidence.

Of course, here again the investigators have the additional responsibility of preventing further crimes. To this end, preventive arrest and detention is an option. However, this can only be taken if there exists a reasonable expectation that the possible guilty person might escape, hinder the investigation, or commit more crimes. And in any case, a person may be held only a total of two months without further approval from the procurator or the courts, which may extend the pre-trial detention to a legal maximum of nine months. Nonetheless, the procurator is obligated to check that the crime actually took place, that no grounds exist for quashing the case, that the investigation was complete, that the charges are supported by evidence, and that the indictment was properly formulated and presented.[17]

The exact criteria of what constitutes a crime are open to interpretation. Action that violates a prohibition in the criminal code is *potentially* a crime, but only if it is serious enough to pose a "social danger," an elusive quality dependent on the exigencies of policy and on the personal dispositions of the investigators.[18] Also, the potentiality is further restricted in three ways: first, crime is viewed as closely connected to the intent of the criminal himself, which if absent is sufficent for no crime to exist; second, a lack of capability vitiates responsibility, which means that mental deficiency or youth (but *not* alcoholic condition) renders an act non-criminal; third, "extreme necessity" and "necessary defense" are loopholes.[19]

This preliminary investigation step is particularly important and receives some degree of attention in the criminal code. Most significant here, besides the power to arrest and detain the suspect, is the right of authorities to collect evidence by interrogating witnesses and authorizing police searches (during the daytime only).[20] It is interesting from a due process point of view that the suspect may challenge the participation of any particular investigator, and has a series of rights of information, despite the absence of an attorney until the investigation is complete (itself a glaring difference from Western legal process). On the other hand, any abuses at this stage cannot be appealed to the courts, but only to the prosecutor himself.[21]

In Lithuania in the 1970s, however, clearly such a complaint to the procurator was futile. For example, the procurator responded to formal dissident complaints about KGB actions by finding that all was in order in their investigations.[22]

This investigative step also requires a decision: whether to prosecute after indictment by the investigator. (The prosecutor can so decide even if the investigator wishes to release the suspect.) If the case moves on, the prosecutor is obliged to refer the case to the proper court and inform the suspect that he is now "the accused" before that court. Again, the prosecutor has the final legal responsibility here, for not only can he overrule the investigator, but the prosecutor himself can be legally prosecuted (by higher authorities) if he knowingly indicts an innocent person.

It is necessary to digress here on court jurisdictions. There are in the Soviet Union three levels of courts: people's courts, regional/oblast, supreme courts. The lowest level, people's courts, numbering about 50 in the Lithuanian republic, with each raion (hereafter, province) and each of the districts of some larger cities like Vilnius possess courts.

In Lithuania and other smaller republics, there are no regional courts: the republic supreme court takes their place. This is of importance in the prosecution of both the category of "especially dangerous crimes against the state" (articles 64–73) and other crimes, including some of the special provisions against dissent (like 190-1) mentioned in Chapter 2. All but the "ordinary" crimes (like theft of state property, and violation of regulations on religion) are investigated and tried at the republic supreme court level (in contrast to the RSSFR, where much is done at the province level).[23] Thus, these "especially dangerous" crimes are *automatically* brought to the attention of the central Lithuanian authorities in Vilnius by virtue of the legal code and the structure of the court system.[24] We shall have more to say about the institutional structures shortly.

Trial

The third step—the trial—actually begins with the preliminary determination by the court that the investigator's/prosecutor's case is strong enough to merit a trial. Conquest[25] notes that since 1958, only when the judge disagrees with some aspect of the indictment or when the conditions of preventive detention—mostly duration—require change does the court hold a preliminary session. This administrative session is attended by prosecutor and defense counsel, each of whom argues for his side, but the guilt of the defendant remains "unjudged," at least in theory. The current Chairman of the USSR Supreme Court, then Minister of Justice Terebilov clarifies this part of the process. He notes[26] that the judge will act alone unless there is disagreement or modification of conditions of arrest, as noted by others, in which case he will be joined by the two lay assessors at a formal "administrative sitting."

The court can return the case to the prosecutor for further investigation or suspend it for an indeterminate time. Generally, however, the case continues; the defendant and his counsel are entitled to review all the materials concerned with the case, and to copy any of the information contained in the prosecutor's evidence. Then the trial engages the two sides to guide the court in its attempt to examine the evidence, and to argue the merits of its view. The rights of the accused are protected at this step by equal rights in introducing evidence and presenting and questioning witnesses, open courtrooms, among others.

According to Bassioni and Savitski, the trial itself unfolds in five steps: opening/preliminary session, judicial inquiry (hearing of evidence and testimony), pleadings, last word of the defendant, and judgment (with sentencing, if necessary).[27] The trial opens at the appointed hour and all rise, as in Western courts. However, the witnesses must be outside the courtroom during the presentation of the case and enter only for their turn, stand when giving testimony, and immediately leave. Before the hearing of such evidence, however, the court asks several procedural questions of the participants, including whether the defense challenges any individuals on the bench (or the prosecution or clerical staff) on the grounds of personal involvement, whether either side requests new evidence or witnesses be added to the case. The court rules on the challenges and requests, and may on its own initiative, bring in further evidence, etc.

The next part of the trial is the judicial inquiry, which begins with the reading of the charges, the arguments of the participants about the sequential order of the witnesses and evidence, and the discussion by the court of each item, before the presentation of any material. Only then does the court actually move on to the actual presentation of evidence and testimony. This presentation is in some respects similar to Western trials. The procurator gives the state's case against the defendant; the defense counsel can put questions to the state's witnesses, call his own in presenting the defense, and can argue over points of procedure as well as over severity of charge and punishment. Official minutes, which may be subject to comments by the participants, are kept by a secretary. The court allows the participants to make supplemental petitions during and after this part of the trial.

However, there are some notable differences from the Anglo-American tradition in trial procedure. First, the court can play an active role in examining and even calling witnesses. Second, there may be one or more participants not found in the West: so-called "social defenders" and "social prosecutors," selected by outside institutions like trade unions and apartment associations. These representatives are admitted to the trial and given the rights of the other participants.[28] Finally, the defendant can play a more active personal role. He can address questions of witnesses[29] and more dramatically, before the court reaches a verdict, he can make a last plea. His "last words" are not to be limited by the court and no questions can be made by the other participants then.

The end of the trial comes with the verdict and, if a guilty judgment is brought, sentencing. We shall discuss sentencing at some length in the next chapter. For now, a brief description of the process will suffice. A simple majority of the court is needed, and a dissenting opinion may be placed in the record for possible appeal. Such an opinion, nonetheless, need not be made public at the trial. What is presented is the evaluation of the charges and evidence. Then a sentence is pronounced for any guilty findings. The sentence is supposed to be based on the findings, the requirements of law, and the several principles of sentencing. These include humanism, justice, expediency, and individuation.[30] If the defendant is found innocent, he is immediately released from custody.

Appeal

If the result of this step is somehow unsatisfactory, either to the defendant or to the prosecutor (or even to the victim), then an appeal, or cassation, is filed, and the case enters the next step. This step is not a retrial: it entails a re-examination of the same materials presented to the original court, and a determination if the judgment was legal and "correct" according to these materials. However, the defendant may participate and may present new evidence, if it has a bearing on the original evidence. No new witnesses and no new evidence from further prosecutory investigation may be introduced.

The original judges, the attorneys on both sides, and the defendant are all called to explain the case and a judgment is rendered. This can be the equivalent of acquittal (vacating of the sentence and termination of the case), upholding the verdict, remand (to either the preliminary investigation or trial step), or amendment of the original sentence. The court of cassation is not allowed to increase the punishment and it is obligated to "vacate" the lower court's judgment under certain specific conditions, including onesidedness of investigation, incompleteness of investigation, lack of evidential base of judgment, violation of procedural law, arbitarily harsh sentencing, etc.[31]

There is a limit of one appeal by the defendant. If the case began in the People's Court, then he may appeal it to the next higher court—in Lithuania, to the republic supreme court. If the case began at the republic level, then the appeal can only be to the Supreme Court of the USSR. In Lithuania, the dissidents who have appealed have had a nearly universal lack of success with the Supreme Court. However, there are three interesting exceptions, all early in the regime's dealings with the post-Khrushchev dissidents, and all exceptions made for idiosyncratic reasons.

In 1965, the Supreme Court reversed the 1964 Svencionys People's Court decision depriving Father Bronius Laurinavicius of some leftover building materials given to him by way of pay for labor in the parish; however, the case was reheard in the People's Court of Ignalina, which held against him, and this time the court did not hear an appeal. We can see a minor court finding being overturned, but only once, and not in the end.

On the other hand, the 70-year-old Kleofa Biciusaite was sentenced to a year, for teaching children religious catechism, by the People's Court of Akmene in 1972. However, the Supreme Court after a month did change the sentence to a moderate fine of 100 rubles. This change, however, did come in the midst of the first wave of petitions against the arrest and imprisonment of priests for the same activity. It seems clear that the regime was feeling its way here, and did not wish to exacerbate an unprecedented situation by the heartlessness of incarcerating an elderly woman.[32]

Finally, in January 1971 the Supreme Court commuted the death sentence of an airplane hijacker to 15 years in labor camps. His initial sentence was causing something of an uproar because of the imminent destruction of his young family, his 22-year-old expectant wife. This would not be a pleasant prospect for many Lithuanians uninvolved in dissent but holding conservative family values. Thus, the time was critical as in the Biciusaite case. Since then, no appeals from Lithuanians have been productive.[33]

Execution of judgment

The last step needs little comment: it is the implementing of the court's decision. The sentence begins after the appeal, if any. The time the defendant has already spent in custody, before the beginning of the sentence, does count in part toward the fulfillment of the term. Most cases do result in sentences, and for most political and other serious crimes, some form of incarceration in labor camps or prison is assigned. The camps and prisons are under the control of the Minister of Internal Affairs, again with the procurator responsible for the legality of operations.[34]

It should be noted that incarceration in prison or labor camp is not the only penalty. There are 11 different punishments, from depirvation of freedom to fine to social censure.[35] However, in the cases of dissidents, it is rare for anything but incarceration to be the outcome.[36] There is, however, a special kind of incarceration that must be mentioned: indefinite confinement in a mental hospital.

The Detours to the Psychiatric Hospital

As mentioned under "Preliminary Investigation," the lack of capability—mental illness or retardation—restricts what can be considered a prosecutable offense. This loophole means that a "mentally deranged" dissident is not held accountable for his actions, and will not be tried and sentenced. This seems humane, but the conditions in psychiatric hospitals, the indeterminacy of detention, and the legal situation of the patient all make this a less "pleasant" option in many instances than a labor camp term.

It is curious to Westerners that almost any deviation from passive political obedience can be diagnosed as mental illness in the Soviet Union. It is well established now that all sorts of non-psychiatric behavior, including the simple exercise of legal rights to defend oneself against the agents of varied institutions, have been taken by Soviet psychiatrists at one time or another as signs of deviation.[37] The justification is often that of "schizophrenia," which is seen to be a biologically based illness that may flare up at any time, for which there is no cure. Indeed, there is even the notion that no symptoms may be visible: "sluggish schizophrenia" and "seeming normality" are two frequently encountered phrases.

Other psychiatric grounds are as vague and even amusing, if it were not for the real suffering that accompanies their appearance in a psychiatric report: "nervous exhaustion brought on by . . . search for justice"; "psychotic paranoia with overvalued ideas and tendency to litigation" (sending appeals to higher courts and complaints to the procurator); "religious delirium"; "reformist delusions"; even "mania for reconstructing society." These phrases make it clear that psychiatry can be used to punish dissidents with internment for their activity, at the discretion of the coercive apparatus, and with few legal safeguards.[38]

The determination of mental illness is made in three steps.[39] First, the investigator must decide during his preliminary investigation of a crime if there is a likelihood of such illness in the suspect, taking into consideration the investigator's own training and experience, the behavior of the suspect, and other evidence (such as testimony of family and friends).[40] Next, a forensic commission of three certified psychiatrists examines the suspect and issues a report. Finally, the report and the investigator's evidence are submitted to a special session of the court, what is sometimes called a "sanity hearing" in the West.

This last step closely resembles a regular trial, but there are some differences. The court is obliged to determine if an otherwise criminal act has been executed by the suspect, if the suspect is ill, and what to do with the ill person. The court can release the suspect if there is insufficient evidence, or if he is adjudged not dangerous, in which case he is released into the custody of family or guardians—nonexistent options in dissident cases.[41] Alternatively, it can put him into a regular mental hospital run by the Ministry of Health, or can confine him to a "special psychiatric hospital" for "especially dangerous" patients, run like a prison by the Ministry of Internal Affairs.[42] The defendant is entitled to a defense attorney, who can appeal any finding of insanity and can complain to the procurator over any procedural errors.

However, this is the defendant's *only* legal protection. The suspect who is presumed to be mentally ill has no right to participate directly: he cannot challenge the court, call witnesses, make petitions during the session, or even give a final word (as he might if it were a regular trial). In addition, he may be excluded entirely if the court decides that his presence might worsen his condition (!). The various documents, such as the commission's report, the investigator's summary of evidence, and even the judgment of the court, may not be shown to the defendant, for similar reasons.

After the verdict of insanity has been promulgated, the defendant becomes a "patient" indefinitely. He is supposed to be examined over six months by a psychiatric commission, whose report goes back to the court for review. Only if a commission later determines a return to sanity will the defendant be released by the court, and even then this release is viewed as potentially only temporary. Thereafter, he must register with the local psychiatric clinic and is subject to later short-term internments if the "social danger" he presents increases.[43]

However, there is another route to confinement, one that has even fewer safeguards, since it does not directly involve the courts or attorneys: "civil confinement."[44] The police (MVD, sometimes acting with the KGB) can participate at the beginning of this path, if the patient-to-be violently resists commitment, or even (as of 1971) if there is a possibility of resistance by the person, his family, or guardians.

Under this procedure, it is possible for a psychiatrist to put anyone into detention for an examination, even if no criminal act has occurred and even if there are no charges made against anyone. Indeed, the procedure of civil commitment allows *no* individual protections, no rights or appeal of any sort, either by the individual or by his family or guardians.[45]

For this procedure, the 1961 directive from the Ministry of Health (approved by the MVD and the Procurator-General) requires the existence of a "clear danger from a [potentially] mentally-ill person to those around him or to himself." The conditions of mental illness that would feed such a danger are not clear in this directive, and the list of conditions itself is expressly "not exhaustive." Moreover, "externally correct conduct and dissimulation" are discounted as possible evidence of sanity.[46] After initial confinement, a three-psychiatrist commission must examine the person within 24 hours and report to the family. Monthly examinations and reports follow until the patient is sane again.[47]

This potential for "insanity" is great enough, but in 1969 it was broadened by a special decree that suggests that long-term *prevention* is a primary goal of civil commitment. This decree shifts preemption away from immediately and physically dangerous acts to more diffuse, enduring "socially dangerous tendencies." The psychiatrist's actions, need not be based on any specific actions, even "seemingly normal" ones, by the patient-to-be. Thus, we have an increasing "medicalization" of dissent in the Brezhnev period, a process that clearly parallels, or complements, the increasing "criminalization" through the changes of laws (noted in Chapter 2) and, as we shall see, in their application.

The expansion of the scope of application has been accompanied by expansion of record-keeping on potentially mentally-ill dissidents displaying these tendencies. This is significant, for it occurs not only in the offices of the local psychiatric clinic, which covertly assigns a level of social danger to each individual, but also in the central and local offices of the Ministry of Health, MVD, and KGB, the last of which makes its own determination of social danger. An investigator in the latter agencies would thus have information on file about the likelihood of "mental illness" and could use this either in intimidation (of witnesses, suspects, defendants) or as an option in the conventional judicial process.

Thus, we have two ways for the coercive apparatus to place a dissident into a psychiatric facility. One, if he is already charged with a crime, he can be judged by a commission and then a court. Here he is deprived of direct impact, although his family, friends, and defense attorney have some legal options for appeal and complaint. Two, a psychiatrist can talk with the dissident for a brief time, in a "neutral environment" like the local Soviet's executive offices or the military commissariat's examination rooms, and then confine him for later commission examinations. Here, there is virtually no recourse for the dissident or the family, unless the monthly reports do not come, in which case some administrative appeals within the Ministry of Health or Internal Affairs might be used.

The first route is judicially based. Those proceedings are in effect trials under somewhat different rules. In the second, mental illness is used as a reason for circumventing trial. In our analysis in Chapter 8 we will consider commitments under the first process as trials. Insofar as the result in either case is *different* from conventional trials, and similar to each other, we will also compare trials to the combined psychiatric routes.[48]

The Role of the Procurator:
Responsibilities, Powers, and Organization

A major feature of the legal process (excepting the civil psychiatric route) is the pervasiveness of the prosecutor, called the procurator. He is consulted, makes decisions, and supervises nearly all the steps in some fashion or another. Formally, at least, the office of the procurator is the lynchpin of the judicial system.

The formal responsibilities of the procurator are many and important.[49] They include:

1. "general responsibility" for the legality of the actions of all institutions, including the various ministries (but excluding soviets and the Communist Party itself),
2. supervision of judicial process and substance of decisions (investigation, trial, sentencing, detention),
3. prosecution of criminals.

Along with these formal responsibilities comes an impressive array of formal powers.[50] Each of the steps in the judicial process that involves supervision by the procurator brings him in to verify that correct procedures have been followed and entitle him to object if any irregularities occur. Such objection (or "protest") is usually directed to the offending agency or its immediate superior. This is not unlike Western prosecutors occasionally dropping cases when legal bounds are not respected.

However, in contrast to the American district attorney, the procurator has powers that go beyond mere administrative appeal. In the early stages of the legal process he can demand any document from all sorts of governmental institutions, even outside the legal system. More importantly, he can "stay" the execution of any penalty for the duration of the protest, and can give investigative agencies directions to be followed, as well as personally conduct any case, remove individual investigators or agencies from the investigation, or finally end the criminal case before it goes any further if he wishes.

At the trial stage, he can give opinions to the court about the legality of its actions and those of the other participants, and suspend any court decision which he considers illegal or inappropriate. This latter power supplements the power to file a formal appeal.

Finally, he can inspect jails and camps, suspend illegal actions taken therein by authorities, and even free anyone illegally detained. Concomitant to these powers, it might be noted, is the express obligation to consider any petitions or complaints by individuals of ill-treatment or illegality at any stage.[51]

In order for the procuracy to fulfill the duties, using the varied powers where appropriate, the office has long ago developed a complex bureaucratic structure, in most respects similar to the other bureaucracies of the Soviet system. There are several levels paralleling those of the courts and police: 1) All-Union (with Procurator-General elected by the Supreme Soviet for a 7-year term), 2) Union-Republic (however, in contrast to many other institutions, appointed by the Procurator-General—democratic centralism), 3) regions/autonomous republics/etc. (appointed by Procurator-General in law—in practice by middle level with the confirmation of the Procurator-General[52]), and down to 4) circuit/district/town. These various levels have chief procurators and are differentiated internally.[53]

One can get a sense for this differentiation by examining the top policy-making body of the highest level, the Collegium of the Procurator-General. This includes the top officials of several subsidiary offices: the Procurator of the RSFSR, the Chief Military Procurator, the Chief of the Department of General Supervision, the Chief of the Department of Supervision of Prisons, the Chief of the Department of Supervision of Investigation of Organs of State Security, Chief of the Department of Control and Inspection, and the Chief of the Department of Cadres, as well as the Procurator-General himself. Each of these subordinate officials heads a staff devoted to a particular part of the operations of the procuracy.

For our purposes the major office is the one connected to the KGB, and two not represented on the policy-making Collegium, a "special department" oriented to especially important cases, i.e., political cases, and a separate department (the militia of the Ministry of Internal Affairs)[54] for the monitoring of the activities of the other police. It should be noted that there also exists sections for juvenile cases, statistics, and analysis of legislation; and "administrations" for investigations and for especially important cases.[55]

Each of the union republic procuracy offices, and their lower levels down to the city and interdistrict units, has similar internal differentiation. Indeed, this specialization sometimes leads the procurators within larger population centers to specialize in different kinds of crimes.[56] This is possible in no small measure because each of the USSR's several thousand districts has at least one procurator, according to Berman and Spindler.[57]

However, there is at least one major way in which the Procuracy differs from most of the rest of the judicial apparatus, except those elements also concerned with direct coercion. The procuracy is clearly military in organization. This bureaucracy is unlike the non-coercive ministries in its cohesive unilinear hierarchy of command: in contrast to them, where the units at each level bear obligations to the legislatures at their levels *as well as* the next higher level of their own ministry, the procurator at each level has obligations only to the next higher level, up to the Procurator-General himself. This means that directives from above function as orders to be obeyed, not as plans toward which one should strive. As Kaminskaya noted, "the state's prosecutor, who behaved with such lordly independence during a trial, was obliged to report in advance on the case and on his handling of it to the District Procurator, and the views of his superiors were binding."[58]

In addition, the procuracy has a hierarchic list of positions, numbers, and ranks, similar to the military or police. For example, the Procurator of a republic may be a "State Councillor of Justice, Second Class" with a rank number 3, as contrasted to the procurator of a district entitled a "Junior Councillor of Justice" with a rank number of 8.[59] This system of ranks is accompanied by badges designating ranks, to be used on duty, as well as official uniforms.[60]

Nonetheless, there is one aspect of bureaucratic life in the Soviet system that the procuracy does share with all the others: the penchant to operate according to plans and statistics. As we have noted above there exist specialized departments for the gathering and analysis of legal statistics, even at lower levels. Indeed, there is considerable evidence that planning and the collection of statistics have produced some marked changes in Procurate behavior: at least one study of campaigns against economic and other crime from 1955 to 1976 notes that there is "a regular ebb and flow of procuratorial activity governed by the economic plan . . . [possibly] the Procuracy is engaged in some 'storming' of its own in order to fulfill its quota of investigations."[61]

The significance of the powers and bureaucratic structure of the procuracy for the individual going through the legal process is great. The procurator is supposed to protect the procedural rights of the witnesses, suspect, defendant, and convict. In the Soviet system, the role of defense attorney is far less conflictual than in Western systems, and the courts themselves are more supine about the operations of the procurators. Yet, Conquest[62] notes that these responsibilities entail several antithetical functions. Particularly, the efficient direction of investigation can conflict with the legality of investigative procedure. Similarly, the successful prosecution of the case may contradict the duty of protection of procedural safeguards.

It is well known that the network of safeguards simply does not cover the dissident; there are many violations of rights and procedures.[63] Among the most significant are: overly long pretrial detention, unnecessary and inappropriate searches and confiscations, harassment and intimidation of family and friends of defendants, falsification of written records about interrogations and statements of witnesses and suspects, closed trials (lack of notification to relatives and general public; police restriction of access to courtroom; "packing" of courthouse by anti-defendant individuals by special pass, even a completely *in camera* proceeding supposedly because of state secrets, etc.), refusal to admit expert and other testimony requested by the defendant, interruptions and restrictions on the statements and questions of defendant and his attorney, and so on.

Lithuanian evidence tends to confirm this pattern in all its details. For example, there is extensive pretrial detention beyond the nine-month limit (in the data we have, this is the case in nearly one half of those trials where there are exact arrest and trial dates). Also, there were many unreasonable searches and seizures, and many examples of blatant harassment by KGB agents of witnesses and suspects. The open trial provisions were also vitiated by KGB and party packing of the court-rooms and the use of KGB and militia to keep potential supporters out. Finally, there were refusals of reasonable requests about the participation of experts and public defenders.[64]

Berman and Spindler do suggest that many of these violations are not strictly illegal, as in the open trial provision.[65] There is, in other words, some degree of contradiction even within the laws providing protection. However, here the point is that the common-sense interpretation of these protections is not the base for procuratorial action on behalf of the political defendants.

Procurator, Party, KGB

Why does the procurator not attempt to protect the dissidents? In Chapter 2 we discussed the general institutional framework of Soviet Lithuania, and there lies the answer, in several interrelated linkages of the Procurator to other institutions, as well as in his office as a bureaucracy, and in the Soviet ideology.

First, consider the recruitment of procurators. These posts are filled under the system of personnel control called nomenklatura, as discussed in Chapter 2. Thus, it is not at all surprising that 82% of all procurators of all ranks in 1973 were members of the Communist Party.[66] This means that nearly all of them are subject to party discipline, thus unwilling to jeopardize membership, career, and even liberty, by seeming to favor politically suspect people. Indeed, a 1966 Soviet text on the Procuracy admits that the party organization formally evaluates the work of prosecutors and investigators for the Procurator at least biennially.[67]

Second, given the hierarchic structure, even if individual procurators, especially among the 20% non-party element, were to attempt to provide protection to dissidents, there would be intervention by higher levels of the procuracy, on the order of the highest levels of the party. Thus, it is rare for an individual procurator to act, as one did in Amalrik's case, to release a dissident from illegal incarceration.[68]

Third, the KGB dominates the investigation of and control over dissidents, as evidenced by its various specialized departments for that purpose. Its influence even at the lowest levels is unchallenged.

So far, it seems that the system operates efficiently to repress dissent, as the totalitarian/authoritarian model would predict. Yet, some Western analysts have sighted signs of "inefficiency" that may be based on intra-elite conflict. First, idiosyncratically, the Amalrik case is one of eventual early release from a labor camp by the procurator.[89] Second, structurally, the creation and continuation of two separate police forces (KGB and MVD) implies some distinctiveness, possible conflict as well as cooperation.[90] One might add a third and fourth set of signs: the last several years have been marked by ministerial changes including the transfer of top personnel from KGB to MVD; finally, there have been trials of MVD officials for economic crimes. Clearly, the Politburo detected an unhealthy MVD autonomy in the control of economic crimes, and decided to end it by use of "more reliable" and "tough" KGB careerists.[91] Yet most of these clues point to material corruption, not differences about the treatment of dissidents. (This may be in the process of changing. See Chapter 8.)

This means that bureaucratic rivalry and the bureaucratic process are less likely to operate to the advantage of dissidents than to the advantage of those engaged in illegal economic activity. Politically tainted dissidents are more troublesome for the legal apparatus and the civil militia, and they are more likely to go along with the KGB on their handling of these cases, as is the procurator.

Certainly, in Lithuania, there is no evidence of rivalry of the police forces, or of the conscientious protection of political defendants' rights by the procurators. Instead, we have seen that the procurator and KGB dominate the process, and the former does not fulfill his responsibilities to protect defendants' rights against the latter. Thus, the results of the judicial process must be seen as the "implementation of public policy" toward dissidents of differing kinds. Let us now examine the results of the process.

Notes

1. CCCL, 1: 3–4. About the response to the arrest of Father Zdebskis in August 1971.
2. The following is taken from several sources, mainly Harold J. Berman and James W. Sprindler, transl., *Soviet Criminal Law and Procedure: the RSFSR Codes* (Cambridge, Mass.: Harvard University Press, 1972), pp. 235–301, articles 108–324; and the summary by Christopher Osakwe, "Due Process of Law and Civil Rights Cases in the Soviet Union," in Donald B. Barry, F.J.M. Feldbrugge, George Ginsburgs, and Peter B. Maggs, eds., *Soviet Law After Stalin* (Alphen aan den Rijn, The Netherlands: A.W. Sijthoff, 1979), vol.

In Lithuania, there is clear evidence from reportage about interrogations, of the significance of KGB authority. There are numerous reports of control over the seminary; cooperation with other governmental and non-governmental bodies on the interrogation of suspects, publicity campaigns against dissent, etc.; and KGB activities undertaken by in-place agents in such mundane locales as the local housing authority in Siauliai in 1980.[69] Of course, the KGB has also conducted many searches and interrogations of dissidents, some of which were directed in provincial towns by high-level agents from Vilnius.[70]

At least one Western study of procuratorial activity found no reported case of protest of KGB investigations in twenty years (1955–1974), although one percent (of the probable several thousands) of procurator's protests were directed against the militia.[71] The absence of such protests seems on the surface all the more remarkable given the vagueness of the KGB's formal authority.[72]

Fourth, this influence at the lower level is, in part, a reflection of the increasing power of secret police at the highest levels, namely in the Politburo, where the symbolism of the full membership of Yuri Andropov (and his eventual succession to Brezhnev) could be missed by no one in the procuracy, or elsewhere in the judicial system, for that matter. Further, before the rise of Gorbachev there was no "legalist" counterweight at this high level. Only at the next level, the Central Committee, did one find the Minister of Justice and the Procurator-General, who *might* speak for their underlings' interests in greater legal constraints on all governmental (including secret police) activity.[73]

Fifth, these features tie in to the party's direct control and socialization links to the procurators, and all other judicial personnel (as well as the nomenklatura system, mentioned above). As part of the system, each party level has responsibilities of supervision and training.[74] There may be spot checks on legal activities by the apparatuses of the Central Committee down to regional committee,[75] justified by the extensive party doctrine on the supporting role which the legal system is supposed to play to the party. Indeed, it is expressly stated that the formal independence of the procurators, investigators, and even judges is not to be misunderstood as autonomy from party leadership and policy-making. To make this abundantly clear, the party devotes energy to the political education of all legal officials and directs continuing propaganda work on legal questions;[76] there are even published exemplars in a text issued by the Central Committee.[77] This means that local party bodies may discuss and even occasionally predetermine the verdict and sentence before trial.[78]

In addition, the higher levels of the party do occasionally "intervene" by issuing directives to the party bodies within the lower levels. Such directives can be infrequent, as in cases involving blatant personalist protection of party members from legal punishments, or routinized as in the category of "politically sensitive" cases here. In the latter eventuality, the KGB is often the "supplemental channel" of direction: it warns and threaten dissident suspects with further legal punishment, it determines who among potential defense attorneys will be allowed to participate in the trial proceedings, and it and the party issue specific orders to local judges about dispositions.[79]

The degree of *direct* KGB and party participation in trial proceedings is difficult to determine, but there is some evidence that in political cases, at least, the final disposition is determined in advance by higher levels. Kaminskaya, for example, cites a former Moscow prosecutor who said that many cases were decided by the district party secretary, her own experience as a defense attorney that the Moscow province committee forced one attorney to withdraw so that its decision would be more effectively implemented, and her sense that the Galanskov trial was pre-ordained by the KGB with the party determining the sentence.[80] There is also some testimony about KGB direction by other lawyers and other participants on the 1964 Brodsky trial and the 1965 Amalrik trial, among others.[81]

Seventh, the selective recruitment and socialization of procurators is complemented by that of other actors in the judicial system. For example, judges are also on the nomenklatura, with predictable results: over 1/2 of 9230 people's judges elected in 1976 union-republic elections were members of the party, and 95% were university educated.[82] Indeed, because public elections are involved, formal party approval of nomination is automatic, as in the elections to the Soviets. This means that the spot-checks mentioned above, and the occasional "hearings" (held by the leadership of the district and province party organizations) into the work of each judge in the jurisdiction, have great impact on the behavior of the judges, especially when it comes to treatment of dissidents and to the sentencing at the end of trials.[83]

There are many ways in which defense attorneys are also under party supervision and control, although there are individual lawyers, like Dina Kaminskaya, who have in recent years attempted to defend vigorously their dissident clients. Only those lawyers approved by the KGB can defend those accused of "especially dangerous crimes against the state," although most often the trials are "open" in that some friends or relatives do attend and hear no state secrets. This restricted access to defense attorneys, limiting the pool of potential defenders to 10% of the total, effectively undermines many dissidents' legal defense. In addition, control over allocation and daily work conditions for these attorneys is in the hands of the Presidium of

their collective: there are no private partnerships, and the "elected (i.e., party-approved) leaders of legal associations have close ties party and state. Indeed, these collegia are directed by party department of administrative organs, local soviets' executive committees, and th department of advocates of the Ministry of Justice. Finally, defens attorneys are simply treated as nuisances at trials if they attempt t refute the procurator's case.[84]

An eighth factor in the non-protection of dissidents is the planning system itself. For each of the major actors there are quotas to be filled. We have noted the Smith study of procuratorial campaigns Also, the courts, the militia, and the KGB all have similar planning functions and produce periodic reports and statistical indices for examination by higher party and state authorities.[85] Such schematic summaries produce pressures for high rates of "success." The goal is to finish off the cases as rapidly and successfully as possible, not giving the individual dissident any major degree of leverage, of course.

Finally, the ideological premises of law reinforce those on dissent and varied social phenomena to make it hard for a prosecutor to sympathize with the arguments of dissidents, especially those who substantively challenge some part or all of the Party's policies and authority. As discussed in chapter 2, dissent is seen as oppositional and tied in to foreign powers' machinations or simple mental illness; such perceptions undermine the credibility of the arguments presented by dissidents. The nationalist and religious dissidents, especially, are viewed as adherents of anti-Soviet positions that undermine the entire system.

The Soviet legal code stresses, in general, collective or societal over individual rights. Article 1 of the criminal code specifies *first* "the protection of the Soviet social and state system, [and] of socialist property" and only secondarily that "of the person and rights of citizens."[86] Moreover, the Code of Criminal Procedure specifies that

> Criminal proceedings must facilitate the strengthening of socialist legality, the prevention and eradication of crimes, and the education of citizens in the spirit of undeviating execution of Soviet laws and respect for the rules of socialist communal life.[87]

The factors of recruitment, organizational structure, party-KGB supervision, other judicial institutions, planning, and ideology all combine to produce "political trials" without effective legal protections for the dissidents. One might summarize this by saying "The Party will permit its own law-breaking in defense of . . . [its] authority, especially in the trials of dissidents."[88]

3, pp. 179–221, esp. pp. 190–196, except as otherwise noted. Cf. Conquest, who sees only three stages—those numbered 2 through 4 here, pp. 55 ff.; and M. Cherif Bassioni and V.M. Savitski, who present six, including "assignment to trial" in addition to those listed below—in *The Criminal Justice System of the USSR* (Springfield, Illinois: Charles C. Thomas, 1979); Samuel Kucherov, *The Organs of Soviet Administration of Justice: Their History and Operations* (Leiden, The Netherlands: E.J. Brill, 1970).

3. This first stage, if no "preliminary investigation" is obligatory, is technically called "inquest," according to Kucherov, p. 377, and "the inquiry" according to Berman and Spindler, pp. 238 ff.

4. Gordon Smith notes that there are six different kinds of institutional control mechanisms: state (e.g. Fire Inspectors), adminstrative (internal departmental), general (procurator), court (police and judges), arbitrazh (economic, involving enterprise activities), and social (citizens' complaints and comrades' courts). Thus, it is clear that all are allowed to participate in the reportage of crime. Gordon B. Smith, *The Soviet Procuracy and the Supervision of Administration* (Germantown, Maryland: Sijthoff and Noordhoff, 1978), p. 3. However, reports from dissidents often get nowhere officially. A chronic complaint is that cases of vandalism, theft, and violence against priests and churches in Lithuania produce no arrests. There were 25 such cases in the Telsiai Diocese alone in the 1977–1980 period. See CCCL, 47: 34–39; 45: 21–24; and for elsewhere in the 1975–1980 period, 46: 43–44.

5. Kucherov, p. 379. See below on restrictions to be enforced by the procurator on the continuation of a case from the preliminary investigation, conditions that apply here as well, as Kucherov notes on p. 434.

6. Conquest, p. 55; Kucherov, p. 392.

7. Kucherov, p. 430.

8. Cf. Bassioni and Savitski, pp. 77–92 and Kucherov who discusses the role played by the investigating "magistrate." (pp. 392–403).

9. Conquest, p.55, cites open, official Soviet sources from 1958 and 1961 on KGB authority here. See Berman and Spindler, p. 84, esp. fn. 22, on "concurrent jurisdiction."

10. CCCL, 48: 128; 48: 5ff; 7: 225.

11. See Chapter 2, fn. 47.

12. See, for example, CCCL, 46: 52–53; 31: 3–7; 6: 239ff; and 45: 41–42.

13. It is argued with some persuasiveness by dissidents that former Commissioner Rugienis and a deputy named Raslanas were secret police agents. CCCL, 6: 239; 33: 23–24; 36: 34; 37: 39.

14. One of the unusual cases of minimal KGB interest reported in samizdat is that of Ramanauskaite in 1979. She was arrested by the MVD, and briefly interrogated by a KGB investigator from Moscow. However, here case was unusual in the openness of the trial, and the resultant light fine of 50 rubles, which the crowd celebrated in song. The fact that neither KGB nor MVD took efforts to restrict access to the courtroom, despite the prevalent pattern of such restriction, suggests how little concerned both agencies, especially the KGB, were with her. CCCL, 40: 10–30.

15. CCCL, 45: 35–36; 7: 267–269; 47: 44–46; 5: 213; 9: 397; 42: 25.

16. Kucherov, p. 379, and Berman and Spindler, p. 225.

17. Kucherov, p. 433.

18. This discussion is taken from Conquest, pp.74–76, and Berman and Spindler, articles 7–14, pp. 127–129.

19. There is a comparable ambivalence about action, character, and social conditions after a trial yields a conviction. See below, and Chapter 6, on sentencing.

20. This stricture on nighttime operations also applies to interrogations, which are prohibited from 10 PM to 6 AM local time, as Kucherov correctly points out, p. 394, fn. 2.

21. Hazard, p. 303.

22. CCCL, 8: 343–344; 9: 395, 405.

23. Berman and Spindler, Article 36, p. 215. This is a simplified presentation of the judicial structure. There are several aspects that are interesting, but not particularly pertinent here: elected "lay assessors," comrades' courts, internal panels in higher courts, the centralized Ministry of Justice, and the short-lived Ministry for the Protection of Social Order (MOOP). For more these features, see works cited elsewhere by Terebilov, Conquest, and others.

24. There is one recorded case of Supreme Court justices "going on circuit" in 1980 to Kaisiadorys for the trial of Janulis and Buzas. The same day another panel of the Supreme Court held the trial of Navickaite and Vitkauskaite in Vilnius. CCCL, 46: 4ff.

25. Conquest, p. 57.

26. Terebilov, *The Soviet Court*, pp. 138–139.

27. Op. cit. The following discussion of the technical details of the trial procedure taken from Berman and Spindler, and Terebilov, pp. 140–145.

28. Conquest, pp. 123–124.

29. Hazard, p. 304.

30. See below, pp. 114–117.

31. See also Conquest, pp. 59–67, for further details on the appeals process.

32. CCCL, 4: 161–162, 1: 46–48; 2: 85.

33. CCE, 17: 80–81; 18: 135, 158; ELTA, 162: 3; 170: 3; 179: 7.

34. For further discussion of the camps, see Amnesty International's report, *Prisoners of Conscience in the USSR* (New York: Amnesty International, 1980), chapters 3–6.

35. Berman and Spindler, articles 21–36, pp. 130–138.

36. This, of course, does not apply to the Administrative Commissions of the local Soviets' executive committees that do levy fines for violations of several varieties of regulations, most notably those on religious organizations. For example, Father Petras Orlicka was fined 50 rubles for playing volleyball with children in 1971 by the Kaunas province soviet's administrative commission (CCCL, 1: 39–40). Father K. Zilys was similarly fined for allowing children in the church choir in 1974 in the Prienai province (CCCL, 9: 412). These bodies, however, are not technically part of the judicial process (although their decisions can be "appealed" to a people's court, and even to the Supreme Court, as Father V. Sakalys did in 1972—CCCL, 3: 122.

37. Amnesty International, loc. cit.

38. Amnesty International, *Prisoners of Conscience*, pp. 184–185; Sidney Bloch and Peter Reddaway, *Russia's Political Hospitals* (London: Futura, 1978), 243–255.

39. What follows is a simplified version of the process, taken from Bloch and Reddaway, pp. 99–105; Medvedev, pp. 156–159; and Berman and Spindler, pp. 149–150 (articles 58–61 of the criminal code), 227 (article 79 of criminal procedure), and 327–330 (articles 403–413 of criminal procedure).

40. Actually, the beginning of the psychiatric determination process can occur anywhere along the judicial process, but Amnesty International (p. 174) cites the investigator as the major initiator, and there is no evidence in Lithuania that any other agency regularly initiates the procedure.

41. Amnesty, p. 177.

42. Amnesty, pp. 190–191. Reforms are in progress. See Chapter 8.

43. Of course, there are violations of all of these procedures. Amnesty International, pp. 174–178.

44. Bloch and Reddaway, pp. 152–158; Amnesty, pp. 178–181.

45. Medvedev implicitly calls for the reinstitution of criminal responsibility for malpractice, the illegal and inappropriate internment of individuals. Op. cit., pp. 156–157.

46. Bloch and Reddaway, pp. 152–153; Amnesty, p. 178.

47. Again, there are widespread violations of procedure in cases of dissidents. See Amnesty, p. 180.

48. For the interned, only the timing of the commission's examinations is different in the two routes. On the other hand, there are relatively few psychiatric detentions: only 44, of which only 15 are definitely criminal. According to J.M. Feldbrugge ("Law and Political Dissent in the Soviet Union," in *Contemporary Soviet Law*, ed. Donald D. Barry, William E. Butler, and George Ginsburgs [The Hague: Martinus Nijhoff, 1974], p. 67) most of the cases of psychiatric internment in the late 1960s and early 1970s were criminal. Here, the undetermined cases may or may not be criminal, but there are no reports of either commission or court evaluations for them. Thus, it is a task simply beyond the data to make a more complete analysis of the psychiatric detentions.

49. Kucherov, pp. 418–440, and Berman and Spindler, pp. 100–101. Thus, this official does not determine constitutionality.

50. The following is taken from Berman and Spindler, pp. 101–104.

51. However, this obligation is at the crux of an anomalous situation. This is discussed at greater length later.

52. See Kucherov, p. 417.

53. The details are taken from Smith, *The Soviet Procuracy*, pp. 15–20, except as otherwise noted.

54. Smith, p. 20.

55. Loeber, as cited by Berman and Spindler, p. 101, fn. 4. Specifically on the department of statistics, see Smith, 4p. 139.

56. Smith, p. 22. See Chapter 6, pp. 125–127.

57. Berman and Spindler, p. 101.

58. Even if the case developed in such a way that the procurator was legally required to terminate the case, he would ask for a recess to refer this to the higher level. Kaminskaya, pp. 14–15.

59. See Smith, Appendix A.1, p. 136.

60. Bassioni and Savitski, p. 20.

61. Gordon B. Smith, "Procuratorial Campaigns against Crime," in Barry and others, *Soviet Law Since Stalin* (Alphen aan den Rijn, The Netherlands: Sijthoff and Noordhoff, 1979), vol.3, pp. 143–167, pp. 152 and 153.

62. Conquest, pp. 42–45.

63. The following summary is taken primarily from Berman and Spindler, pp. 87–89. There are numerous other places that elaborate at greater length these and other violations. See, for example, Amnesty, Chapters 1–2; Roy Medvedev, *On Socialist Democracy* (New York: W.W. Norton, 1977), pp. 148–163; and Osakwe, pp. 209–214. In addition there are many samizdat, tamizdat "published abroad"), and emigre works detailing the specifics of such violations in individual cases. For two of the more unusual of such accounts, see Dina Kaminskaya's *Final Judgment: My Life as a Soviet Defense Attorney* (New York: Simon and Schuster, 1982) and the tape transcripts of the trial of the Jewish doctor Mikhail Stern, *The USSR v. Dr. Mikhail Stern*, ed. August Stern (New York: Urizen Books, 1977).

64. Cf. various issues of CCCL. Of the 43 cases in the 1969–1981 period with exact dates for either arrest or trial, and at least month and year for the other, 21 (48.8%) have pre-trial detentions beyond 9 months (279 days of a 365-day year), and 18 (41.9%) beyond 300 days.

65. Berman and Spindler, p. 89.

66. Smith, *The Soviet Procuracy*, p. 25. Cf. Peter H. Juviler, "Some Trends in Soviet Criminal Justice," in Barry and others, vol.3, pp. 59–87, especially p. 67 and fn. 43 on p. 84. A dramatic example of the close personal link between the two at the middle levels is cited by Juviler (p. 62): the director of the Procuracy's Research Institute on the Causes and Prevention of Crime had been the deputy head of the Central Committee's important Department of Administrative Organs.

67. Conquest, p. 42, cf. also his pp. 112–113.

68. Juviler, op. cit.

69. On the seminary see examples in CCCL, 38: 40, 43: 4–6; for cooperation with the Young Communist League and local soviet officials, see CCCL 3: 118–119; for cooperation with the military commissariat (with responsibilities, among other things, for the military draft), see CCCL, 47: 63–64, 36: 38–39; for joint visit with the Council for Religious Affairs, see CCCL, 8: 358–359; for a talk at a school, see CCCL, 47: 64; for the housing authority incident, see CCCL, 48: 51–52.

70. For example, cf. CCCL, 4: 160; 7: 277–278; 43: 12–14; 44: 15ff; 45: 26, 29–31.

71. Smith, p. 20.

72. Despite the formal authorization noted above, Osakwe notes that the KGB can intervene at its own discretion, no matter the charges. The enabling

articles 117 and 125 of Criminal Procedures do not enumerate the exact border of its jurisdiction. Osakwe, p. 209, and fn. 76, pp. 220–221. Articles 64–73 and 190.1, etc., can be so widely interpreted as to include all sorts of non-deviant behavior, as has been well documented by Amnesty International, ibid., pp. 3–64. However, it is likely that some secret legal directives do specify this area. Such unpublished laws seem to be frequent.

73. Boris Meissner, "The Relationship of the CPSU to the Ministry of Justice," in Barry and others, vol.3, pp. 393–398, p. 397. Smith, *The Soviet Procuracy*, includes a discussion of a 1972 survey of 243 procurators in the RSFSR on the question of procuratorial supervision. Well over one half of them agreed that existing laws were insufficient for this function, p. 130.

74. Robert Sharlet, "The Communist Party and the Administration of Justice in the USSR," in Barry and others, vol. 3, pp. 321–392, esp. pp. 322–331.

75. Cf. also reference in Juviler in Barry and others, fn. 42, p. 84. There is some slight indication that there may be regional differences in the legal process, with some cities and provinces being less harsh than others, due to differing local party leadership. However, this variation seems to occur where individual party members are somehow personally involved, a mode of interference separate from political cases (where it is routinized). See Sharlet, p. 369. These may develop in part because the higher levels have far fewer personnel for such spot-checking, and depend on district and province "instructors" who are themselves insufficent to the task of continual monitoring. Sharlet, p. 381. Also, Kaminskaya, p. 35, notes that outside Moscow, the further away from the capital, the more the party controls, and the less the impact of the defense on the operations of the court at the trial.

76. Conquest, p. 110; Sharlet, p. 326.

77. Juviler in Barry and others, p. 68 and fn. 47, p. 84.

78. Ibid., pp. 68–69. However, Sharlet notes that such intervention in individual cases is frowned upon by higher levels. Sharlet, p. 341 et passim; Conquest, pp. 113–114.

79. Sharlet, pp. 364–368. He suggests that higher party intervention comes mostly from local party contravention of central legal policy, rather than from capricious desire to manipulate every case for maximum impact, p. 382.

80. Kaminskaya, pp. 61, 171, 181–182, 210, 299.

81. Sharlet, pp. 354–355, 364–369. Yet, Amalrik's lawyer did successfully appeal to the RSFSR Supreme Court. Ibid., p. 355.

82. Bassioni and Savitski, p. 12, fn. 14.

83. Kaminskaya, p. 57. To be noted also is the appointment of a special official within each party organization to monitor the local court and procuracy between such hearings.

84. Conquest, 32–39; Kaminskaya, pp. 25, 31–32; Juviler, pp. 66 and 68, especially fns. 49–51, pp. 84–85. Conquest notes some unspecified geographic variation in the level at which the collegia are supervised—pp. 32–33.

85. Sharlet, pp. 345–346.

86. Berman and Spindler, p. 126. Cf. also article 7, "The concept of crime," p. 127.

87. Ibid., article 2, p. 206. Note: there are similar provisions in the law on court organization—articles 1 and 2, p. 336.

88. Juviler, p. 67.

89. Peter Juviler, *Revolutionary Law and Order: Politics and Social Change in the USSR* (New York: Free Press, 1976), fn. 201, p. 223.

90. Amy Knight, "The Powers of the Soviet KGB," *Survey* (112) (1980): 138–155.

91. For more on the transfer of KGB chief Fedorchuk to the MVD (and its link to the anti-corruption campaign), the introduction of political officers in the MVD, and the purge of 160 Communists (and several in the MVD) in the Bashkir Autonomous Province, see the *New York Times*, December 18, 1982, 1:3; December 4, 1983, 4, I, 4:1; and January 28, 1984, I, 2:4.

5

Political Justice in Action: The Targeting of Nationalists and Hybrids

Soviet law prescribes the implementation of elaborate procedures for the processing of criminals. Yet as we saw in the last chapter, for dissidents this processing is highly politicized because of the roles of the procurator and the KGB. In this chapter we will see that judicial policy on dissent does not involve automatic punishment for "crimes." Indeed, the courts are used sparingly in general; their use is directed against certain groups of dissidents.

Specifically, the data on interrogations, arrests, trials, and psychiatric detentions indicate certain patterns of "targeting" and "relative immunity." We will examine the data by type of dissent and then by type of activity. We will discover several foci of repression: intellectuals, students, and white-collar workers are special targets (and priests are not); nationalists and a combined category ("hybrids") are targets (and religious and human rights activists are not); acts of violence and samizdat are targets (and petitions are not). Finally, an unanticipated policy toward women is revealed: the frequent interrogations of women are used as a "deterrent" to further activity.

In this chapter we will examine the numbers of dissident cases that travel through the system, and delineate some of their major features. The analysis will concentrate on the characteristics and activities of dissidents who move through the various stages of the judicial system. The focus will be on four types of events, three initiated by the system and one by dissidents. The following figure shows the presumed sequence of the typical case.

The data used will be limited to the 1969–1981 period for several reasons. First, for idiosyncratic reasons, the reportage on the second event (interrogation) is nearly exclusively from this period. Yet the analysis that follows assumes that the events are in some sense linked.

Figure 1

The Judicial Process of Filtering

1. Dissident acts
        ---> some do not involve judicial repression;
        ---> some lead to legal action, starting with Interrogation

2. Interrogations
        ---> some produce nothing further;
        ---> some yield more interrogations;
        ---> some bring about arrest;

3. Arrests
        ---> some do not proceed; result is release;
        ---> some end in trial or psychiatric detention;

4. Trials
        ---> no acquittals (although a rare suspended sentence is
                seen);
        ---> some end in indefinite psychiatric detention;
        ---> most end in some form of incarceration.

To include, therefore, the arrests, trials, and dissident acts that predate this period would render analysis more difficult. There would be no interrogations associated with them at all. Second, there is far more information in general on events in this period. This means that the other events are also more completely described in the sources. Third, the period is cohesive in general political climate: there are no major leadership shifts comparable to 1953 and 1964 to complicate the analysis. In a later chapter, however, we will discover some interesting differences rooted in these leadership shifts.

In addition, we will examine the psychiatric detention, in comparison to the trial. As noted above, the detentions in which there is mention will be included in the trial figures in most of the following tables. However, for this last comparison, the court-assigned detentions will be excluded from the trial figures. For the moment, let us turn to the process of targeting by social group.

Social Groups: Priestly Immunity and Literate Focus

Perhaps the most interesting aspect of the entire process, is how the largest groups of dissidents—priests, students, and intellectuals— are handled. In Table 1 we see a sophisticated appreciation of the informal and organizational strengths and weaknesses of these dissidents. This is most evident in the targeting of all *but* the priests.

The white collar, intellectual, and student groups are significantly targeted for interrogations, arrests, and for trials:[1] each group gets considerably more attention from the judicial apparatus than its numbers or proportion of dissident acts committed by it might warrant.

TABLE 1

JUDICIAL PROCESSING BY SOCIAL GROUP

	Events							
	Dissident Acts		Inter-rogations		Arrests*		Trials*	
Social Group	N	%	N	%	N	%	N	%
White Collar	33	5.5	61	15.0*	24	15.4	21	23.8
Intellectual	55	9.2	78	19.2	33	21.2	20	22.7
Student	70	11.7	132	32.5	41	26.3	18	20.5
Priest	366	61.2	72	17.7	17	10.9	6	6.8
Worker	66	11.0	61	15.0	40	25.6	21	23.9
Peasant	2	0.3	2	0.5	1#	0.6	2	2.3
Total+	598	100	406	100	156	100	88	100

*Here and in subsequent tables, marked differences of more than 5.0% from the dissident act percentages will be underlined for emphasis.

#One peasant was tried in 1969 after an arrest sometime before.

+Here and in subsequent tables, this is the number of cases without missing data, which varies by type of event and variable.

These dissident groups are numerically and structurally weaker than the priests, as noted in the previous chapter. This is in some measure due to the absence of extensive dissident organizations, and even legal bases for activity, like parishes and other church bodies available to the priests.

However, there are some differences among these three groups. White collar workers represent a larger and larger proportion of those processed at each succeeding judicial stage. The proportion of students, on the other hand, drops at each stage, as many are not prosecuted further. Intellectuals are present in each judicial stage to about the same extent, roughly double that of their dissident activity.

These differences can be attributed to relative strengths. White collar workers have no organization whatsoever, and their position in the social-economic hierarchy is the lowest of the three. Intellectuals have some associations with and some personal connections into the establishment by virtue of their jobs, but are neither numerous nor cohesive in any dramatic way. Students, however, do have student associations, some cohesiveness within their institutions, and are often the children of more than simple workers. Students are also younger and presumably more impressionable; this may lead to their recantation,

TABLE 2

TOLERANCE BY SOCIAL GROUP

	Events		
Social Group	Dissident acts per arrest	Dissident acts per trial	Arrests per trial
White Collar	1.6	1.4	1.1
Intel- lectual	2.8	1.7	1.7
Student	3.9	1.7	2.3
Priest	61.0	21.5	2.8
Worker	3.1	1.7	1.9
Peasant	1.0	1.0	0.5*
Total	6.8	3.8	1.7

*See note "#" to table 1.

cooperation, and some willingness by the authorities to be more tolerant of "misguided youth." (Youth is also a mitigating factor at the end of the judicial process, in sentencing; we will examine this in the next chapter.)

On the other hand, priests are clearly *not* targeted for further judicial treatment. Their dissident activity, person for person, is far greater than that of other groups, yet few are even interrogated and successive stages of the judicial process see a continuing dramatic decline in their representation. The overall pattern of relative clerical immunity can be summarized in the following table. The leeway that the regime grants priests in their dissident activity is clearly shown, for they commit on the average far more acts before an arrest is considered essential, and then are arrested more times before actually being brought to trial.

Here there seems to be an intention to avoid confronting this group whether by temporary incarceration, or by show-trial. This is probably due to the organizational, cultural, and ideological strength of priests, as opposed to other, less unified groups.

This has come out dramatically in the current history of dissent in Lithuania. As discussed in Chapters 2 and 3, the last major trials of priests in the 1970s occurred at the beginning of the decade. The incarceration of Fathers Zdebskis and others for teaching cathecism to children did nothing but exacerbate priestly discontent, and fire up their parishioners. These trials led to the signing of dozens of petitions with thousands of names, and were in some sense "the last straw" for Lithuanian activists who proceeded to create the *Chronicles* the following year to record and publicize any further repression of the Church. The petitioning actions have recently been replicated after the arrests (and subsequent trials) of two other activist priests in the early 1980s. Clearly, the regime knows that every such trial generates forces among Catholics in Lithuania that might get out of hand: better to wear down and intimidate most of the priests in a less dramatic fashion, if possible.[2]

In addition, one must cite the direct resistance of priests to the judicial process in explaining the relative absence of priests in interrogation, the preliminary stage. That resistance is, literally, simple refusal to answer summons for interrogations.[3] The refusals render the entire judicial process cumbersome, for the arrest of priests on grounds of hindering investigation of other dissidents would make the clerics into even more popular martyrs for even those who are not particularly religious, for example, the human rights type of dissident.

It is interesting that workers, a small group of dissidents, do have high rates of arrests and trials. With arrests and trials at nearly double their share of dissident acts, they are numerically tied with students and intellectuals for tolerance of dissident activity per trial, and slightly better than intellectuals in dissident acts per arrest.[4] Why? It is difficult to try *workers* when they are supposedly the social basis of the socialist state, especially given the ideological claim that "bourgeois remnants" are responsible for dissent. The risk of workers striking in their enterprises might be a constraint on the trial of any large number of workers. (However, counterbalancing these factors, the workers do not have the elite connection of either of the other two, nor the autonomous network or popular support of priests.)

The relative absence of peasants in activity and judicial action is striking. This suggests a low level of participation in formal actions, but one must remember that the massive petitions about the Klaipeda cathedral (mentioned in chapter 3 under religious dissent) were unavailable for the data-collection. It is likely that of the over 100,000, many were peasants with strong religious feelings.

There is one general lesson from this, a lesson that might be too easily lost in the detail. It is simply this: there is no automaticity in the judicial process. Dissident acts generally do not produce arrest, much less trial. There is no pattern of the KGB, procurator, and court moving into action at the slightest provocation. Indeed, there are signs that the regime does make efforts to use the courts sparingly, in relation to numbers of dissidents and their activities. Moreover, the regime does differentiate among various social groups, more or less along lines of the resources on which each group's activist dissidents can draw.

Violence, Samizdat, and Unusual Activities

One ought not to infer that the actual actions of dissidents are totally irrelevant to the movements of the judicial apparatus. As we shall now see, the overall pattern of targeting also relates in part to the tactics used by each group, that is the particular type of dissident activity. After all, it is a fundamental premise of Soviet law that "crime" is behavior that violates law and presents a social danger; clearly, "social danger" would vary by the type of action.

The major trigger acts for arrest and trial seem to be 1) violent acts and 2) somewhat unconventional events, such as religious processions and courthouse gatherings. These comprise over a half of the triggers to arrest and trial. (See Table 3.) One can see the relative immunity of priests by examining more closely these and other triggers leading to trials.

Students and workers predominated among users of violent acts (each 6 of 13), suggesting that some relationship exists between social background, action, and response. Yet, the largest users of "other" acts were priests (21 of 59, or 35.6%), who were tried in only two of the "other" act trials (or 15.4%). This indicates some leniency toward priests committing these acts.

Secondary triggers are "flag incidents" and samizdat actions, which account for another one-fifth of the triggers. ("Flag incidents" include the raising or waving of traditional pre-Soviet Lithuanian flags, as well as the lowering of and other forms of "disrespect" for Soviet flags.) Students predominate in the trials over flags (8 of 11 such incidents). All groups, especially intellectuals and workers participate in some samizdat.

Individual and mass petitions are relatively safe acts. These brought about only a fifth of the trials, although they were the overwhelming bulk of the dissident activity (80.1%). Here too we can notice the ameliorating effect of social group on prosecution.

The two types of petition are the preferred tactics of priests (77.8% of their actions). However, they also are preferred by intellectuals (78.1%), white collar individuals (69.7%), and even workers (59.1%). (Only students have a marked predisposition away from individual petitions [7.2%], in favor of "other" activities [14.5%].) Yet, only 1 of the 12 trials for petitions and mass petitions involves a priest,

TABLE 3

JUDICIAL PROCESSING BY DISSIDENT ACT

Type of Dissident Act	Dissident Acts		Event Interrogations*		Arrests*		Trials	
	N	%	N	%	N	%	N	%
Demonstration	9	1.3	3	4.1	5	6.5	0	0.0
Flag	14	2.0	5	6.8	9	11.7	5	9.4
Mass Petition	441	62.0	8	11.0	4	5.2	6	11.3
Petition	129	18.1	26	35.6	12	15.6	6	11.3
Violence&	23	3.2	1	1.4	18	23.4	17	32.1
Other+	82	11.5	25	34.2	22	28.6	13	24.5
Total	711	100.	73	100	77	100	53	100

---

*These are the trigger acts most immediately prior to the judicial event, for interrogations and arrests these occur the same month or the month before; for trials, the trigger may occur as long as two years before, because of the strong tendency noted on p. , for pre-trial detention to exceed nine months, as well as the possibility that a trigger dissident act may have occurred some time before.

&This includes riots, hijackings, physical resistance to militiamen, etc.

+This category includes such actions as waiting in a group outside courthouses, walking in a religious procession, and other non-illegal activities.

although priests were involved in over half of the individual petitions (56 of 96) and nearly three-quarters of the mass petitions (287 of 391). Most of the tried priests were involved in ongoing activities—teaching cathecism—or simply symbolic support of *other* dissidents being tried, namely, standing outside the courthouses during their trials.[5]

Nationalist and Hybrid Targeting

Given what we have suggested about the various social groups, it would not be surprising that the types of dissident concentrated in these groups would be targeted by the judicial apparatus. Indeed, the following table shows this.

Given the leniency with priests, it is not surprising that the relative participation of religious dissidents generally falls at each succeeding step of the process, as the religious dissidents, especially priests, are

TABLE 4

JUDICIAL PROCESSING BY TYPE OF DISSENT

	Dissident Acts		Events Inter- rogations		Arrests		Trials	
Type of Dissent	N	%	N	%	N	%	N	%
Religious	233	34.6	123	29.7	47	19.1	26	22.0
Nationalist	59	8.7	37	8.9	57	23.8	44	37.3
Human Rights	34	5.0	24	5.8	11	4.6	5	4.2
Hybrid	103	15.3	189	45.7	76	31.8	29	24.6
Total	674	100	414	100	239	100	118	100

filtered out at the earlier stages. However, the number of religious dissidents who are tried is still substantial. This suggests that non-priests within the religious movement, particularly students (who are the second largest group within this type of dissent) and others are being used by the regime to intimidate the priests, who are personally treated so gingerly. (We shall have more to say on intimidation below, in the discussion on women.)

However, a pattern of special judicial attention is clear for nationalists (notably in arrests and trials) and the hybrid dissidents (most dramatically in interrogations but also at both later stages). The attention paid to nationalists is partially due to the types of activities, as we will see below. This suggests that the dynamic of repression for nationalists is rooted in the implicit challenge of nationalism to the integrity of the USSR and in their actual behavior, which is indeed more obviously and directly threatening to the social order.

Nationalists characteristically use three modes of protest, each making up about one quarter of their dissent: flag incidents (13), violence (16), and "other" (14 of their 59). They were nearly exclusive users of the first (with only one non-nationalist involved), as well as dominant users of violence (69.6% of the 23 violent acts). This activity relates to their social background, of course, for over a half of the nationalists are students, with another 1/3 workers and intellectuals, as noted in chapter 3. These groups are the ones that predominate in the use of violence, and to some degree "other" activities.

Descriptions of hybrids' careers indicate that their interrogations center on intimidation plus information-gathering on the various wings of the movement. This is a reflection of the degree to which communications, morale, coordination of the movement are important to them. This dynamic differs from that of the nationalists; for the hybrids, there is no clear pattern of judicial action based on activity. Their dissident acts were similar to those of the religious dissidents: mass and individual petitions (with hybrids using them 85.5% of the time, and religious using them 93.9%).

However, hybrids tend to choose samizdat activity (they committed 9 of the 13 acts in this category), as well as the other subcategory, joining dissident groups (9 of 10). Note, however, that these activities have a common goal: the creation and maintenance of connections, the precise characteristic of hybrids that bothers the regime. For hybrids, activity, not social group, is important. As we saw in the last chapter, hybrids are spread through the social groups from 29% priests, to 22% white collar to 13–18% for the remaining groups.

In contrast to the other types, the pure human rights dissidents are neither particularly targeted nor particularly protected. They have a pattern of dissident activity nearly identical to that of religious dissidents, a pattern characterized by the absence of any acts of violence, yet their participation in the judicial process does not decline as does that of the religious type. Why? This seems to reflect the intermediate position of the intellectuals, who dominate human rights dissent, as discussed in Chapter 3. They have greater links to the establishment than do the religious dissidents, but less group influence and cohesion because of their small numbers and low degree of social organization.

Thus, we have noted among the differing types of discontent a continued pattern of social targeting, combined with some response to particular types of acts. The priestly immunity, and targeting of other groups, contributes markedly to the relative tolerance of religious dissent, and the judicial focus on nationalists and hybrids.

Kaunas and Vilnius: Increasing Work of Justice

As we saw in Chapter 2, there is some concentration of white collar, intellectual, and student dissidents in the two major urban areas. It is not surprising then that a similar concentration should appear in judicial operations.[6] (See Table 5).

Although there is a strong tendency to focus on both provinces, the smaller, more volatile Kaunas is the target of more *repression* (especially for trials) per dissident act. This pattern exists despite the notably greater rate of actual dissident *activity* for Vilnius. One explanation may be the countervailing effect of the size of Vilnius and deliberate attempts to deter mass dissent, like demonstrations, which are far more common in Kaunas.[7]

TABLE 5

JUDICIAL PROCESSING BY PROVINCE

Events

Province*	Dissident Acts		Inter- rogations		Arrests		Trials	
	N	%	N	%	N	%	N	%
Kaunas	76	11.4	145	25.4	66	29.7	46	41.1
Vilnius	155	23.3	143	25.1	82	36.9	39	34.8
Others	433	65.2	282	49.5	74	33.3	27	24.1
Total	664	100	570	100	222	100	112	100

---
*Residence, not locale of event, which may infrequently differ. Note that trials of certain kinds, "especially important crimes against the state," are held in the republic supreme court in Vilnius, except for one case, held "on circuit," no matter the location of the arrest, interrogation, or dissident act.

TABLE 6

JUDICIAL PROCESSING BY GENDER

Events

Gender	Dissident Acts		Inter- rogations		Arrests		Trials	
	N	%	N	%	N	%	N	%
Male	620	87.1	380	61.1	207	79.9	117	84.8
(without priests)	264	74.1	308	56.8	190	78.5	111	84.1
Female	92	12.9	242	38.9	52	20.1	21	15.2
(without priests)	92	25.9	242	43.2	52	21.5	21	15.9
Total	712	100	622	100	259	100	138	100
(without priests)	356	100	560	100	242	100	132	100

Women, Information, and Intimidatory Interrogations

Table 6 reveals that the patterns of judicial processing by gender tend to parallel those by dissident activity. The vast bulk of such acts and later judicial intervention into the lives of dissidents is male-centered.[8] The only major variation is at the interrogation stage, where the women are interrogated at three times the rate of their activity. One reason for this is rooted in statistics, another in the judicial process.

Statistically, the disproportionate percentage of women in the total interrogated can be explained in part by a simple statistical fact also related to the position of priests; namely, the scarcity of priests interrogated decreased the pool of males interrogated. Thus, the potential absolute number of men fell, without any corresponding decline in the number of women. However, the near absence of priests from the trial stage (in comparison even to the interrogation stage) is not accompanied by a rise in the females tried. Thus, there is more than mere priestly immunity involved here.

Another reason for the anomaly in interrogations is the nature of that part of the process. Interrogations are fundamentally part of the investigation into the nature of purported crime. Both suspects and witnesses (including eyewitnesses and character witnesses) are subject to questioning. Thus, a number of those who know the suspect, or who may have heard of him would be questioned to gain information.

Thus, there can be a non-investigative purpose to interrogation: intimidation of dissidents. As Turk notes in his work on political crime, there are two other functions of "political policing." These are "neutralization" (which is "specific deterrence" against individual political resisters) and "intimidation" (which is "general deterrence" against all actual and potential opponents).[9] In this instance, we see neutralization in the arrest and trial of specific dissidents, in which women are not particularly targeted, and intimidation through interrogation.

This can take several forms: interrogation of an imprisoned dissident's family and friends to threaten *him* indirectly with dire consequences, interrogation of the dissident to threaten his family and acquaintances unless he cooperates, and interrogation of the dissident's more vulnerable associates to blackmail him into cooperation. In the Lithuanian case, there is a considerable amount of direct family-and-friend intimidation: there are around 170 such interrogations of family and friends, non-dissidents. This is only part of the answer to the question of why women rarely go further than the interrogation, because this friends-and-relatives group is not markedly more female than interrogated dissidents (69 of the former, a little over 40%).

There is also a somewhat less direct form of intimidation that derives from the relative immunity of priests. Many of the women interrogated were brought in for questioning because of their supportive role in the samizdat network, especially that of the *Chronicles of the Catholic Church in Lithuania*: over a third (251) of the interrogations were of individuals related to samizdat in some fashion. The role of women as middle level support for activist priests in the dissident movement is clear: possession of a typewriter and samizdat led to interrogation in 60 cases, of which over half (35) were women. In addition, in another 41 cases there are interrogations in which samizdat is somehow mentioned; of them, 21 are women.

This suggests that the police are interested in getting more information about samizdat networks (in which there are extensive reports of priests' activity), but not necessarily in direct punishment of women involved or suspected. The support function of women makes them useful to the regime as "hostages": if priests are rarely punished, the more active supporters in their parishes, especially women with families, may be threatened by interrogation, a possible first step to arrest.[10]

It is necessary to remember, in any case, that once past this stage, with its multifunctionality, the rest of the cycle is more nearly exactly representative of the gender distribution. There appears to be a somewhat greater arrest rate, but the exclusion of priests from the data reveals a decline at later stages, despite their rate of dissident activities. Thus, the implied threats to the supporters of priests and other activists do not seem to be executed, at least along lines of gender.[11]

One might say that there is some leniency for females, "humanism" based in family values or sexism. The table indicates some care in arresting women, in at least one way: whereas one third of the males arrested are tried, two-fifths of the females arrested were thus processed. The varied "dissident" specialists in the judicial system try to make sure that the women who are arrested will be tried and convicted, presumably to avoid "unnecessary" unrest, if large numbers of women were to be arrested, not merely interrogated.

The Psychiatric Route

The Soviet judicial system filters out different kinds of people at different stages. The party clearly makes policy decisions about dissent, and the secret police puts them into effect. In this chapter we have examined the ways in which people are "selected out." However, before we summarize and discuss the implications of this process, it is necessary to examine the other paths mentioned earlier: those to psychiatric internment.

As we mentioned above, in many respects psychiatric detention is a judicial affair, although one possible way to the psychiatric hospital—civil commitment—eludes the courts entirely. Of course, the number of civil detentions is relatively small, and thus the findings must be more sketchy and tentative.

If we compare conventional trials to all psychiatric detentions, we discover a general similarity of targeting. (See Table 7.) The targets

TABLE 7

TRIALS VS. PSYCHIATRIC DETENTIONS

Variable	Trials* N	Trials* %	Psychiatric Detention N	Psychiatric Detention %
Occupation				
White Collar	20	25.97	5	18.52
Intellectual	16	20.78	7	25.93
Student	16	20.78	8	29.63
Priest	6	7.79	0	0
Worker	18	23.38	6	22.22
Peasant	1	1.30	1	3.70
Total	77	100	27	100
Type of Dissent				
Religious	24	22.86	4	10.53
Nationalist	42	40.00	6	15.79
Human Rights	5	4.76	1	2.63
Hybrid	24	22.86	15	39.47
Other	10	9.52	12	31.58
Total	105	100	38	100
Province				
Kaunas	42	42.42	9	24.32
Vilnius	33	33.33	16	43.24
Other	24	24.24	12	32.43
Total	99	100	37	100
Sex				
Male	106	84.80	37	86.05
Female	19	15.20	6	13.95
Total	125	100	43	100
Type of Act				
Demonstration	0	0	0	0
Flag	5	10.87	3	18.75
Mass Petition	5	10.87	1	6.25
Petition	4	8.70	5	31.25
Samizdat	5	10.87	2	12.50
Violence	17	36.96	0	0
Other	10	21.74	5	31.25
Total	46	100	16	100

*Excluding psychiatric detentions

among social groups, types of discontent, sex, and trigger acts are generally the same.

To be sure, there is a slightly greater focus of psychiatric detention on intellectuals and students, with flag incidents as triggers. The desirability of immediate and indefinite removal of those youngsters who would publicly confront the regime with so potent a symbol seems to account for this slight emphasis.

However, there is somewhat less medical action in Kaunas and against nationalists per se, which is tied in to the reluctance to respond to violence with such a "medical" action. This complete absence of the trigger act of violence was unexpected. It clearly seems that to Soviet authorities it is "crazy" to oppose the system by writing illegal complaints (individual petitions are a target of such detentions, new from our discussion of the regular judicial process), but not by rioting, hijacking airplanes, or attacking militiamen. Indeed, the concept of "hooliganism" in Soviet law is one that would encourage such "acceptance" of violence as criminal but not "sick."

Hybrid dissidents are the targets of psychiatric detention even more often than they are of conventional trials. This is perhaps to be explained by the complete isolation that internment brings about, cutting the ties that are so important to the hybrids. In addition, the hybrids are predominantly intellectuals, who must have a horror of the mental and psychological tortures of this particular form of incarceration. The authorities would realize that the mind-numbing effects of isolation, drug-treatment, and continual hospitalization could well intimidate intellectuals who might only hear rumors of such internments. Just as the interrogation of women was intended to function to affect other dissidents, so too the psychiatric internment of intellectuals who are "hybrids" would be useful. Their detentions might operate as "general deterrence" of other intellectuals, as well as "specific deterrence" in destroying communications lines.

This would explain another anomaly, the complete absence of priests and the near-absence of religious dissidents generally, from the ranks of the psychiatrically interned. They are likely to possess considerably more emotional resources to bear the effects of psychiatric detention, and to pray—if not petition and protest—for those who might be interned. Thus, the deterrent value of detention is slight for the religious, and particularly priests.

Again, the main point about psychiatric detentions is the overall similarity to regular trials. The targets of detention are not markedly different, although the relative frequencies do vary. If anything, the data seem to show a marked sophistication in the regime's appreciation of the vulnerability of differing groups, and consistency in targeting.

Targeting and Differing Functions

In the previous pages, we have examined a great deal of data. The socio-demographic and behavioral concomitants of the judicial and psychiatric internment processes have been detailed at some length. There are several major lines of findings.

First, the automatic and mechanical repression of dissidents suggested by some Western analyses does not really occur anywhere near as consistently as may have been thought, at any point in the process. For example only 132 of the 620 arrests were important enough to produce trials. Thus, the various stages of the process itself were used differently (and against different groups) by the KGB in the struggle against dissent.

Second, the process of filtering out of the judicial process is related to socio-demographic characteristics. Priests are especially active, and yet are infrequently interrogated, rarely arrested and tried. Students, intellectuals, and workers, on the other hand, are foci of the attention of the apparatus.

Third, although there is some relationship of judicial treatment to the specific activity of the dissident, that relationship is not immediate and unvarying. We have seen, for example, how petitions are not particularly trigger acts for trial; and, of petition-related trials, the vast majority are *not* of priests, despite the clear dominance of priests in petition activity. Thus, priestly immunity holds up, even controlling for type of act.

Fourth, there is a connection between type of dissent and repressive acts. Generally mediated through social group and type of dissident activity, this relationship overall is clearly seen in the striking targeting of nationalists and hybrids, especially in the cases of trials and psychiatric detentions.

Finally, the targeting at differing stages seems in part to depend on the desired function of repression. The interrogation of women is a prime example of how an otherwise untargeted group may find itself the object of a great deal of regime attention at one stage of the judicial process because of the "beneficial consequences" for the regime's purpose of the general deterrence of greater dissent as well as the collection of further information on samizdat activities.

In the last chapter the theoretical significance and implications for the future of these and other patterns of repression will be analyzed at greater length. Suffice it to say at this point that we have demonstrated that the coercive apparatus does not act in an *exclusively* arbitrary way when it comes to dissent.

Of course, there are violations of the rights of individuals, and there is an inconsistency in the action undertaken when the same types of "crimes" are committed by different (and even the same) kinds of "criminal." However, there are discernible patterns of targeting, that produce regularities of treatment in the judicial process. Those regularities seem to be tied to policies that take account of the resources of differing groups, the kinds of activities engaged in by the group, and other features. The next question is to what degree this patterned regularity is to be found in the disposition of those dissident cases that are actually taken to trial. In the next chapter we will examine the patterns of sentencing.

Notes

1. This contrasts to the standard studies of crime in general in the Soviet Union. Lower educational groups, especially workers and unemployed youths, are the bulk of the criminals processed, according to several Western specialists: see Connor, pp. 89–93; Shelley, p. 220.

2. However, there has been a recent trend in the brutalization and murder of priests. Also, more recently—since the completion of the data collection for this study—trials of priests have begun again, with Fathers Tamkevicius and Svarinskas receiving lengthy camp and exile terms for their activities as leaders of the Catholic Committee for the Defense of the Rights of Believers. See Chapter 8.

3. An interesting example is that of Father Tamkevicius who even refused a summons from the more foreboding cental KGB in Moscow. CCCL, 44: 16.

4. On the other hand, see fn. 1, above.

5. Priests are 15.4% (2 of 13) of those tried for "other" trigger acts, yet they participated in 43.8% of them (21 of 48 identified with group).

6. Interestingly, there is a similar concentration in common crimes, according to official Soviet statistics. Shelley, p. 214, notes that in areas with more economic development there is more crime; especially, in urban areas there is 40% more than rural. Of course, she also points out that the crime figures generally differ by republic, with the Baltics higher than many others, slightly greater that of Moscow, pp. 218–219.

7. It must be remembered that mass dissident acts are not included in the figures in these tables, except for those individuals who have been named specifically in the various sources. Thus, there were far more demonstrators, rioters, and even mass petition signers than the tables suggest. However, we are using the data quite conservatively here. For a discussion of the overall numbers of acts, etc., see chapter 7.

8. Curiously, the gender distribution is quite similar to that for common crimes in the USSR generally, about 12% female. Cf. Connor, p. 152; Shelley, p. 217. However, Shelley on p. 270 suggests that half of the Baltic crime is by juveniles, and about of that, she suggests, is female, for a rate for females of at least 25%.

9. Austin T. Turk, *Political Criminality: The Defiance and Defense of Authority* (Beverly Hills: Sage, 1982), chapter 4.

10. In the special case of possession of typewriter and samizdat arrests, due to the illegality of such possession according to current official interpretations of "anti-Soviet agitation and propaganda," the proportion of women remained the same, 18 of 31.

11. This "general deterrence" seems to go beyond priests. If one draws a sociogram of the relationships of dissidents, the results are several clusters,

with one of 148 being clearly the largest, the others not exceeding ten in size. In the large cluster, only 11 of the links of the 56 women were interrogations about priests. However, interrogations about other women surpassed this: there were 18 about Vitkauskaite and Navickaite alone. Thus, the deterrence seems to be directed at *women*, rather than priests.

6

Crime and Punishment:
Determinants of Sentencing

The Soviet coercive apparatus selects among different kinds of dissidents (who have committed different dissident acts) for processing from interrogation to trial. We have seen that the regime is particularly concerned with nationalist and hybrid dissident. However, the more intense form of coercion of dissidents begins at the end of trial when dissidents are sentenced to long labor camp terms, usually hundreds or thousands of miles from family, friends, and homeland. What is particularly interesting about this sentencing aspect of repression is that some of the implied policies are at variance to those seen earlier in the process, suggesting even greater and more sophisticated differentiation of countermeasures.

The growing literature on the Soviet judicial system has described not only "law," but also "crime" and the courts. The operations of Soviet courts have only in recent years become the object of empirical study. Increasing numbers of studies of Soviet criminals, with Soviet specialists themselves attempting to describe the characteristics of the "criminal," have appeared. Western specialists depend on these studies in their own work, and in the case of non-political offenses have demonstrated differential rates of conviction and differential sentencing along several dimensions, such as age and gender, that may be pertinent to the "politicals."

Because criminologists in the Soviet Union are subject to a particular set of ideological-political constraints, the "political offender" is sorely neglected by Soviet criminologists.[1] Part of the reason is that the Soviet regime denies the very existence of "political prisoners"[2] (although "crimes against the State" are in the legal codes and part of the ongoing sociological record analyzed by Soviet legal specialists). Thus, this chapter's examination of the sentencing of "political prisoners" has no precedent in the study of Soviet law. As such, any finding would be of interest; but we do discover significant patterns of punishment, especially an unanticipated adherence to legal rules about severity in cases of "especially dangerous crimes against the state."

The regime attempts to deal with the Lithuanian dissident movement by incarceration of differing lengths according to dynamics dependent on the article of the criminal code, which make other factors such as prior record, activity, social group, and type of dissent relevant in complex ways. Only for those "especially dangerous crimes" do we find evidence that the legal provisions on determinants of sentencing have any major impact. This ultimately suggests a political underpinning to the sentencing process which is amenable to policy and leadership change.

Soviet Sentencing Policy: Aims and Principles

Soviet legal theory recognizes several causes of crime, but the primary one has always been "capitalist remnants."[3] In other words, violations of laws and concomitant threat to the social order are seen as something beyond the individual and beyond the essence of socialist society. To be sure, there have been recent additions to the list of causes, medical/mental deficiency and "incomplete socialization" to socialist ideas,[4] but the major factor is supposed to be the continuation of certain anti-socialist attitudes among some (small) parts of the populace. Thus, it is logical that Soviet legal theory proclaims the aims of law to be protection against the behavioral manifestation of such attitudes, the deterrence of further such acts, and the reeducation of these errant citizens.[5]

Thus, too, it is unsurprising that legal punishment for crimes is viewed as multifunctional. "Chastisement" is the first of many aims explicitly mentioned in Article 57; to it are added "correcting and re-educating" as well as "preventing the commission of new crimes by both the convicted persons and by other persons."[6] Indeed, the functions are even seen to reinforce one another: as Terebilov puts it, "the more exact and just the punishment for the acts committed, the greater will be the educational value of a court sentence."[7]

The formal intent of Soviet law is to tie punishment to *several* dimensions of criminal cases. As Bassioni and Savitsky note,[8] the sentences meted out by the courts are supposed to implement four principles—justice, humanism, individuation, and expediency. However, according to Western sources, most of these principles seem to be honored more in the breach for all Soviet dissidents.

The first principle—justice—is based on the premise that innocent people who have done nothing wrong (and who pose no threat to society or themselves) are not to be convicted. According to Supreme Court chairman V. Terebilov, "punishment is meted out only to persons who have committed socially dangerous acts either willfully or through negligence, . . . acts which are strictly defined and recognized by the law as a crime."[9] Of course, as we have seen in the previous chapter, for dissidents the court system in practice does not allow the defendant procedural rights by which to challenge the assertions of the procurator and to demonstrate their "harmlessness," if the act in question is irrefutable.[10]

The principle of humanism suggests that torture and inhumane penalties are not to be imposed; thus, article 20 of the criminal code states, "punishment does not have as its purpose the causing of physical suffering or the lowering of human dignity."[11] This principle has a policy implication which is not followed through in the case of dissidents: respect for safety and nutrition. It is clear that punishment in labor camps, prisons, and psychiatric hospitals does induce physical suffering, especially through malnutrition, and degrades the dignity of imprisoned dissidents.[12]

The third principle is "individuation": the assessment of the pe-culiariities of the individual's case. First, the penalty must bear some relationship to the exact nature of the criminal act. In this context, the primary consideration is "social danger." As noted in the last chapter, acts that are violations of the law but not "socially dangerous" are not legally crimes. Those acts that pose some risk are to be punished, but the sentence ought to in some way be proportional to the danger posed.[13] However, social context having little to do with the act itself may affect this evalation. For example, the frequency of the type of crime and the quality of the crime (e.g. theft of rare art works) may be enough for the danger to be seen as high.[14] This seems to be the basis for harsh punishments for such relatively minor dissident actions as typing up essays in the privacy of one's own home, in that such actions may spur on other, unrelated individuals to disseminate their own samizdat, or even make public proclamations or demonstrations.

A second aspect of individuation is that the personality and social condition require consideration in sentencing. This allows some mit-igation of responsibility for the crime, and may yield a lesser sentence than the maximum called for by law. We have already seen one aspect of this "liberalism" in the use of psychiatric detention, supposedly employed in those cases where the individual's personality is perverse in a medical way. One can add here such mitigating factors as the predisposition of the defendant to crime (as indicated by a prior criminal or psychiatric record), and his current attitude to the criminal act in question, i.e., whether the defendant has confessed and is remorseful, is willing to make recompense, voluntarily surrendered, etc.[15]

Prior records have been institutionalized in article 57. However, these are supposed to be automatically cleared if no further crimes are committed within a certain time period, with the exception of 10-year-or-greater sentences, which only a court can clear.[16]

There is a special provision for "especially dangerous recidivists." This category includes a) those who have been previously convicted for especially dangerous crimes against the state (among others) and had then received at least a five-year term, and b) anyone previously sentenced twice for these crimes (no matter the length of term) who is again sentenced for a term of more than three years for one of these crimes. The determination of this status is done by a court, which is charged with taking into account all the factors of individuation mentioned here.[17]

The implications for dissidents of this principle of individuation are mixed. Prior records are common but not universal among dissidents. Also, even partial confessions are rare. This would mean that this provision would not be applicable to Lithuanian and other dissidents.) On the other hand, there is little information on the labelling of "especially dangerous recidivists."

The *social* conditions considered under this individuation principle include the family circumstances (number of dependents, whether there are grave problems, whether a female defendant is pregnant, etc.), the age and state of physical health of the defendant, and (implicitly) the degree of "public" involvement in the case (i.e.,indignation at the crimes, expressed in the newspaper and public forums).[18]

Age is to be factored into judgments at both ends of the continuum. For those under 18, the maximum sentence for all crimes with a usual 15 years' maximum is lowered to 10, and there is no death penalty under any circumstances. Also, youth itself is listed as one of the possible mitigating factors.[19] For those who are elderly and infirm, discretion is allowed, and the expectation is that they too will be given milder forms and degrees of punishment.[20] Again, reports in the West are that such principles have not resulted in lesser punishment for numerous aged and ill dissidents, even those with "good" records.[21]

The fourth principle is that of expediency. Penalties are to take into account practical needs, of *both* society and defendant. From this comes the preference for *labor* camps over simple prisons, for both common criminals and dissidents. They can "benefit" from labor, and society can derive economic surplus value for the good of all, not "wasting" it in mere incarceration.

It is this principle that provides for reduction of charges, or even suspended sentence, under certain conditions. If punishment is not needed for correction, if there is no longer any social danger, if the crime is a first offense—under such conditions it is not beneficial for society to incarcerate criminals, at least for long periods of time.[22]

Thus, the sentencing policies of the Soviet Union are founded in several principles that allow for fair, humane, differentiated penalties. Such principles take account of the social background, personal features, and behavior of the individual defendant, as well as the actual crime. These features are significant in that they create the official possibility of *different* kinds of sentencing practice. In the sections that follow we will discover that the patterns of sentencing of dissidents in Lithuania do conform to some of the legally based aspects of individuation, although the particular parameters of punishment do *not* seem connected to common-sense understanding of the social danger of different kinds of acts.

The Data-Set: The Trials and Sentences

This chapter will analyze all trials mentioned in the sources, from 1969 to 1981, excluding those without specific dates given. The focus of this chapter will be sentencing. We will compare average sentences for several groups along differing variables. The major dependent variable is length of sentence, calculated as the simple sum of years in labor camps and years in exile (if any) for each individual. A common sentence for dissidents is the combination of a labor camp term *and* a following term "in exile," meaning enforced residence in remote parts of the Soviet Union for as much as five years time.

One could simply drop the exile terms without major distortion of the results, because no dissidents received *only* an exile term, although Soviet law allows this possibility for nearly all major offenses. However, it does make intuitive sense that the addition of exile is roughly comparable to a longer camp term, although the two conditions are somewhat different. The simple addition of the two in forming the variable "sentence" has the virtue of simplicity and does not produce results markedly different from those using the camp term alone.[23] Trials with fines and non-incarceration sentences (like corrective labor without imprisonment), as well as psychiatric detention are excluded from the analysis, as these are qualitatively different from conventional imprisonment and exile.[24]

The following sections examine the factors that may have an influence on this combined length of sentence for dissidents. These factors form a complex mosaic, the most important part of which is the criminal charge against the defendant. From the prosecutor's selection of a charge flow a number of consequences, namely, whether other aspects of the case will have any role to play, and exactly how they may do so.

Sentencing and Social Danger

Given the scope of the dissident movement, its degree of organization, and the variety of its activities, the regime does target the dissidents differentially, as we saw in the last chapter. It is to be expected that it would use the courts to punish dissidents harshly, by charging them with serious crimes and sentencing them accordingly to long terms in camps and prisons. This connection of sentence to formal criminal charge is one that can be found in the Western courts, where several studies have demonstrated the importance of formal charge. To the degree that the Soviet leadership since the revolution has stressed the need for "socialist legality"—this particularly after the death of Stalin—the application of coercion ought to be associated with the formal requirements of punishment, to demonstrate the "legality" of the repression of dissent.

For similar reasons, one would expect the regime to modify its sentencing on the basis of the nature of the dissident act and of the dissident's prior criminal/dissident record. For the regime to ignore these factors would appear arbitrary and non-legal, and thereby undermine claims that the courts had overcome the "cult of personality," under which Stalin had dominated the institutional structures of the entire society and his "paranoia" supposedly "distorted" their operations. His successors have claimed to have corrected these problems.

Also, Western specialists on Soviet law and on dissent have suggested that the dissidents *have* been punished according to the law. Dissidents are charged with harsh crimes and sentenced to the maximum allowable terms—and no more. Also, the introduction of article 190.1 ("slander of the Soviet state"), as we noted in Chapter 2, was specifically seen as an attempt to provide some charge more lenient than "anti-Soviet agitation and propaganda" with which to punish dissent.

Let us now examine the effect of charge, nature of the crime, and prior record on the sentencing of dissidents. The empirical patterns will show that the general wisdom only holds so far: these factors are important, but not exactly as one would reasonably anticipate.

Table 1

Sentencing by Article
of the Criminal Code

Article	Average Sentence	Maximum Possible	N
Treason (no.64)	13.2	20.0	9
Anti-Soviet agitation and propaganda (70)	5.8	15.0*	31
Slander of the State (190.1)	2.0	3.0	9
Religious articles --Separation of Church and State (142)	3.3	3.0*	7
--Violations of Rights of Non-Believers (242)	3.8	5.0	2
--both together	3.4	3-5	9
Others&	1.7	2-7 years	24
None reported	2.6	----	11
OVERALL (all trials)	4.5	2-15	93

*These maxima are special ones for recividists, expressly mentioned in the article. See Berman and Spindler, op. cit., for all the maximal terms.

&Includes charges such as 190.2, 190.3, resisting the militia, hooliganism, residence violations, draft evasion, etc.-- all very infrequent charges in the data set.

N.B.--Death sentence is possible for treason and some crimes in the "other" category. Fines are possible in slander of the state, separation of church and state, and some of the "other" articles. Both these outcomes have been omitted from the above calculations for reasons of non-comparability.

Charge

The article most often used against dissidents has been anti-Soviet agitation and propaganda, article 70. (See Table 1.) Next is "treason," article 64, followed distantly by slander of the state, article 190.1.

The charge determines upper limits to the sentence, and the courts seem to press for those limits in many "political" cases. In other words, maximum sentences are frequent, while suspended sentences are quite rare. The highest average is for treason: Article 64 (with its 20 year limit and average of 13.2 years). Lesser charges also yield lesser terms. For example, "anti-Soviet agitation and propaganda" yields less than half the average sentence of treason (5.8 years), and slander of the state one third of that (2.0 years).

Surprisingly, the anti-religious article sentences are harsh compared to the political charge of slander of the state. Previous chapters have shown that religious dissidents are not targeted for judicial processing as often as some other types. This apparent contradiction is explained in part by the fact that of the religious dissidents who actually ever came to trial, two-thirds were Jehovah's Witnesses, not Roman Catholics. The Witnesses, with their very public proselytizing activity (often on street corners), represent a special case of religious dissent to the regime. As a result, Witnesses are often charged with violating the separation of church and state (Article 142) for engaging in "education" (the Soviet authorities would say "mis-education") of youth in public places. This charge is less frequently and less severely applied to Catholics.[25]

This suggests that, indeed, factors in addition to formal charge must be closely examined. These factors may have a major effect on sentencing through the modification of sentence under similar charges. Before we consider these and other variables such as socio-demographic features of the defendant, however, it is necessary to describe briefly the patterns related to other "criminal features" that the legal establishment is supposed to consider along with charge to determine the degree of gravity of the social danger; namely, prior criminal record and the nature of the trigger act.

Prior Record

Although the relationship of punishment to the dissident's prior record (previous arrests and trials) is not clear because of sketchy data, a few limited generalizations may be made. Table 2 suggests that prior arrests and trials *generally* do not make a difference. The aggregate averages are not very far apart, and vary in erratic directions.

Only in trials involving article 70 ("anti-Soviet agitation and propaganda")—an "especially dangerous" crime does a legal concern for social danger hold. Length of sentence does increase with number of previous arrests and trials. Thus, the Soviet regime treats these trials differently from the others: the legal consensus for harsher penalties to those with lengthier criminal records also overcomes a possible tendency to allow other factors to diminish sentence.

The few cases for slander of the state (190.1) suggest just the opposite: prior record seems to *ameliorate* sentencing. This must be explained by a confounding variable: the social-political context of the time of trial. Earlier trials occurred during the early days of the emergence of the social movement, and the later mass organizational efforts of petition drives and similar activities may be seen as offering

Table 2

Sentencing by Prior Record
and Article

Article	Number of Prior Arrests			Number of Prior Trials		
	0	1	2 or more	0	1	2 or more
64*	13.0	15.0	--	13.0	--	15.0
(N)	(8)	(1)		(8)		(1)
70	5.2	6.5	7.0	5.2	5.5	11.5
(N)	(22)	(6)	(3)	(23)	(6)	(2)
Religious arts.	3.7	--	1.0	3.5	5.0	1.0
(N)	(8)		(1)	(7)	(1)	(1)
190.1	2.2	2.0	1.5	2.2	1.7	--
(N)	(6)	(1)	(2)	(6)	(3)	
Other	2.6	0.7	1.5	2.0	1.0	1.3
(N)	(14)	(5)	(5)	(16)	(6)	(2)
None reported	2.6	--	--	2.6	--	--
(N)	(11)			(11)		
Overall	4.6	4.6	3.1	4.6	3.1	6.9
(N)	(69)	(13)	(11)	(71)	(16)	(6)

*For the names of these articles see the prior table; for some discussion of their content, see Chapter 2.

some limited degree of protection to those tried under this article. This effect does not seem visible for other articles (except to a very limited extent for the residual "other" category). More must be said about this specific historical context, and we will investigate it further in the next chapter.

There are two implications of this complex relationship of sentencing to prior record. First, trials under different articles may be driven by different dynamics in sentencing. The legal consensus on prior record seems to operate mainly in the case of this one type of more serious "political" trials. Indeed, prior arrest and conviction can be nearly automatic grounds for the "especially dangerous recidivist" classification and a harsher sentence. The trials under the less "political" articles seem to involve different pressures to overcome the logical predisposition to punish more persistent criminals.

The second implication of the exceptionalism of article 70 is the possibility of a differentiated bureaucracy not rooted in geography. Article 70 trials may be understood as trials so important to the regime that specific central directives would override the "normal" workings of the judicial system. In other words, on lesser charges the local procurators, judges, and police would have greater autonomy, and would tend to move in more differentiated directions; this would wash out the close relationship of sentence to prior record. Of course, it would be oversimple to maintain that the central authorities (in either Moscow or Vilnius) were completely disinterested in the "less political" trials. However, in article 70 trials, the regime would want especially to demonstrate "legality" of the process and the seriousness of the defendants' crimes.

Thus, we have seen that although articles of the criminal code are generally significant in themselves, in setting upper limits to sentences, the criminal record of the defendants seems important only in one kind of trial, namely anti-Soviet agitation trials. In other trials, it is not.[26] This indicates different dynamics of sentencing under different charges, with the possibility of some degree of autonomy for trials under certain less political charges.

Dissident Activity

Given the required assessment of "social danger," the nature of the trigger act leading to arrest and trial should also be a factor in determining punishment. Indeed, Barghoorn suggests that in the current, post-Khrushchev period (from which most of the data is drawn), the policies of repression have been quite sophisticated in linking punishment directly to *activity*. He attributes to the regime a policy of measured, incremental response to dissent that allows individual dissidents many opportunities to escape harsher repression by ceasing further dissent.[27] On the other hand, Rein Taagepera evaluates Soviet repression differently. From his analysis of the case of Estonian dissident Juri Kukk and Estonian dissidents in general, Taagepera characterizes repression as "softening without liberalization." That is, the regime is *inconsistent*: it does allow *some* dissidents sometimes to engage in limited dissident activity *sometimes*, but accompanies this limited tolerance with harsh arbitrary repression. The regime has softened to the degree that it of tolerates some dissent for a short time, but it has not philosophically or practically reconciled itself to the continuing existence of dissent; erratic softening has not brought about any systematic "liberalization."[28]

The spotty data suggest that neither Barghoorn nor Taagepera may be completely correct: the degree to which the social danger was endangered by the trigger act may be important, albeit in a non-obvious way. While punishment does vary according to activity, it does not do so incrementally. We can see this in the sentencing patterns for actions that differ by degree of violence, politicization, and number of participants.

Since Soviet law sees the "dangerousness" of the crime as of prime importance, we would expect the more violent, highly political, and mass (multi-person) crimes to produce higher sentences than the less violent, less politicized, or more individual crimes. However, the aggregated data suggest that violent trigger acts generally drew *shorter* sentences than non-violent acts. Similarly, mass crimes (unless they involved what could be interpreted as a conspiracy—even if it were a mass demonstration or riot), usually resulted in *lighter* punishment than did single-person crimes. In contrast, the most highly politicized (that is, not a personalized expression of discontent, such as the spontaneous soccer riots) crimes produced higher sentences than the less politicized. (See Table 3, overall figures.)

As with prior record, the article with which the defendant is charged is important, this time in nearly completely "washing out" apparent effects. First, there are simply no big differences on the violence dimension within any major article. (Only for treason is punishment much greater for violence, yet even this is for a total of three cases.) The general lack of harshness toward violence seems due to the readiness of the Soviet regime to punish *any* "opposition" harshly, but this finding is quite tentative given the small numbers of cases.

This suggests that the full force of the judicial establishment may be used against peaceful groups writing petitions expressly acknowledging the legitimacy of the Soviet system, as much violent rioters. To understand this, we need to discuss the role of non-violent "conspiracy" within the Bolshevik tradition.

Lenin and his followers were only a small conspiracy for much of their pre-revolutionary existence. It was a primary "point of faith" that the revolution could come about only if a tightly-knit organization of professional revolutionaries were to prepare for it; not mass electoral politics, not bomb-throwing, but covert organizing was the way to the future. This prescience was accompanied by the call in *What is to be Done?* for an underground newspaper to combat the establishment ideology: surely dissident samizdat composed and distributed by small underground groups resonates strongly with contemporary Communists, at least implicitly. The state is not entirely safe as long as conspiracies, with the goal of massive change and with the essentially peaceful tactics of organization and communication, continue.

Thus, just as the context for an art theft entails the rarity of the works stolen, no matter their objective value, so too the actions of small groups entail counterrevolutionary prospects, no matter their expressed intent. They can be just as "dangerous" as riots and hijacking. This is especially the case because small groups acting peacefully can build and maintain a mass "social movement" over a long period.

Table 3

Sentencing by Feature of Trigger Act and Article

		Violence*			Political&		Number of Participants#			
	no act	no	yes		no	yes	1	small group	mass group	samiz.
64	13.1	12.5	15.0		10.0	15.0	10.0	15.0	--	15.0
(N)	(6)	(2)	(1)		(1)	(2)	(1)	(1)		(1)
70	6.2	5.7	--		6.7	6.4	6.7	8.0	4.8	6.3
(N)	(6)	(25)			(7)	(15)	(6)	(1)	(3)	(15)
Religious	4.1	1.0	--		1.0	--	1.0	--	--	--
(N)	(7)	(2)			(1)		(1)			
190.1	2.4	1.9	--		1.5	--	1.5	--	--	2.0
(N)	(2)	(7)			(2)		(2)			(5)
Other	3.9	1.6	2.2		1.4	1.9	0.9	0.9	2.3	2.6
(N)	(3)	(14)	(7)		(7)	(12)	(6)	(3)	(8)	(4)
None reported	2.5	.04	3.2		.04	4.4	.04	3.0	3.3	--
(N)	(5)	(1)	(5)		(1)	(5)	(1)	(1)	(4)	
OVERALL	6.0	4.0	3.6		3.7	4.4	3.5	4.8	3.1	5.2
(N)	(29)	(51)	(13)		(19)	(40)	(17)	(6)	(15)	(25)

*Samizdat, petitions, mass petitions, etc. are considered non-violent, while riots, airplane hijacking, and similar acts are classified as violent.

&Politicization was determined from content of dissent: orientation toward changes in policy or structure was considered political, whereas amelioration of individual condition, or expression of religious or other belief was not. Those cases without known content were deleted from this part of the table.

#Samizdat is separated out from the number categories for other acts because it is impossible to determine how to treat the physical reproduction and dissemination of such journals: they are individual acts when the retyping is done in the privacy of one person's apartment, they are small-group in the editing process, and they are mass acts in the numbers ultimately involved.

In this connection, samizdat itself may be viewed as socially dangerous even if the act of possession of one's own work does not harm anyone else. Especially, the laborious retyping of multiple copies of essays, poetry, and novels on onion-skin sheets of paper is seen as potentially as harmful as the issuance of revolutionary calls for the overthrow of the Soviet regime.

The perceived threat of general samizdat activity can be noted in the overall higher sentences drawn by dissidents arrested for such actions. (See Table 3.) This harshness seems more to be a result of selective charges against them, weighed heavily toward anti-Soviet agitation, slander of the state, and miscellaneous non-political charges, but in the last two categories there is some evidence of disproportionate penalty for samizdat.

This brings us to the question of number, for samizdat is created, reproduced, and distributed by any number of dissidents. When one considers the number of participants in the trigger act, one finds some worsening of sentence, once more than a single person is involved, although not automatically more the greater the number of others.

The reason for the lack of uniform differentiation in sentencing by number lies in the interpretion of the regime of the nature of dissident activity, especially relating to samizdat production. Samizdat itself can involve one, a few, or a large number of individuals. A solitary person might write a denunciation of government policy after a petition, but not circulate it. This makes no difference for the regime: to have written it is sufficiently dangerous. A small number of persons may circulate their own poetry, life stories, and essays among themselves, without going beyond a person's living room; for the regime, this is as dangerous as standing on a streetcorner passing out pamphlets. Likewise, a large network of people may be involved in the continuing production and dissemination of an underground journal, yet this may not disturb the authorities as much as the original creation of the journal.

Similarly, dissident acts may vary in social danger by degree of "politicization." Acts oriented to pressure leadership toward policy change, as opposed to private demands for individual grievances, might be perceived as more threatening to a regime opposed to any mass "spontaneity." In practice dissident calls for revolution are rare; rather, mass or individual petitions for the release of incarcerated dissidents are far more common. Nonetheless, these petitions do differ from nationalist riots in their intended maximum effect: individual restitution as opposed to structural change of the body politic.

On this dimension, Table 3 shows *no* major aggravating effect of politicization on sentencing (only 3 cases for treason being the exception). And there is no significant differentiation prior to trial in selection of charges. Religious articles and slander of the state are not used for politicized trigger acts, but the numbers are not great enough to imply a clear policy on this. This non-finding on politicization may be due to the possibility that the coercive apparatus may view all of the dissidents in this file as "political."

Another aspect of the context of dissident activity ought to be mentioned: the differing organizational and political strengths of dissent in various parts of the country. These differences may impel

Table 4

Sentencing by Province
and Article

Article	Overall	Province Vilnius	Kaunas	Other	Not reported
64	13.2	--	--	15.0	12.7
(N)	(9)			(2)	(7)
70	5.8	7.0	5.3	4.9	3.8
(N)	(31)	(12)	(7)	(7)	(6)
Relig. articles	3.2	--	4.5	1.0	5.0
(N)	(9)		(5)	(3)	(1)
190.1	2.0	5.3	1.9	2.5	--
(N)	(9)	(6)	(4)	(2)	
Other	1.7	1.7	1.7	1.4	--
(N)	(24)	(8)	(12)	(5)	
None reported	2.6	1.5	3.8	3.0	2.3
(N)	(11)	(2)	(4)	(2)	(2)
Overall	4.5	4.4	3.2	4.1	7.6
(N)	(93)	(24)	(32)	(21)	(16)

procurators to move for harsher or softer punishments, or different kinds of trials (achieved by basing them on different articles of the criminal code), according in part to what the possible local dissident reaction would be, as well as what the prior history of dissident activism has been. Thus, charges for dissidents from the capital (Vilnius) and for those from the second largest city (Kaunas) should vary in the charges dissidents are tried under, and in sentences meted out.

Table 4 shows some support for this. Dissidents from the capital Vilnius were given harsher terms for both anti-Soviet agitation (article 70) and slander of the Soviet state (article 190.1). But dissidents from Kaunas were tried on religious charges (while none from Vilnius was) and given far longer terms than those in smaller provinces.

Why? The capital and the second largest city are show-places for the regime. Trials in those cities have a greater "educational" value because more people live there and would be more attuned to them by infrequent press coverage and more frequent word of mouth. In addition, the danger of dissent in those cities would be markedly higher, even for the same number, type, and activity of dissidents, for the same reason. Thus, the regime would move to punish them harshly for serious crimes in a draconian fashion to preempt further growth of dissent.

Yet the dangers of dissident contagion would be somewhat different. In general they would be greater in larger, more anonymous Vilnius, but more so for religious dissent in more "traditional" Kaunas with its surviving seminary. Thus, the difference in sentencing.

Thus, the behavioral characteristics of the "crime" have only a limited, idiosyncratic effect on sentencing. More violent, public, and collective crimes do not lead systematically to greater punishment. Instead, only certain kinds of criminal charges, like treason, show any effect of crime on punishment. Finally, the local context is important for the trials on many charges, including anti-Soviet agitation and propaganda, slander of the state, and religious charges.

Differential Sentencing

There are considerable differences in average sentence along all the demographic and cultural dimensions analyzed in prior chapters. This should not be surprising because the rationale of targeting implies that the end-point will produce differentiated results for the targets.

Gender

In the aggregate, males receive sentences twice as long as females. This pattern implies that the coercive apparatus does "take mercy" on women in sentencing, conforming to the "tolerance" and emphasis on intimidation-through-interrogation seen in the last chapter. The percentage of women among those actually sentenced (11.8%) is lower than that of their participation in the dissident movement (27.9%). Thus it seems that women are "allowed" more leeway before the authorities act to isolate and punish them.

According to Amnesty International,[29] "it is difficult to detect a coherent pattern of leniency for such persons [such as women]" in political cases. It is difficult to ascertain one way or another the correctness of this description because of the low number of women charged under particular articles. Fragmentary data indicate only slight signs of leniency for the religious articles and slander of the state, but only 4 women were convicted under these provisions. For other articles there is virtually no difference.

The aggregate difference seems to be due solely to the *distribution* of charges. Almost all those charged with the more serious charges with heavier possible sentences (like treason and anti-Soviet agitation) are male, while women are charged with the less serious "slander"

Table 5

Sentencing by Gender and Article

Article	Male Years	N	Female Years	N	Overall
64	13.2	9	--	0	13.2
70	5.7	30	6.0	1	5.8
Religious arts.	3.5	8	2.5	1	3.2
190.1	2.1	6	1.8	3	2.0
Other articles	1.7	20	1.8	4	1.9
None reported	2.8	9	1.5	2	2.6
OVERALL	4.7	82	2.2	11	4.4

and "others" somewhat more frequently than their numbers would otherwise warrant. Only in the *selection* of charges is there clear evidence of gender-based leniency, not in the sentencing.

Age and Social Group

Like the supposed gender-based "humanitarianism," there is a leniency for certain age groups, according to Soviet legal provisions. In the practice of non-political cases, the legal provisions relating to age do seem to carry some weight; Connor notes that length of sentence in non-political criminal convictions does vary in part with age (and offense).[30]

Here, too, Amnesty International argues the absence of "leniency" in political cases.[31] Partial data imply that Amnesty is basically incorrect: the average sentence for those under 21 years of age at the time of sentencing—0.6 years (for six cases)—is markedly different from the overall average of 4.4. For those over 60 (four cases), the average is 0.5. With such small numbers, though, it is not possible to take this analysis further.

The question of age is tied to that of occupational category: the younger defendants are preponderantly but not exclusively students, and the older are often, but not entirely priests. There is a large range of average sentences (from 0.9 years to 15.0) among the different occupational groups, but the least punished category is that of the students.

Table 6

Sentencing by Social Group
and Article

	Worker	Student	Intel.	Peasant	Cleric	White Collar	None reported
Article							
64	15.0	--	--	15.0	--	15.0	12.3
(N)	(2)			(1)		(1)	(4)
70	7.0	3.9	7.2	--	--	4.5	4.4
(N)	(3)	(4)	(12)			(3)	(9)
Relig. arts	--	--	--	--	1.0	--	4.9
(N)					(3)		(6)
190.1	1.8	--	3.0	--	2.0	2.3	1.7
(N)	(2)		(1)		(1)	(2)	(3)
Other	1.8	2.5	2.5	--	.04	2.3	1.5
(N)	(9)	(3)	(2)		(1)	(3)	(8)
None reported	.03	.02	--	--	.04	--	0.8
(N)	(1)	(1)			(1)		(6)
Total	4.2	2.9	6.3	15.0	0.9	4.4	3.9
(N)	(17)	(8)	(15)	(1)	(6)	(9)	(36)

*There is one "other" social group case. It is a 10-year article 64 trial that has been omitted from this table.

The lighter terms for students on the harsh article 70 suggest a leniency and chance for redemption, as well as a confidence that the myriad levers in the komsomol/educational system network will prove effective in the long run. Paradoxically, one can argue that this aim is also served by non-leniency on the less serious charges in the "other" category: they serve as an inoculation that is painful but that prevents a more serious illness.

This is in tune with our findings on the selection process itself: students are among the targets, but at each successive stage in the process their proportion of the repression falls noticeably. Because the students are, reluctantly, limited targets of the regime, there is some predisposition to "go easy" on them. To be noted here is the pattern of lesser charges being chosen for students: there is no treason or anti-Soviet agitation for them.

The effect of social group does not end with students, as we would guess from our discussion of the filtering process in Chapter 5. The regime understands the potential explosive nature of trials of clergy, and has decided to use this route infrequently (6 times in 40 years). Trials on religious charges would highlight the priests' religious roles, organization, and popular support. (For other charges, there are simply too few cases of priests to make reasonable comparisons.)

However, the main lesson of Table 6 is differential selection of articles of the criminal code. As with gender and other variables, the different social groups do seem to be slotted into different kinds of trials. Intellectuals and students are most often charged with anti-Soviet agitation, priests with religious articles, workers with other criminal acts, and white-collar with either anti-Soviet agitation or "other" crimes. The differences among groups on the same charges generally seem slight, except as noted above.

Thus, students and priests are handled leniently by the courts, at least through the selection of lesser charges and only exceptionally by lesser sentences for the same charges. This is to be expected given the policy of limited targeting of the former and the filtering out of the latter. The same rationale that avoids putting them on trial also sentences them mildly. We also found that white-collar, worker, and intellectual groups are dealt with more of a mailed fist, notably on the political charges.

What needs to be investigated further is the effect that content of dissent has on sentencing. We noted in Chapter 2 that there are historical connections of priests to religious and nationalist sentiments, in Chapter 3 that there are some contemporary connections (in the persons of hybrids) among the differing kinds of dissidents, and in the last chapter that a clear targeting of nationalists and hybrids could be seen in the filtering process in the judicial system.

Type of Dissent

The Western literature on dissent frequently suggests that type of dissent is significant for repression. For example, Rudolf Tokes expressly labels Baltic nationalists and religious dissidents as "low status" and suggests that because of this they "received unusually harsh sentences." Ludmilla Thorne also found in a study of fragmentary data from 1978–1980 that Lithuanian (and Ukrainian) nationalists "usually draw the longest sentences."[32]

Given the targeting of nationalists and hybrids, we should expect a harshness of punishment for them. They should receive even harder penalties, to reinforce the "educational" and deterrent value of their trials. The data do show that those participating in nationalist dissent average camp and prison sentences as much as three and a half years longer than those received by participants in either religious or human rights activities. This harshness confirms that the regime is most concerned about the power of nationalism in the Lithuanian Republic.

Table 7

Sentencing by Dissent Type
and Article

Article	Relig.	Nat'l.	Human Rights	Hybrids	Others	N/A
64	--	13.1	--	15.0	--	12.0
(N)		(12)		(1)		(1)
70	6.0	5.0	10.0	5.9	4.5	3.5
(N)	(3)	(5)	(1)	(14)	(5)	(3)
Relig.arts	3.3	--	--	3.0	--	5.0
(N)	(6)			(2)		(1)
190.1	1.8	2.0	--	2.0	2.2	--
(N)	(3)	(2)		(1)	(3)	
Other	1.4	2.0	1.5	1.8	1.4	1.0
(N)	(4)	(7)	(1)	(8)	(3)	(1)
None reported	1.0	5.5	.04	--	--	4.3
(N)	(4)	(4)	(1)			(2)
OVERALL	2.6	6.0	3.8	4.5	3.0	4.6
(N)*	(20)	(30)	(3)	(26)	(11)	(8)

*These numbers are fewer than in Table because trials
without sentences have been omitted.

The intensity of repression of nationalist dissidents derives from the prosecutorial decision on charges, not from the legal basis of "social danger." As may be seen in the table, nationalists in the contemporary period do *not* receive higher sentences than non-nationalists for any article, with the exception of the general "other" crimes category.

Only nationalists (and one hybrid) have been charged with treason in recent years and have not been sentenced under religious articles. Yet, hybrids have been disproportionately charged with the somewhat less harsh anti-Soviet agitation, and religious dissidents have modally faced the even less punishing religious articles. Thus, it is in the selection of charges that greater punishment is doled out to nationalists and hybrids.

That the religious dissidents are not charged so often with harsher articles suggests that the regime does not go out of its way to be vindictive toward religious dissidents on any article; rather, it allows local prosecutors autonomy on them. The religious dissidents, then, are filtered out in great numbers, but when those left do get to trial, they are not subject to close scrutiny, and are not "made examples of."

A word on human rights dissidents: they are generally sentenced on any but anti-Soviet agitation charges. Unfortunately, there are simply too few cases in this category for any meaningful comparison to be made.

Thus, the type of dissent is important in selection of charges, but not in the implementation of those charges in sentencing. This suggests that type of dissent is significant prior to trial, but not in the denouement.

The Politics of Sentencing

Sentences in dissident cases are more than simple reactions to the "violation" of the law. The legal code allows for individuation, and we have found limited evidence that some factors do play a role. Prior record does have a slight effect, at least for a few charges, but generally there is no relationship of such individuation in sentencing.

Unfortunately, it is not simple to account for these patterns. There has been no theoretical, and little empirical work done on the determinants of sentencing in the Soviet Union or any Communist country. However, there *is* a large literature on the working of Western (and particularly the American) courts, especially on the question of sentencing of different groups, that can shed light on Soviet patterns.

One recent overview of that literature[33] outlines the four preponderant theories about sentencing. These are the "legal consensus," "conflict," "labelling," and "prosecutory subsystem" theories. They stress, respectively, the nature of the action for which the accused is brought to trial (and the offense charged), the class or social background of the individual, the perceived threat of the group to which the criminal belongs, and finally the characteristics of the prosecutors and the pressures under which they work. We can see from our findings that sentencing in political trials in Lithuania are illuminated by all but the conflict models.

The "legal consensus" theory focuses on the nature of the offense, i.e., its seriousness as defined by law. In a general sense, we have found that more serious charges do yield longer sentences, as the major pattern seems to be that article of the criminal code accounts for much of the variation in average sentences among differing categories.

However, as we have seen, the official interpretation is that the "gravity of the crime" is supposedly one of the most important considerations in sentencing, regardless of the charge. The nature of the dissident act that "triggered" arrest and prosecution (and for which the individual is charged) should officially be significant. Thus, more violent, more politicized, and more collective "crimes" should yield more punishment, especially given the fact that those crimes are so frequently followed by arrest. Indeed, Barghoorn asserts that there is a correspondence between dissident behavior and regime response: more militant and fundamental opposition produces harsher treatment.[34] Yet, there are no signs of this being a consideration.

In addition, the prior criminal record is also as important in the legal consensus. Recidivism should be viewed negatively, and prior trials (or arrests or dissident activity) would be contributory factors to higher sentences. Here there are signs of a special pattern: only one type of "especially dangerous crime"—anti-soviet agitation—seems subject to legal consensus on the exacerbation of social danger. Thus, legal consensus seems operational in constraining sentencing only, with the partial exception of article 70 trials, where recidivism does matter.

The second theory suggests that the class and social background status of the defendant are the important variables. In the current case, the age, sex, and social class of the dissident could be posited to have an aggravating impact on harsh sentences. Youth, women, and non-intellectuals (especially peasants, workers, and clerics) have the least potential prestige and power, and thus should receive longer sentences than middle-aged, male intellectuals. On *none* of these is there great evidence in the expected direction. There is *no* difference for women or youth, and at least some of the non-intellectuals are not more harshly treated. The most severe sentences can be found on many articles for intellectuals. Here the critical factor seems to be the pre-trial selection of charges—determined long before trial—rather than the "social danger" of the individual act or actor.

Another theory of sentencing suggests that the values of the "deviant" and how they are regarded by the authorities are the critical factors. This "labelling" perspective suggests that the regime may be responding to the *type* of dissent and thus to perceived differing threats to the regime's core legitimating values.[35] National and human rights dissent are perceived by the Soviet government to involve "national sovereignty" and "territorial integrity" of the Soviet Union directly and indirectly[36]: nationalism can lead to demands for secession, and human rights platforms may produce international "interference" in the "internal affairs" of the Soviet government. The past history of the Baltic republics does suggest that nationalism may be dangerous, as we saw in Chapter 2. Also, "hybrid" dissidents may be seen as strategically vital to the growth of a potentially dangerous social movement, as discussed in Chapter 3.

The interrogation and arrest processes discussed in the previous chapter are oriented to these particular brands of dissent, as we have seen. The labelling theory predicts that those nationalists and hybrids who *were* considered sufficiently dangerous to be arrested and put on trial would receive heavier sentences than other types of dissidents would because of the more general structural "threat" of nationalism and of the broader social movement to the Union of Soviet Socialist

Republics. Again, this occurs, but only through the selective use of harsher articles of the criminal code, rather than through the fine-tuning of sentencing.

The fourth theory of sentencing, the prosecutory process, suggests that *political* variables are necessary to explain sentencing. The dynamics of political conflict within the bureaucratic/institutional framework of prosecution are supposed to be the most significant factors in punishment. In the current case, we would have to go beyond mere intra-office rivalry and local ambitions, because of the nature of the Soviet system and the clear signs of central supervision and policymaking. In this form this theory does account for much noted here.

How? The most important .factor is the charge made against the dissident. It is especially amenable to political pressures. In the last chapter we saw that there is no automaticity of punishment, or even automaticity of movement through the criminal justice system as a result of dissident activity. In addition, it has been well established that Soviet trials of dissidents do not allow for effective defense based on the nature of the activity (for example, of the actual *content* of an essay typed and kept in an intellectual's desk drawer). The rules of evidence in Western trials are simply not applicable.

Selection of charges involves political choices. The regime faces a social movement composed of different groups, with different kinds of activity. As it tries to avoid priests generally, the regime only puts them up on lesser charges. As it focuses on hybrids and nationalists, it punishes the former under a slightly less arduous article (anti-Soviet agitation, rather than treason).

The subsidiary but limited pattern of article 70 exceptionalism implies a bureaucratic/political consideration. As one of the "especially dangerous crimes against the state," this article entails the possibility of longer terms, as well as of extra-ordinary classification for recidivists. These articles, in contrast to the others considered here, have special units at the republic center to watch over implementation of the law. There are distinct divisions within the bureaucracies of both the procurator's office and the KGB charged with the prosecution of these crimes. Each of these units has its own plan to fulfill, its own investigators, personal ambitions, etc., as we noted in Chapter 4.Thus, the exceptionalism is a sign of unusual centralism within a system marked by extreme centralization of direction in general, a sign of bureaucratic differences within the judicial system itself.[37] Unfortunately, one cannot account for the absence of such exceptionalism for other "especially dangerous crimes," except for the small number of cases (9 for article 64).

The prosecutory process theory of sentencing implies that certain bureaucratic imperatives and constraints that operate on the major actors in the judicial process, especially the prosecutor. In the Soviet context, the imperatives and the constraints are ones that emanate from the political center, Moscow, more than from anywhere else. Thus, the major question now remains to what degree these factors are related to macro-level policies Does the pattern of repression, centrally directed, but administered in the republic, change as the political climate in Moscow or local political conditions change? Moreover, since repression interacts with dissent itself, how does this interaction develop over time? These questions are investigated in the next chapter.

Notes

1. Walter D. Connor, *Deviance in Soviet Society* (New York: Columbia University Press, 1972); Louise Shelley, "Crime and Delinquency in the Soviet Union," in *Contemporary Soviet Society,* ed. Jerry G. Pankhurst and Michael Paul Sacks (New York: Praeger, 1980), pp. 208–226. Indeed, the very scope of crime and especially "political crime" in the Soviet Union is problematic, as indicated by Frederick C. Barghoorn, "The Post-Khrushchev Campaign to Suppress Dissent," in *Dissent in the USSR,* ed. Rudolf L. Tokes (Baltimore: Johns Hopkins University Press, 1975), p. 85; and others (e.g., Amnesty International, *Prisoners of Conscience in the USSR* [New York: Amnesty International, 1975], p. 51), for the number of political prisoners (particularly from the 1940s) is indeterminate.

2. Amnesty International, p. 50.

3. Robert Conquest, *Justice and the Legal System in the U.S.S.R.* (New York: Frederick A. Praeger, 1968), p. 72.

4. F.T. Cullen, Jr., and J.B. Cullen, in their "The Soviet Model of Soviet Dissidence," *Pacific Sociological Review* (20)(3) (1978): 389–410, suggest that the major thesis of Soviet theory on this is unicausal: incomplete or defective socialization of individuals, with some supporting role played by external propaganda and capitalist "vestiges."

5. Conquest, pp. 72–74.

6. Harold J. Berman and James W. Spindler, *Soviet Criminal Law and Procedure: The RSFSR Codes* (Cambridge, Mass.: Harvard University Press), p. 130; Conquest, pp. 77–79.

7. Berman and Spindler, p. 151.

8. M. Cherif Bassioni and V.M. Savitski, *The Criminal Justice System of the USSR* (Springfield, Illinois: Charles C. Thomas, 1979), pp. 167–176.

9. V. Terebilov, *The Soviet Court* (Moscow: Progess Publishers, 1973), p. 151. Note, as mentioned in the previous chapter, that article 7 of the criminal code specifically exempts those acts that are not dangerous, even if "against the law." Berman and Spindler, p. 127.

10. Also to be noted here is the degree to which even in theory the determination of "danger" and the evaluation of evidence in general depend upon the "revolutionary law consciousness" of the judge, a loophole for political rather than technical justice. See Samuel Kucherov, *The Organs of Soviet Administration of Justice: Their History and Operation* (Leiden: E.J. Brill, 1970), pp. 593–599.

11. Berman and Spindler, p. 130.

12. According to Conquest, p. 80. The death sentence has been abolished three times, but since 1950 it has been occasionally extended, especially in 1961–1962, when grand larceny, counterfeiting, foreign currency violations, attacks on militiamen, aggravated rape or bribery were added.

13. See Kucherov, pp. 600–609, for an interesting discussion of the legal debate over "social danger" as opposed to "objective evidence" and the judicial quest for "absolute truth."

14. Conquest, p. 77.

15. Bassioni and Savitski, p. 168. Cf. article 38, Berman and Spindler, pp. 138–139.

16. Conquest, p. 84.

17. Article 24–1, Berman and Spindler, pp. 133–134.

18. The last-named is one that is less clear in the law, but clear in practice, as Kucherov noted, pp.619–620.

19. Terebilov, 27, 152. In addition, the age for liability for major crimes is now 14, and for lesser crimes to 16. Conquest, pp. 82–83. See also, articles 10, 38, 55, and 63, in Berman and Spindler, pp. 127–128, 138–139, 146–148, 151.

20. Article 38 also lists "grave personal or family circumstances" which could include health problems, as well as pregnancy, as mitigating factors. Berman and Spindler, pp. 138–139.

21. Amnesty International, p. 82.

22. Bassioni and Savitski, pp. 170–176.

23. The intercorrelations of camp terms with this additive index and two others (with camp/prison term added to one-half or one-fifth of the exile term) are 0.992 or better.

24. Moreover, in common criminal cases, incarceration is the primary form of punishment. Connor notes that only 4% of the sentences were fines.

25. The three Roman Catholics received an average of 1.0 years, while the six Witnesses drew 4.6 years (obviously each charged with several counts).

26. It might be noted that Soviet literature says little about the role of prior record, beyond mentioning that recidivists account for 6–8% of offenses, but 12–13% of camp terms (Connor, pp. 141–142.

27. Barghoorn, loc. cit.

28. Rein Taagepera, *Softening Without Liberalization in the Soviet Union: The Case of Juri Kukk* (New York: University Press of America, 1984).

29. Amnesty International, p. 34.

30. Connor, pp. 127–128.

31. Amnesty, loc. cit.

32. Tokes, "Dissent," p. 29; Ludmilla Thorne, "Three Years of Repression in the Soviet Union: A Statistical Study," *Freedom Appeals*, 9 (March-April 1981): 30.

33. Douglas W. Maynard, "Defendant Attributes in Pleas Bargaining: Notes on the Modelling of Sentencing Decisions," *Social Problems* 29 (4) (April 1982): 348–349.

34. Barghoorn, p. 65.

35. Peter Reddaway, "Soviet Policy Towards Dissent Since Khrushchev," RFE-RL Report, no. 297/80 (21 August 1980), p. 8.

36. Thomas Buergenthal, ed., *Human Rights, International Law, and the Helsinki Accord* (New York: Allanheld, Osmun, 1977).

37. Apart from the question of their enforcement and application, the laws *themselves* are also particularly "vulnerable" to Soviet authorities: laws can be introduced or amended with great ease in any one-party system. Unfortunately, the data are not complete enough to allow a full-scale examination of the earlier years, when the laws were considerably different from today in several respects.

7

Politics in Command:
Leaders, Policies,
or Dissent Itself?

Judicial institutions act within political-historical contexts. The Soviet courts, police, and mental hospitals are no exceptions. The way they interact with dissidents is conditioned by more than the individual dissident's own actions and characteristics. More specifically, the political context of leadership, policy, and mass political activity are fundamental factors which need to be examined.

In previous chapters we have seen that the Lithuanian dissidents form a social movement of diversity with some specialization by social group and type of dissent. We have seen that the regime responds to this movement by interrogating, arresting, and trying dissidents from these groups, with differing rates of repression and intensity of punishment for each group. The differences in treatment represent policy decisions made by political authorities about how to deal with the social movement. Clearly, the greater context of politics must be considered. This chapter will examine exactly that broader context.

This chapter considers the possible relationship of several political factors to patterns of dissident and regime activity from 1969–1981. Two elite-level factors, factionalism and general repressive policy, are *not* found to be related to those patterns. Instead, the mass-level dynamics of the Lithuanian social movement yields short-term patterns of repression. It also reinforces a structural, long-term decline in punishment, partially rooted in a shift to less onerous charges. This implies that under certain conditions legal proscriptions may partially protect dissent. (In Chapter 8 we examine developments up to mid-1987.)

The Aggregate Historical Data

The aggregate data that will be discussed in this chapter is drawn from the same sources as the individual-level data analyzed in previous chapters. A separate data-file was created; it was composed of reports of collective activity in which all the participants were not named in the source. Thus, in Table 3, for example, (below, p. 212) a separate column on aggregated individual dissident acts and the columns on repressive acts are drawn from the data-set discussed in Chapter 3 (pp. 56–60). We have included a new column, mass dissident acts.

Problems of small numbers of arrests and trials per year, especially given the occurrence of missing data for other variables, prevent us from any systematic examination of the covariance of several variables on a yearly basis. Therefore, we will look at data grouped by several year periods, using times suggested by prominent Western scholars. Then we will examine yearly patterns for occurrence of these events and for the average punishments of sentencing.

Factionalism

In Western studies of the Soviet Union, the most frequent object of analysis or explanation of phenomena is the nature of the top political elite. This is not surprising given the great concentration of power in the Communist Party's Politburo. However, changes in the decision-making dynamics of that body do not account for the patterns of repression and dissent. The subtle twists in the workings of factionalism during the Brezhnev era do not provide us with a useful understanding of the activities of either dissidents or their state monitors.

The post-Stalinist era is generally seen as one in which arbitrary power in the hands of a single tyrant has been displaced by rule by committee. The Brezhnev years were marked by a form of "collective leadership" that paradoxically maintained both elite stability and conflict. Brezhnev dominated but other Politburo members retained their positions even after occasions of conflict with him. The case of Kosygin is well-known. Thus, personal rivalry for power continued.[1]

Although this struggle entailed attempted manipulation of policy by rivals, of course, the elite dynamics of the times forced a more sophisticated and abtuse form of factionalism than in the 1950s. Infrequently did major personnel changes mark the shifts of power, and even less often were there dramatic policy innovations because of new power alignments. Instead, the 1970s saw more subtle shifts in emphasis in policy.

This suggests that repression was neither introduced nor eliminated by factional ebbs and flows. Instead, a swing in power to more "conservative" elements like the military and the KGB might lead to a growing intensification of attacks on dissidents (which might in turn generate more dissent). Variation is likely to occur within the limits of a broadly anti-dissident stance accepted by all the major factional leaders, with differences being the result of disagreements about implementation.

Unfortunately, although many Western scholars have used the factionalist concept to analyze the Brezhnev regime, there are no studies of the relationship between factional activity and anti-dissident policy. Usually, factionalism is a factor briefly mentioned or implied within discussion of dissent and repression, or vice versa. A recent careful and detailed study of factionalism nonetheless worth pursuing is Breslauer's analysis.[2] He sees four subperiods: 1964–1968 (political succession), 1968–1972 (Brezhnev ascendant), 1972–1975 (reaction), and 1976–1981 (consolidation).

My data covers all but the first period. It shows that although there are some signs of repressive change from one period of factional activity to the next, they do not correspond to the differences in factional activity.

We must use the 1969–1972 period as a base line for change, because data on earlier times is not comparable. Before the early 1970s there was no systematic samizdat. Events from those earlier years are decreasingly well reported, the further back in time one goes. We must then concentrate on the second and third periods.

Fortunately, Breslauer argues that the real shift came at the end of the first period, in 1972–1973 when Brezhnev retreated from a more consumerist, optimistic program to ally himself more conclusively with the conservative, military-heavy industry factors in the party. This move away from populism was associated with the official linkage of dissent with treason in 1973–1974 and an intensification of repression.[3]

When we compare the second to the first period in Table 1, we can see that Brezhnev's turning to the KGB and military for support was reflected in a 50% increase in the rate of arrests and trials.[4]

However, data on the last period—"consolidation"—reveal a bit different story. The arrest rate did jump another 50% as one might expect with "law and order" leadership more completely in control, but the trial rate was nearly halved, moving to levels even lower than in 1969–72, when the coercive apparatus had less factional power.

The argument that fewer trials were necessary to *maintain* a secure conservative establishment against its more "liberal" factional rivals

Table 1
Factionalism under Brezhnev:
Rates of Repression and Dissent

	Breslauer's periods		
	1969-72 Ascendance	1973-75 Reaction	1976-81 Consolidation
Numbers of arrests per annum	11.3	16.7	24.2
Number of trials per annum	8.8	13.0	7.2
Indiv. diss. acts p.a.	13.0	29.3	95.2
Mass diss. acts p.a.	13,216	21,456	37,589
Number of years	4	3	6

ignores the likelihood that a conservative consolidation will be marked by a full-fledged implementation of more conservative policy preferences, namely a fiercer anti-dissident campaign, in the face of a more threatening situation in Lithuania. Instead, we find fewer punishments despite the "objective" need for them from an authoritarian perspective, as expressed in the multiplication of dissident activity, in both indvidual and collective forms (Table 1). We shall have more to say about this growth of dissent and lessening of punishment later.

Thus, it seems clear that factional dynamics do not account for the general patterns of repression and dissent. One must turn elsewhere. Logically, a second elite-level factor needs investigation, that is, changing anti-dissident policy as decided on by the leadership regardless of factional maneuvering.

General Policy and the "Autonomy" of the Lithuanian Movement

The Brezhnev period generally was seen in the West as a time of bureaucratization and conservatization. The de-Stalinizing reformism of the 1950s and early 1960s gave way to rigidity and "ossification."[5]

Western analyses of the Soviet legal system under Brezhnev have noted this increase of repression. For example, Cutler characterizes this time as one of reassertion of authority. Controls over dissent increased, official mass mobilization continued, and the range of legitimate disagreement narrowed, as human rights and political demands were expressly delegitimated.[6] These imply a greater constraint on dissent within a routinized network of repression.

Yet the data suggest that the constraints established by the regime at the center may be overcome by local developments. These may form an autonomous motor for development separate from, although influenced by, the vagaries of central policy (or the rise of dissent in other parts of the USSR).

The literature on repressive policy is characterized by little data or systematization. It is mostly historical description, with few studies even advancing to empirical data collection or tentative categorizations. Kowalewski and Alexeyeva have presented some figures on the arrests and trials of dissidents, but with no underlying categorization of anti-dissident policy, and with contradictory results (the former finds an intensification of repression, the latter greater "taboo-breaking" by the dissidents entailing a lessening of penalties).[7]

One interesting formulation based on an historical analysis of the repression of dissent in both the Soviet Union and Eastern Europe was done by Robert Sharlet.[8] He sees a somewhat different emphasis in the anti-dissident policy during each "phase": 1965–1970 as a time of "high visibility eliminationist trials," 1971–1976 as one of "low visibility containment," and from 1977 on as a return to the eliminationist strategy of intense, widespread repression.[9] The data in Table 2 reveals that the vagaries of general repressive policy under Brezhnev do not hold for Lithuania.

For arrests, we have a continuing increase in rate per year over the three periods, although one might have expected a marked decline during the middle period—"containment." For trials, we have a noticeable increase in the 1971–76 period, followed by a slight decline thereafter. We should have seen the decline and then rise of this indicator from the second to the third period. Indeed, one might have expected a dramatic increase in the last period, given the explosive growth of dissent. Nonetheless, higher levels of repression were not implemented in Lithuania.

Thus, general repressive policy does not account for the vagaries of dissent and repression in Lithuania. We can say that the Lithuanian movement does not seem to have been treated in the same way as its allies—real or potential—in other republics. (However, the final word on this must await further data on the dissident activity of and state counteraction against these potential allies in the Ukraine, the Russian Republic, Uzbekistan, etc.) The Brezhnev period was a time of regime hesitation in the face of Lithuanian dissident growth. It is to that factor that we now turn.

Table 2

Repressive Policy under Brezhnev

Sharlet's Periods

	1969-1970	1971-1976	1977-1981
	High visibility Eliminationism	Low visibility Containment	Return to High Repression
Numbers of arrests per annum	7.0	17.7	24.0
Number of trials per annum	4.0	10.5	8.0
Individual dissident acts p.a.	3.5	27.5	107.8
Mass dissident acts per annum	224	19,625	44,953
Number of years	2	6	5

The Dialectics of Dissident and State

Many scholars have noted the *interaction* of dissent and repression. Sharlet specifically refers to "the recurring cycle of repression and dissent" and the "dialectic of dissidence and repression," beginning with the 1966 Daniel-Sinyavsky trial. Tokes agrees: a new, broader "national movement phase" was triggered by that trial. That phase featured a partial convergence of different types of dissent—pragmatic and moral—during the years 1966–1970. Increasingly differentiated dissident demands, growing non-Russian national sentiment, and heightened religious activities blended together and the regime replied with repression. Vardys sees a similar beginning of the Lithuanian "religious protest movement" in 1968 as a consequence in part of the "heavy-handed Soviet treatment of religion," and a parallel expansion through partial merging with nationalist discontent.[10]

Thus, we would expect growth of *both* dissent and repression. We find evidence for both a short-term co-occurrence of these two processes, and a longer-term acceleration of dissent despite state repression.

The two data-sets on Lithuania demonstrate that dissent is a growing phenomenon. In Table 3, we can see the growth of dissent in numbers of both individual and collective dissident acts. There is a marked jump for individual dissent in 1971 and for mass dissent in 1972,

Table 3

Yearly Aggregate Dissent and Repression

Yearly figures

Year	Dissident Acts		Repressive Acts		
	Indiv. Acts	Mass Acts	Arrests	Trials	Psychiatric Detentions
1969	4	140	5	2	1
1970	3	109	9	6	1
1971	17	24088	8	11	6
1972	28	28527	23	16	4
1973	12	62154	26	15	4
1974	27	69	10	15	3
1975	49	2144	14	9	3
1976	32	768	25	3	3
1977	68	3328	29	10	4
1978	57	5025	13	4	4
1979	238	166232	20	5	4
1980	102	13914	46	19	5
1981	74	36268	12	2	2
Total	711	342766	240	117	4

N.B.   The peak years are underlined.

followed by a high plateau for each, with only 1974 mass acts returning briefly to earlier levels. Thus, we confirm the specific findings of Kowalewski and Remeikis on dissident activity.[11]

These numbers imply that individuals in Lithuania were increasingly willing to express their discontent. This willingness led to the development of numerous organizations and the expansion of samizdat networks. As early dissident activity of differing types emerged, other potential dissidents were stimulated by force of example, at least.

Specifically, nationalist activity starting in 1970 blossomed in 1972. It then expanded into 1) new organizations from 1973, 2) demonstrations and riots from 1974, and 3) new nationalist samizdat from 1975. Similarly, the religious petitions of 1968 by individual priests and parishes soon mushroomed in 1971 and 1972, and continued at a high level for every year thereafter, reaching the 100,000+ level in the 1979 drive to obtain the return of the Klaipeda Cathedral.

It should be noted that the "autonomy" of Lithuanian dissent from external processes found earlier is borne out here too. The peaks do *not* relate to the general patterns of repression in the 1970s, according to Alexeyeva. Her data indicate that 1969–1970 and 1974 as the major trial years, not particularly high years for Lithuania. Moreover, she found no increase in arrests in the Soviet Union generally after 1972, despite the increase in dissident activity, clearly a finding incongruent to the Lithuanian plateau of high arrest years beginning in 1972 through 1980.[12]

Relatedly, the growth of the Lithuanian movement is not attuned to that of other dissident groups. The peaks and valleys of Lithuanian dissent are not synchronized with the non-Lithuanian dissidents. Reddaway, for example, indicates that the 1974–1976 period was one of "impressive growth"—not decline— for the Moscow-based "mainstream human rights movement," yet Table 5 shows a short-term decline. In addition, Kowalewski's data on collective protest indicates two major peaks in the 1965–1978 period, in 1971 and 1977. The former is a Lithuanian mass dissent peak, but the latter is certainly not. From 1974 to 1978 there is a *valley* of low years, during which time only 11,334 of over 300,000 such acts occurred (barely 3%, as opposed to Kowalewski's 39%).[13]

However, since dissent is intimately related to repression, the local increase of the one should be accompanied by the interacting local growth of the other. One can trace a long path through the entire period. The illegal catechism of 1969 led to the arrests and trials of Fathers Seskevicius, Zdebskis, and Bubnys in 1970 and 1971; petitions in 1971 and 1972; interrogations and the creation of the *Chronicles* network in 1972. This continues with more petitions in 1973, arrests in 1973, trials and new petitions in 1974 and 1975, more arrests and the creation of the Lithuanian Helsinki Group in 1976. Then, more arrests and trials in 1976 and 1977 were followed by more samizdat and mass acts in 1977; new trials and petitions in 1978; new petitions and arrests in 1978; more arrests, trials, and petitions in 1980; and petitions in 1981, the end of the data-set.

This interaction between local occurrences of repression and dissent is evident at the aggregate level. As we can see in Table 3 (above), arrests remained stable until 1972, and then increased in three waves through 1980, with new peaks being reached in 1977 and 1980. As noted, the 1972 arrest peak corresponds to 1) the increased *quantity* of dissent in 1971–1972; 2) the qualitative development of the social movement accomplished by the establishment of the *Chronicles of the Catholic Church in Lithuania* that year.

Similarly, the 1977 and 1980 arrest peaks reflect *responses* to dissent. The 1977 arrests and trials followed the creation of more samizdat and organizational networks. Especially important here for the regime was the hybrid Lithuanian Helsinki Watch Group, the hybrid journal *God and Country*, and the numerous clerical petitions on the proposed 1977 Constitution. The 1980 peak was a response to the massive Klaipeda petition, the clerical petition drive, and the further proliferation of samizdat (three nationalist and one religious journals).[14]

A significant aspect of the interactive growth of dissent and repression bears further thought. In both aggregate and individual aspects dissent and repression rise in waves with each subsequent crest higher than the preceeding. Individual dissident peaks grow from 28 in 1972 to 238 in 1979 (with 49 in 1975, 68 in 1977). Mass dissident acts are less consistent but still grow from 62,154 in 1973 through 166,232 in 1979 (the intermediate peak in 1975 is low at 2144, as is the 1981 peak, which may only be the rising part of the next wave). Arrests crest perfectly from 9 in 1970 through 46 in 1980 (with 26 in 1973, 29 in 1977), although trials act somewhat less uniformly in that the middle peak is lower (16 in 1972, 10 in 1977, and 19 in 1980).

The dialectic thus seems to reinforce itself in an "unstable" way here as each side pushes the other harder. A threshold may have already been reached where one side stops growing in response to the other. Theoretically, either the dissidents will convince the state that further escalation will be too costly (for its own elite consensus and socio-economic rationality), *or* the state will intimidate the dissidents, eliminating major leaders and paralyzing followers (by the prospect of further, useless sacrifice). As we shall now see, in practice, the former emerges in the data.

Thus, repression and dissent co-occur in the short-run, but the longer-term relationship is cyclical, with both ratcheting upwards at differing rates, favoring the dissidents. Both effects reflect the power of the Lithuanian social movement. Long-term effects reinforced by this power can be found in the frequency of repression and the sentencing of dissidents.

Increasing "Tolerance" and "Leniency"

As we saw in the previous tables, the policy of repression had proven ineffective in preventing dissent. The regime was confronted with an intolerable choice: expand and intensify repression, or tolerate more activity. Because the leaders did not want to encourage the further development of the social movement and did not wish to reinstate massive Stalinist terror—a dangerous alternative to the elite— they continued *selective repression*. However, those arrests and trials were unconvincing either to the regime or to the dissidents. Thus, the movement continued to grow.

By default, the regime acquiesced in growing dissent. This is revealed in a steadily increasing "tolerance" of dissident acts, whether we use the factionalism or policy periodizations. In Tables 4 and 5, "tolerance" as measured by the number of dissident acts per repressive act clearly increases. This change was linear and dramatic, no matter which ratio

Table 4
Growth of "Tolerance"
Despite Factionalism

Ratios	Breslauer's periods		
	1969-72	1973-75	1976-81
	Ascendant	Reaction	Consolidation
Individual dissi-dent acts per arrest	1.2	1.8	3.9
Individual dissi-dents acts per trial	1.5	2.3	13.2
Mass dissident acts per arrest	1,170	1,285	1,553
Mass dissident acts per trial	1,502	1,651	5,221
Number of years	4	3	6

Table 5

Growth of "Tolerance"
Despite General Policy

	1969-1970	1971-1976	1977-1981
	High visibility Eliminationism	Low visibility Containment	Return to High Repression
I.d.a. per arrest	0.5	1.6	4.5
I.d.a per trial	0.9	2.6	13.5
M.d.a. per arrest	32	1,109	1,873
M.d.a. per trial	56	1,869	5,619

is used. The third period was from 1.5–200 times more tolerant than the first period, depending on the periodization and ratio.

Thus, the Brezhnev regime retreated before the rising social movement. Accompanying this "tolerance" is an increasing "leniency" towards dissidents in sentencing.[15] Graph 1 shows a major decline of length of sentence after 1972. From a range of 5–10 years in the first three years to one of 3–4 years for the rest of the period, the average shifts downward with only one major exception, 1978. That year saw the two trials of the internationally and domestically well-connected and visible Lithuanian Helsinki Group. The defendants were clearly seen by the state as more than just Lithuanian dissidents,

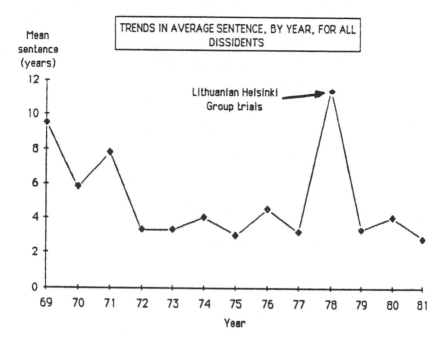

Mean
sentence
(years)

TRENDS IN AVERAGE SENTENCE, BY YEAR, FOR ALL
DISSIDENTS

Lithuanian Helsinki
Group trials

Year

and the excessive sentences given to them were aimed at greater audiences than the Lithuanian movement alone.

The dissidents did not have an entirely unfettered position in the later years. The regime attempted to maintain some degree of control over the growth of the movement in two ways. First, it continued show trials for some onerous political charges, to demonstrate that dissent remained unaccepted, and made the punishments even harsher. Second, for many cases the regime chose "depoliticization," the application of clearly non-political criminal articles, to discredit the leading dissidents.

Table 6 shows that the harshest charge—article 64—disappears after 1971, except for three trials in the late 1970s. In its place arise less serious charges of 1) articles 70 and 190.1 and 2) "other" non-political crimes. For 190.1 and "others" one can see a direct substitution: they appear in 1972 just as article 64 leaves. (Thus, the big drop in range seems directly tied to the abandonment of article 64 and the displacement of cases into lesser charges.)

For these lesser political charges there is some *growth* of punishment, contrary to the general decline shown in the graph. For article 70 this is dramatic (from 2.5 in 1971 to 15 in 1978), but inconsistent (with 1977 and 1980 being deviant years). For 190.1, the growth is entirely consistent, but marginal in magnitude (from 1.5 to 2.3).

Table 6
Trends in Sentencing, By Charge

Year	Charge					N/A
	Art.64	Art.70	Art.190.1	Anti-relig. articles	Others	
1969	15 (1)	4 (1)	--	--	--	--
1970	12 (1)	3.3(3)	--	1 (1)	--	--
1971	13.5 (5)	2.5(1)	--	1 (2)	--	3 (1)
1972	--	--	1.5(2)*	5 (1)	2.6(6)	--
1973	--	2.8(3)*	--	4.4(5)**	1 (1)	4.3(4)
1974	--	4.3(8)	2 (1)	--	2.8(2)*	6 (1)
1975	--	6.3(3)**	--	--	0.7(3)	.04(1)
1976	--	7 (1)	2 (1)*	--	--	--
1977	15 (1)	5 (1)	2 (1)*	--	0.8(2)	0.8(3)
1978	15 (1)	15 (1)	--	--	4 (1)	--
1979	15 (1)	--	--	--	0.5(3)	.04(1)
1980	--	5.1(8)*	2.3(4)	--	1 (4)*	--
1981	--	--	--	--	2.8(2)	--

*One more case has unknown sentence.
**Two more cases have unknown sentences.
N.B.--The actual number in each category is in parentheses.

There is, in addition, another substitution, of "other" non-political criminal charges. These yield more erratic sentences—it is a residual category after all—but almost always these are much less than the political articles.[16]

This "criminalization" of dissent represents an attempt to "de-politicize" the social movement. By 1972 the social movement was already crystallizing. The magnitude of individual and mass dissident acts that year and the creation of the *Chronicles* mark this evolution. The movement thus had some initial strength, and the regime worried about further growth. To slow that growth it sought to avoid directly antagonizing undecided citizenry by moving away from harshly punitive, political show-trials.

The necessity to deal with and limit the social movement combined with the need to maintain the power balances within the Brezhnev leadership. The movement could not be ignored, and the KGB had to be respected (but not "unleashed"). Thus, the courts were to be used, sparingly, to undermine but not immediately eradicate the social movement. The results were no appreciate effect on the development of that movement.

Another consequence of the regime trying to deal with this difficult situation was the avoidance of excessive sentencing of priests and other leaders of the social movement, even though that many had been arrested before. The fear that any such treatment would spark even more widespread discontent and crystallize the movement even more was clearly important. Yet by so doing it allowed these people maneuvering room and gave their followers encouragement.

Ironically, the regime's desire to limit dissent meant implicitly recognizing some limits to repression. This recognition in turn allowed dissidents to become a social force promoting legal constraints on the state.

Conclusion

It is difficult to accept Reddaway's characterization of the contemporary period: "both policy toward dissent and the application of this policy have changed remarkably little."[17] Although we found little evidence of the impact of factional politics or the subtle shifts in general policy, we did discover change in the application of that policy in Lithuania at least.

The Brezhnev era was a time when arbitrary repression lessened, despite and indeed in part because of the growth of the social movement. More and more, the leadership had to take into account the dynamics of a movement outside its control. The meaning of this development for subsequent leaders I will examine in the next chapter.

Notes

1. There is a large literature on factionalism among the Soviet elite since the death of Stalin: cf., for example, Robert Conquest, *Power and Policy in the USSR: The Struggle for Stalin's Succession, 1945–1960* (New York: St. Martin's, 1961); and Carl A. Linden, *Khrushchev and the Soviet Leadership, 1957–1964* (Baltimore: Johns Hopkins University Press, 1966), for two of the "classics." More recent work has also included specific studies of the possible linkages of factional conflict to foreign policy: Philip G. Roeder, "Soviet Policies and Kremlin Politics," *International Studies Quarterly* 28 (1984): 171–193; and Harry Gelman, *The Brezhnev Politburo and the Decline of Detente* (Ithaca, New York: Cornell University Press, 1984).

2. George Breslauer, *Khrushchev and Brezhnev as Leaders: Building Authority in Soviet Politics* (London: Allen, Unwin, 1982).

3. Nonetheless, Breslauer maintains that the "conservative reaction" of the Brezhnev years generally entailed a two-fold modification of relation of citizen to state: the conservative introduction of new laws and a new constitution stressing citizen duties and sanctioning actions against dissent, but also the development of specific legal norms to make the state seem less arbitrary and more responsive (pp. 214–215, 263).

4. The yearly number of psychiatric detentions was small and relatively stable (see Table 3, p. 145). Thus, we have excluded them from this analysis.

5. Seweryn Bialer, *Stalin's Successors* (Cambridge: Cambridge University Press, 1980), Chapter 3; J.F. Hough, "The Bureaucratic Model and the Soviet System," *Journal of Comparative Administration*, 5 (1973): 13–67; Alfred Meyer, *The Soviet Political System: An Interpretation* (New York: Random House,

1965), especially pp. 467–476; Daniel Tarschys, "The Soviet Political System: Three Models," *European Journal of Political Research*, 5 (1977): 287–320; John Reshetar, Jr., *The Soviet Polity* (New York: Harper, Row, 1978), pp. 344–346, 349–358.

6. Robert M. Cutler, "Soviet Dissent under Khrushchev," *Comparative Politics*, (October 1980): 30–31. Bohdan R. Bociurkiw, "Political Dissent in the Soviet Union," *Studies in Comparative Communism*, 3(2) (1970): 74–105, and Peter Reddaway, "Soviet Policy Towards Dissent since Khrushchev," Radio Free Europe-Radio Liberty, RL 297/80 (August 21, 1980) each agree.

7. David Kowalewski, "Trends in the Human Rights Movement," in *Soviet Politics in the Brezhnev Era*, ed. Donald R. Kelley (New York: Praeger, 1980), pp. 166–167, on intensification from 1972 to 1975 of numbers of detentions and light judicial sentences; and Ludmilla Alexeyeva, "The Human Rights Movement in the USSR," *Survey*, 23 (4) (Autumn 1977–1978): 82.

8. All three are based on an underlying unity of a Brezhnevite, authoritarian "relegalization" of repression (a "pro-state, anti-deviance orientation" as compared to Khrushchev's "pro-individual, anti-arbitrariness direction"). The net result is the increasing import of law except for political cases, where "political expediency may usurp formal legality." Robert Sharlet, "Dissent and Repression in the Soviet Union and Eastern Europe: Changing Patterns since Khrushchev," *International Journal*, 33 (4) (Autumn 1978): 763–795. The phrase "relegalization" is from his work in *Soviet Law After Stalin*, ed. Donald D. Barry and others (Germantown, Maryland: Sijthoff and Noordhoff, 1978), p. 320ff.

9. Sharlet, "Dissent and Repression in the Soviet Union," *Current History*, October 1977: 776–788, 794. In the next chapter we will discuss 1979 as a critical policy year. (See below, pp. 156.)

10. Sharlet, "Dissent and Repression," 112–13; cf. also Bociurkiw 1970. Bociurkiw, "Political Dissent," and Jacob S. Dreyer, "Soviet Intellectual Dissent, in Julius Jacobson, ed., *Soviet Communism and the Socialist Vision* (New Brunswick, New Jersey: Transaction Press, 1972), p. 10, also agree on 1965–1966 as the critical period. However, Valerii Chalidze, in his *To Defend These Rights: Human Rights and the Soviet Union* (New York: Random House, 1974) sees 1968 as one benchmark and 1972 as another (pp. 54–55). (Rudolf Tokes, "Dissent: The Politics for Change in the USSR," in *Soviet Politics and Society in the 1970s*, ed. Henry W. Morton and Rudolf L. Tokes (New York: Free Press, 1974), p. 11 dates the "'retrenchment and polarization' phase" from 1971. Cf. V. Stanley Vardys, *The Catholic Church, Dissent, and Nationality in Lithuania* (Boulder: East European Quarterly, 1978), p. 127 et passim. Cf. also Thomas Remeikis, *Opposition to Soviet Rule in Lithuania, 1945–1980* (Chicago: Institute of Lithuanian Studies, 1980).

11. Kowalewski's study of collective dissent indicates that fifty-one protest demonstrations occurred in Lithuania in the 1965–1978 period. In general, the number increased steadily each year. Cf. Kowalewski, "Lithuanian Protest for Human Rights in the 1970s: Characteristics and Consequences," *Lituanas* (25)(2)(1979): 43–57; and his "Dissent in the Baltic Republics: Characteristics

and Consequences," *Journal of Baltic Studies*(10)(4)(1979): 309–319. Remeikis shows a linear increase, steady and dramatic growth throughout the 1970s, of samizdat production: from 1 journal to 8, from 4 issues to 31, from 170 pages to 1500. See Remeikis, *Opposition*, Table 4, p. 121.

12. Alexeyeva, p. 82, fn. 2. The decline after 1972 is supposedly because the taboos had been broken and the system simply did not view many activities as seriously as it had before. Of course, she does contradict the description—but not the explanation—in then suggesting an increase in repression in 1977–1978, because of the rise of a new threat, the Helsinki Monitors. Also, her data indicate peaks for psychiatric detention in 1970–1972 and 1974, while in Lithuania the pattern was fairly stable, albeit with arithmetic peaks of 6 and 4 for 1971–1973.

13. Reddaway, "Soviet Policy," p. 15; Kowalewski, "Protest Demonstrations in the Brezhnev Era," paper presented at the Annual Meeting of the American Association for the Advancement of Slavic Studies (Philadelphia, Pennsylvania: 1980), Table 3, p.15. Also, Kowalewski's data do not suggest any peaks during the 1972–73 years, although it is clear in Lithuania. Kowalewski finds that 30.9% of all demonstrations from 1965 to 1977 took place before 1971, whereas barely *one-tenth of one percent* of the mass acts (n=249) occurred during 1969–71 (with very few acts in the overall data-set occurring prior to this).

14. The pattern for trials is similar, but less volatile. The peak years were 1972, 1977, and 1980. However, after the first peak a plateau continued for another two years.

15. The increasing sophistication of juridicization can be seen in the final stage of targeting discussed in chapter 6, sentencing. (A direct comparison of the filtering processes of the differing periods would have been preferable but the data available are not appropriate. However, we can examine sentencing: the data is sufficient for further analysis because these are high-profile events. However, very small numbers make this section highly exploratory.)

16. The elimination of the anti-religious charges from the arsenal of the state after 1973. These less punitive articles were available to the procurator if he wished to end up with lesser sentences—the clear pattern—yet they were not used. The source of this avoidance seems to be the Lithuanian social movement's strong religious component.

17. Reddaway, p. 21.

8

Dissent and Repression
in the 1980s

In December 1986, a remarkable event occurred. Andrei Sakharov, the dean of Soviet dissidents, and his wife Elena Bonner were allowed to return to Moscow. Sakharov was released from a seven-year long administrative exile to the industrial city of Gorky (a punishment of dubious legality because of the absence of a trial). He was permitted to take up a semblance of normal life again, without any recantation, without a regime triumph over the dissidents who had looked to him for leadership for nearly two decades. Astonishingly, his return from exile was prepared by a phone call from General Secretary Mikhail Gorbachev himself.

This drama was the beginning of a new policy on dissent, the outlines of which are still emerging. The policy marks a break with the past of major proportions. It is important for us to discuss what preceeded this break, given the patterns of repression in Lithuania and other factors, before we try to understand what it means for the future, which we shall do in the last chapter.

We now pick up the thread of the dialectic at the end of the 1970s. We must discuss what happened during the uncertain times of transition from Brezhnev's leadership to the assertion of power by Gorbachev, including the years of age and illness of Mssrs. Andropov and Chernenko. Then, we can consider the full dimensions of the domestic transformation engineered by the currently dominant reforming faction.

The Late Brezhnev Period

In the last chapter, we used the periodization of Sharlet on repressive policy change, in which 1977–1981 was a time of high-visibility repression. Lubarsky goes beyond this, seeing continuity from the early 1970s through the 1980s, "only small oscillations in the fundamentally repressive Soviet policy."[1] However, for most analysts, 1979 was a turning point, rooted in 1) Western reaction to Afghanistan invasion,[2] 2) West European decisions to deploy Pershing and Cruise missles, 3) turmoil in Poland, and 4) the Soviet apparat's fear of unrest during a time of elderly leadership. These factors lowered the international costs of greater action against dissent (by eroding East-West relations) and raised the perceived domestic costs of inaction.

Thus, that year saw a new wave of repression. Alexeyeva compared that wave to earlier ones in the 1960s and 1970s and noted several distinctive features in 1979. The targeting was different, with open groups, leaders, samizdat activists, and women being hit more often. In Lithuania, the first three groups had been of interest to the regime throughout the 1970s; the last was a new priority.

Also, the timing and location of repression changed. Several types of dissidents being hit simultaneously, and repression noticeably radiated outwards from Moscow. On the other hand, in Lithuania earlier, there had been simultaneity and geographic spread beyond the capital.

Finally, there was harsher judicial behavior penalties. Most blatant were longer sentences and the resentencing of political prisoners (mainly starting in 1982).[4] The former ran contrary to the pattern in Lithuania; we cannot speak to the latter, for they are outside the data-set. (Other changes at dissident trials included the frequent denial of the defendant's last word and the increase in trials where no defense attorney was present.)

All in all, this round of repression marked a more intense *policy* of repression, although not one completely divorced from prior practice in Lithuania. This policy included, in addition to the continuity of the above features of the 1979 wave:[5] a broadening of the laws against dissent;[6] increasing repressive attention to religious dissent;[7] the arrests of dissident family members, the ill, and the elderly; criminalization of repression against political and religious dissidents; and the rise of unofficial violence against and murder of dissidents.[8]

This harder policy endured to 1985. It was pursued under the leadership of 3 General Secretaries, all old, ill, and concerned with heirs apparents and rivals. Thus, through the 10 November 1982 death of Leonid Brezhnev and the 9 February 1984 death of Yuri Andropov, up to the 10 March 1985 death of Konstantin Chernenko, the broader, deeper repression of dissidents continued.

For Lithuania in the late Brezhnev period, the new policy in all of its ramifications meant the continuation of the dialectical cycle of dissent-repression-dissent, especially for the religious. The interaction of regime and dissident activity has been shown to be strong from

1979-early 1981 in the Table in the last chapter. From mid–1981 to the end of 1982, there was no change in this. In 1981 religious festivals and processions were major dissident activities,[9] provoking several severe counteractions by the regime. These included widespread interrogations that summer; the August arrest and beating of a priest (Fr. Cerniauskas), detained for several days for his sermons and organizing a religious retreat for youth,[10] the blocking of the Siluva processions by police in August and September; and the arrests and beatings of procession marchers in September and October.

Organizing efforts were also punished through the arrest in March and trial in June of processional leaders (and Helsinki Monitors) Vytautas Vaicunas and Mecislovas Juravicius on 190.1 charges. They were sentenced by the Lithuanian Supreme Court to 3 and 2.5 years, respectively.

The CCDRB denounced this trial and pressed demands for unrestricted religious processions; and a mass petition for religious freedom was signed in February 1982. These protests were in turn followed by a successful procession of 50,000 believers in Siluva in August 1982. The regime responded with the October arrest of former prisoner Jadvyga Bieliauskiene for organizing religious study groups and collecting petition signatures, the concomitant arrests and interrogations of secondary school student Daiva Naikelyte and her mother, and the interrogation of several students about Bieliauskiene.

Older religious issues remained salient. Petitions specified the restoration of the Klaipeda cathedral (in December 1981), KGB interference in the seminary (in May 1981), destruction of religious-nationalist shrines (in April and June 1982), greater restrictions on religious activity, pressure on religious instructors of the young, and the heightening press campaign against religion (July-August 1982).

More ominously, there was considerable and increasing unofficial violence against the Church. The killing of three priests in a little over a year (October 1980-November 1981)[11] was a dramatic development causing great concern among the dissidents, demonstrated in part through mass funeral services for priests, such as the ones for Fr. Adomas Milerius (in October 1981 with 10,000 mourners and 100 priests) and Fr. Bronius Laurinavicius (in November). Also, thefts from churches and interference with religious services led to considerable protest through samizdat and petitions.

Beyond the religious agitation, nationalist activity continued. Despite the harsh sentence of human rights/nationalist dissident Algimantas Andreika in early 1982 on article 70 charges (4 years in camp plus 5 in exile), nationalism erupted again in May and September 1982. Those incidents involved pamphlet distribution (by burst balloon), graffiti on the outer wall of a castle, and another soccer riot-turned-march in Vilnius. As in prior riots, the last led to arrests of only a handful of the thousands who participated.

Attempts to leave were also clear. In September 1981, Pentecostalist Eduardas Bulachas received a year term for his emigration demands. In May 1982, Marija Jurgutis participated in a hunger strike (in Moscow with several others) to gain support for family reunification. At about the same time, Jonas Pakuckas and several of his family were tried for a plot to escape via Sweden, with Pakuckas gaining a harsh 12 year sentence.

Finally, there were some activities on the human rights front, even after the functional end of the Lithuanian Helsinki Group (the trial of Vaicunas and Juravicius mentioned above). Several youths engaged in writing campaigns to political prisoners in 1982, trying to keep the latters' spirits up. These youths were subjected to interrogations in the second half of the year, but nothing worse.[12]

The Andropov Period

When Leonid Brezhnev died in November 1982, the ex-KGB chief and party bureaucrat Yuri Andropov became General Secretary. This seriously ill leader did try to shake up the old system with his anti-corruption campaign, purging of some Brezhnevites, and pro-discipline campaign in the workplace. However, in terms of dissent, this succession "resulted in, if anything, a worsening of Soviet human rights practices." [13]

This deterioration was evident in a tightening spiral of repression and religious dissent,[14] which accelerated after the shift of Andropov's KGB successor (Fedorchuk) to MVD, and his replacement by Chebrikov. In November, Jonas Sadunas, the brother of a woman who had been convicted in an earlier *Chronicles* case, was subjected to interrogation, arrest, and psychiatric detention for 2 weeks while 468 of 701 priests protested in petitions against new regulations on religion. In December there were interrogations of Dalia Tamtutyte about her activities on petitions and the *Chronicles*, and of Fr. Benedikas Urbonas on his petition against a fine for teaching children and on his alleged foreign ties.

A milestone occurred in January 1983—the first major arrest of a priest since the early 1970s. Fifty-five-year-old Fr. Alfonsas Svarinskas, a CCDRB founder and former prisoner, was charged initially on an automobile incident, although TASS later denounced his anti-Soviet sermons, meetings with his parishioners, and sending "false" materials on religious abuse abroad.

This arrest marked a major change of policy in Lithuania. It was a direct challenge to the Catholic dissidents, given the explosion of dissent that had accompanied the 1970–1971 arrests and trials of Frs. Seskevicius, Bubnys, and Zdebskis for religious catechism of children. The Svarinskas arrest was part of KGB pressure that included interrogations that month of other CCDRB members, of priests who had praised him in sermons, and of *Chronicles*-connected Sadunas.

As in the decade earlier, the immediate response of dissidents included petitions to Andropov in February and March. As before, these were to no avail. In May, Fr. Svarinskas was convicted under article 70 for compiling the *Chronicles* and for giving anti-Soviet sermons. He was given a particularly drastic 7 years in camp and 3 in exile. As before, dissent grew rapidly.

There was a demonstration outside Svarinskas' courthouse, during which his housekeeper Monika Gavenaite was arrested (later sentenced to 10 days for hooliganism for trying to get in to the trial). Starting that month, petitions were collected in numbers rivalling those of the peak years in the late 1970s. Priests drew up their own: 2/3 of them signed. Signatures on some mass petitions numbered more than 50,000 by September; on one to Andropov, 123,000 by early 1984. This petition movement was supplemented by new processions, such as one in January 1984 to the town where Fr. Svarinskas had worked prior to his arrest (an entire busload of passengers were arrested then, because it was evidently suspected that the first anniversary of his arrest was to become a new dissident date of mourning).

This activism was all the more dramatic given the regime's desire to intimidate. There were arrests and interrogations of those collecting signatures, in May, July, and August.[15] These were supplemented by other high visibility trials (of Beliauskiene the same month as Svarinskas, on article 70 for petitions and educating children; of Sadunas for personal libel in reporting on repression, also that month; and in November of Fr. Sigitas Tamkevicius, a co-founder of CCDRB, who had been arrested at Svarinskas' trial), and systematic interrogations. These interrogations focussed two groups, other members of the CCDRB (Fr. Algimantas Keina in May, June, and August, after which he left the committee; Fr. Leonas Kalinauskas in June and December; Fr. Kazimieras Zilys in June, when he too resigned; and Fr. Vincas Velavicius and Fr. Vaclovas Stakenas in July), and personal supporters of Fr. Tamkevicius (his brothers, other priests, and children who knew him in May and in September).[16]

This wave of interrogations and arrests was amplified by those of other Catholic dissidents on other actions. In July there were searches of Sadunas' residence that uncovered samizdat, including the *Chronicles*, and led to interrogations of him and his wife on that literature and on the whereabouts of his sister (who had hid from the authorities for years). In September the search and confiscation of religious items led to the arrest of Petras Cidzikas. In November the search and confiscation of *Lithuania's Future* and various notebooks yielded interrogations of Aldona Raizyte, ex-prisoners Jadvyga-Gemma Stanelyte and Vytautas Vaiciunas, and four others. In January 1984 religious meetings in apartments were broken up by arrests and interrogations of young Catholics. In one case, ex-prisoner Genovaite Navickaite (in whose apartment some meetings had taken place) was also tried for "resisting police," and sentenced to 10 days.

At the same time, there was a marked press campaign against cleric dissidents. The Lithuanian party daily *Tiesa* published a vitriolic article on Svarinskas' trial within a few days and a similar one after Tamkevicius' trial, in which the *Chronicles* were mentioned for the first time in the official press. The Chief Justice of the Lithuanian Supreme Court even went onto television to warn that signature on a dissident petition was a crime leading to imprisonment.[17]

This media attack paralleled media and legal attacks on dissent generally. At the June 1983 Plenum of the Central Committee, General Secretary Chernenko warned of the dangers of foreign ideas and of the need to eradicate them. In December the extension of prisoners' sentences was legalized (in article 188.3), and in January 1984, a tightening of law on state crimes was put into effect. Treason was broadened to include use of money and parcels, giving economic secrets to foreigners was codified in the new article 13–1, anti-Soviet agitation and propaganda was expanded to include any form; labor camp discipline was made harsher, and in article 83, border crossing maximum was raised.[18]

In this climate in early 1984 an underground section of CCDRB began to operate. That group continued the Committee's functions without risking its public members, then under severe pressures as we have seen. This transformation was all the more necessary because of the death in December 1983 of Ona Lukauskaite-Poskiene, the last Lithuanian Helsinki Group member at liberty.[19]

The Chernenko Period

Yuri Andropov died in February 1984. One-time border guard and party bureaucrat, Konstantin Chernenko became General Secretary and initiated an attempted return to Brezhnevite stability. After a period of transition, the "new" leadership seemed willing to return to the standoff of the 1970s in Lithuania.

Although in February 1984, Vladas Lapienis, an elderly religious dissident who had served time in 1976 for the *Chronicles*, was again arrested (along with a church organist and a teacher) and the pressure on the CCDRB proceeded with the interrogation and warning of Fr. Velavicius, in March there was no juridical repression of religious dissent. Thus, in the spring of 1984, the regime and the Catholic dissidents called a respite in their conflict.

From March to October, other groups were the focus of investigatory efforts. First, human rights dissidents unaffiliated with any human rights organization were attacked. In July the search and confiscation of Ludas Dambrauskas' prison memoirs led to his to interrogation and arrest, and his subsequent trial on article 70 in October, when he was sentenced to 3.5 years in camp and 2 in exile. Also, in June, there were interrogations of 5 dissidents who were collecting signatures for a letter on political prisoners. In July, one of those interrogated in June was again brought in after a search led to confiscation of letters from her husband in camp, letters which had appeared in Western outlets; also, the wife and son of prisoner Gintautas Iesmantas were interrogated about activities on his behalf.

Second, there was some repression of a small number of Lithuanian Pentecostalists trying to leave the USSR. This had begun sporadically under Andropov (in the spring of 1983 several Pentecostalists were interrogated after a few had fled to Turkey, and in August, 4 Pentecostalists were "warned" by the KGB about this case). It continued in March-April 1984, when searches led to interrogations and one arrest.

Finally, German refusniks in Lithuania were active. In April 1984, several were arrested trying to get into the West German embassy in Moscow. In July two were again arrested (Woldemar Volker and Hugo Krieger); both were tried in September for passport violations and given 2 years and 1 year in camp, respectively.

This new agitation on visa matters, along with the possible connections of Edita Abrutiene with Western human rights groups made greater restriction on foreign contacts seem quite sensible. The May 1984 Decree set limits on interaction with foreigners, making it difficult for dissidents to maintain ties with them.

In November 1984, the repression of Catholic dissent was reinvigorated with the Vilnius arrest of a fourth priest, Fr. Jonas-Kastytis Matulionis, another former prisoner from the 1976 *Chronicles* case. A priest of the underground seminary, he was taken into custody after giving last rites, and accused of organizing an All-Saints' Day procession. His sacristan, a student named Romas Zemaitis, was also arrested for the same action.

They both were convicted in January, Fr. Matulionis receiving 3 years in camp for public disorder and resisting police, and Zemaitis, 2 years for resisting police. Contemporaneous to that trial, Lapienis was again arrested (for his camp memoirs and religious essays), as were 2 other Catholics (Murauskas and Jonulis) for running an underground religious printing press.

To make things more difficult for dissidents like Fr. Matulionis, Lapienis, and others who had prison records and therefore difficulties finding employment, the regime adopted a Decree on Parasitism in December 1984. It made unsuccessful job hunting even more unpleasant.

Yet in February 1985, there were two events of note: a new underground Lithuanian group (the Lithuanian Youth Association) was formed, and Secretary Gorbachev publicly and vigorously thanked the voters for their feedback.[20] The first demonstrated the durability of Lithuanian dissent, especially in hybrid forms. The second hinted at a potential populist-reformist shift in political orientation among the top leaders, an especially significant development in light of the impending death of Chernenko in March.[21] Why should there have been any shift?

The Repressive Policy of 1979–1985

The successes of the intensification of repression were many, as Alexeyeva has noted.[22] The numerous Helsinki Monitor Groups were eliminated through incarceration, exile, and emigration. The Pentecostalist emigration movement seemed broken, as well as the Crimean Tatar and Meskhi homeland movements. The unregistered Evangelical Baptists were decreasing in number.[23] Most overt dissident organizations were eradicated. Generally, information on repression was thereby reduced to a trickle to the West.

On the other hand, this policy had numerous failures. To begin with, Lithuania remained a center of activity, still producing new organizations, samizdat, and leaders, as we have seen above. In other republics, the situation was also not completely to the regime's liking: in Georgia, there was a resurgence of dissent after 1980 with leafletting, demonstrations, hunger strikes, receiving repression, but with many concessions and releases; Estonian dissent intensified after 1978 in the rapid rise in samizdat activity, beginning of high-school dissent with flags, mass demonstrations, the creation of an armed group in 1979, and the increased participation of intellectuals; in Latvia, dissent reemerged in the 1980s with slogans, flags, appeals, groups, samizdat, and leaflets against Afghanistan; in the Ukraine, dissent went underground. Various other dissident groups continued despite repression, including Armenian nationalists, Soviet German and Jewish refusniks, Russian Orthodox dissidents, young musicians, hippies, and Hare Krishna followers. In some ways most ideologically difficult, Marxist and socialist dissent reappeared in late 1970s.[24] Clearly, it was time for a change; the tougher policy had not yielded permanent results.

The Gorbachev Period

On 10 March 1985 Secretary Mikhail Gorbachev became General Secretary. A party technocrat with law degree, he renewed the Andropov campaigns against corruption and lack of work discipline that had slowed during Chernenko's interregnum, and intensified the anti-alcoholism drive. Fundamentally a reformer, he had pressed these themes in late 1960s, and in 1978 he gave public support to agrarian experimentation. Yet the West was unprepared for the extent of his reformist policies as General Secretary, in part because of the rapidity of the "generational succession" and his skill in consolidating his position.[25]

The major parts of Gorbachev's reform program are *glasnost, perestroika*, democratization, and legal reform. *Glasnost* means openness, publicity, or exposure. The policy is historically derivative of earlier anti-corruption/pro-discipline campaigns. Public revelation of egregious examples of poor behavior by elites and masses provides both with inspiration to work harder within the established rules. A series of criticisms, discussions, and proposals have appeared in all the media: news articles on social problems (in *Ogonyok, Oktyabr, Literaturnaya Gazeta, Pravda, Moscow News*); public reports of the 1986 Kazakh riots and disasters like Chernobyl; anti-Stalinist novels, including *Dr. Zhivago* (scheduled for 1988)[26], plays including one partially rehabilitating Trotsky and Bukharin, films released after being "on the shelf" for years; television shows, concerts, and records of unofficial jazz and rock musicians, and a call for more open social science data in *Pravda*.[27]

The result of domestic mistrust (leading to increasing popular use of Western radio and rumors) and a foreign image of "defensive totalitarian regime" undercutting its peace offensive in Western Europe, glasnost seems to be aimed at developing support among the intelligentsia for further reforms, and improving the regime's image abroad.[28] Given the dissident goal of greater information about repression and social problems, glasnost has the potential of coopting dissent, yet its limits have included the denial of the existence of political prisoners, a refusal to mention the names of political prisoners, and the non-appearance of any direct criticism of Gorbachev or the party,[29] thus preventing any major reincorporation of the dissatisfied through openness.

Glasnost leads logically and in practice did lead to economic, then political reforms, including legal reform.[30] *Perestroika* means restructuring, and implies economic reorganization to increase the authority and responsibility of lower-level units. Primarily, it entails the de-emphasis of central direction, the decline of Gosplan, the use of market mechanisms in supply and pricing decisions, and the acceptance of private initiatives in the service sector. Its aim is the revitalization of the economy, due to a general slowdown and slippage in technological race with the West.[31]

To the degree that republic and provincial governments gain influence over economic activity, and that consumers can apply pressure, this reform could lead to a vitiation of dissent on ecological, historical preservation, and even cultural/linguistic grounds. Also, openness to joint economic ventures could have positive human rights consequences. J. Hough has even suggested that decentralization may allow ethnic and religious groups to produce their own foods and artifacts in international religious ventures.[32] However, so little economic reorganization has as yet occurred, that its future impact remains unclear.

Third, democratization is meant to shake up the party bureaucracy without the party losing legitimacy or overall dominance. This complements the first two parts of the reform program and is essential to their full realization. Thus, there have been multiple-candidate experiments, proposals for secret ballots by committees and a return to the Khrushchevite innovation of regulated "rotation" of elites, a new affirmation of the right to criticism, a planned party conference in 1988 on reform. If effective, democratization might undermine dissent on the arbitrariness of government and party, by eliminating it. Of course, its limits are maintenance of the party's institutional monopoly and eventual stability in the Politburo once Gorbachev's reinvigoration is complete. Here, too, so little has been done, it is difficult to assess potential impact.

Most pertinent for us, the Gorbachev program has eventually included a 4th component, legal reform. This reform addresses many of the abuses in the judicial process examined in chapter 3, the basis of considerable human rights and other dissent.

First, a move to increased legality is apparent in the actions taken against some of those who blatantly abused the investigative, arrest, and medical powers of the coercive apparatus. The trial of policemen and prosecutors in Latvia in January 1986 for coercing a confession was followed by a series of firings: MVD and procuratorial investigators in Latvia in July 1986 for violation of a drunken suspect's rights; of judges and procurators (and the arrest of an investigator) in Uzbekistan that same month for false arrest, incorrect indictment, and unjustified conviction of an engineer; procurators, judges, and the Republic Minister of Justice in Belorussia in October 1986 for improper prosecutions; and prosecutors and the provincial KGB chief in the Ukraine in November 1986 for harassing a reporter; and others. In addition, several officials involved in psychiatric abuse were removed.[33]

Second, since late 1986 there have surfaced proposals to change the judicial process itself. The defense attorney's role may be expanded and strengthened, the number of lay assessors may be increased, the judicial abuse of defendants' rights has been denounced, and citizen access to the courts on problems of the illegal actions of government officials has been affirmed.[34]

Lastly, there are proposals to change laws of concern to dissidents. Emigration, for example, has been more institutionalized, but with some greater limits; and crimes against the state are currently under review for possible revision.[35]

This legal part of the Gorbachev program is intimately tied to a new policy on human rights and dissent, what has been called a "human rights offensive."[36] This campaign has been extensive. Beyond the new and proposed legislation, and the major components mentioned above, it includes the releases of prisoners, mostly high-profile dissidents during the amnesty of early 1987; and a restraint on repression, especially of Jewish refusniks, none of whom had been arrested since June 1986. [37]

However, this campaign is less than it appears. C. Fitzpatrick of the US Helsinki Watch Group has characterized it as "commercial operations in international markets" because its limits seem determined by international supply and demand.[38] Although high-profile dissidents were released, many were not. Two dozen Helsinki monitors were too "expensive" for the "market." Several groups were untouched. Baptists who were without major international support were excluded, as were other Christians and Moslems, who were technically omitted by the amnesty's limitation to articles 70 and 190.1 prisoners. Yet such prisoners who were nationalists and those in psychiatric detention were not sufficiently valuable "currency" to be put forward.[39] Of course, no *new* groups were allowed to join Jews and Germans to gain visas, even with restrictions.[40]

In addition, the juridical and administrative status of the released remains unclear and variable. All returning Muscovites have received residence permits, while several Leningraders have not. Many but not all had to ask for a pardon or sign statements admitting degrees of guilt or promising no future criminal activity. Some were released only after hunger strikes or demonstrations by their families.

These differences in coverage of different groups and in implementation ought not to be surprising. Earlier chapters have shown such differential policy in Lithuanian repression in arrest, trial, psychiatric detention, and sentencing. It is entirely plausible that any formal program of release should reveal such features.

To some degree, these objections about the limits of amnesty may soon be moot. Another dramatic amnesty was announced in June 1987. It should cover 3/4 of known political and religious prisoners (excluding those in psychiatric detention). The major categories included are veterans, medal-winners, pregnant women, women with underage children, men and women over retirement age (60 and 55, respectively), the disabled, women beyond the first third of a sentence of up to 5 years, and men serving up to 3 years. The major exclusions are those sentenced under articles 64, 70, 80, 83, and those convicted of "malicious violation of [camp] regime." Those not eligible for immediate release will have their remaining time reduced by one half to one third after serving the first one third, unless convicted of the above "malicious violation of regime."[41]

Also, there has been movement on the psychiatric front. About 20 political "patients" have been released (with approximately 100 others yet unaffected); glasnost has reached psychiatric abuse in the form of major newspaper and journal articles in *Izvestia*, *Sotsialisticheskaya Industriya*, and *Meditsinskaya Gazeta*; and the medical establishment has been reconsidering the international isolation of its psychiatric practitioners, with some indication that an American monitoring visit is not out of the question as a preliminary for re-admission to the World Psychiatric Association.[42]

Lithuania under Gorbachev

What has this time of reform meant for Lithuanian dissidents? For the first 21 months the struggle of regime and dissidents slowly wound down.

Interrogations of Catholic activists kept the pressure up from March 1985 through December 1986. They focussed on samizdat, with 2 priests, a soldier, and more than 20 others asked about the *Chronicles* and other, religious samizdat. A variety of other activities continued to interest the authorities: the catechism of children, religious processions, contact with imprisoned priests (even carrying photographs of them), collecting signatures on petitions. These subjects are a reflection both of the crucial role of samizdat in the dissident communications network, and of the diversity of resistant behavior that persisted. (More on this behavior in a moment.)

Despite this flow of interrogations, there were only two trials of Catholics. In March 1985, Lapienis was tried in Kaunas on article 70 for writing his memoirs and a collection of religious essays, and given 4 years in camp and 2 in exile. In January 1986, there was the Lithuanian Supreme Court trial of 5 activists for using an illegal printing press for the manufacture and sale of religious postcards, calendars, and prayerbooks over the course of 7 years. They were charged with article 162, "prohibited trade," and assigned sentences of from 3 years in camp down to 1 year, suspended. The trial was clearly meant to intimidate priests, 60 of whom were called as witnesses (only 2 actually showed up). The journal *Sovietskaya Kultura* had denounced the defendants as profiteers, alcoholics, a parasite, and an embezzler, thus making the priests appear to be allied with common criminals.[43]

There were arrests, but no major wave. With the exception of Fr. Matulionis (re-arrested after his evidently mistaken release in June 1985), the handful arrested were soon released after interrogation on religious samizdat, photographing KGB men at a religious ceremony; collecting Klaipeda Cathedral petition signatures.

Through these months, violence against church property and cemeteries were ongoing, spilling over once again in the August 1985 kidnapping and assault on Fr. Stakenas. This parallel to the attack on Fr. Jerzy Popieluszko in Poland did not end tragically, but no police action was undertaken either.

Yet, Catholic dissent maintained itself. The petition movement was strong. Nearly 50,000 signed one on Fr. Matulionis' imprisonment in March 1985, when there were also clerical and parish petitions on a number of matters, activities continuing into July and then renewing itself in March-June 1986. Religious festivals drew large crowds in May, July, August, September 1985, and June 1986, without approval, but generally without official reaction, too. Catechization of the young moved apace, triggering harassment and further dissent.

Nationalist dissent appeared episodically also, but was consistently repressed. In February 1986, there were more traditional flags and nationalist leaflets distributed on Independence Day, about which Arunas Rekasius was questioned. In May, searches in Kaunas brought the interrogation of the editors of *Ausra*, Algirdas Patackas and Petras Kimbrys, and 10 others in Kaunas and Vilnius; in June, 20 more were questioned in several towns (and in August, yet another 12). Then in July, Patackas was arrested for his samizdat editing and for writing a nationalist book.[44]

The more exotic religious strain of dissent, Krishna followers, was increasingly severely dealt with, on the other hand. In August 1986, searches in Kaunas produced religious tracts of the sect, and Dainis Vaicunas was interrogated. Saulius Dagys was arrested and put into psychiatric detention, as he had been the prior September and would be again that coming October. One other Lithuanian Krishna-ist was hospitalized in September (Vidas Vosilius).

There were two small positive signs in 1986: the November release of Bielauskas and Jaskunas (9 months after the first early release of a dissident, and the 9th of the year),[45] and the December release of Antanas Terleckas and Lapienis (the latter without his appeal, although his wife had asked for his pardon). The scarcity of such gestures seems incongruent to the changes occurring on the all-union level—the unfolding of glasnost beginning with the Central Committee commitment at Gorbachev's ascension, the optimism of the November 1985 Summit, the prisoner swaps leading up to it, the 27th Party Congress in February 1986, Yevgeny Yevtushenko's April 1986 criticism of dogmatism and persecution, the June 1986 Writers' Congress calling for further reform. Of course, we have seen in the last chapter that earlier all-union policy changes were not automatically related to Lithuanian events.

The year 1987 marked a major break in repressive policy—releases, non-arrests for most groups,[46] absence of criminal prosecutions, discussions of illegality and reform. In January, as Gorbachev called on the Central Committee to legalize glasnost, a new Decree on Emigration was issued, Sakharov was easily interviewed by Western press, a review of prisoners for "anti-Soviet activities" was announced, and a KGB official was fired for harrassing a reporter, the previously targeted Krishna-ists peacefully attempted to register their religious community in Vilnius, although unsuccessfully. In April, they were allowed a press conference in Moscow; also, one of their number (Dagys) was among the few psychiatric detainees to be released.

That Krishna-ist's release was part of the larger move to neutralize international attention and mobilize domestic support of intellectuals through systematic amnesty. It brought some limited relief to other Lithuanian dissidents. Several were released early: Dambrauskas and Vytautas Skuodis (after he wrote his own release statement) in February; Gedimintas Jakubcionis and Patackas (both from pre-trial detention with their cases dropped), and Algirdas Statkevicius (from a psychiatric hospital) in March; Andreika in April; Abrutiene in May. However, two very important prisoners, Frs. Svarinskas and Tamkevicius, were not, evidently because they refused to sign statements upon their temporary transfer to Lithuanian prisons prior to possible release. Ironically, here we may have an inverse to the priestly immunity of the 1970s, a priestly handicap in the releases.[47]

There have been no new trials or prosecutorial proceedings initiated since the amnesty began. In two special cases, there were arrests. On 2 April 1987 after a search and the confiscation of *Chronicle* number 73 (which was in the process of being printed), Nijole Sadunaite was arrested, but soon released. (She had been hiding from authorities for 5 years since her release from camp and was then threatened with charges of non-compliance with admininstrative surveillance.) Then on 10 July, 3 Lithuanian Krishna-ists were arrested after publicly distributing religious literature in a Moscow park, and released later that evening. To be noted, there were also only two interrogations, of Gintautas Sakevicius in February and of Birute Briliute in April, both about the *Chronicles*.

Thus, after the winding down of repression in 1985 and 1986, the regime has almost completely withdrawn from juridical repression in Lithuania. There have been few arrests and no trials.[48] The Gorbachev reforms have meant an amelioration of conditions for dissent.

Nonetheless, the regime concentrated on what had been a secondary line of attack, social pressure against dissidents through negative publicity. On 16 May, a Lithuanian newspaper ran a recantation by Kostas Meidunas, a samizdat editor of *Vytis* since 1982. On the following day, there appeared a *Moscow News* attack on dissident Balys Gajauskas (and one other); and on 28 May, *Tiesa* published a letter from recently-released Jaskunas denouncing fellow inmates and Western human rights organizations that had spoken out on his behalf.[49] These followed several April attacks on other dissidents in the Russian Republic. The sharp edge of glasnost was to be directed against dissidents, not the sledge hammers of the people's court and psychiatric centers.

This implies no end to the struggle of the Lithuanian dissidents. Their activity does seem to have been reduced markedly in 1987, possibly the result of a "wait-and-see" attitude. The only report of Catholic dissent is of a widespread, week-long series of prayer protests (in May) for the imprisoned priests.

What is clear is the low level of confrontation since the January 1987 breakthrough in regime policy. Both sides have stepped back. Both sides still try to discredit the other through their own channels, but neither seems willing to return to yesterday. Even the situation of the early months of Gorbachev now seems undesirable.

Reform, Opposition, and Commitment

In the 5 years since Brezhnev's death, a sea change has occurred in Soviet politics. The older, post-Stalinist generation that came to power with Khrushchev is now gone.[50] In its place are men and women who experienced de-Stalinization as young adults and the swing back to stolidity under Brezhnev at the start of their careers. They now have their chance and under Gorbachev's leadership are moving to major transformations in process and policy.

For the dissidents, the meaning of this shift has become more and more positive. Although religious prisoners have not done well, the coercive institutions have taken a "soft" line on them and others in the last 6 months. The "openness" of Sakharov's apartment in Moscow is indicative of a new "hands-off" policy (of course, his support for the reforms and official arms control proposals does give the regime more reason for tolerance). A line does exist, across which dissidents wander at their own risk. The June trial of Kazakh rioters did feature several harsh sentences, including one death penalty. Yet the Politburo and the KGB must realize the potential feedback effects of the release of political prisoners, namely, the raising of the taboo that had linked national security and uniformity of political opinion.[51]

One might ask why the breakthrough occurred in 1987, rather than earlier in Gorbachev's stewardship. It is clearly premature to offer definitive explanations, but one may now posit several plausible reasons.

On the narrow issue of the amnesties, the cost/benefit equation does seem to have been changing in 1985–1986. The Soviets had used "swaps" and releases successfully to its considerable international advantage, even spurring the US to summit meetings. Moreover, the deaths of many well-known dissidents in camps in this period were a growing burden to that same diplomacy. Especially problematic was the death of Marchenko following a hunger strike in late 1986.

On a more general level, one can note that it has taken time for the older, conservative factions in the party to be dislodged from the top. Perhaps, the question might be rephrased to how did the reformers move so *fast*, given the endurance of some of the non-reforming elements in power.

Indeed, Gorbachev and his colleagues did press on reform from the start, even in the waning days of Chernenko's General Secretaryship. His commitment has been strong from his first moments and has become more so. In his 19 June 1986 speech, Gorbachev called for the "clashing of opinions" and underlined his position: "if not now, when? if not us, who?" At the 27 January 1987 Central Committee

Plenum, he talked of the need to "make fundamental change of direction" and of the absence of any "place to retreat."[52]

It seems likely from their early speeches and proposals that the reformers learned that isolated, piecemeal change would not work. In the course of 2 years, they came to realize that dramatic, simultaneous recasting of several sectors of Soviet society was called for.

The process of liberalization is not merely composed of one decision, promulgated and then implemented.[53] It is a series of decisions, ever-widening as the momentum of change builds and the inertia of bureaucratic unresponsiveness obstructs. This interplay expanded the need for reform and led the Central Committee into the unchartered waters of a limited bottom-up liberalization to supplement their fundamentally top-down program, to prod bureaucratically sluggish officials at middle and lower levels.[54]

Apparat rebellion against reform is increasingly evident. Already at 27th Party Congress in March 1986, while Gorbachev promoted the glasnost policy, his colleague on the Politburo Ligachev distanced himself from it.[55] That October the Central Committee began directly to attack the "resistance from those who, out of selfish interests, are trying to preserve outmoded procedures and privileges." It even went so far as to state that those who resist central reformist directives "will be held personally accountable to the Party."[56]

This is not to say that internal opponents to reform were thereby intimidated into acquiescence. Half a year later, with obvious high-level support, conservative writers countered by associating "time-servers, speculators, mediocrities, and some very shady people" with restructuring (although only "sometimes" this was supposed to be the case). One arts bureaucrat went so far as to charge that "certain active groups of artists and art critics . . . are [intent on] . . . channeling restructuring in the field of fine arts into the discrediting and overthrow of realism." This, he claimed, was part of a larger "offensive of alien ideas" against Soviet culture.[57]

The reformers, in turn, have upped the pressure on the recalcitrants. In April, Gorbachev denied the existence of "political opponents" (denying them any legitimacy and affirming his commitment to reform by foregoing Stalinist anti-factional purging). He did warn of those from the Central Committee downwards who "accustomed to the old way of life . . . do not want to revise it or are changing it very slowly." In May, his group invoked attempts in the 1950s and 1960s to condemn Stalin and "administrative-voluntarist methods." Linking their current opponents to those who defeated the earlier attempts, the reformers imply the immediate responsibility for the contemporary stagnation and decay lies with the bureaucratic "old thinkers," and hint at the possible dire consequences of any lasting defeat of reform this time.[58]

Although there are few signs of such resistance on issues of repression,[59] the dissidents are aware of it and are concerned. For example, participants in the March and April sessions of the "Peace and Social Research" Group noted the problem and Gorbachev's need to use "strong grassroots pressure" to overcome it; the editors of the new journal *Glasnost* warned "these forces should not by underestimated."[60] Should the conservatives defeat the reforms, there is every possibility of a return to pre-Gorbachev levels of repression, perhaps even worse. We must now ask, what is the future of the Soviet system?

Notes

1. Cronid Lubarsky, "Changes in the Categories of Soviet Political Prisoners," *Fifth International Sakharov Hearings: Proceedings, April 1985*, ed. Allan Wynn, Martin Dewhurst, and Harold Stone (London: Andre Deutsch, 1986) p. 37. Although he says that "neither the structure nor the scale of this repression has changed in substance," he does see differences in the "structure" of repression. See below, fn. 7.

2. Cathy Cosman, "The Helsinki Process and Beyond," in Wynn, Dewhurst, and Stone, pp. 156–157. Alexeyeva also notes the coincidence of repression and Afghanistan and the end of detente in 1979. Ludmilla Alexeyeva, *Soviet Dissent: Contemporary Movements for National, Religious, and Human Rights* (Middletown, Connecticut: Wesleyan University Press, 1985), p. 85.

3. Alexeyeva, pp. 368–370. To these one must, of course, add the January 1980 banishment of Sakharov. Cosman, p. 157.

4. U.S. Department of State, *Implementation of the Helsinki Final Act: Thirteenth Semiannual Report*, Special Report No. 105, p.11; Alexeyeva, pp. 368–370.

5. Cosman, pp. 156–157; Marita Sapiets, "The Baltic States," in Wynn, Dewhurst, and Stone, p. 101; US Department of State, p. 11. Cosman also pinpointed some of the Alexeyeva analysis of the 1979 wave, and the increasing intensity of arrests. Peter Reddaway gives different view on arrests, however. Big increases began during 1979, from 94 in 1978 to 145 in 1979 to 257 in 1980 as per Edward Kline, "The Helsinki Process: A Balance Sheet," in Wynn, Dewhurst, and Stone, p. 183. Also, according to Lubarsky, during the years 1982–1984, the number of psychiatric detentions went *down* 20% after international attention. This decline was due to the release and non-rearrest of high profile dissidents, not to a decline in the use of this mechanism. Ibid., pp. 37–39.

6. These changes included the September 1981 law establishing criminal liability among service workers, the October 1982 act making the law on parasitism harsher and more broad, the December 1983 law on crimes in the military, and the January 1984 laws creating a new article (13–1) for

economic secrets to transmitted to foreigners, extending article 70, and tightening camp discipline. See Dina Kaminskaya, "Changes in Soviet Criminal Legislation since the Helsinki Final Act," in Wynn, Dewhurst, and Stone, pp. 19–20.

7. Lubarsky points out the shift to religious prisoners, especially Baptists, Pentecostalists, 7th Day Adventists, and to human rights activists. The nationalists slipped from first to second place. In addition there were more Moslems, Russian Orthodox believers, and Georgians, and fewer Ukrainians and Estonians. Lubarsky, pp. 37–39. According to Bourdeaux, the new campaign against religion begun in 1979 led to the creation of underground groups for all major religions, and was continued by Andropov and Chernenko, by camp discipline legislation (making it difficult for believers to function therein with artifacts and rituals) and by public ideological attacks (for the first time in years by a top leader). Michael Bourdeaux, "The Church in the USSR— Prospects under the New Leadership," in Wynn, Dewhurst, and Stone, pp. 59–60.

8. Fr. Antanas Bitvinskas was assaulted in September 1980; also see fn. 11. Other features of the policy were severe reduction of emigration; the resumption of the jamming of Western radio broadcasts; and the deterioration of camp conditions, leading to more camp deaths (9 in 1985 a post-Stalinist high). Irwin Cotter (chairman of the Canadian Helsinki Watch Group), "The Soviet Human Rights Offensive," "Human Rights" Conference.

9. The following overview of Lithuanian events is taken from *USSR News Briefs*, ELTA, LIC news releases, and *CCCL*, except where otherwise noted.

10. Oddly enough, this month saw the early release of religious dissident Jadvyga-Gemma Stanelyte, after only half of her term.

11. Fr. Leonas Sapoka was killed in October 1980; his three killers were sentenced to death, 15 years, and 15 years at the August 1981 trial that was discussed in the party daily *Tiesa*. Fr. Leonas Mazeika was killed the month of that trial, but there was no mention in *Tiesa* on the January 1982 trial of his murderers, who were sentenced to death and 4 years, respectively. Fr. Laurinavicius killed in November 1981, just 3 days after a *Tiesa* attack on him.

12. Dissent temporarily took on a stronger internationalist flavor. In September over 3 dozen Lithuanian dissidents sent a message of support to Poland's Solidarity through the nationalist *Ausra*. In October, a major proposal for a nuclear-free Baltic area was presented by 38 Baltic dissidents.

13. US Department of State, *Implementation of the Helsinki Final Act: Thirteenth Semiannual Report*, Special Report No. 109, p. 9.

14. The only Lithuanian nationalist event under Andropov was minor. At the end of 1983 a Lithuanian soldier (Musikevicius) was convicted for anti-Soviet statements (conversations on political topics with other Baltic soldiers), article 64. The only purely human rights events related to Abrutiene, the wife of a prisoner concerned with her husband's repression and with the possibility of a visa. In December 1982 a search and confiscations of her statements and other human rights documents led to her arrest on article

190.1; in July 1983 she was given 4 years in camp and 2 in exile for article 70.

15. The August arrests were protested the next month in open letters on police treatment by those involved: Sukyte, Zemaityte, Bumbulis, Kazalapskas.

16. In September Fr. Antanas Grazulis was briefly arrested for interrogation purposes.

17. LIC, 27 Feb 84. The Procurator General's response to one delegation bringing a petition was "Fr. Svarinskas is an enemy, and so are you and all believers." Sapiets, p. 102.

18. According to Alexeyeva (p. 81), the Lithuanian Helsinki Group was destroyed for all practical purposes with the arrests in March 1981 and the killing of Fr. Laurinavicius.

19. US Department of State, *Implementation* . . . , No. 109, p. 9; *USSR News Briefs*, 1984, 3–4.

20. After praising the "vital creativity of the people," at the meeting of voters of the Kiev district of Moscow, he then said, "I am deeply grateful for the trust, the warm reception and the businesslike words of advice that have been heard in this hall today." "On a Course of Unity and Solidarity," *Pravda* and *Izvestia*, 21 February 1985, p. 2. Cf. Grigory Romanov's more traditional speech in Leningrad, "Fully Armed with Experience, Move on to New Successes," *Pravda* and *Izvestia*, 15 February 1985, p. 2 (and the fuller version in *Leningradskaya Pravda*, same date). (For these and subsequent Soviet press references in this chapter, see *Current Digest of the Soviet Press* volumes 37–39, except where noted.)

21. Sometime in late 1984 or early 1985 Gorbachev not only ran Secretariat for Chernenko, but also chaired the Politburo in the latter's absences due to illness, according to Archie Brown, "Gorbachev," *Problems of Communism* 34 (3) (May-June 1985): 8–9.

22. The following summary is taken from Alexeyeva, pp. 372–382, 230, 152 ff., 163–164, 214, 381–382, except where noted.

23. Yet, arrests and trials for running Baptist printing presses continued into early 1980s, implying the continued dedicated samizdat activism by some. Alexeyeva, p. 211.

24. Alexeyeva, pp. 106–120; 88–96, 97–105, 56–58, chapters 6, 9–10, 14, pp. 390–398, 423–426.

25. Cf. Brown, 11–12; also his "Gorbachev's First 2 Years," talk at the Harriman Institute, Columbia University, 3 March 1987.

26. One by Chingiz Aitmatov, *Chopping Block*, portrays the main character an ex-priest favorably, according to Donald Treadgold, "The Soviet Union and Asia Today," Spring Symposium, Washington DC Chapter of American Association for the Advancement of Slavic Studies, Washington, DC: 15 May 1987.

27. "Restructuring and Sociology," *Pravda*, 6 February 1987, pp. 2–3.

28. Ellen Jones and Benjamin Woodbury, "Chernobyl and Glasnost," *Problems of Communism* 35 (6) (November-December 1986): 29; CSCE, *Phase II of the Vienna Review Meeting of the CSCE* (Washington, DC: GPO, 1987), p. 6.

29. CSCE, pp. 5–6.

30. One early call for openness (which mentions the March 1985 Plenum's continuing commitment) is the *Pravda* editorial "Openness in Work," 27 March 1985, p. 1. "Openness" began earlier on practical questions and the purges of inefficient personnel. Viz., A. Durzenko, "Speaking out about Openness," *Izvestia*, 19 June 1985, p. 1; Yu. Zhigulev, "About Adherence to Principles and Public Disclosure," *Pravda*, 15 October 1984.

31. Although Gorbachev once said, "I would equate the word restructuring with the word revolution," even on that occasion he spoke mostly of economic management. "Restructuring is an Urgent Matter that Affects Everyone and Everything," *Pravda*, 2 August 1986, pp. 1–2.

32. "Panel II: The Future of Human Rights in American-Soviet Relations," "Human Rights in the USSR" Conference, NY: Columbia University, 27 March 1987.

33. G. Tselms, "A Supplementary Ruling that Was Never Made," *Literaturnaya Gazeta*, 15 January 1986, p. 14 (Latvian trial), "In the Bureau of the Belorussian CP Central Committee," *Sovietskaya Belorussia*, 4 October 1986, p. 1; "Good Name," *Pravda*, 25 October 1986, p. 3 (Uzbek affair); "In the USSR Prosecutor's Office," *Pravda*, 29 November 1986, p. 6 (the Ukraine); V. Chebrikov, "Overstepping the Limit," *Pravda*, 8 January 1987, p. 1 (the Ukraine also); "Punished for Red Tape and Conniving Incident 22 Kilometers Out," *Izvestia*, 23 July 1986, p. 3 (Latvia). Cf. further reports on Bashkiria in *Pravda*, 6 May 1987, p. 2, and on the Russian Republic Procurator, *Izvestia*, 13 June 1986, p. 6. On the firing of psychiatric personnel, see CSCE, p. 6.

34. Cf. I. Petrukhin, "The Force of Law," *Moskovskaya Pravda*, 17 May 1987, p. 3; O. Chaikovskaya and G. Anashkin, "Slander? I Don't Believe It," *Literaturnaya Gazeta*, 15 April 1987, pp. 11 ff.; "Plenary Session of the USSR Supreme Court" (a remarkable official enumeration of abuses), *Izvestia*, 12 December 1986, p, 3; A. Vaksberg, "Look Truth in the Eye" (one of the most direct, most pithy criticisms of "open lawlessness" in the judicial system), *Literaturnaya Gazeta*, 17 December 1986, pp. 13 ff.; V. Savitsky, "The Prestige of the Bar," *Pravda*, 22 March 1987, p. 3; "Justice and the Times," *Pravda*, 25 October 1986, p. 3; "On Further Strengthening of Socialist Legality and Law and Order and Increasing the Protection of Citizens' Rights and Legitimate Interests," *Pravda*, 30 November 1986, pp. 1–2.

35. Cf. *USSR News Briefs*, 1986, 24–4; 1987, 3–21, 3–22. Indeed, in its first meeting (7 July 1987), the dissident "Glasnost Press Club" focussed on the "political articles" of the criminal code and issued an appeal for the repeal of articles 70 and 190.1 in particular. *The Press Club Glasnost* (New York: Center for Democracy, n.d.—apparently July 1987), pp. 2–3

36. The following is based on Cotter, ibid.; except where noted.

37. According to Cathy Fitzpatrick, there were no new political arrests in Moscow, Leningrad, and Kiev since November 1986, but *USSR News Briefs* reported arrests in Moscow and in Leningrad (see fn. 49). Fitzpatrick, "Panel II," "Human Rights" Conference.

38. Fitzpatrick (ibid.). She also noted Soviet acceptance of political rights as topics of discussion since Ottawa review. Cotter (ibid.) also includes arms

control initiatives as having human rights implications. On the reversibility of the amnesty because of these limits, see Tania Mathon, "Glasnost selon Gorbatchev et repression," *La Nouvelle Alternative* 6 (June 87): 58.

39. According to CSCE (ibid.), there were few believers and few nationalists released. Cf. *USSR News Briefs*, 1987, 8–1, 11/12–1, on the release of a small number of Baptists and Pentecostalists.

40. However, Armenians continued to be allowed to leave also. CSCE, p. 6.

41. *USSR News Briefs*, 1987, 11/12–2.

42. Robert van Voren, *Changes in Soviet Psychiatry* (New York: Freedom House, n.d.—evidently July 1987); "US Group Seeking to Visit Soviet Mental Wards," *New York Times*, 10 August 1987, p. 6.

43. S. Murauskas, the head of an art workshop; his brother Z., an excavator; Jonutis, a railroad worker; Vaicekauskas, skilled worker; and Mitkas received 3 years, 2 (suspended), 2, 2 (suspended), and 1 year (suspended), respectively. LIC, 14 Feb 86.

44. Only 1 pure human rights event occurred in this period: the interrogation of folklorist (Ruzas) and his wife in October 1985, for his possession of the memoirs of a former prisoner.

45. *USSR News Briefs*, Special Supplement, 15 July 87, p. 1. Jaskunas evidently capitulated to the KGB; see text, p. 248, and fn. 49.

46. Also, Vaiciunas, Jurevicius, and Viktoras Petkus—Helsinki Monitors with strong Catholic connections—were not released, although Statkevicius was.

47. Reportage is undoubtedly less than complete for the first seven months of this year. This period is far too recent.

48. Some actions were taken against other groups *elsewhere* in the USSR in 1987. Baptists (January); refusniks (February-April); peace activists (February); artists, hippies, and human rights dissidents (all in May) were arrested, but generally released shortly thereafter. There were very few trials: Baptists (in January, a Latvian, who was placed into a psychiatric ward; in February, of 3 in Tashkent), a Ukrainian refusnik (who in February was also taken along the psychiatric route), and Kazakh rioters (January and June). But these were few and far between, especially given the burgeoning of dissent in Moscow and elsewhere.

49. *USSR News Briefs*, 1987, 10–15, 10–19. Mathon notes that glasnost has not constrained the regime from "a violent diatribe" against religious dissidents and believers in general. "Glasnost," 58.

50. As of March 1987, one could note that only 59% of the 26th CPSU Congress delegates were reelected in 1986, that 9 of 12 Secretaries were Gorbachev appointees, and that 5 of 11 full and 6 of 8 candidate members of the Politburo were selected under Gorbachev's leadership. Brown, "Gorbachev's First 2 Years."

51. Mathon, "Glasnost," 58.

52. The rhetorical questions from the 6 June 1986 Gorbachev speech to the Central Committee (cf. the account in the *Washington Post*, 18 June 1986,

p. A 31; and "On the 5 Year Plan of the Economic and Social Development of the USSR for 1986–1990 and the Party's Organizational Tasks for its Realization," *Pravda*, 17 June 1986, pp.1–4) are cited by William Corey, "Panel II." The 17 January 1987 Plenum quote (from the tough, specific, and lengthy denunciation by Gorbachev—cf. *New York Times*, 28 January 1987, I, p. 6, 8) is from Peter Juviler, "Panel II."

53. T. Oleszczuk, "The Commanding Heights and Liberalization," *Comparative Politics* 13 (2) (January 1981): 171–185.

54. "In the Central Committee," *Pravda* and *Izvestia*, 1 October 1986, p. 1.

55. Jones and Woodbury, p. 30.

56. "In the Central Committee."

57. "Restructuring is Will, Courage, and Responsibility," *Literaturnaya Rossiya*, 27 March 1987, pp. 2–4; "In Step with the Times" (the report on the Russian Republic Artists Union, by the first secretary of its board, V. Sidorov), *Pravda*, 20 May 1987, pp. 1 and 5.

58. "Opposition to Gorbachev," *Washington Post*, 17 April 1987, p. A 25. Cf. also Jean-Marie Chauvier, " 'Transparence des debats opacite des reforme: Le 'Printemps' de Moscou," *Le Monde Diplomatique* 398 (May 87): 1, 10. As one of Gorbachev's reform economists, A. Butenko, put it: ". . . restructuring is proceeding slowly so far because the very same forces that prevented the complete implementation of the decisions of the 20th CPSU Congress— which dethroned and condemned the personality cult— and . . . interrupted the process of the renewal of out life [thereby] do not want changes and are impeding them now, too." "In the Light of Openness," *Moskovskaya Pravda*, 7 May 1987, p. 3.

59. "Summary of a Discussion Conducted by the Discussion Club of the Peace and Social Research Seminar on March 21, 1987" and "Summary of a Discussion Conducted by the Peace and Social Research Discussion Club of the Friendship and Dialogue Group on April 19, 1987" in *Information Bulletin Glasnost* (Moscow) 1 (June 1987) (translated and edited by K. Szczepanska and others; printed by the Center for Democracy; New York, New York), p. 5.

60. "On the Information Bulletin *Glasnost* and the Anthology *Glasnost*," *Information Bulletin Glasnost*, 1 (June 1987), p. 1.

9

Political Justice
and the Future

Many Western discussions of post-Stalinist dissent and regime response have suggested that the underlying characteristics of repression are arbitrariness and unrelenting pursuit. Yet, measures against dissidents in Lithuania were not completely arbitrary. Major judicial institutions have acted in predictable, rational ways when dealing with dissidents. Our expanded judicial process approach, incorporating concerns for both juridical institutions and socio-political factors, has helped us discover the connection of this rationality to the development of the dissident social movement itself.

Previous chapters demonstrated a dialectical, feedback relationship between the regime and its opponents. In Chapter 2 we saw that the historical context of the absorption of Lithuania into the Soviet Union reinforced the ideological and legal bias against autonomous activity. Religion and nationalism were (and are) considered dangerous as throw-backs to capitalism. Lithuanian history distinctly combined the two into a strong anti-Russianism threatening to the Russian-dominated leadership and probably to most of the Russian populace. Many laws against such dangers were created or already existed at the time of the rise of Lithuanian dissent: anti-Soviet agitation and propaganda, treason, slander of the state, violation of the rights of believers, violation of the separation of church and state, and numerous non-political criminal charges. Finally, dominance by the Communist Party over governmental institutions ensured that these ideological and legal biases were unopposed from within.

In Chapter 3 we found that dissent in Lithuania occurred despite the vast power of the state and its efforts to prevent such activity. The dissidents of Lithuania were drawn from every sector of society, although disproportionately from intellectuals, students, and religious leaders. Although divided into religious, nationalist, and human rights

179

varieties, dissent in Lithuania formed a social movement of protest in which the realization of common values by cooperative efforts was the basis for organized activity. Dissident actions, statements, and organizations; the socio-demographic features of dissidents; and dissident "careers" all show the interconnectedness of the parts of the whole.

The Soviet state did not ignore this movement, which emerged in response to its own repressive activities in the late 1960s and early 1970s. It used the legal system for the social control of this "deviant behavior." As we saw in Chapter 4, the legal institutional setup and its formal processes were on paper designed to emphasize the implementation of legal norms within the limits of state legitimation; i.e., law was also to educate the population to the finer side of Soviet life, to inculcate obedience to the state and the Communist Party. Therefore, although the procurator bears the most responsibility for the defense of legal norms and the protection of the rights of individuals, his position as representative of the state prevailed. In many cases in that chapter legal safeguards were disregarded. Blatantly arbitrary interpretations of laws *and* personal behavior went unchallenged by the procurator, who was recruited and supervised by the party organization. This ignoring of rules and logic is the germ of the charges of arbitrariness leveled against Soviet law.

This arbitrariness is shown in chapter 5. We saw there that individuals facing the powers of Soviet law were dealt with "unfairly" in substantive terms, given their activities. The type of activity that precedes arrest and trial (or even interrogation) bears no clear relationship to the possibility of repression. Although violent and less conventional acts do predominate among the known triggers for arrest (and trial), most of these actions do *not* themselves lead to such responses.

In addition, chapter 6 indicates that the final disposition of the trials of dissidents was only indirectly tied to the "facts" of the cases. Although "social danger" is supposed to be an important determinant of sentencing regardless of the charge, length of sentence—and the short-circuiting of public judicial proceedings by psychiatric detention—was almost exclusively based on the early decision to book individuals on specific charges, decisions themselves empirically associated with different triggers. In other words, the sentence did not vary according to offending act, except to the limited degree that more serious acts might lead to more serious charges.

Although of real merit, the accusation of arbitrariness misses a deeper level of Soviet reality, the *regularity* beneath the chaos. The selection of dissidents for interrogation, arrest, trial, and psychiatric detention was *not* "senseless" in general, no matter how irrational from a formalist-legalist perspective in almost all the individual cases. Judicial institutions targeted certain kinds of dissidents for differing treatment. Women were pulled in for interrogation, but seldom arrested and tried. Religious clerics were nearly immune to judicial persecution, but their supporters among other groups were commonly brought to "justice." The big targets were intellectuals, students, and white-collar workers, especially those who espoused nationalist demands or who had connections to differing dissident groups. These differences are strongly associated with the differential location of the groups within the social movement, a pattern that suggests strong utilitarian rationality by judicial institutions in dealing with a potential adversary.

In sentencing too we notice some degree of "rationality" of the coercive apparatus making decisions about different groups of dissidents. The charges did vary by social group, gender, and basis of dissent. Thus, the regime did differentiate along these dimensions, charging some more harshly and dealing out longer sentences accordingly.

These differences were also based on the strengths and weaknesses of the Lithuanian social movement. Its leadership with strong organizational and emotive resources—the priests—were generally tenderly handled in this time period, for fear of arousing more dissent. Relatedly, religious dissidents generally were less harshly punished, while nationalists and hybrids received longer terms, or psychiatric detention. On the other hand, intellectuals being slightly more isolated did obtain more and harsher penalties on anti-Soviet agitation, as did workers, who also were more often charged and sentenced under the treason article. (For somewhat different, idiosyncratic reasons, students are more leniently treated.)

The lesson of these patterns of differentiation is political calculation by those directing repression. Surprisingly, this calculation has transcended more "mundane" political factors, like factional conflict and policy vacillation; it answered instead to a more general dialect of dissent and repression. In Chapter 7 we found that elite conflict at the highest levels in Moscow during the Brezhnev leadership was unrelated to the degree of repression, as was the vacillation of anti-dissident policy at the highest levels. Neither the fortunes of putatively more repressive leaders nor the swing toward more repressive show-trials throughout the Soviet Union (and Eastern Europe) were then systematically at the base of the interactions within Lithuania.

Of course, in the last chapter we noted that the all-Union reformist swing under Gorbachev has been paralleled by a winding down of the dissident-regime confrontation in Lithuania. This implies a convergence in recent years between all-Union and republic processes, temporarily obscuring the "autonomy" of Lithuania from elite conflict and policy change.

This finding of the occasional "autonomy" of processes from such direct political factors was one big surprise of this research. Of course, it would hard to deny that these factors play a *background* role in the decision-making regarding all dissidents in the Warsaw Pact, but the data clearly indicate that that role was far less important than the nature of dissent in Lithuania itself, a logical but hitherto unstated proposition.

This is not to say that the Lithuanian case has no message for all-Union developments. Given that the dynamics of Soviet repression were affected by the dynamics of Soviet dissent, there are clear systemic implications. Chapter 7 showed the rise of the social movement to be accompanied by a most untotalitarian increase in tolerance and decline in punitiveness. The example of a dissident movement having some social power—despite its lack of legal or political legitimacy—suggests the possibility of similar movements in other regions surviving, given favorable conditions of language, culture, and social organization.

It is not clear how many (or how few) of the other nationalities have such a positive configuration of history and society. One might easily be pessimistic: the Lithuanian experience might not be replicated anywhere else in the Soviet Union. The social-political potential of other dissident groups, starting with the nationalities, certainly remains a fertile area of future research for Soviet specialists. However, occasional repression and unrest among many other national and religious groups[1] suggest that a summary dismissal of the Lithuanian case as "atypical" would be too precipitous.

Constraints: Why Not the Heavy Hand?

Although the existence of a non-official social movement has produced an enduring, sophisticated policy of repression, one can argue that such dissent places—or reinforces—constraints on the regime. In the particular circumstances of Lithuania, much more repression would be necessary to *attempt* to eradicate dissent entirely, yet this attempt is unlikely because it might yield other results undesirable from the elite's perspective.

First, the power of the KGB would be magnified greatly in society at large. This would almost automatically lead to increased political clout at the highest levels. That prospect cannot be pleasing to those high-level bureaucrat-politicians with few direct ties to the KGB to protect them.

In addition, the suppression of the Lithuanian social movement might be economically costly. The republic could become a seething area of turmoil, with disruptive work stoppages and student riots cutting into production activities, at the least. A major introduction of massive military/secret police occupation itself would not be costless. Even action involving less than a complete military occupation would have considerable practical costs: bugging, paying secret policy salaries, maintaining files, etc.

The costs would be especially high if other national, religious, and human rights dissidents expressed some solidarity with the Lithuanians. This non-zero probability event is not terribly likely given the weakening of leadership caused by continuing repression and emigration among some of these other groups.

The application of any more comprehensive sanctions against the social movement faces other costs as well. The concern of the leadership for high-technology development implies a concern for the productivity of scientists and technologists, who will not directly support a particularist cause like that of Lithuania. However, such groups do not work at their optimal efficiency in a climate of coercion, even in the mild coercion of Western bureaucraticized firms. Should the use of coercion be continuing but limited to more "legitimate" forms, like occasional show trials, there is less chance for this economic-technical boomerang.

However, there is a somewhat different danger here, forming a less tangible constraint on the use of the judiciary in this fashion. Continuing trials of Lithuanian dissidents over the course of years and decades— without the full-scale mobilization of the rest of Soviet society to uproot the so-called dangers of ideological subversion—could lead to a down-playing of the importance of dissent *and* repression. After all, if life goes on "normally" or even improves with no real effects due to dissent and repression, dissent might be seen as no real threat at all, as a minor irritant to be ignored. This trivialization by the masses might make *support* less dangerous, just as the decline of Brezhnev's vitality in his last years led to trivialization of his *personal* power and to the rise of numerous political jokes about him in the Soviet Union. The overuse of judicial repression undercuts the political educational lesson of the trials, and may even delegitimate the trials themselves.

The Soviet authorities face Medusa here. If they move too far with mass repression, they endanger themselves and the economic system, at least. If they move instead toward greater judicial repression without mass mobilization, they endanger the judicial system and support for their anti-dissident policy (if it does exist). If they include increased mass propaganda activities, the social movement itself may well be energized, as the waverers and silent supporters of the movement are pushed into its defense.

There might be international repercussions. Relations with the US and Western Europe would likely become strained, given the immediate challenge to Western values of free expression, religious worship, and legalism. This prospect did not deter martial law in Poland, of course, or the invasion of Dubcek's Czechoslovakia, but tense relations with the most technologically advanced states could endanger useful trade and scientific acquisitions by the USSR.

Direct attacks on the Roman Catholic Church could incite Catholics in Poland (and elsewhere) into anti-Soviet demonstrations. This in turn could endanger ties to France, Italy, and Latin America. Such a violent anti-religious campaign could well ruin continuing economic and political ties with Western Europe, (for even the martial law government of Poland took particular care with its religious opposition).

Thus, there have been some external and internal constraints on the full application of coercive power against the Lithuania dissidents. The social, economic, and political costs were reinforced by the strengths of that movement, namely, its organization and rootedness in Lithuanian society. This leads us to a more refined view of the Soviet political system.

Models of Soviet Politics

The several models of Soviet politics yield insights of differing worth, given this study of repression. Some features of some models are invisible or only faintly pertinent to Lithuania.

Rationality, autonomy, constraints, and differentiation imply that totalitarian schema is not useful except at a philosophic level. The concentration of coercive power is not absolute, arbitrary, and atomizing. Such power is limited and independent political behavior is possible; judicial proceedings are routinized and some attention is paid to written norms.

Ideology seemed to play only a limited role, primarily in the regime's analysis of the situation and in the mass legitimation of repression. The repression of a dissident movement—not accepted formally, denounced publicly, and subject to countermeasures—is justified as "defense" of socialism against its enemies. Yet, the regime rarely reported its political trials and subjected them more to ad hominem attacks than to detailed ideological exegesis. Religion and nationalism in Lithuania were decried in ideological terms in many publications, *but* this attack was episodic and did not lead to a psychology of

seige, and a rigorous attention to Lenin and Marx. The strengths of
the movement are indirectly recognized.

Other models, which suggest some degree of political conflict and
interaction between rulers and ruled are more appropriate.[2] Two based
in the structural-functional mode of analysis—bureaucracy and modernization—offer considerable insight into the structure and functioning
of the repressive apparatus.

As one would expect of "bureaucracy," the Soviet system possesses
differentiated institutions for the monitoring and control of dissent,
as we saw in chapters 2 and 4. Those legal institutions contain
specialized roles into which only select individuals are recruited. Their
behavior is regulated by detailed written rules, but as in all bureaucracies unwritten norms govern many situations, here the processing
of political suspects.

Like social systems moving toward greater complexity, economic
interdependence, and sophisticated modes of compliance, the Soviet
legal system shows elements of "modernization" as well. Patterns of
repression were quite complex, interdependence and sophistication
were suggested by the changes in behavior examined in chapter 7.
There we found indications that elements of the bureaucracy attempted
to protect themselves through the routinization of that process and
the amelioration of the uncertainty associated with the dissident
movement outside its immediate purview.

"Modernization" also implies some degree of diffused power, even
in undemocratic systems. Although the Soviet system has a dictatorial
nature, it is not "apolitical" in the sense of an absence of actors.
Even dissidents had indirect influence in the autonomy of their
activities, and in the existence of their nationalist/religious "contra-
system."[3] The limits to regime power were rooted in strength of that
contrasystem *and* in internal transformations of previous periods,
"liberalization." This was so even though repression "intensified"
when the first waves of "de-Stalinization" ended. The elite fear of
an unleashed KGB is an essential ingredient to this limit, which
continues into the 1980s, especially as General Secretary Gorbachev
attempts to revitalize Soviet life.

The model of "empire" provides to us in some ways the most
important insight, at least for dissent. The regime has not only not
eliminated nationalism as a source of tension among its citizenry, it
has promoted it through increased education (viz., the large numbers
of intellectuals and students among Lithuanian dissidents) and through
its own anti-nationalist policies, seen through the eyes of the dissidents.
This suggests a fundament of structural weakness, lines of fragmen-

tation appearing in the multiethnic base of the Union of Soviet Socialist Republics.

The concept of empire is a good one for understanding the rise and continuity of Lithuania's movement. It also suggests the ethnic dilemma of repression in today's USSR: fear of contagion to other non-Russian groups counterbalanced by a fear of sympathy for an oppressed nation by those groups.

We must see the Soviet Union, then, as a country with nationalist problems, with which the central authority must deal within the realities of limited power and opposition. The underlying trends seem favorable to the dissident opposition, but they too are only part of the picture. The regime leadership and its choices must be considered, as must mass response.

This brings us to the question of the likely consequences of the continuance of both repression and dissent in Lithuania. They are difficult to ascertain, but we may discern several possible paths.

The Future: Paths of Political Developments

For decades, many scenarios for the future of the USSR have been presented by Western scholars. Possibly the best articulated, best known, and most extensive set of scenarios was done by Zbigniew Brzezinski.[4] Our task is made somewhat simpler because his delineated paths are implicitly based on the most common "models" of Soviet politics of the post-war period.

Our above discussion of constraints and costs implies that Brzezinski's "militant fundamentalism" path is improbable. As Western analysts have noted in "applying" the totalitarian concept, there is now simply no sign of the Marxist-Leninist ideological fervor, even among elites, that would be required to legitimate a more highly centralized, mobilizational leadership. Instead, there is a more pragmatic understanding of the dilemmas of power. However, one cannot rule this path entirely out, in the short-run at least, because of the dangers of another path, which might under severe conditions appeal to a panicked leadership. That transitional course is *political disintegration*.

The complete collapse of the Soviet leadership's ability to rule seems the least likely of Brzezinski's possibilities. Internal elite paralysis, helplessness in face of mounting dissent are not major aspects of the political system today. Institutions remain strong, leadership united on systemic survival (and increasingly reform), and citizenry generally passive. Yet, in the long-term, the Lithuanian movement has demonstrated a limited and local regime incapacity that may promote other, more widespread movements and may immobilize the leadership. The short-term success of Gorbachev's program may have similiar effects if economic conditions deteriorate further and dissent becomes common.

More research on other Soviet nationalities, their dissidents, and their potentials is needed. Lithuania is not likely to be a major problem for Soviet leaders, even if they continue with the spiral of dissent and repression. It is a small republic with a small population. However, if the other national groups are vulnerable to the power of example, the situation becomes much more serious, as recent events in the Caucasus and Kazakhstan show. Without such research we cannot imply disintegration is in the immediate future of the Soviet system.

A third possibility also seems improbable, if only because the system seems to have "outgrown" it. "Oligarchic petrifaction," in which the party and state elite continues to promote stability and its own rule at the expense of needed policy innovation, seems unlikely given clear evidence outside this study of the breakup of the personnel logjam of Soviet-style gerontocracy. Elite changes in the last five years have been extensive. (Also, our examination of Lithuania indicates a spiral of repression and dissent, an inherently unstable condition.)

What this means for anti-dissident policy per se is becoming clear. The new leadership twenty years younger than the previous one is trying some important innovations. Dissent has endured. The threat in Moscow and Leningrad, at least, seemed to have peaked in the mid–1970s, after which they were effectively frozen out politically, their organizations were dispersed and their leaders jailed or exiled. But the releases of prisoners and the new atmosphere of change have meant a great deal more activity in the capital and elsewhere than only a few years ago.

One cannot rule out new use of old means of social control. Expansion of psychiatric facilities, broadening of the limited opportunities to emigrate, or even some restricted forms of cooptation (e.g., easier approval for church maintenance or construction, to divert energies into more physical, less political projects) are all possibilities open to the new leadership. Nonetheless, for the moment the Politburo has staked its legitimacy on this second wave of liberalization since the death of Stalin.

"Technological adaptation" of politics is also appearing in the USSR. Expertise, efficiency, discipline are all becoming more valued inside the party and out. As the society becomes more advanced economically, the new technocrats are more important to the successful accomplishment of official and unofficial tasks. Concomitantly this group comes into political favor. For Brzezinski, this path is different from the second in that use of high-tech means of repression is not excluded. The bounds of debate might widen but only to include tolerance of scientific intellectual debate on narrow policy questions. This path would entail the "technocratic" model of Jacques Ellul and others, in which political values lose ground to technological values of productivity and innovation, without implicitly liberal-democratic acceptance of the universal right to public disagreement.

In this study there are few signs of this path. Although the intellectuals were a major social component in the Lithuanian movement, they were linked to the others by "hybrid" dissidents who personally represented the differing kinds of dissent, by organizations which supported the demands of others, and by an underlying set of common dissident values centering on Lithuanian dignity and anti-bureaucratic individualism.

Yet, although the scientific dissent elsewhere in the Soviet Union was eradicated as far as samizdat, petitions, and similar activities are concerned, the release of Sakharov and the rise of technocratic reformers may reinvigorate such dissent. Balancing this, the reforming leaders is attempting to integrate technocratic concerns with the legitimacy of political institutions through all the new proposals.

In Lithuania the government and party face a major challenge to their claim to represent the best interests of all Lithuanians. Official policies come into too great a conflict with the traditional values and institutions of Lithuania. The continuity of Lithuanian tradition lies, instead, in the Catholic Church and in the persons of recalcitrant priests.

The Soviet regime bases its legitimacy on the promise of socialism and the threat of capitalism. However, the "internationalism" of the Communist Party is not free of Russian domination. The dissident movement, on the other hand, possesses an anti-Russian traditionalism that rejects many of the fundamental premises of Marxism-Leninism.

As Tucker has noted, dissent is a "belief movement" arising at a time of "crisis in society." The dissidents' ideas provide the opportunity for a "recovery of belief" in an environment of the lack of belief in the official ideology. Thus, the dissident movement has a long-term capacity to survive repression. There is no socio-psychological or spiritual alternative, and repression reinforces the movement's "righteousness."[5] This suggests the possibility of a long-term qualitative change in the political system.

According to Brzezinski, "pluralist evolution" entails the rise of differing interests within the party and state apparatus, each articulating increasingly distinctly its own policy preferences. This quantitative change in decision-making toward overt and conflictual debates would accompany the decline of ideology as a major shield behind which leaders could defend their positions and as a major emotive force for both elites and masses. In such a climate, less energetic repression would be natural, as the bounds of acceptable expression widen to include at least some of the policies or criticisms of those branded as "dissident" today.[6]

Although there have been and continue to be criticisms of "bourgeois nationalism"—a concept that could be used against Russification—the emergence of a free area of debate is as yet barely discernible. Individuals and their organizations are still monitored and repressed at various times for even the covert expression of views that expressly accept the long-term legitimacy of "Soviet power."

Our findings about Lithuanian dissent and repression imply the beginnings of such an arena, outside the party-state environment that might produce internal changes there. Although the official interpretation of diverging viewpoints of dissidents is still hostile, the constraints placed on mass coercion allow for a widening area of "free" expression (increasingly manifested now in the policy of glasnost). Even under Brezhnev, thousands had articulated religious, nationalist, and human rights demands without major repression. For them, at least, the trend from the 1940s through the 1980s has been one of evolution toward some kind of pluralism. These "areas" are not sacrosanct—activists were occasionally arrested and convicted, non-activists were harassed in non-juridical ways. Yet the social movement itself has given thousands of individuals courage, and they have often acted without the adverse consequences of the Stalin years. As it continues, it is difficult to see how the party could prevent "contamination" within its ranks, especially because of glasnost, legal reform, and perestroika.

Changes in sentencing policy implementation may at first have been rooted in local bureaucrats' fears of mass discontent or central anticipation of them. On the other hand, the Lithuanian dissident movement responding even to smaller sentences may be turning into an important component in the political reformist alliance for the "rule of law." The Lithuanian movement already acts as a small social force pressing for legality along with "liberals" within the legal apparatus. Lithuanian dissidents demands' for human rights including bureaucratic respect for the Constitution and the criminal codes, may provide support for their potential allies within the party, spokesmen for legalist positions who have played important policy-making roles on legal questions.[7]

The prospects for an overt coalition are dim, but a de facto alliance could come about as increasing demands by dissidents might be used as an argument to respect legal norms to undercut this basis of discontent. This is a definite possibility, given the oft-noted "juridification of society—a greater role and rule of law"[8]—that parallels the increasing political use of the courts. This juridification is the outcome of the influence of the legalists at many levels of the party.

Whether this coalition emerges depends on several other factors. One such factor is the multiplicative potential of nationalist threats.[9] Already there are indications of a Russian nationalist movement (in the form of the *Pamyat* Society), renewed activity of Crimean Tatars and discontent among Armenians.[10] Should this phenomenon of the social movement appear in great strength among other nationalities (even the Ukrainians alone), then the immediate response might well be a strengthening of the party's control over social life, or even a move in the direction of military control if the party proved insufficient to the task, a move down the militant fundamentalist path. What cannot be predicted now is if the integrated social movement of dissent will appear elsewhere, much less when or if in conjunction with other groups' dissident mobilization.

However, given what we have suggested about the nature of power in the relationship of dissident and state in the Lithuanian context, the use of the military (or a reinvigoration of the coercive apparatus under the control of the party) would form a *major* change in the political system that would also threaten the position of major elements of the elite. It seems highly improbable. No hint of a coercive resurgence is visible despite the numerous demonstrations in Moscow and elsewhere through the first five months of 1988.

There are major changes at work in the Soviet dictatorship. We must disagree with Solzhenitsyn, who sees only disintegration or external force as ways in which the Communist system will change.[11] Even before the current reforms, Soviet laws did constrain the regime in limited ways (in sentencing and in the use of arrest and trial). The routinization of repression and the emergence of clearer limits to dissident activity are in process; in other words, the pluralist path is open.[12]

Law in the Soviet Republic of Lithuania is put to political use in dissident cases, but there are limits to its use and the social movement survives. The regime has tried to be sophisticated in its targeting of segments of the movement, in its selection of articles of the criminal codes, in its use of psychiatric internment, and in its adhering to the terms set by statute for various crimes. The leadership is not completely arbitrary in its treatment of dissidents. It wishes legitimacy, legality, and an end to dissent. It has not achieved all of these goals, and will most likely continue to face the challenge of dissent.

The potential of contagion spreading to other republics during turbulent times needs further research, but Lithuania demonstrates that given favorable conditions, dissent can survive repression. General Secretary Gorbachev certainly hopes to make the issue moot by spurring stagnant institutions dynamic, leadership youthful and bold, and the populace enthusiastic. Whether dissent can outlive the regime— successful reforms or not—remains for history to answer.

Notes

1. See fn. 48 of chapter 8, and fn. 10, below.

2. This discussion draws upon John Reshetar's useful compilation. *The Soviet Polity* (New York: Harper, Row, 1978), pp. 336–361.

3. Robert Sharlet, "Dissent and the 'Contra-system' in the Soviet Union," in *The Soviet Union in the 1980s*, ed. Erik P. Hoffman (New York: The Academy of Political Science, 1984), pp. 135–146.

4. *Between Two Ages* (NY: Penguin, 1970), pp. 164–176. Cf. Seweryn Bialer, *Stalin's Successors* (Cambridge: Cambridge University Press, 1980); George W. Breslauer, *Five Images of the Soviet Future* (Berkeley: University of California— Institute of International Studies, 1978), etc.

5. Robert C. Tucker, "Swollen State, Spent Society," *Foreign Affairs* 2 (Winter 1981–1982): 414–435, as reprinted in *The Soviet Polity in the Modern Era*, ed. Erik P. Hoffmann and Robbin F. Laird (New York: Aldine, 1984), pp. 41–67.

6. The underlying assumption of this view is a structural-functionalist one: any society as large and varied as the Soviets' must at some point allow the interdependence and interaction of all its parts, without an artificial uniformity, or it will not survive.

7. Peter H. Solomon, *Soviet Criminologists and Criminal Policy: Specialists in Policy-Making* (New York: Columbia University Press, 1978).

8. Peter H. Juviler, "Some Trends in Soviet Criminal Justice," p. 80, in *Soviet Law After Stalin*, ed. Donald D. Barry and others (Leyden: A.W. Sijthoff, 1980).

9. Zbigniew Brzezinski, "Soviet Politics: From the Future to the Past?", in *The Dynamics of Soviet Politics*, ed. Paul Cocks and others (Cambridge, Mass.: Harvard University Press, 1976), pp. 337–351, 414–415), as reprinted in *The Soviet Polity in the Modern Era*, pp. 69–83.

10. *USSR News Briefs*, 1987, 9–31 and 10–34 on the Pamyat Society, and 13–22 on the Crimean Tatars. Most recently, Armenians have also become active.

11. Aleksandr I. Solzhenitsyn, *The Mortal Danger* (New York: Harper, Row, 1981), pp. 1–71, as reprinted in *The Soviet Polity in the Modern Era*, pp. 5–39.

12. Of course, this is contingent upon the activities of the masses and political and socio-economic requirements. "Medicalization" via inappropriate psychiatric incarceration and "thuggery" remain minor alternatives to the conventional judicial process, but these are little used for reasons similar to the application of widespread coercion discussed above.

Appendix:
Bias and Coverage

In the last 15 years samizdat materials from the Soviet Union have flooded into the West. They have specified the relations of the Soviet government and its dissidents. Although occasional histories of Soviet dissident groups have been based on this samizdat, few empirically-oriented, social science studies have appeared.[1] For the most part, these empirical studies have subjected the data to only the most rudimentary statistical analyses.[2] This is not surprising given the disagreement over the value of these materials as anything more than anecdotal evidence of individual encounters with the Soviet coercive apparatus. This appendix takes a closer look at the usefulness of samizdat for the more complex empirical analysis of the Soviet political system. We find that samizdat is useful, with some expected bias that can be countered by using several sources.[3]

Without public statistics by the Soviet government on the numbers of prosecutions of dissidents each year, or of Soviet sociological studies of "political offenders,"[4] the assessment of samizdat as an alternate measure or source takes on special importance. Until the time that something comparable to an updated "Smolensk file"[5] becomes available—and perhaps not even then—scholars in the West will have to depend heavily on dissident sources for information about this aspect of Soviet politics. Thus, a clear understanding of the essential soundness of that information is important. That understanding can come from a close examination of the characteristics of data collected from samizdat as opposed to non-samizdat sources.

Scholarly opinion on the use of statistics drawn from samizdat is divided. One scholar maintains that the economic statistics used in samizdat articles are unreliable or distorted.[6] Another has argued that while an analysis of the scope of repression using all relevant available sources would be "most useful," such work cannot succeed because of the indeterminate number of unpublicized political prisoners.[7] A third has suggested that at least one kind of data drawn from samizdat—

figures on protest demonstrations—is complete, reliable, and generally appropriate for more complicated analytical techniques.[8]

They may all be correct. Dissidents in their writings may not have accurate estimates of economic activities, there may be large parts of the political prisoner population (especially from the 1950s) about whom we know nothing, and yet samizdat may still be a fertile field for research.

The soundest area of samizdat reportage may be related to its greatest weakness, the operations of the judicial apparatus against dissent. Although the past actions of the Soviet regime have produced an "indeterminate" number of political prisoners, one *express intent* of samizdat journals with lengthy publication records has been to record the *current* actions taken against dissidents. This appendix will focus on types of events about which these sources can be presumed to be particularly careful, events that formed the basis of investigation for this book: arrests, trials, and interrogations.

Considerations of the substantive utility of such information can outweigh the objections of the methodological purist if care is taken to delineate the flaws, real and imagined, of the data. The near impossibility of getting information on all the historical cases of repression against dissidents does not mean an end to research in this area, even before it is properly begun. In several interrelated areas in political science, the "universe" of "events" similarly *cannot* be known conclusively. The lessons of the scholars studying methodological problems there can be applied here.

The study of sources used in the analysis of "event data" has a particularly well-developed literature in international relations. There have been numerous articles on the acceptability of data on events of international significance in the foreign relations of states,[9] as well as domestic conflicts.[10] The major questions have focussed on source coverage, bias, and the representativeness of findings.

First, disagreement centers around whether some kinds of sources provide *more* information than other kinds (international oriented Western newspapers, as opposed to indigenous regional newspapers or historical documents), and whether one source alone may do an acceptable job, thus cutting the time and fiscal cost of research tremendously.

Second, there is also some question about the quality of data. Many studies of bias in the reportage of differing types of newspapers and other sources have attempted to determine whether visible biases undermine the reliable of the data derived from them.

Finally, studies have compared the results of statistical analyses of data from different sources, in the belief that less-than-complete coverage and clear bias may not render a source worthless if the results are the same as those derived from more complete and less biased sources. Substantive usefulness of a source—its "representativeness" of the real phenomenon—may ultimately count more than the extant imperfections that must be counterbalanced.

Each of these three questions (coverage, bias, representativeness) will be investigated in the following sections. We will follow the explicit advice of two scholars who have worked the evaluation of sources of event data. Burrowes and Spector say that "the best test of the adequacy of any particular source is a *systematic comparison* with a number of other sources."[11] The substance of this method in the current case is the examination of the relative strengths and weaknesses of several sources, the juxtaposition of samizdat to non-samizdat sources, and the comparison of both to a data-set compiled from all the sources.

These comparisons suggest that the sources used in this book span the major types of informational sources one might use in this research area. The samizdat sources are good, despite some bias and underreporting. Single samizdat sources can yield significant data that represent the underlying tendencies for some variables, yet the combination of two such sources produces such good results that further data collection is unnecessary (although for this book all the sources have been used, and the data-base is the overall file).

The Sources

The kinds of sources used are the ones a researcher might consult for information on repression in the Soviet Union. (The more specialized sources are directly concerned with the affairs of only the Lithuanian part of the Soviet Union, but if one were to study another group or geographic area, there would usually be counterpart "specialized" sources.) The different types of sources are: 1) specialized samizdat, 2) general samizdat, 3) emigre organizations' publications and archives, 4) the publications and files of human rights organizations with a particular interest in the Soviet Union, and 5) nationally reknowned newspapers. There is at least one source in each of these categories.

The specialized samizdat examined here is the major journal of the Lithuanian movement itself, the *Chronicles of the Catholic Church in Lithuania*.[12] This journal, dedicated to the reporting of the events within Lithuania to the world outside, has survived several waves of arrests and trials explicitly oriented to its extinction.[13] It is readily available in English language translation from the Lithuanian Roman Catholic Priests' League of America. Although on the surface only a religious publication, it contains summaries of the contents of many other samizdat journals circulating in Lithuania,[14] as well as reports of dissent and repression of non-Catholics and non-Lithuanian Catholics in Byelorussia and Moldavia. Issues 1–49 were used here.

The more generalized samizdat examined here is the well-known, Moscow-based *Chronicles of Current Events*. Established in April 1968, in part in response to the optimism of Dubcek's Czechoslovakia, it has since the early 1970s become something approaching an all-Union dissident "newspaper," reporting on events from ever-wider areas. It has been interrupted only once, from October 1972 to May 1974, in response to the authorities' threat to add to the eventual prison terms of two prominent dissenters in custody if any more issues appeared. One of them collaborated, however, and the onus shifted, allowing "publication" to resume with so direct a moral dilemma.[15] Readily available in English translation from Amnesty International, the CCE has been put in over 60 issues. The first 58 are included here.

Third, there are two emigre sources used, one political and one non-political. The Lithuanian National Foundation publishes a bulletin of news events in Lithuania called *ELTA*. Originally composed mainly of the diplomatic and military remnants of the interwar Lithuanian government (before 1979, it was called the Supreme Committee for the Liberation of Lithuania, with the initials "VLIKo"), this organizatin has a strong anti-Communist and anti-Russian bent. It has devoted its energies in recent years to publicizing the economic, social, and political conditions in Lithuania to mobilize Western public opinion and political elites to action.[16] Its bulletin dates back to 1956 and since 1973 has included excerpts from various samizdat materials, and letters and commentary from recent emigres. Numbers 1–124 and 161–275 were included here.

The other emigre organization is less political, although it too attempts to influence public opinion through publicity. The Lithuanian Information Center, located in Brooklyn, New York, collects information on events in Lithuania, aids in the translation of samizdat, and maintains files on dissident prisoners. In contrast to the Lithuanian National Foundation, the LIC focusses its attention on the dissemination of information through publications, lectures, and related activities, and not on the intensive lobbying of Congress and the Executive. The LIC is affiliated with the Lithuanian Roman Catholic Priests League and with the Lithuanian American Roman Catholic Relief Services, established in the late 1940s to coordinate humanitarian aid to Lithuania.[17] Its card files and lists for 1980 and 1981 (the only lists available at its offices) were used.

The three human rights organizations with particular interest in the Soviet Union differ from one another. One is primarily a research institution with some concern for publicity, Keston College (Keston, England), which is a private agency established by a circle of prominent religious leaders of the major faiths of the United Kingdom to collect information on the state of religion in Communist countries generally. It devotes considerable effort to preparing reports[18] and lists of prisoners in the Soviet Union, specializing in Christians of various denominations (leaving Soviet Jews to many other specialized organizations). It has put out lists in 1977, 1979, and 1981, all of which are used.

The second human rights organization is a private news collection service limited strictly to the Soviet Union and its dissidents. Established and run by emigre dissident Cronid Lubarsky, this service disseminates information in two major forms: a yearly list of "political prisoner" (in which religious dissidents are also included) and a biweekly newspaper, *Vesti iz SSSR*.[19] *Vesti* is the product of the centralized collation of reports from literally dozens of emigre groups, individuals, and human rights organizations, and includes within its pages all the latest materials to be incorporated in subsequent lists of prisoners, based on a lengthy card file updated with each issue. This work includes the issues from 1/1978 through 12/1981, and the lists from 1978, 1980, and 1981.

The third human rights organization is similar to Lubarsky's. Khronika Press in New York publishes, among other things, the journal *Chronicles of Human Rights in the USSR* beginning in 1973. It was intended to fill the gap left by the suspension of the publication of CCE (note the close similarity of title), but it continued to be issued even after CCE resumed. Edited by another emigre, Valery Chalidze, CHR follows the model of CCE in format and reportage. It does not aspire to replace it and as a consequence only summarizes the reports of CCE and other samizdat publications, including CCCL. Instead, it attempts to add information from other sources, such as Western newspapers and recent emigres' books and articles. Issues 1–41 are included here.

The last type of source is the daily press. Perhaps the most internationally oriented American newspaper, the *New York Times*, was selected, among other reasons because several studies of international events have done likewise.[20] Certainly, the interactions of regime and dissident in the Soviet Union are a form of domestic conflict.) For this book daily reports from 1 January 1968 through 31 December 1981 were employed.

TABLE   1

OVERALL COVERAGE OF DATED EVENTS BY SOURCE

Percentage of total reported+

Event type	N	CCCL	CCE	LIC	ELTA	Vesti	KC	CHR	NYT
Arrests	496	46.4	39.5	28.6	29.4	22.4	4.4	5.6	1.8
Interrogations	630	83.2	42.2	2.9	35.1	3.7	0	2.9	0
Trials	236	26.7 (30.9)*	36.4 (63.6)*	41.1 (64.0)*	54.7 (54.7)*	6.8 (34.3)*	5.5 (7.2)*	12.7 (12.7)*	3.4 (3.4)*
Total	1362	818 60.1%	548 40.2%	257 18.9%	496 36.4%	150 11.0%	35 2.6%	76 5.6%	17 1.2%

+Indicates the percentage of events in the file which have been reported by
the source; does not sum to 100% because some events have been reported by
two or more of the sources.

*Includes trials to which the source alludes, but without giving the specific
date.

TABLE   2

COVERAGE FOR 1970-1981 PERIOD

Percentage of total reported+

Event type	N	CCCL	CCE	LIC	ELTA	Vesti	KC	CHR	NYT
Arrests	23	45.3	58.5	30.9	45.8	25.9	8.5	11.0	3.8
Interrogations	617	2.9	42.8	2.9	35.3	3.7	0	2.9	0
Trials	115	42.6 (46.1)*	54.8 (62.6)*	33.9 (54.8)*	61.7 (61.7)*	11.3 (33.0)*	11.3 (14.8)*	23.5 (23.5)*	7.0 (7.0)*

+Indicates the percentage of events in the file which have been reported by
the source; does not sum to 100% because some events have been reported by
two or more of the sources.

*Includes trials to which the source alludes, but without giving the specific
date.

Extensiveness of Coverage

Any consideration of the utility of samizdat must begin with the
amount of coverage of events. If this source ignored most of the
known events, then one would have to look elsewhere for information.
The actual coverage summarized in Tables 1 and 2 suggests that, to

the contrary, samizdat sources (here CCE and CCCL) report on repressive events as well as or better than other kinds of sources.

Table 1 indicates that both samizdat sources reported more arrests and interrogations than any other source. Both exceeded the reported arrests of each of the others by at least 10%, interrogations by at least 7%. This means that the emigre, human rights, and newspaper sources did not consider these events as significant as the samizdat sources did, and thus the former either omitted them or did not seek out information on them. (Emigre sources (ELTA and LIC) were superior on their reportage of trials, but samizdat came in second, covering more trials than any of the remaining four sources.[21])

This pattern of samizdat excellence in coverage is repeated with slight differences if one focusses on events in the recent period (1970–1981, the time frame of this book), as shown in Table 2. The advantage of samizdat in arrests and interrogations is replicated.

One major change is the dramatic improvement in coverage of trials for almost all sources. Here the excellence of samizdat is reinforced: they are surpassed only by ELTA.[22]

The juxtaposition of the last two tables suggests that samizdat sources are among the most comprehensive ones available. More important, most of the events reported in either samizdat or non-samizdat date from the post–1969 period. Despite the arrests and exile of thousands of Lithuanians in the 1940s,[23] only 260 arrests from that period were reported in any source. Thus, *all* sources suffer from underreportage of events less recent. Barghoorn seems correct about this problem of the unknown numbers of political prisoners from this time who may still survive in the prison and psychiatric systems.

Thus, caution ought to be used in the analysis of pre–1970 events, at least on their "scope." That is only common sense given the relative lack of samizdat in that earlier period. One would not reasonably expect the underground writings of the 1970s to be as extensive on events of three decades before when so much current information existed to report. Thus, the analysis of this book has been limited to the post–1968 period.

More generally, one can say that samizdat sources actually surpass most or all other sources in the numbers of repressive events reported, depending on the event, time, and specific source. Certainly, given these figures, it seems somewhat less than just to attack samizdat for being incomplete, for the current period at least. Of course, how accurate and unbiased the reports are is another question.

Quality of Reportage: Bias

There are several kinds of potential bias in samizdat that may be isolated for empirical analysis. They include 1) distortion based in the vulnerability to personal repression of those participating in the production of samizdat, 2) the scantiness of reportage in the earlier stages of the development of informal communications networks, 3) the "noise" of the process of secret and personalistic reporting, and 4) the selection of certain types of events by the editors because of their limited resources and their judgments about the interests of their audiences. Let us examine each of these possible biases.

First, there may be varying coverage over time due to the vulnerability of the compilers and underground "correspondents" of samizdat to arrest and trial for their samizdat activity.[24] During the years when the KGB has targeted CCCL or CCE,[25] and arrested several of those dissidents it connected to those journals, the reportage of the repressive activities might suffer.

If a samizdat journal loses several of its activists without replacement, then the coverage for those years may be expected to deviate from usual patterns in serveral ways. The range between minimum and maximum numbers of repressive events in a year would be lower, as the sweep would pick up "chroniclers" unable to report on their own arrests and trials, much less on the numerous arrests and interrogations taking place while they are under arrest. In addition, there ought to be fewer repressive events overall reported, for the same reason.

Samizdat does not show marked signs of such a bias for either of these posited "vulnerability effects." Simply put, for yearly maxima, CCCL exceeded all the others in arrests and interrogations, and came in tied for second with CCE for trials.

This pattern of greater numerical coverage despite KGB efforts is repeated in the total numbers of events. Once again, for arrests and interrogations, samizdat is unexcelled by other sources; it was superior to all but ELTA for trials. Despite occasional setbacks, samizdat continued to report the greatest number of various events.

The implication of these tests for vulnerability is that repression does not seem to under the *reportage* of samizdat. What must happen is that the lost activists are replaced by new ones or compensated for by higher levels of activity by the remaining dissidents. In either case, the reportage goes on.

A second kind of potential bias is related to the social growth of samizdat communications networks. In the earlier days of the existence of an underground publication even the compilers could not be sure how long the project would last.[26] As a journal survives and people

TABLE 3

VULNERABILITY EFFECTS, 1970-1981

	Source							
	CCCL	CCE	LIC	ELTA	Vesti	KC	CHR	NYT
Maximum number of events in a single year								
Arrests	35	21	21	9	23	7	5	2
Interrogations	106	51	15	42	19	0	13	0
Trials	14	14	12	19	10	6	9	3
Total number of events								
Arrests	107	129	73	67	64	20	16	9
Interrogations	512	264	18	218	23	0	18	0
Trials	49	63	39	71	12	14	26	8

TABLE 4

MATURATION EFFECTS

	Number of events reported by file and samizdat sources					
	File		CCCL		CCE	
	1970-75	1976-81	1970-75	1976-81	1970-75	1976-81
Arrests	89	147	37	70	54	80
Interrogations	252	365	232	280	137	127
Trials	72	43	27	22	41	22

become more familiar with it, more and more individuals send along information for inclusion. Slowly informal channels of communication develop. This pattern of growth has been noted in the geographic widening of reportage, as well as the expansion of coverage to new groups.[27]

For these "maturation effects" to be noticeable as bias, one would expect to find an increasing percentage of known events reported by these sources over the years. A comparision of the first and second halves of the contemporary period in Table 4 reveals a somewhat more complicated pattern than for the previous type of bias. Here there is some, ambiguous evidence of the bias.

For interrogations neither samizdat source has the expected increase in percentage, but for the other two events CCCL has the increase, implying that its networks consolidated and grew. For CCE, the percentages for trials and arrests *fall* somewhat.

Although it is difficult to account for the lack of uniformity for the different events, it is highly unlikely that different networks specializing in different events would exist, for these events frequently co-occur as arrest is followed (or preceded) by interrogation and then trial. Passing along information on the individual's interrogation while omiting information on arrest and trial seems an improbable action for those risking arrest by participation in samizdat. (The decline in the interrogation percentage might be related to the editorial judgment that more significant, more dramatic items deserve higher priority. We will look into this possibility below.)

What can be said is that for trials and arrests, there are clear signs of the "maturation" of social communications in the particularist CCCL, where bonds of social solidarity are likely to be strongest (among co-religionists and others of one's ethnic group). For the more general CCE, there are no such signs.[28]

The maturation effects of CCCL indicate that the reportage of repressive events in the first several issues of a new specialized journal is likely to be less complete than in later issues. Thus, just as the overall figures in the first section on coverage implied caution in using data from before the 1970s, the maturation bias confirms that some care should be taken with these earlier samizdat reports. Certainly one would want to cross-check those reports with other sources, an option mentioned above, and used for this book.

A third basis for bias may be rooted in the distortions and inaccuracies engendered by the secretive and personalistic process of samizdat production and dissemination. Late hours, fatigue, and partially illegible carbon copies to be retyped may yield typographical errors and thus contradictory reports of events. This process has been noted by several authors, including those personally involved in samizdat.[29] Also because of limited time and energy, and the potential costs of delay (a sudden knock at the door may prevent the information from getting out via the issue being produced), less important or less severe cases might be dropped entirely, resulting in fewer cases each marked by higher degrees of repression.

Thus, one would expect two different features in the data because of such biases. Neither is present, as is shown in Table 5. The "error rate" or percentage of incorrect reports[30] is *not* higher for samizdat. Indeed, except for the *New York Times*—which had so few reports to begin with— they had the lowest rate. The conclusion can only be that those working in the reproduction of samizdat are aware of the problem[31] and wish to overcome it because of the understood importance of an accurate record. This would lead to a high degree of care, "overcompensating" for fatigue and the noise of poor copies.[32]

There is also no particular bias due to limited resources leading to selectivity. One would expect to find that there would be some selectivity in reportage by degree of drama: the more repressive events

TABLE 5

INCORRECT DATES REPORTED

Event type	CCCL N of errors	CCCL % of total	CCE N of errors	CCE % of total	LIC N of errors	LIC % of total	ELTA N of errors	ELTA % of total	VestI N of errors	VestI % of total	KC N of errors	KC % of total	CHR N of errors	CHR % of total	NYT N of errors	NYT % of total
Arrests	3	1.3	4	4.7	5	3.5	11	7.5	5	4.5	2	9.1	2	7.1	0	0.0
Interrogations	0	0.0	0	0.0	0	0.0	0	0.0	0	0.0	0	0.0	0	0.0	0	0.0
Trials	1	1.5	5	2.6	5	5.2	13	10.1	2	12.5	1	7.7	1	3.3	0	0.0
Total	4	0.5	9	1.6	10	3.9	24	4.8	7	4.7	3	8.6	3	3.9	0	0.0

Source

TABLE 6

AVERAGE SENTENCES, BY SOURCE
(1970-1981)

	Source							
	CCCL	CCE	LIC	ELTA	Vesti	KC	CHR	NYT
Average of yearly average sentences								
Camp	1.9	3.6	6.6	3.4	5.6	2.5	2.1	0.9
Exile	0.1	0.2	0.2	0.7	1.3	1.1	0.7	0.0
Individual average sentence								
Camp	2.4	4.1	5.7	3.5	6.3	4.1	3.1	5.8
Exile	0.7	0.4	0.8	0.7	1.5	1.8	1.1	0.0

being reported more than the lesser ones. Thus, trials ought to be reported more frequently in samizdat than arrests, and arrests more than interrogations, and trials with higher sentences more than trials with lower sentences.

Referring back to Table 3, we can see that samizdat sources have more trials overall than almost all other sources. The samizdat sources did not drop less significant cases. Also, they reported more arrests and interrogations, although these events are less dramatic than trials with their nearly-inevitable camp sentences.

Table 6 shows that samizdat sources do not skip those trials with lesser sentences. The average yearly camp sentence reported by CCCL is the second *lowest*, and that by CCE is the sixth lowest. Likewise, for individual sentences over the entire 1970–1981 period, CCCL yields the lowest camp average, with CCE in fourth place. In other words, it is the other sources, not samizdat, that drop the cases with lesser sentences.

The fourth kind of bias is based on selectivity of a different kind. There may be distortion rooted in the probable "audience" of samizdat.[33] The compilers may make decisions to report on some events and exclude others because of their perceptions of what might interest their readers. This may take the form of one of three patterns. First, editors may select trials with charges carrying greater potential punishment or with explicitly political aims, more than trials held on other articles of the criminal code. Second, the religious-oriented CCCL may feature more trials on the articles restricting the practice of religion than other sources would.[34] Third, CCCL may report on fewer events concerning non-Catholic dissidents than do other sources.

The first two "audience effects" are examined in Table 7. For the first, political charges, one can note that CCCL did report a higher percentage of "anti-Soviet agitation" trials than did the overall file, but no more so than most of the other sources. For the other major

TABLE 7

AUDIENCE EFFECTS: TRIALS ON VARIOUS ARTICLES

AS REPORTED BY SOURCES

	File	CCCL	CCE	LIC	ELTA	Vesti	KC	CHR	NYT
						Source			
Article 70									
Number	33	20	19	21	17	19	12	8	0
% of total trials	38.8	47.6*	38.8	35.0	44.7*	43.2*	80.0*	34.8	0.0
Article 190									
Number	13	7	18	8	8	7	2	6	0
% of total trials	15.3	16.7*	36.7*	13.3	23.3*	15.9*	13.3	26.1*	0.0
Both 70 and 190									
Number	46	27	37	29	25	26	14	14	0
% of total trials	54.1	64.3*	75.5*	48.8	65.8*	59.1*	93.3*	60.9*	0.0
Article 142									
Number	11	4	0	1	4	0	0	5	0
% of total trials	12.9	9.5	0.0	1.7	10.5	0	0	21.7*	0.0
Article 227									
Number	2	0	0	0	0	1	1	0	0
% of total trials	2.4	0.0	0.0	0.0	0.0	2.3	6.7*	0.0	0.0
Both 142 and 227									
Number	13	4	0	1	4	1	1	5	0
% of total trials	15.3	9.5	0.0	1.7	10.5	2.3	6.7	21.7*	0.0

*Indicates percentage higher than in the overall file.

political article, "slander of the state," CCCL reported about the same percentage as the file, while CCE (and several other sources) exceeded that to some degree. For both articles together, samizdat *and* almost all non-samizdat sources exceeded those of the file. (Indeed, the most "selection by political article" seems to be by Keston College, with 93.3% of its trials falling into this category.) Thus, editorial selection based on audience interest in more dramatic articles does seem to exist but it is not substantially greater than in non-samizdat sources.

The anti-religious articles of the criminal code do not bias the two samizdat sources at all. As may be seen in the bottom part of Table 7, the samizdat sources actually underreport these articles. This may seem surprising for CCCL, but some of the gap can be explained by the third pattern, the underreportage of non-Catholics, namely Jehovah's Witnesses, who are subject to the anti-religious articles as much or more than Catholics.

There is a clear bias in CCCL here. It is difficult to determine precisely the religion of many dissidents, but from time to time some explicit identification by label or behavior can be made of many others. For the entire file, there were only 16 obvious non-Catholics— 10 Jehovah's Witnesses, 3 Protestants, and 3 Jews. A total of 9 arrests,

13 trials, and 2 interrogations involved them in the 1970–1981 period. CCCL reported on *none* of these individuals and on *none* of these events.

This bias of CCCL does not necessarily indicate any prejudice against non-Catholics. A simple perusal of some issues shows that, instead, the concern for Catholic matters simply allows for less attention to non-Catholics. It must be kept in mind that these excluded individuals and events comprise a small part of the overall file: 1.9% of the individuals, 3.8% of the arrests, 0.3% of the interrogations, and 11.3% of the trials. Also, the overwhelming majority of the Lithuanian population is Catholic. Nonetheless, the proselytizing Jehovah's Witnesses have been tried and sentenced to imprisonment for "violating the rights of non-believers" and ignoring the "separation of church and state" more than Catholics have.

Thus, of the four kinds of bias, our tests have discovered only some signs of maturation and audience distortions for CCCL. These biases do not seem to exist in great degree. In any case, as Scolnick correctly states,

> Perfect and complete reporting is an ideal and it is unrealistic to expect perfection from any source . . . . A researcher should be alert to the possible variety of errors in different sources and should take them into account when deciding what to use as his sources . . . .[35]

To take the maturation and audience biases into account involves assessing the degree to which they interfere with obtaining acceptable findings. It remains to be demonstrated that these biases do not constitute major obstacles to empirical analysis.

Quality of Reportage: Representativeness of Findings

In the international relations literature on the "validity" of sources of event data, the approach to the question of usefulness of sources has moved beyond coverage and bias to a research-based knot of questions on how to *use* sources. Whether one, two, or many sources ought to be used in testing hypotheses is the underlying problem. The answer varies with the investigator, his research questions, and his criteria.

To use more than one source can be expensive in time and energy, and is potentially wasteful in a research climate of increasingly scarce resources. Using many different statistical techniques and kinds of sources (often including *The New York Times* specifically), scholars

TABLE 8

CORRELATIONS WITH FILE FINDINGS OF
YEARLY AGGREGATES, 1970-1981

Source

Item	CCCL	CCE	LIC	ELTA	Vesti	KC	CHR	NYT	CL+CE
Arrests	.796	.906*	.822	.356	.790	.777	.082	.198	.962
Interrogations	.964*	.644	.184	.876	.595	.000	.432	.000	.989
Trials	.979*	.425	.782	.785	.469	.345	.513	.232	.780
Camp terms	.408	.859*	.362	.759	.663	-.058	.356	.640	.800
Exile terms	.226	.456	.588	.899	.369*	.564	.913	.000	.722
% Article 70	.523	.652	.352	.519	.541	.590	.720*	.000	.681
% Article 190.1-3	.830*	.544	.823	.553	.750	.007	.162	.000	.948

*Highest correlation for this item by a single source

assessing the representativeness of their sources ("validity") have in recent years analyzed the usefulness of the *findings* derived from them.

Following this latest approach, we will examine one type of finding—yearly figures derived from each source—and compare them to the totals produced by the overall file. We will thus establish each source's relative accuracy, with the file itself as the base-line. The yearly figures include the totals for each type of event, averages for length of labor camp sentences and exile sentences, and percentages of trials on charges of violations of articles 70 and 190.1–190.3, some of the major political "crimes."

The yearly totals will be used because one aspect of repressive activity, timing, is of great potential interest, as we saw in chapter 7. Thus, we will look at the statistical "fit" of the yearly pattern from 1970–1981 found in each source to the pattern of the overall file.

The most common statistic used in social science to indicate the "tightness" of such a fit is the correlation coefficient (Pearson's r). This number tells us how close the set of numbers from the individual source is to that of the underlying pattern. In other words, the correlation indicates the correspondence between each year's totals in source and overall file. (This correlation itself does not suggest the possible numerical direction over time of either source reports or the file's. That possible mathematical relationship is a separate, substantive question discussed in chapter 7.)

Table 8 shows the correlations of the sources' figures on number of events and other variables to the file. Samizdat sources once again prove to be good on the relative changes over time in the number of events. Within CCCL, the fit is closest for interrogations and trials despite the problems discussed in earlier sections, coverage (the relative incompleteness in trial reportage) and bias (maturation for trials and slight audience effects in favor of Catholics). Within CCE the fit is best for arrests, despite its lower coverage of such events. Thus, for the patterns of occurrences over time, the two samizdat sources taken separately for individual events would come the closest to predicting the underlying changes.

The story is mixed in the more qualitative trial-related measures, where samizdat outperforms non-samizdat on only two of four variables. For the yearly reports of the relative importance of the political articles, CCCL does fit well on articles 190.1–190.3, while CCE does well on article 70 (although bested by CHR). On average camp sentences, CCE achieves the highest correlation of any source (CCCL is fifth). However, on exile terms neither samizdat sources does well, ranking fifth and seventh.

These relative poor correlations on exile terms are related to two facts. First, samizdat has a weaker coverage of trials. The missing-data problem is not all that serious when considering the number of occurrences; the event is either known or missing. Even if a substantial proportion of cases are missing, the distribution may reflect the underlying pattern if those missing cases are spread over the time period forming a "random error." The effect of missing data is greater for variables which are *averages*, such as the exile term. If in a given year the highest term is missing, the average of the known terms will be lower than the real average; in another year, the lowest term being missing would artificially inflate the average. This problem is exacerbated by the second fact, the small number of exile terms (13). Many years had only 1 or 2 such terms and the absence of a report is particularly grievous then.

Thus, for occurrences of events, samizdat did much better than any other source, but they were less accurate in figures related to particular dimensions of trials. Even so, samizdat did perform well on two of four variables related to those dimensions.

Enhancing Representativeness: Using Multiple Sources

The previous sections suggest that while samizdat produces good results for some variables, other sources are better for other variables. In addition, Table 8 indicated that almost every source could make an appropriate prediction (a correlation of .50 or better) for at least one variable. However, the best source differed from one variable to

Appendix

TABLE 9

REPRESENTATIVENESS OF FINDINGS

FOR SELECTED COMBINATIONS OF SOURCES*

Item	CCE	CCCL +CCE	CCE +ELTA	CCE +Vesti	CCCL +CCE +ELTA	CCCL +CCE +Vesti	CCCL +CCE +V+E
Arrests	.906	.962	.918	.927	.972	.949	.970
Interrogations	.644	.989	.811	.770	.993	.992	.995
Trials	.425	.780	.815	.766	.788	.792	.803
Camp terms	.859	.800	.878	.850	.805	.734	.742
Exile terms	.456	.722	.464	.458	.684	.414	.414
Article 70	.652	.681	.659	.700	.687	.680	.680
Articles 190.1-3	.544	.948	.770	.531	.947	.948	.948

*Correlations as in Table 8.

the next. Without the kind of intensive analysis herein undertaken, one would not know which sources provide the highest correlation for which variable. This is especially an obstacle if the researcher is interested in more than one variable. However, it is not insurmountable: the judicious selection of the two best sources taken together could provide an acceptable file to analyze, as we shall now see.

Table 9 shows the correlations on occurrence and dimension figures for various combinations of sources. One might reasonably start with the general CCE, given its availability and broad coverage. If a specialized samizdat source like CCCL is added, the fit for both occurrences and qualitative dimensions is excellent, from .68 to .99.

Interestingly, these correlations are *not* markedly improved by the addition of either the best emigre source, ELTA, or the best human rights source, *Vesti*. Thus, for those studying other groups it seems likely that the costs of adding several more sources would likely outweigh the benefits of the marginal increase of such correlations. Of course, for this book all the data had already been collected and the marginal costs had thus been "paid."

What about researchers interested in groups without a continuing, specialized samizdat source, like Armenians or Estonians? All is not lost. Table 9 also shows that the addition of either an emigre source (here ELTA) or a human rights source (like *Vesti*) does improve the fit over CCE alone, even if the correlations are not as high as those produced by tandem samizdat research. For all variables but exile terms, the fit is good for CCE-ELTA and CCE-*Vesti* (this latter also is a bit weak on articles 190.1–190.3).

Conclusion

Repressive data of a representative nature on a specific dissident group in the USSR in the 1970–1981 period could be obtained by simple recourse to the *Chronicles of Current Events* plus *one* of the following: a specialized journal concentrating on the group; the reports of a major emigre organization associated with that group; or the records of a human rights organization particularly concerned with the USSR. This possibility is of major importance to those doing research on dissent and repression, for it means that time and money can be efficiently used while still obtaining meaningful quantitative data by mining only two sources, including one readily available at major university libraries (CCE).

The single-v.-multiple source controversy can be resolved by noting the correctness of both sides. Some individual sources can be used along for single variables; however, combinations of variables require two sources, CCE plus one other.

One might wish to go beyond these two for other reasons, of course. The number of cases yielded by the two source might be too small for more complex analyses. "Too many empty cells" is the bane of those working with small data-sets. More sources would yield more cases. (Thus, even using all the sources for this book, I found it frustrating that the analysis of variance, multiple linear regression, and other statistical techniques could not conveniently be used.)

Moreover, one might wish to collect information on all known cases for non-statistical reasons. The exact names and numbers of dissidents might be needed for the preparation of human rights initiatives.

If the limitations of coverage, bias, and representativeness ofthe data are kept in mind, data collected from samizdat sources can prove fruitful substantively. This book is evidence of the usefulness of such data.

Notes

1. Joshua Rubenstein, "The Enduring Voice of the Soviet Dissidents," *Columbia Journalism Review*, 27(3) (1978): 32–39; Cornelia Gerstenmeier, *The Voices of the Silent* (New York: Hart Publishing Company, 1972); and others

fall into the first category. Ludmilla Alexeyeva, "The Human Rights Movement in the USSR," *Survey*, 23(4) (1977–1978): 72–85; David Kowalewski, "Lithuanian Protest for Human Rights in the 1970s: Characteristics and Consequences," *Lituanas*, 25(2) (1979): 43–57; and Ludmilla Thorne, "Three Years of Repression in the USSR: A Statistical Study," *Freedom Appeals*, 9 (1981): 29–31, fall into the latter.

2. David Kowalewski, "The Protest Uses of Symbolic Politics in the USSR," *The Journal of Politics*, 42(1980): 439–460, is one of the rare exceptions to the rule of quite simple use of additive totals of varying kinds.

3. A shorter, somewhat different version of this appendix has appeared in *Soviet Studies* (January 1985). That article is solely devoted to bias, whereas here problems of coverage are also examined.

4. Louise Shelley, "Crime and Delinquency in the Soviet Union," in Jerry G. Pankhurst and Michael Paul Sacks, ed., *Contemporary Soviet Society* (New York: Praeger, 1980); Walter D. Connor, *Deviance in Soviet Society* (New York: Columbia University Press, 1972).

5. These official internal Soviet documents were brought to the West surreptitiously during the 1940s as unintended spoils of the war. The most thorough, yet greatly incomplete use of these documents is to be found in Merle Fainsod, *Smolensk under Soviet Rule* (New York: Vintage, 1958).

6. Rudolf L. Tokes, "Varieties of Soviet Dissent: An Overview," in his edited *Dissent in the USSR* (Baltimore: Johns Hopkins University Press, 1975), p. 9, fn.7.

7. Frederick Barghoorn, "The Post-Khrushchev Campaign to Suppress Dissent," in Tokes, p. 85; and *Detente and the Democratic Movement in the USSR* (New York: Free Press, 1976), p. 125.

8. David Kowalewski, "Protest Demonstrations in the Brezhnev Era," paper presented to the Annual Meeting of the American Association for the Advancement of Slavic Studies, (Philadelphia, 1980), p. 2.

9. See, among others, Edward A. Azar, "The Analysis of International Events," *Peace Research Reviews*, 4(1) (1970); Azar and others, "The Problem of Source Coverage in the Use of International Events," *Insternational Studies Quarterly*, 16 (1972): 373–388; Philip M. Burgess and Raymond W. Lawton, *Indicators of International Behavior: An Assessment of Events Data Research* (Beverly Hills: Sage, 1972); Charles W. Kegley, Jr., and others, *International Events and the Comparative Analysis of Foreign Policy* (Columbia, SC: University of South Carolina Press, 1975); Don Munton, ed., *Measuring International Behavior: Public Sources, Events, and Validity* (Halifax, Canada: Centre for Foreign Policy Studies, Dalhousie University, 1978).

10. Joseph M. Scolnick, Jr., "An Appraisal of Studies of the Linkage between Domestic and International Conflict," *Comparative Political Studies*, 6 (4)(1974): 485–509; Robert W. Jackman and William A. Boyd, "Multiple Sources in the Collection of Data on Political Conflict," *American Journal of Political Science*, 23 (2)(1979): 434–458.

11. R. Burrowes and B. Spector, "Conflict and Cooperation within and among Nations," paper presented to the annual meeting of the International Studies Association (1970), p. 11.

12. The title is sometimes translated as *Chronicles of the Lithuanian Catholic Church*. I have chosen to use the version of the major translating and publishing body mentioned above.

13. See CCCL 51: 19–21; and Richard J. Krickus, "Hostages in Their Homeland," *Commonweal*, 107(3)(1980): 78–79.

14. For summaries of other Lithuanian samizdat,see V. Stanley Vardys, "Lithuania's Catholic Movement Reappraised," *Survey*, 25(3) (1980): 66–69; and "The Underground Periodicals in Lithuania," ELTA, 261 (1981): 9–13.

15. Rubenstein, pp. 37–38.

16. Paul Wasserman and Jean Morgan, ed., *Ethnic Information Sources of the United States* (Detroit: Gale Research Company, 1976), pp. 417–418; Stephan Thernstrom, ed., *Harvard Encyclopedia of American Ethnic Groups* (Boston: Harvard University Press, 1980), pp. 674–675.

17. Thernstrom, pp. 671–674.

18. Michael Bourdeaux and Michael Rowe, *May One Believe—In Russia?* (London: Darton, Longman and Todd, 1980), for example.

19. For the last few years, the publisher has been Das Land und Die Welt, in Munich.

20. Scolnick, p. 491.

21. Indeed, if one includes *implied* trials (reports of arrest dates with specific prison sentences), then one of the two samizdat (CCE) is nearly identical to the best emigre source (LIC), at 63.6% and 64.0% respectively. Thus, even for trials samizdat is among the best available.

22. Again, if implied trials are included, CCE virtually ties ELTA.

23. Vardys, *The Catholic Church, Dissent and Nationality in Soviet Lithuania* (Boulder: East European Quarter, 1978), pp. 45–51, 60.

24. Peter Reddaway, "The Development of Dissent and Opposition," in Archie Brown and Michael Kaser, ed., *The Soviet Union since the Fall of Khrushchev* (New York: Macmillan, 1975), p. 147; CCCL 51: 19–22.

25. Tomas Venclova, "The Chronicles of the Lithuanian Catholic Church," *Chronicles of Human Rights in the USSR*, 30(1978): 39; Vardys, "Lithuania's Catholic Movement Reappraised," p. 62; Rubenstein, op. cit.

26. CCCL editors anticipated only about 12 issues before imprisonment. See CCCL 51: 23.

27. Alexeyeva, "The Tenth Anniversary of a Chronicle of Current Events," CHR 29(1978): 58–62; Venclova, p. 39–40; CCCL 51: 19.

28. The relative deterioration of percentage for CCE may well have been an artifact of the increasing reportage from other areas, i.e., the maturation effects of *other* groups' samizdat networks, something that cannot be dealt with here.

29. For example, Julius Telesin, "Inside 'Samizdat,'" *Encounter* 40(2) (1973): 25–33; Rubenstein, op. cit.; CCE 7 as reported in Peter Reddaway, ed., *Uncensored Russia* (New York: American Heritage Press, 1972), pp. 58–59; CCCL 51: 19, 23.

30. "Incorrect" reports are contradicted by other sources. They are in practice easily determined to be incorrect by the number, detail, and currentness

of the reports contradicting them. Of course, this particular method of measuring such error does understate it: an objectively incorrect report found only once in all the sources cannot be so labelled. There is no solution to this underestimation.

31. CCCL 51: 23.

32. Note that a somewhat different "cost effect" of secrecy is that of KGB "disinformation," as noted by Tokes, "Varieties," pp. 9–10. A likely sign of that effect would be high error rates for samizdat sources because KGB disinformation would have as its goal the confusion and discrediting of these sources in the eyes of their audiences. Structurally, the posited effects on this data-set are no different from the cost effects of fatigue and noise.

33. See Sophia Peterson, "News Selection and Source Validity," in Munton, pp. 43–66, on such effects in Western newspaper coverage.

34. Vardys, *The Catholic Church,* pp 57–58 and 65–66; and Venclova, pp. 39–40, argue the opposite, however.

35. Scolnick, p. 493.

Topical Index

Index of Names

Abrutiene, E. 161, 168, 173 (fn. 14)
Afghanistan 11, 54, 156, 162, 172 (fn. 2)
Alexeyeva, L. 143, 145, 156, 162
Amalrik, A. 84, 87
Andreika, A. 157, 168
Andropov, Yu. 86, 155, 156, 158, 160, 161, 163, 173 (fn. 7)
Ausra 30 (fn. 30), 57, 66 (fn. 53), 167, 173 (fn. 12)

Barghoorn, F. 122, 132, 193, 199
Bashkiria 94 (fn. 91), 175 (fn. 33)
Berman, H. 7
Bialer, S. 13
Biciusaite, K. 76
Beilauskiene, J. 157, 159
Bielauskas 168
Bitvinskas, Fr. A. 173 (fn. 8)
Bonner, E. 155
Breslauer, G. 141, 142
Brezhnev, L. 3, 27, 50, 79, 86, 140–144, 148, 150, 152 (fn. 8), 155, 156, 158, 170, 181, 183, 189
Briliute, B. 169
Brzezinski, Z. 3, 186–190
Bubnys, Fr. P. 50, 146, 158
Bukharin, N. 163
Bulachas, E. 158
Bumbulis, Fr. A. 174 (fn. 15)
Buzas 90 (fn. 24)

CCCL (Chronicles of the Catholic Church in Lithuania) 37, 39, 40, 41, 51, 67 (fn. 61), 105, 146, 160, 161, 166, 195–197, 199–202, 204–206, 208, 209

CCE (Chronicles of Current Events) 37, 39, 196, 197, 199–202, 204, 205, 208–210
Cerniauskas, Fr. R. 157
Chalidze, V. 197
Chebrikov, V. 158
Chernenko, K. 155, 156, 160, 162, 163, 170, 173 (fn. 7), 174 (fn. 21)
Chernobyl 163
CHR (Chronicles of Human Rights in the USSR) 39, 197, 208
Comintern 15
Cox, E. 44, 95 (fn. 34)

d'Encausse, H. 13
Dagys, S. 168
Dambrauskas, L. 161, 168
Daniel, Yu. 22, 144
Dubcek, A. 184, 196
Dziaugis, A. 29 (fn. 9)

ELTA 38, 196, 199, 200, 209
Eucharist Society, Friends of 51

Fedorchuk, V. 21, 95, 158
Fitzpatrick, C. 165
Friedrich, C. 3

Gajauskas, B. 169
Gavenaite, M. 158
Gorbachev, M. 155, 162–166, 168–172, 174 (fn. 21), 175 (fn. 31), 181, 185, 187
Gorky 155
Gouldner, A. 44
Grazulis, Fr. A. 174 (fn. 16)

THE
BOY in the BOX

MASTER MELVILLE'S MEDICINE SHOW

BY CARY FAGAN

❋ CLARION BOOKS ❋
HOUGHTON MIFFLIN HARCOURT
BOSTON · NEW YORK · 2012

For the whole house—Rebecca, Rachel,
Emilio, Sophie, and Yoyo

Clarion Books
215 Park Avenue South
New York, New York 10003

Text copyright © 2012 by Cary Fagan
Illustrations copyright © 2012 by Erwin Madrid

The text in this book was set in Pastonchi.
The illustrations were executed digitally.

Clarion Books is an imprint of Houghton Mifflin Harcourt Publishing Company.

www.hmhbooks.com

Library of Congress Cataloging-in-Publication Data
Fagan, Cary.
The boy in the box / by Cary Fagan.
p. cm.—(Master Melville's Medicine Show ; bk. 1)
Summary: A misfit boy finds an unexpected second life
after being kidnapped by a colorful traveling medicine show.
ISBN 978-0-547-75268-6 (hardback)
[1. Juggling—Fiction. 2. Kidnapping—Fiction. 3. Medicine shows—Fiction.] I. Title.
PZ7.F135Boy 2012
[Fic]—dc23   2011049590
Manufactured in the United States of America
DOC 10 9 8 7 6 5 4 3 2 1
4500378468

Contents

WHICH IS A MORE SHAMEFUL CALLING,
TO BE A JUGGLER OR A THIEF?

⤲ Old saying ⤳

THE HALF-CASCADE

F^{or} OR the first time in his life, Sullivan Mintz, standing in his underwear, was doing a half-cascade with *four*
balls. He was trying not to become so excited that he
would overthrow a ball, or look down at his hands, or
make any of the million tiny moves that would throw
him off.

The half-cascade is the classic pattern of juggling,
the balls crossing one another as they rise up and fall
again into the juggler's hands before being thrown once
more. It is an elegant sight when done well, the juggler

appearing to move as effortlessly as if he were raising a glass of water to his lips.

The truth is, just about anyone who works at it can learn to do a half-cascade with three balls. Kids, middle-aged men, grandmothers. But four balls — that's something else entirely, a whole new level of difficulty. It takes a leap of courage and coordination, not to mention speed. It takes far more practice — weeks, sometimes months. But done well, it looks not only elegant, but wondrous.

Sullivan had started juggling six months ago, but it was only in the last five weeks that he had attempted four balls. And until this moment, Sullivan had messed up every time. Yet he had persisted, obsessively practicing before school, after school, at bedtime, any chance he got. He took his soft juggling balls to school and practiced at lunch, in an empty classroom where nobody would see him. Even when he wasn't practicing, it felt as if he were, the balls rising and falling in his mind, his fingers opening and closing the way people sometimes moved their lips silently when they read.

Five weeks. Five weeks, every chance he got. And now he had it.

Sullivan, who was eleven years and seven months old, was once called by a teacher "the most average kid I've ever known." And it was true that his grades were

average across the board, his height was average, even his hair color was somewhere between blond and brown. The remark had been made to another teacher, but Sullivan and several other students had overheard, including a beefy kid named Samuel Patinsky, who was always on the lookout for somebody to torment. From that day forward, Samuel had started calling Sullivan "Mr. Average." Sullivan despised the nickname, but he didn't see what he could do about it. His friend Norval had suggested that he call Samuel Patinsky "Mr. Below Average." But Sullivan had no desire to get punched in the face.

He had taken up juggling on the advice of Manny Morgenstern, one of the oldest residents of the Stardust Home for Old People. Manny was eighty-one. He had suggested juggling one afternoon when Sullivan was feeling pretty unhappy about just about everything. Like having only one friend at school. And being taunted by Samuel Patinsky. And having the kinds of chores that other kids didn't have. And having a mother who was known by the embarrassing title of the Bard of Beanfield. And having a little sister who everyone thought was adorable when, in fact, she was the slimiest, most scheming creature alive.

Manny might have suggested all kinds of things, such as learning guitar or taking karate lessons. He was trying to think of something that would improve

Sullivan's coordination and perhaps give him some confidence. And that wouldn't cost his parents, whose business was having what is politely called a cash flow problem, very much money. But juggling just seemed right.

"Once you start," Manny had said, "you'll want to juggle all the time. Your parents are going to have to tell you to stop. You're going to drive everybody crazy."

"I really don't think so," said Sullivan. Manny, who was very thin and always wore a suit and tie and stood remarkably straight despite his age, had been standing in Sullivan's doorway. He still had his hair, which was now the color of ivory, and a little goatee — an empire, Manny called it. Sullivan had been sitting on the end of his bed, sulking. Having an eighty-one-year-old man as your friend was kind of neat, but having him as your closest friend wasn't neat. It was pathetic.

"Juggling would be just about the dorkiest thing I could do," Sullivan had said. "It would be like wearing a sign that said YES, I REALLY AM THAT BIG A LOSER. Besides, I'd be terrible at it. All I'd manage to do is drop things on my head."

And yet here he was, keeping four balls in the air at once. (Or so it looked. The balls were never actually all in the air at the same moment. There was always one in his hand, just caught or about to be thrown.)

"Sullivan!" came a voice from behind him. "I've already called three times. Now, please come for dinner."

The sound of his dad speaking made Sullivan miss a ball. The others rained down around him. Entering the room, his dad sighed as he helped pick them up. "Juggling again? Having a hobby is one thing, Sullivan. But having a hobby that interferes with your chores is another. You're keeping forty-eight hungry people waiting."

"Sorry, Dad. I guess I didn't hear you."

"And, Sullivan, put on some pants."

Sullivan placed the balls in the bottom drawer of his dresser. It used to be his sweater drawer, but he had moved the sweaters up one, cramming them in with his shirts. Now the drawer held all his juggling stuff—larger and smaller balls, clubs, plates, and in-structional books. On his walls he had posters, not of baseball players or bands or movie stars, but of great jugglers of the past. There was Salerno, whose real name was Adolf Behrend and who was known as the "gentleman juggler" for dressing in tails and using hats and canes. There was Enrico Rastelli, maybe the great-est juggler of all time, who was known to practice con-stantly for the sheer love of it. There was the American Bobby May, who used comedy and was famous for his returning-bounce ball tricks. Sullivan even had a poster

of ancient Egyptians juggling, from a painting inside a tomb. None of them had been easy to find. It wasn't as if you could walk into a poster shop and ask for the juggling section. He'd saved his small allowance and then ordered them from acrobatic supply companies that he found using the Internet at the public library.

Sullivan pushed the drawer closed and pulled on his cotton pants (his parents didn't like him to wear jeans at dinner). He was about to leave his room when something caught his eye through the window.

Sullivan moved over to it, put his hands on the sill, and leaned forward. There was something unusual moving down the street. It was dusk and the streetlights hadn't gone on yet, but in the gloom, moving past the worn-down houses on the other side, he could see a wagon. That would have been strange even if it wasn't being pulled by a horse. And it wasn't a wagon exactly, thought Sullivan. It was something else. A caravan. Yes, that was the word. An old-fashioned wooden caravan, the likes of which he'd never seen before except maybe in pictures in some book.

The caravan had large wheels that turned slowly as the horse pulled it along. There was a sort of ornate carving around the top and sides. It looked like it belonged in the time of western cowboy movies or in Victorian London. On the side, painted in fancy lettering,

were the words *Master Melville's Medicine Show*. And under the arc of words was a picture of a narrow glass bottle with a stopper in it. Around the bottle were stars and lightning bolts.

It was only after he read the words that Sullivan noticed the figure on a seat at the front of the caravan, holding the horse's reins. The figure was hunched over and wore a big coat and a stovepipe hat. The face was hard to make out in the gloom, but Sullivan thought he saw a mustache and beard. There may have been somebody seated on the man's other side — he couldn't be sure.

The sight of the horse and driver and caravan was so strange that Sullivan felt as if he were looking backwards through time. But as he watched it pull out of sight, he heard another of his father's exasperated calls, and the spell was broken. He ran out of the room.

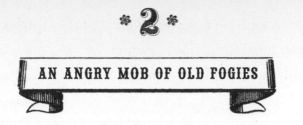

AN ANGRY MOB OF OLD FOGIES

SULLIVAN and his family lived on the top floor of a three-story house on the outskirts of the town of Beanfield. The other two floors made up the Stardust Home for Old People. To get to the dining room of the Stardust Home, Sullivan had to run along the hall and down two flights of stairs that creaked underfoot.

"Hurry up, Sullivan," said his mom. "Grab a tray." She rushed by, putting down hot dishes of breaded sole and cooked carrots and rice. A lot of the residents could eat only soft food, so most of the meals his

father cooked—or rather, overcooked—were mushy. Sullivan hurried into the kitchen to load up a tray of his own. As he came out again, he saw a sheet of paper tacked to the bulletin board. He knew right away that his mother had written another poem. She wrote lots of poems, sometimes two or three a day, and she left them tacked on the board, or taped above the toilet in the bathroom, or pinned to a door. Once a week the local paper published one of her poems under the heading *The Bard of Beanfield*. But the residents of the Stardust Home were his mom's most devoted readers. Sullivan stopped a moment to read her latest.

> *I'll tell you then, I'll tell you now,*
> *of all the beasts, I love the cow.*
> *With eyes so pretty and breath so sweet,*
> *she gives us both our milk and meat.*
>
> *But I do feel bad, I must admit,*
> *when into a burger I have bit*
> *and I think I hear a call—but who?*
> *Could it be the sound of "moo"?*

No wonder they were having fish tonight. His tray loaded, Sullivan headed into the dining room. There were eight round tables covered in white cloths, each

with six people—six white-haired or bald, liver-spotted people, some with trembling hands, others with watery eyes or shifting dentures—waiting for their dinner. It used to surprise Sullivan how eager old people were to get their dinner, even if they never ate very much, but by now he was used to it.

Sullivan went straight to table number seven, where Manny Morgenstern was talking to Elsa Fargo and Rita Cooley, two widowed sisters who always sat on either side of him.

"It's true. I really was a professional boxer," Manny was saying. "Of course, this was sixty years ago. My job was to lose and make my opponent look good. Which I was happy to do. Except for this one fight. You see, the five Trepovsky sisters came to see me. And I didn't want to look bad in front of them, because naturally, I was in love."

"But which of the Trepovsky sisters were you in love with?" asked Elsa.

"I can't remember. It was either sister number three or sister number five. My opponent was Hank 'the Crusher' Hopster and he looked like a gorilla, only he was hairier and uglier. I knew that my only chance was to surprise him with a knockout blow."

"And did you?" asked Rita breathlessly. "Did you knock him out?"

"I guess I wasn't as in love as I thought. I took one look at the Crusher, jumped over the rope, and ran out of the gym. I never boxed again. Instead, I got a job on a riverboat. Oh, Sullivan! I haven't seen you all day. What have you been working on?"

"Four balls," Sullivan said, putting down their plates.

"And?"

"Kept them up for twenty throws."

"Brilliant. You'd better keep serving or you'll have an angry mob of old fogies after you. Now, Elsa, Rita, did I ever tell you about the time I lived in Come By Chance, Newfoundland, testing rubber boots?"

Sullivan served two more tables and then sat down with his mother, his father (who was just taking off his apron), and his little sister, Jinny. "So how was school today?" his mom asked.

"Super great," said Jinny, who was only in first grade. "I made up a poem, just like you do. It's about a frog. Want to hear it?"

"No," said Sullivan. Jinny was always getting attention from their parents. It wasn't as if Sullivan wanted to be the center of attention, but still, it was annoying as anything. Now she was just sucking up to his poetry-loving mom.

"Of course we do. Go ahead," his mother said.

Jinny put her hands together and made her face look serious. She recited:

A frog is the special-est thing in the world.
More than a brother, a nail, or a bird.
All the frogs love me, it really is true.
But not brothers, because they smell like—

"Now that's enough, Jinny," his dad interrupted.

But Jinny insisted on shouting the last word out.

"*Glue!*"

"Did anyone ever tell you that you're a genius, Jinny?" asked Sullivan. "Because if they did, they were lying."

His dad sighed. "Can we have some peace at the table, please? Otherwise I'll never be able to digest my food."

Sullivan's parents, Gilbert and Loretta, had been the managers of the Stardust Home for eight months. Before that they had run a diner, an old movie theater, a hair salon, and a beadery, and each time they had gone bankrupt. "Not," Sullivan's dad once admitted, "something to be really proud of." His parents worked hard, they got along with people, they always provided a good service. But the Mintzes just weren't competent at running a business. They paid too much for

supplies and never charged enough for whatever they were selling. When people couldn't pay, they gave the meal (or the ticket, or the haircut, or the beads) away for nothing.

The Mintzes had hoped that the Stardust Home would be different. For one thing, they could save on expenses by living in the house themselves. For another, they could use the skills that they had learned running the other businesses. They could cook for all the residents, show movies and other entertainments in the evening, even cut hair and hold art workshops. They liked old people, who had so many fascinating stories to tell, and thought that it would be good for the children to be around them. And now that Sullivan was older, he was able to help a lot more.

But as always, things hadn't worked out as planned. For one thing, Sullivan's parents found running a home full of old people exhausting. There was a never-ending stream of chores—shopping, cooking, laundry, cleaning, pills to dispense, bored or lonely or irritable residents to cheer up, doctor's appointments to arrange. For another, Gilbert and Loretta seemed to attract people who had very small pensions or limited savings and could not afford to pay very much. In fact, if things continued on as they were now, the Stardust Home, like the other businesses, would soon go bankrupt. But

this time, not only the Mintzes would suffer—all the residents would find themselves without a place to live.

Sullivan knew about these problems because he sometimes heard his parents talking at night when they thought he and Jinny were asleep. Sullivan was a natural worrier anyway. When he was five years old, he asked his parents what would happen if the sun didn't come up in the morning. When he was seven, he would look up at any airplane in the sky and watch until it passed over to make sure it didn't crash into their house. But the financial problems of the Stardust Home gave him something real to worry about. He would lie awake at night trying to come up with schemes that might help. He was too old to believe that a lemonade stand or selling all his comic books would be enough, as he used to think when his parents' other businesses were going under. But he wasn't too old to imagine he might earn enough money by juggling.

Was there some way that Sullivan could make money with his hobby? He couldn't remember ever seeing a juggler on television or in the movies. Maybe he could become a busker, one of those people who performs on a street corner or at a market while other people throw money into his hat. Sullivan would much rather be a busker than a dentist or accountant or any of the other things that his parents said were good

careers. Could he make enough to help his family that way? And even if he could, was he good enough? Probably not. Not yet, anyhow. Even if he was, there was no way his parents would let him do that.

And then there was the little matter of stage fright.

For the truth was that Sullivan was seriously afraid of performing in front of people. Oh, he could juggle in front of his parents, or even Manny Morgenstern. But an audience — that was a different matter altogether. Just the thought of it made his hands sweat and his body begin to tremble. And yet the weird thing was that he *wanted* to perform for people. In fact, he wanted to so badly that it felt like something he would one day *have* to do. It was one of the things that kept him practicing every chance he got. But how could he ever perform, when he was terrified?

Sullivan's father pushed back his chair. "Showtime, folks," he said — it was what he always said when it was time to clear the plates and bring out dessert. When Sullivan reached Manny's table, his friend said to him, "So how about a little juggling for the old codgers tonight, Sullivan? I'm sure we could use some diversion."

Sullivan felt perspiration immediately spring to his forehead. "I've got a lot of homework," he said. "Maybe another time."

"That's what you always tell us," Elsa complained.

"Now, now," said Manny. "The boy has homework, didn't you hear? He'll juggle for us one day. When he's ready."

Good old Manny. Sullivan returned to his family's table to eat his own wedge of chocolate cake. His thoughts drifted back to the strange sight outside his window. Looking down at that caravan, he'd felt for a moment as if it were a hundred years ago. He had heard of medicine shows, but he wasn't exactly sure what they were. Then his thoughts were interrupted by his dad saying, "You'd better get down to that homework right after dinner. Your mom and I will do the dishes. When you're done, you can fold bed sheets. There's a mountain of them in the laundry room."

"Okay," Sullivan said. He didn't look forward to folding a zillion sheets. It was hard to get them properly square and flat. He hoped that he could finish the chore quickly enough to leave some time to practice before bed.

"I have homework, too," Jinny said.

"You're in first grade," Sullivan scoffed. "What homework do you have?"

"Coloring."

"Exactly."

"It's hard."

"I'm sure it is."

"Harder than learning Italian."

"I don't take Italian."

"It's still harder."

"Why are you talking to me, anyway?"

"Sullivan," said his dad. "Be nice to your sister."

"I'm the sort of person everybody just adores," said Jinny.

Sullivan rolled his eyes. He got up, took his plate into the kitchen, and went to do his homework.

* 3 *

A CROW gave a lonely caw and flew over the Stardust Home, past the last houses of the town, to a field that had not been plowed in years. The night was almost black, the moon and stars hidden by a dense layer of cloud. But the crow saw something down below that made it bank its wings and wheel in a circle. A horse was pulling a caravan over the uneven ground. The bird dropped lower, but then the man holding the horse's reins looked up and shook his fist. The crow flapped hard and pulled away.

The horse, clearly exhausted, breathed heavily and shook the bit in its mouth. "Come on, you mangy thing," said the man with the reins, and he cracked his whip against the horse's flank. "Don't give out on me yet. We're almost there."

The man wore a black stovepipe hat and a long black coat with the collar pulled up. A slighter figure next to him, sitting upright and wearing a hat ornamented with black feathers, was as unmoving as stone. The horse pulled the caravan along a stand of birch trees that stood ghostly in the dark, and the man pulled on the reins. "This'll do," he said. "We've gone far enough for tonight. Don't you think so, my dearest darling? I'm sure we've left that unfortunate little incident well behind."

"Cold," the other figure said. It was a woman's voice, breathy and shrill. "Damp. Uneven. Ugly. Yes, it'll do, you stupid excuse for a man. Next time let me pick the new talent. Now help me down."

"Of course, my sweet," the man said and he hurriedly jumped down, only to put his foot into a crumbling mound of old cow dung. But he said nothing, only came around to the other side of the caravan's seat, swung down a little wooden stair, and offered his hand. The woman took it with her own gloved hand and put one narrow, pointed black heel on the step.

Even in the dark her pale skin, shining black eyes, and ruby lips were visible.

"I'll get the urchins to make us a fire and a spot of late dinner, shall I?" the man said.

"Just make sure that no one has thoughts of running off."

"Oh, they all have thoughts of running, my dearest darling. Of course they do. But they *don't* run off. That's the thing. They wouldn't dare — I've seen to that. No need to worry your pretty head."

"Speak to me like that again and I'll take off your own head."

"Of course, my love. I well know who is the intelligence behind this enterprise. I assure you, I know that."

The man hurried to the back of the caravan, taking mincing steps in case there were any more cow patties. He took a large set of jangling keys from his inside pocket, found the one he needed, and slipped it into the padlock that secured the back door. He pulled on the lock, swung open the door, and, after taking a box from his outside pocket, struck a match.

The flame cast its feeble light into the caravan. Three young faces, eyes blinking, stared out. Dazed faces. Hungry faces.

"Don't just stare at me like a row of bobbleheads,"

said the man. "You know we had to pack up quick. Now Mistress and I want some dinner. And see to that worthless horse. Then it's back to bed. We've got a show tomorrow and I want you in good shape. Performances are getting slack. They've got to tighten up, do you hear? Now get on with it."

One by one the three children climbed out of the caravan. First a girl with long red hair, then a small boy, and last, an older boy. They did not speak, but, taking equipment from inside the caravan or strapped underneath or on top of it, they set up a cookstove, a table, folding chairs. The girl went to unharness the horse, whispering, "That's okay, that's all right" in its ear and patting its moist and shivering neck. The younger boy poured wine into two goblets, sniffling a little as if from a cold or perhaps holding back tears.

"I hate that noise," said the woman. "Make him stop."

"Of course, my buttercup." He stepped over to the boy and said, "You stop that right now. There's no need. Not when you're so well taken care of. Not when we've made your dreams come true. Hush up or there'll be no share for you and you can sleep on the ground under the caravan."

The man's voice sounded harsh, but he put his hand gently on the boy's shoulder. He took up the two

goblets of wine and gave one to the woman. "Let us have a toast," he said. "To our great success!"

"Success?" the woman said. "You promised me the world. You promised me riches. Fame and glory. And look where we are. Look *what* we are. You are nothing but a disappointment to me."

"Ah, but things are looking up, my love. I sense a change in the air. I've got good instincts, and I can feel it!"

"Damn your instincts," she said, and swallowed her wine.

The older boy did the cooking. The sound of sizzling came from the stove, and the smell of oil, garlic, potatoes, and cheese made all three children painfully aware of their hunger. The woman said, "Well, I suppose you all need to eat as well. Let them get plates."

"You heard Mistress," said the man. "Go on now. And don't look so glum. We're all a little upset. But we'll be right as rain in a day or two. We'll be a jolly family once again. You'll see that I'm right!"

The girl brought out three more plates and the older boy served up the meal. The man and woman sat while the children stood. The horse pawed at the ground. "Yes," the man repeated, putting a forkful of hot potatoes into his mouth. "A jolly family once again."

❋ 4 ❋

TOMATO PANTS

SULLIVAN Mintz liked the Stardust Home better than any of the apartments they had rented in the past. Everyone was nice to him at the home. Even the most disagreeable resident, Dunstan Macafee — who complained that the food was too bland, that the other residents snored too loudly, and that the wallpaper looked like it was older than the residents — was nice to Sullivan. "Come over here, Sullivan," Mr. Macafee would call from his wheelchair. "Stand by the mark

on the wall. Yes, I declare that you've grown at least an inch."

"I don't think I grew an inch since last week," Sullivan always said, for he knew that he wasn't growing very quickly at all and that Mr. Macafee was only trying to make him feel better.

"Don't disagree with me, young man. I was a tailor for fifty-seven years. I could eyeball a customer and tell you his exact height, not to mention his waist, seat, and inseam. And I say you're an inch taller."

Though everyone at the Stardust Home liked Sullivan, it was a different matter at Beanfield Middle School. Of course, the teachers were glad enough to have a student who did his work on time and never disrupted class. And he got along well enough with the other kids, even if he hadn't gotten to know many of them, since he could never go to their houses after school or stay for a club or dance. He had to hurry home and help his parents, something they took for granted, as if every kid had to help run the family business. But Sullivan's life at school was miserable. And for one reason.

Samuel Patinsky.

"Samuel Patinsky is a classic bully," said Norval Simick at lunch on Friday. Norval and Sullivan were friends, if you could call somebody you never saw

outside of school a friend. They ate lunch together and tried to get picked for the same team in gym class, which wasn't always easy. Sullivan usually got picked somewhere in the middle, but Norval was always the last one chosen. To Sullivan the amazing thing was that Norval didn't mind. At least, Norval liked to say, he was known for *something*. And it was true, Sullivan thought. Nobody ever remembered who got picked in the middle.

"I don't know what you mean by 'classic,'" Sullivan said, looking suspiciously between the slices of bread of his sandwich. Usually his lunch consisted of whatever they'd had for dinner the night before, stuck between two pieces of pasty bread. Today it was a breaded sole sandwich.

"What I mean is that Samuel is a lunkhead, a dumb-bell, a cretin. He feels stupid and therefore bad about himself. He's also fat."

"He's not fat. He's just big."

"He's fat. And his parents fight all the time."

"How do you know that?"

"Wouldn't you fight if you were Samuel's parents?"

"So you're saying that I should feel sorry for Samuel Patinsky when he picks me up and shoves me inside my locker. When he pours my drink over my head. When he gives me a wedgie in gym. I should say, 'That's okay,

Sam, I know you have self-esteem issues. I hope torturing me makes you feel better.'"

"Pretty much."

"Hey, we've all got problems. I've got to serve forty-eight people dinner every night. Do you know how old they are if you add their ages together? I figured it out. *Three thousand eight hundred and seventy-three.* That's what *I* deal with every day."

"I thought you liked them."

"That's beside the point. I'm not going to feel bad for a Neanderthal like —"

"What are you gabbing about, Mr. Average?"

And there he was, Samuel Patinsky, playing a game on his cell phone even as he leaned over Sullivan and leered, his face as big as a pie. Sullivan could smell his breath. Peanut butter and onions.

"We were just having a fascinating discussion about recycling," said Norval in his most innocent voice. "Want to join in? Maybe you have an opinion about aluminum cans. And by the way, you're not supposed to use cell phones in school."

"Who was talking to you? I'll stick your head in a can if you don't shut up. So, Mintz," he said, turning back to Sullivan. "Guess what my mother put in my lunch today?"

"I don't know."

Samuel had a paper bag tucked under his arm. He reached into it and pulled out three small tomatoes. He held them up so that they were almost touching Sullivan's nose.

"Very nice," said Sullivan.

"No, not very nice. I hate tomatoes." He put them down on the table. "They're like eating the inside of a frog. I'm trying to decide what to do with them. You have any ideas?"

Norval leaned close to Sullivan's ear. "Now's your chance. Juggle the tomatoes. You'll amaze him. You'll amaze everybody in the cafeteria."

Norval knew about Sullivan's interest in juggling, just as Sullivan knew that Norval was into model rocketry. But Norval had never actually seen Sullivan juggle. Sullivan always said he would show him another time.

"What are you whispering about?" asked Samuel.

Sullivan picked up the three tomatoes. He felt them in his hands. They weren't too ripe and might not break if he tossed them carefully.

He put them back on the table.

"Sorry. I can't think of a thing to do with them."

"Then I guess I'll have to figure out something myself. Wait, I've got it! Stand up, Mintz."

"I'm not finished with my lunch."

"I said, stand up."

Sullivan stood up. He watched as Samuel picked up the tomatoes and put them down on the seat of Sullivan's chair.

"Sit down again."

"I don't think that's a good idea."

"Sit *down.*"

Sullivan lowered himself carefully. Then Samuel grabbed him by the shoulders and pushed him down, hard, into the seat.

"That can't feel very nice," Norval said, making a face.

It didn't feel nice. But Sullivan didn't say anything. He couldn't think of anything clever—in fact, he was holding back tears. "Have a great day, Tomato Pants!" said Samuel, walking away. Sullivan's shoulders slumped and his head lowered almost to his chest. Norval started saying something to him, but he didn't hear a thing.

It is a sad truth that all too often the victims of people like Samuel Patinsky keep it a secret. Sullivan had considered telling his parents; in fact, he'd been on the verge of telling them several times. But something always came up. Last time it was Jinny insisting they all sit down and watch her pretend to be a sunflower opening up to the sun. And even if his parents did

have a moment, Sullivan believed that they wouldn't really listen to him. "That's nice," they would say, no matter what he told them, "and by the way, did you empty everybody's trash can? And water the plants? And take those eight bags of shrimp out of the basement freezer?" Anyway, what would he say this time, that Samuel Patinsky made him sit on some tomatoes? If his parents complained, the whole school would learn about it. Most of them wouldn't even know who he was, but then kids would start pointing him out. They'd all start calling him Tomato Pants, which was even worse than Mr. Average.

At least, that was what he believed would happen. The reality was that Sullivan was not the only boy being bullied by Samuel. If he had told, as Norval often encouraged him to, he would have found himself with several new friends and general gratitude from the student population.

✻

Norval had a pair of sweatpants in his locker and lent them to Sullivan. At home after school, Sullivan threw his own pants into the laundry and then began his chores. He sorted the mail and delivered it to the residents in their rooms, politely chatting with each. He got Jinny a snack of crackers and jam because his father was out food shopping and his mother

was at the bank talking to the manager again. (Jinny complained that he didn't use enough jam.) He emptied wastepaper baskets in the common rooms. Only then could he finally do what he was longing to, the one thing that helped him to forget about Samuel Patinsky and about how his parents never listened and that he was so uninteresting and average that nobody even knew who he was.

Taking three balls from his drawer, Sullivan began a regular cascade, the balls weaving past each other in the air. He switched to a shower, with the balls chasing one another up and down again. He paused—one ball balanced on his arm, one on his shoulder, and one on his foot. Then he tossed a ball up with his foot and set them all in motion again.

Over the shoulder. Under the leg. Over the arm. Behind the back. Then a column, with two balls tossed straight up with one hand and a third ball with the other. He caught them, added a fourth ball, began again, dropped a ball, began again, dropped a ball again, began once more. When he dropped two balls he threw them all into the drawer and took out his wooden clubs.

At first he had found using clubs especially hard. Just the idea of throwing them up into the air and trying to catch them scared him. Unlike balls, clubs had to

turn just the right number of times so that they came down with their handles facing him. The smack when they met his hands stung. Even though he'd gotten better, he was still afraid of conking himself on the head.

He got the three clubs into an easy pattern and then threw them higher. The ceiling was covered in scuff marks from throws that were too high. He wanted to try a 360-degree spin, whipping around in a circle before catching the clubs again. But he was a split second slow and they rained down on him. "Ow!" he cried, protecting himself with his arms. When he looked up, he saw Manny Morgenstern watching from the doorway.

"Did you have to witness that particular moment?" asked Sullivan.

Manny said, "When you mess up, it's a sign of progress. I once saw a juggler in a vaudeville theater back in the old days. He juggled three clubs while going up and down a flight of stairs on a unicycle. It took him months to learn how to do it."

Sullivan put his clubs away in the drawer. "What was vaudeville like?" he asked.

"Of course, I didn't see vaudeville in its heyday. It was already dying out. What was it like? You would go to the theater and buy a ticket—you could go in any time of the afternoon or evening because it didn't

really have a beginning or an end. Just one act after another, all day long. You might see a comedian, a juggler, a bunch of clowns, a lady singer, a short play, a snake act. There was a little orchestra of four or five musicians playing the popular tunes of the day and also the music for the acts. It was great, it was lousy, it was silly, it was funny . . . it was always changing. I loved it. Of course, I loved all kinds of performances. Dramatic plays, musical comedies. The circus, when it came into town.. If it was on a stage, any stage, I tried to see it."

Sullivan asked, "Did you ever see a medicine show?"

Manny rubbed his little goatee while he thought. "No, I don't believe I did. But I've heard of them. They're long gone, died out even before vaudeville. I bet there hasn't been a medicine show for seventy or eighty years."

"What are—I mean, what *were* they?"

"A kind of traveling show, I suppose. Often with a wagon that went from town to town, or village to village, the small places that didn't get regular theater shows. They'd set up a little stage and have some kind of act—singing, dancing, mind-reading, banjo playing, you name it. And of course there was the pitchman."

"The pitchman?"

Manny didn't seem to hear him. "I suppose it was

phonographs and radio and the movies that killed off medicine shows, just like they did vaudeville. And they'll never come back. Nowadays people are used to special effects, light shows, 3D, watching images on big screens and tiny screens, all kinds of nonsense. But that was some entertainment, Sullivan. That was the real thing. People performing right before your eyes."

Sullivan had a lot more questions for Manny, but at that moment he heard his mother calling for him to come and help set the tables for dinner.

"I'll give you a hand," Manny said. "I hear it's fried chicken tonight. I just live for that fried chicken. Which is funny when you consider that the chicken died for it. Listen, Sullivan — I've got a thought. How about you put on a little juggling show for the residents after dinner tonight? I'm sure they'd love it."

Manny made the suggestion as if it were the first time, as if he didn't make it every day. Sullivan hesitated. Every night he lay in bed and imagined performing for people, but the chance to actually do it made him turn ice cold. "I don't think I'm ready yet," he said. "Soon, though."

"Whatever you say. But don't wait for perfection, Sullivan. Or you'll be waiting a very long time, I'm afraid."

※

Only later in the evening, after dinner was cleared away and the residents had moved on to playing cards or listening to music or watching television or visiting with their relatives or sitting in their rooms doing nothing at all, did the Mintz family get some quiet time. They sat in their small third-floor sitting room with the castoff sofa and armchairs and a fireplace that didn't work. Sullivan's dad found that knitting helped him relax at the end of the day, and he was working on a sweater for Jinny. Sullivan's mom sat at a small desk with the account books open before her. Sullivan sat on the other side of the desk, doing his homework. Jinny was lying on the rug, looking at some picture books from the library.

"I don't know how we're going to keep this place running past the end of the year," his mom said, as if she had forgotten the children were present. Unless, Sullivan considered, she was trying to prepare them, which meant that the situation was even worse than he had thought. "The man at the bank says he can't loan us another cent without permission from the head office."

"Perhaps we could think about it another night."

"Gilbert, you always say that. And then we go bankrupt."

"It's a good point, dear. I do always say that. Jinny,

stand up so I can put this sweater against you and see how it's going to fit."

Jinny stood up and held out her arms. "I could make lots of money," Jinny offered.

"You could?" said her dad, checking the sleeve length. "Well, that's just wonderful. And how will you make lots of money?"

"That's easy. I'll find treasure."

"A fantastic idea. And how will you find treasure?"

"Oh, that's easy, too, Daddy. You can bury it and I'll find it."

"Now, why didn't I think of that?"

Sullivan got up from the desk and looked out the window. There was nobody outside, only a broken chair by the curb across the road. At least his sister had an idea, he thought, even if it was one that made no sense. Sullivan wished again that he could find a way to bring in money. If he could only get over his fear of performing in front of people, maybe he really could make money juggling. Maybe he could join a circus. They still existed, didn't they?

"The mood is far too gloomy in here," his dad said. "Sullivan, why don't you take Jinny for a walk to the corner store. You can get yourselves a treat."

"It worked!" Jinny cried. "I was thinking, *Let us have*

a treat, let us have a treat. I sent my brain message to you."

Sullivan said, "Mom and Dad let us get a treat lots of nights."

"Well, I for one think it's amazing," his dad said. "Keep an eye on your sister, Sullivan."

"Oh, he will," said Jinny. "'Cause he *loooves* me."

"Dream on, sis."

His dad fished around in his pocket and came up with four quarters. Sullivan put them in his own pocket. A dollar wasn't going to buy them much of a treat. He wished that he could be more like Jinny. He wished a treat made everything wonderful for him, too.

A HUMBLE STAGE

THE Stardust Home had once been owned by the richest family in Beanfield. They had owned the sawmill and the undergarment factory and the newspaper. On a local history website, Sullivan had seen an old photograph of it as it had been back then — prettily painted, with a fine manicured lawn and men in top hats and women with parasols strolling about or sitting on the veranda. It had been built on the outskirts of town, and Beanfield hadn't grown much since then. There were still farms and fields behind the now

rundown house. The little store that Sullivan and Jinny walked to was the very last building in town.

Yesterday had been cold, but as if by some miracle, Sullivan stepped out into the sort of fresh spring evening that made him feel that something good, even extraordinary, was going to happen; something that he couldn't possibly guess. He breathed the sweet air and saw how the sun was already low between the distant houses.

"You need to hold my hand," Jinny insisted.

"Ugh, your hand is sticky. I don't need to hold it. I can see that you're right beside me."

"Okay, I'll lick it all over. Yum-yum-yum. There. It isn't sticky anymore. You can hold it now."

"That's worse! Give me your other hand, at least."

None of the other houses on the street were anywhere near as large as the Stardust Home, but they were all nearly as old. They were also poorly kept up, in need of paint, mortar between the flaking bricks, and porch repairs. Sullivan saw a blind go down in a second-floor window and a cat stretch itself on a sagging porch chair before closing its eyes again. A breeze came up and stirred the leaves on the big trees. It made a newspaper flutter down the road and a Styrofoam cup roll and bounce. A long and narrow sheet of paper

did a loop in the air, skittered along the sidewalk, and plastered itself against Sullivan's legs.

He leaned down and peeled the paper off, then held it up.

— MEN, WOMEN, BOYS, GIRLS! —

Step back in time and see the one and only

MASTER MELVILLE'S MEDICINE SHOW

Witness the mystifying conjuring effects of

✳ **FREDERICK**, the Boy Wonder!

Gasp at the mind-boggling intelligence of

✳ **NAPOLEON**, the Chess-Playing Automaton!

Roar with delight at the antics of

✳ **SNIT & SNOOT**, the World's Worst-Trained Dogs!

Swoon at the sheer poetry of

✳ **ESMERALDA**, Angel of the Air!

And the cost to you? Absolutely nothing!

Sunset, south end of Reingold's Field

⌒ **PLAYING NOW!** ⌒

"Let me see it, let me see it!" Jinny said.

"You can't even read." Sullivan kept his eyes on the paper.

"Then what does it say?"

"It's some sort of show."

"Oh, goody. When is it?"

"It says at sunset, over in Reingold's Field. That's just about now."

"Let's go! Let's go!" Jinny started pulling at Sullivan's shirt.

"Stop that. This could be from yesterday, or a month or a year ago."

"But it isn't! It's now! It says right on it. Let's go, Sullivan!"

Sullivan shrugged. Yet he, too, was excited by the chance of seeing a show. The name — Master Melville — was the same as on the caravan from the night before. Reingold's Field wasn't far past the store. Sometimes kids played ball games there, although all Sullivan ever did was watch from the side. There couldn't be any harm in going just to see. He took Jinny's hand and began walking quickly. They passed the store and kept going to the end of the sidewalk and through the first open field where an old barn stood, its roof collapsed.

A barbed wire fence ran along the border of the next field, but it had fallen down in several places so it was easy for them to step over. Weeds and stray grasses and wildflowers grew along the old furrows. There was a creek on one side, and along it a billboard had been planted into the ground with wooden stakes. COMING

Past it a line of trees began, and beyond them Sullivan
could see a small crowd of people.

"There it is!" he cried. "Let's hurry." He began to
run, pulling Jinny after him. He caught his foot in a
groundhog hole and almost fell, but picked himself up
again. Jinny began to cry that she couldn't go so fast, so
he put his arm around her and half carried her the last
stretch.

They joined the small crowd of thirty or so people, their backs to Sullivan and Jinny as they faced the
side of the caravan. And yes, it was definitely the same
caravan that Sullivan had seen on the street the night
before. So there really was still a medicine show, even
if they were supposed to have been long gone. Could
this be the extraordinary thing that he had felt in the
spring air?

He didn't recognize any of the people in the crowd.
They must have been from the nearby farms or from
houses whose kids went to the school in the next district. It wasn't like Sullivan to be pushy, but he was so
eager to see the show that he held Jinny's hand and
worked his way to the front.

He could see that the long wooden side of the caravan had been let down to form a sort of stage. There
was a curtain painted with a scene of green hills and a

distant, ancient city in ruins. A kerosene lantern hanging on either side cast a yellow light.

Jinny, who had been hopping from one foot to the other in anticipation, slowly grew still. She grasped the edge of Sullivan's shirt with her fingers. "Sullivan?" she said. "Maybe we should go home. I don't like it here. And it's getting dark."

"What do you mean? This could be good."

"It feels funny."

"What are you talking about? Shhh. The show's going to start."

Sullivan heard a rhythmic beating. From around the side of the caravan came a woman dressed in black, her face slim and pale and beautiful, her lips a deep red. She had a big bass drum strapped to her back; a washboard and cowbells on her front; a banjo-ukulele in her hands; a metal contraption holding a harmonica, a kazoo, and a whistle before her mouth; and a cymbal on a little shoulder perch. As she walked, a rope on her foot made the bass drum boom, while on her other ankle a tambourine rattled. She began to strum the banjo-ukulele while buzzing the jazzy melody of "Five Foot Two, Eyes of Blue" on the kazoo, her cheeks puffing out. Sullivan knew the song because Manny liked to hum it.

And then a cymbal crash and silence. At that same

moment the curtain was pushed aside and a very tall, very thin man came out. His face was gaunt, his pockmarked cheeks visible through his scraggly beard, eyebrows heavy and eyes quick and shining. He wore a suit that was not black, as Sullivan had thought looking through the window the night before, but rather a deep purple, with yellow stitching and a waistcoat beneath the jacket that was a wild paisley of gold and red. The silk scarf knotted about his neck was green. He removed his stovepipe hat and made an exaggerated bow.

"Dear friends," the man said. "Yes, although we have not met, I consider each and every one of you a friend. For are we not all sons of Adam and daughters of Eve, all part of one family?"

A honk from the side of the stage. Sullivan looked over to see the woman who made the music holding up a bicycle horn and scowling.

"But I get carried away," he said, stroking his thin beard. "It is excitement, sheer excitement over what we shall offer you good people this evening. A show, certainly, but not just any show. For we have gathered together, on this humble stage, a band of uniquely talented *artistes*. Performers who, although tender in years and fresh of face, have already reached the pinnacle of their particular *métiers*. Each one of them could have

already found fame and fortune on the greatest stages of the world—in London, Paris, or New York. Yet they have all chosen to dedicate themselves to an older and more intimate form of theatrical expression. That is"—the man motioned to the curtain behind him—"to the small stage of a traveling show. They have only their honest talents to hold your attention."

The man lowered his head a moment and cleared his throat with an awful rumble. He looked up again. "But I know that you are all eager for the show to begin. Dear friends, my name is Montague Melchior Melville—Master Melville, as my colleagues in the impresario trade have declared me out of deep respect. And that divine creature to my left," he said, gesturing to the woman bound in musical instruments, "that vision of loveliness is the one dearest to my heart. My own wife, Mistress Eudora Melville, is a woman of most sprightly melodic agility."

Master Melville looked at the woman as if expecting her to thump her drum or strum her banjo-ukulele or toot something in recognition of his compliment. But she merely continued to examine the edges of her long, painted fingernails. So he said, "Let me please insist that the taking of photographs or videos is strictly forbidden. No cameras, no cell phones, no modern geegaws or what-do-you-call-its of any kind. Each of

our performances is meant to exist only for the moment and then in the golden haze of memory, like the wondrous shows of old." Several people put away their phones. "Much obliged. And now let me introduce the first act. Rest assured, I will be back. For I have a message for you all. A message that could make all the difference to each and every one of you . . . that may mean the difference between a life of misery and a life of bliss."

Jinny tugged again at Sullivan's shirt. "He sure talks a lot."

Sullivan ignored her. "But enough for now," Master Melville went on. "Without further delay, I give you a boy on the brink of manhood, who not long ago shaved the fuzz from his upper lip for the first time. And yet he is a conjurer so masterful that the famous magicians of our time have fallen at his feet, begging for his secrets. Ladies and gentlemen, you are about to be astonished, astounded, and awestruck. For I give you . . . *Frederick, the Boy Wonder!*"

With a flourish of his hand, Master Melville commanded the curtain to open. Mistress Melville began to play a jerky waltz. The curtain started to move, got stuck, and then flew to the sides to reveal a boy of thirteen or fourteen with blond hair sticking out from under his black silk hat. He looked uncomfortable in

a tuxedo that had been turned up at the trouser cuffs and sleeves. He gazed at the audience without smiling, as if, thought Sullivan, he was mad at them all just for being there.

"I'm supposed to entertain you," the boy said. "Only I forgot to bring any playing cards. That's how much I care. But I don't have much choice, since you're here, so I'll just have to get some. Of course to do that I need to make a door. Let's see. Up here looks like a good place."

The boy stretched out his hand and with a finger he traced a square in the air just higher than his head. Then he pretended to grasp an invisible knob and open the door. "All I need to do now," he said, "is take what I want." He raised his hand again and reached "through" the door, and as he pulled it back a playing card instantly appeared in his hand. He held it out for the audience to see. Then he took off his hat, dropped the card in, and reached through the door again. He snatched another card from the air and dropped it into the hat. He did it again and again, one card after another, until he had at least a dozen.

"That ought to be enough," the boy said. He picked all the cards out of the hat and put the hat back on. He fanned them out to show their faces—they were all red—and then waved them through the air, turning

them black. He passed them *through* his hat. He threw one into the air, where it vanished, only to appear in his pocket. He tore one to bits, swallowed the pieces, then drew it out of his mouth whole again. He dropped the cards into his upturned hat and fluttered his fingers over them, coaxing them to float into the air one after another. And after they dropped back into the hat, he picked them up one at a time, reached through the invisible doorway in the air, and made each one vanish again.

The crowd clapped and whistled.

"I'm bored of doing this," the boy said. "I don't give a hoot what you think. But I'll do one more because I feel like it. I'll try something different, something I've never done before. You see, even though I'm still a kid, I'm going to buy my first house."

A few titters from the crowd. Sullivan looked down for a moment to see Jinny staring expectantly at the boy on stage. He continued, "The problem is, the house I want to buy is haunted."

"Haunted?" whispered Jinny.

"Let me show you the house. I've got it here."

The boy, Frederick, went to the side of the stage and brought out a giant sheet of cardboard with the simple front of a house drawn on it. The audience laughed. He brought out another sheet meant to be the side

of the house and he propped the two together. He brought out a third and a fourth sheet, making a sort of cardboard play house. Sullivan looked down at Jinny again and saw that she wasn't scared; she was smiling. He knew what she was thinking—that it would be fun to play inside the cardboard house.

"To get the ghost out of the house I'm going to have to trick him," said Frederick. "But first I'm going to have to make him think I'm another ghost."

The boy went to the side of the stage again and this time he came back with a rolled-up sheet. He unrolled it and showed the crowd that there were two small holes cut in the center. Sullivan knew they were eye holes, and sure enough the boy draped the sheet over himself to become a Halloween ghost.

"Not bad," Frederick said, holding out his arms and turning around. "Now all the house needs is the roof." He walked once more to the side of the stage, this time coming back with a sheet of cardboard that was bent down the middle to have a peak like a roof. He lowered it onto the walls.

But as soon as the roof was on the house a terrible moaning and groaning came from inside. Then knocks and screams and the sound of breaking glass. Had the ghost inside become angry? Jinny grabbed Sullivan's

arm and held it tight. Sullivan himself wasn't scared, not really, and he couldn't stop watching.

The boy slowly picked up the roof again.

As he did so the ghost in the house — or at least somebody in another bed sheet costume — rose up, too. The boy put down the roof, grabbed the ghost's sheet, and pulled it off.

And underneath the sheet was . . . *the boy!*

But how could that be? Frederick, the boy magician, was the one *outside* the house! Sullivan couldn't understand. Were they identical twins? The boy standing inside the house now grabbed the sheet of the ghost outside the house and pulled *it* off.

And underneath was . . . *a girl!* Not the magician at all, but a girl maybe twelve years old, with long red hair and freckles, wearing a white satin gown. How had the boy ended up in the house? How had the girl ended up where the boy had been? It really was amazing. Sullivan pulled his arm from Jinny's grasp so he could join the enthusiastic clapping of the crowd.

The curtain closed — from his spot near the stage, Sullivan could hear it creaking. The woman in black, Mistress Melville, boomed the drum, crashed the cymbal, and began a military march, her arms flailing at the banjo-ukulele, her legs pumping up and

down to keep the drum and tambourine going, her mouth blowing into the whistle. Out stepped Master Melville, grinning and nodding.

"Wonderful, just wonderful," he said. "If only the lad would smile, but you know how moody kids are at that age. And what an attitude! If he were to take some of these drops, his disposition would improve immediately, I assure you."

From his inside pocket, Master Melville pulled out a small glass bottle with a paper label and a stopper in its neck. It looked like the same kind of bottle Sullivan had seen painted on the side of the caravan the night before. "Yes," the tall man went on, holding it up. "If he would only take a daily dose of Master Melville's Hop-Hop Drops, young Frederick would be smiling away. Certified organistic, one hundred percent anti-parsinomic, Master Melville's Hop-Hop Drops are just the thing when life's got you down. They are like nothing you can buy from a pharmacy or get from a doctor's prescription. They are all natural, they disperse all acidity and acrimony from the bloodstream, they facilitate remification and inhibit ramification. And they are guaranteed — guaranteed right on the bottle — to make you a happier person."

Master Melville took in a deep breath and smiled warmly as he looked around. Sullivan felt for a moment

that Master Melville was looking not just at him but *through* him. "But let me tell you about these miraculous drops later. I'm sure you would like to see our next performer. Although, to tell you the truth, I don't know if I can call *it* a performer at all. Ladies and gentlemen, allow me to present to you the most astonishing piece of machinery ever produced by humankind. Over two hundred years old, it is run by the simple mechanistic laws of cogs and wheels, springs and screws. And yet, it can think. It can reason. And it can win. Introducing the Chess-Playing Genius . . . *Napoleon!*"

Once more the curtain opened, showing the bare stage. A moment later Frederick the magician wheeled out a strange object. It was a figure, or more precisely the top half of a figure, sitting on a low wooden cabinet. A sort of model or mannequin, it had a painted wooden head that looked a little like Napoleon the French emperor, and it was wearing a tricorn hat, a red and blue military jacket, and white gloves.

"Yes, ladies and gentlemen," Master Melville continued as he walked over to the figure, "Napoleon plays an amazing game of chess. It has defeated Russian grandmasters and French champions. It has amazed kings and queens in courts all over Europe. And it is nothing but clockwork inside. Let me show you."

Master Melville opened a little door in the front

of the cabinet. Inside, Sullivan could see wheels and gears, a rubber belt, and a metal cylinder with little studs on it like the workings of a music box. Then the man and the young magician turned the cabinet around on its wheels and opened the back door to show more wheels and cogs and springs. "You see? There are no wires or chips, no twenty-first-century electronic thingamajigs. Only what you'd find on the inside of your grandfa-ther's watch. Indeed, it was constructed by a watch-maker of the old school. But his secrets died with him, and now only one such automaton exists. For years it was believed lost forever, but after a lifetime of search-ing, I found it—where, I cannot say."

Frederick and Master Melville turned the automa-ton to the front again, and as the magician left the stage, Master Melville opened a drawer at the bottom of the cabinet and took out a set of black and white chess pieces. He placed them on a board that lay on the cabinet in front of Napoleon.

"Is there by any chance a chess player in the crowd? Someone adept at this ancient game that requires deep thinking? Don't be shy now—here is your chance to show off before all these good people."

Sullivan waited. After a moment a man in overalls, a baseball cap on his head, stepped forward. "I'm par-tial to a game of chess," he said.

"You're good, too," said the woman behind him. "Nobody around here can beat you."

"Then you are just our man!" said Master Melville. "Would you like to play Napoleon?"

"Don't mind if I do."

"Excellent. All I need to do is wake it up."

Master Melville pulled from inside his jacket a set of keys. He went to the side of the cabinet, inserted a key, and with much effort began to wind up the automaton. There was a noise of whirs and gears and then the wooden head turned to the left, the right, and back again. The left hand of the figure lurched upward. It moved forward and the fingers opened to pinch the top of a pawn. It placed the pawn two squares forward and lurched back again.

"Your turn, if you please," Master Melville said to the man, holding out a hand to help him onto the stage.

Sullivan wasn't much for games, and he was a poor chess player. But he found it intensely interesting to watch the man play against the machine. Even Jinny, who didn't understand chess, watched with rapt attention. The man in the baseball cap would move a piece. Then a whirring sound would come from Napoleon and its wooden eyeballs would move back and forth as if it were thinking. Its arm would lurch forward again

to make its move. The whole audience watched in silence. Napoleon picked up a bishop and moved it across the board to knock over the man's king. Bells and whistles sounded inside the automaton and the left hand pinched the three-cornered hat and raised it off the wooden head and back down.

"Checkmate!" cried Master Melville. "Napoleon wins!"

Everyone clapped except for the man in the baseball cap, who sheepishly slipped off the stage. The curtain closed, the clanging music started up (a polka this time, with harmonica), and Master Melville stood before the audience once more. "Oh, dear," he said. "Nobody likes to lose, especially to a pile of junk. But if this gentleman would only take a sip from a bottle of my Hop-Hop Drops, his mood would change in moments. The world would look sunny and bright again. That, my dear friends, is the natural effect of this remarkable infusion.

"Ladies and gentlemen," Master Melville went on, "modern medicine is a wonder. I do not denigrate our doctors, our hospitals with their beeping machines, our X-rays and laser surgeries, our capsules and injections. And yet there is much that the wise healers of the past can teach us. Perhaps you can't sleep since your teenage son ran away. Or you feel worthless for

having lost your job. Or you suspect that the person you married twenty years ago no longer loves you. Can modern medicine cure any of these ailments?

"The drops in this bottle"—again he pulled it from his pocket—"are a very old concoction, once known to the ancient Egyptians, then to the great healers of the Mayan civilization, and last to the Chinese of the Ming Dynasty. A recipe lost for generations until discovered by myself in a musty tome and refreshed and revitalized with the addition of certain modern ingredients to make it even more powerful. Ingredients, to be frank, that are available to each and every one of you in the corner grocery store, the field and the stream. But what are they and in what combination? How are they prepared? That, friends, is the secret that I hold. And that I keep to myself for fear of misuse and malevolence. Why, I'm so confident in these drops that I shall give a bottle away for free to the man who went down to defeat only moments ago. Here you go, sir!"

And with that Master Melville tossed the bottle into the air. There were chuckles as the man in the baseball cap caught it. He looked embarrassed, but he slipped the bottle into the big pocket of his overalls.

At that moment Mistress Melville struck up a lively tune, bashing on her instruments and blowing

hard into the kazoo. Master Melville began to dance. He lifted his arms, rose on his toes, and kicked out one leg as he spun around.

"Sullivan! We have to go." Jinny began smacking her brother on the back with her hands.

"Ow! Stop that."

"Mom and Dad are going to wonder where we are. It's dark. I don't like walking in the dark."

Sullivan had to admit that Jinny was right. Their parents were going to start worrying. He hated the idea of not being able to see the rest of the show, but there didn't seem to be anything else to do. "All right," he said, grabbing Jinny's wrist. He began to pull her aside, out of the crowd.

When he looked up he saw the woman, Mistress Melville, her arms pumping wildly as she played her instruments. She was already looking at him — looking straight at him with such intensity that he silently gulped. She took her mouth off the kazoo and said, "You, boy. I have a feeling about you. Come back to-morrow."

"Tomorrow?" Sullivan said, astonished.

But she was looking at the stage again, strumming furiously on the banjo-ukulele and swinging her leg to bang the drum.

* 6 *

SOME LITTLE TALENT

THE town of Beanfield got its name for a good reason: almost all the surrounding farmers grew beans. The importance of beans to the economy of the town wasn't lost on Beanfield Middle School. Every year there was a special presentation in the gym. The morning after Sullivan and Jinny's trip to the medicine show, they sat with their classes and watched a PowerPoint presentation called "Is the Bean the Greatest Vegetable Ever?"

Sullivan could hardly concentrate on the screen, or

on any of his classes afterward, for his mind whirled with memories of the medicine show. It was as if he'd been waiting all his life to see something like it, maybe even to see this very show. He could hardly wait to go again tonight. The woman herself had invited him!

After school, Sullivan had his usual chores, and after dinner, too. Then he went to find Jinny, who was in her room posing in front of the mirror in a pair of her mother's high-heeled shoes and singing at the top of her lungs.

I'm a great singer and dancer too!

Also a great swimmer, pole vaulter, piano player, gum chewer—

"Hey, Jinny," Sullivan interrupted. "Mom asked me to read some stories to you tonight. But I want to go back to the medicine show. How about you look at some picture books by yourself?"

"Nope."

"Please?"

"Only if you play with me now."

"I'll play anything you want."

"Okay, let's play Baddy-Waddy Widdle Boy."

Sullivan groaned. "I hate that game."

"You said *anything.*"

"Fine."

"Yes!" Jinny cried.

And so for the next hour they played Baddy-Waddy Widdle Boy. Jinny was the school teacher, Miss Mintz, and Sullivan was the boy who was always getting into trouble. He didn't do his homework, he didn't listen, he never knew the answer when Miss Mintz called him to the blackboard. Naturally there were, as Miss Mintz said with exasperation, "con-see-quences." He had to stand on one leg in the corner. He had to write "I'm a Baddy-Waddy Widdle Boy" a hundred times on the blackboard. He had to answer questions like "What happens when you mix dishwashing soap with rocket fuel?"

Finally Sullivan broke away to find his parents in the sitting room. His father was knitting, his mother, with her notebook in her lap, was writing a new poem. Sullivan hesitated, for it wasn't like him to outright lie to his parents. He forced himself to speak quickly.

"So I was thinking of putting Jinny to bed myself."

His parents looked up. "You mean you're offering?" asked his dad.

"I thought, you know, that it would be good for us. Bonding. Jinny wants me to. Is that okay?"

His parents looked at each other. "That will be a first," his mom said. "Sure. It's really nice of you, Sullivan. You're a wonderful big brother."

Sullivan wished his mother hadn't said that. He

turned around and went back to Jinny in her room. She was sitting on the edge of the bed, waiting for him.

"Aren't we going to play some more?"

"No, I have to go. The medicine show must have already started. You can look at your books now."

"I changed my mind. I want to go with you."

"Come on, Jinny. It's late. And dark outside."

"I can bring my Super-Explorer flashlight."

"All right, but you can't tell Mom and Dad. And hurry."

Sullivan had to wait while Jinny hunted for the flashlight. Then they crept along the hall and down the stairs to the ground floor. All the residents were in their rooms and the living room lights were off. The furniture cast long shadows in the dark. Suddenly, a light right in Sullivan's eyes blinded him.

"Hey, what are you doing?"

"You said I could use my flashlight."

"Outside! And don't point it in my face."

Slowly, Sullivan opened the door and they slipped out. Jinny turned her flashlight back on and pointed it at the ground as they began walking.

"Is this an adventure?" Jinny asked.

"You don't have to whisper anymore. And yes, it's an adventure."

"Good, because I always wanted one."

They didn't speak much as they continued to walk, past the store and then the abandoned barn, over the barbed wire fence and past the creek to Reingold's Field.

"There they are," Jinny said, although Sullivan had already seen the people gathered just past the trees. A glow came from the lamps on either side of the caravan stage and the music drifted toward them. They walked more quickly now, half running until they reached the back of the crowd, which was smaller this time. Sullivan tried to move them forward but could only get to the side. Master Melville was dancing just as he'd been when they'd left the night before. He did one more turn and stopped.

"But you haven't come to watch me do a jig!" the tall man said breathlessly. "Let me introduce our next act, Clarence and his incorrigible canines *Snit* and *Snoot*, the World's Worst-Trained Dogs!"

The music galloped on as Master Melville danced himself off the stage. Then the woman in black began another tune, one that Sullivan recognized as "How Much Is That Doggy in the Window?" This time the curtain opened very slowly to show a small boy standing between two even smaller dogs. The boy had straight bangs across his forehead and large eyes, and wore *lederhosen*—leather shorts—with suspenders.

The two dogs were white with dark patches and had little tails and small ears that flopped down. Jinny was making noises about how cute they were.

"Hello, everyone," said the boy, giving a little wave. "Tonight I'm supposed to present a dog act. There have been many great dog acts. Unfortunately, this isn't one of them. That's because the two dogs here, Snit and Snoot, won't do anything I say. For example, they won't ever jump—"

At that moment the dog on the boy's right side did jump—right over his head! But the boy didn't seem to notice. He went on, "—or do anything I ask. It would be nice if they listened to me once in a while and jumped when I asked them."

The dog on the left jumped over him. Again, the boy didn't seem to notice. It barked and wagged its tail. The boy looked at the dog and just shook his head.

"Let me give you an example. Watch this. Okay, Snit and Snoot. Roll over!"

The two little dogs stood up on their hind legs. They walked in little tippy-toe circles.

"See what I mean?"

The dogs went down on all fours again and nodded their heads, as if to say, *Yes, we know just what you mean.* Sullivan laughed along with everyone else.

"No, no, please don't laugh. It only encourages them. Let's see if I can teach them to do a basic trick. First, I'll show them how it's done."

The boy got down on his hands and knees. He said, "Paw, Snit!" He held up one hand to show the dog what he meant.

Snit scratched his foot on the ground like a bull. Then he took off and jumped onto the boy's back. He stood on him like a billy goat on a hill. Everyone clapped.

"Please don't clap!" said the boy. "You can see what bad dogs they are."

Now the other one, Snoot, came forward. He hunched down and squeezed under the boy as if he were a bridge. And stayed there.

The woman in black began to play "For He's a Jolly Good Fellow."

"No, no! No music!" the boy pleaded.

The music ground to a halt. Snoot came out from under the boy and began to lavishly lick his face.

"Ugh! Stop kissing me! And Snit, you get off!" The boy struggled to his feet, pushing the dogs away. He stepped forward to the edge of the stage and held out his hands in a gesture of wanting sympathy.

"Ladies and gentlemen, I apologize for this terrible

act. I really expected things to go better today. I can only hope that you enjoy the other acts more than this one . . ."

While he talked, Snoot left the stage and came back pushing a large red ball. Behind the boy's back, he rolled the ball to Snit. Snit tossed it up in the air with his nose and Snoot knocked it back. Snit stopped the ball, jumped on top of it, and moved his feet so that the ball rolled across the stage with him on top while Snoot ran circles around it.

"What are you laughing at?" asked the boy. "I'm trying to apologize. I'm being serious here." People shouted at him to turn around. "What's that? Turn where?" Finally, he did, and saw what the dogs were up to. "You bad dogs!" he shouted, and chased them off the stage. The curtain closed, music struck up, and everyone clapped. Jinny and Sullivan clapped, too.

Master Melville bounded forward. "That poor boy doesn't look very happy about his dogs, does he? But I can tell you, one sip of Master Melville's Hop-Hop Drops will make the world of difference for him after the show. Because, yes sir, they're absolutely safe for children. No doubt some of you out there feel that life could be a little better. A little happier. Some of you no doubt suffer from anxiety, depression, fears, dyspepsia, bad moods, no zip, flatulence, or just gen-

eral grumpiness. Then these drops will help you. And they are available exclusively from yours truly — for a mere ten dollars a bottle. But first, we have one more act to lighten your heart, for it is our desire to bring you happiness in all its manifestations. And after that, Mistress Melville and I will be glad to part with some of our precious supply of drops. Please remember, no pushing, and there is a limit of five bottles per person. But now, let me present to you another young performer, a true artist in her chosen calling, the Angel of the Air, *Miss Esmeralda!*"

Master Melville stepped aside. The audience grew quiet. The music began, a single scratchy note, and Sullivan saw that Mistress Melville had hung the banjo-ukulele on a hook at her waist and had taken up in its place a violin. She began to play something classical (not very well, Sullivan thought), and he turned his gaze back to the stage as the curtain opened. A rope had been suspended across it, perhaps three feet off the ground and sagging slightly in the center. The violin began to play faster, if no less scratchily. From one side of the stage, a bare pointed foot appeared. The foot glided forward along the rope, attached to a slim leg clad in pink tights. Then a ruffled skirt or tutu of a peculiarly bright orange appeared, followed by a small, limp hand and a thin wrist, then a leotard top

of black and yellow polka dots, and finally the rest of the girl with the red hair — the same girl who had appeared outside the magician's haunted house the night before. She had pale skin and long, almost white eyelashes and countless freckles.

The girl walked slowly, almost effortlessly, to the middle of the tightrope, wobbling only a little. At the center she raised one foot, brought her arm down, and then she was standing on her hands, legs straight up in the air. She did a couple scissor kicks before coming back to her feet as the audience clapped.

After that the girl struck a series of ballet-like poses, holding each for several seconds before moving again. She then *ran* along the rope, back and forth, fluttering her arms rather like, Sullivan had to admit, a chicken trying to get away from the farmer's ax. And then she did something quite extraordinary; not exactly artistic, maybe, but certainly unusual. She lay on the rope, hands clasping it at one end and ankles at the other, and then in this horizontal position proceeded to spin around it, like a bead turning on a string. She went faster and faster, and the music became more and more frantic, until she flung herself up into the air and then landed in a split.

There was a great roar of approval from the crowd,

and much whistling and stamping of feet. "She's splen-derful," said Jinny.

Sullivan thought that Jinny was right. The girl was "splenderful," in just about every way. He watched as she curtsied, smiled, and ran off the stage. The curtain closed.

"This humble show of ours," said Master Melville, reappearing once more, "is presented free of charge, gratis, with our compliments. If it has lightened your evening a little, filled your inner vessel with a cup or two of joy, then we have succeeded in our self-appointed task. And I want you to know without equivocation that I don't want you to even consider buying a bottle of Master Melville's Hop-Hop Drops if you never feel down in the dumps, out of sorts, or just plain sad. If you are one of the lucky few, one of the truly happy people of this world, then my drops can do nothing for you. But for all others, take note that we will be selling bottles at the side of the stage. There will be no need to push or jostle, we have enough for everyone. I shall dispense the bottles while my better half, the companion of my life and one of the great beauties of our time, Mistress Eudora Melville, will handle all financial transactions. I do not know when next we shall grace your fair village, as our work takes

us to the most far-flung destinations. But until we meet again, may I say good luck, good health, and great happiness!"

Master Melville made a very deep bow. People were already stepping past Sullivan to get to the side of the caravan. He took Jinny's hand and the two of them watched as Mistress Melville, who had taken off her musical suit of armor, now placed herself at a small table with a little metal money box on it. "Is she a princess?" Jinny asked. "Or maybe she's a witch. Do you think those drops would make Mom and Dad happy? They seem awfully worn out."

"I don't know," Sullivan said, although he'd been wondering the same thing. "Anyway, we don't have ten dollars."

Jinny sighed. "One day," she said, "I'm going to have a machine that makes ten dollars whenever I want it."

"That's counterfeiting."

"It is? Now I know what I want to do when I grow up. I want to be a counterfeiter."

But plenty of other people had lined up and were handing the woman ten- and twenty-dollar bills. Her blood-red lips never smiled or spared a word. Next to her, Master Melville pulled the little glass bottles from a wooden crate and handed them over with a word, a grin, a handshake.

"Let's go home," Jinny said, looking up at the sky.

Sullivan, too, saw how the evening had turned. Distant trees and fences had become black silhouettes. But Sullivan didn't want to go yet. He felt held there as if by a strange power, a magnetic force almost. "We'll be just another minute," he said.

He joined the line, Jinny sulking beside him. Each time the woman at the table took a bill, she held it to the light of the lantern before putting it in the metal box. Each time Master Melville handed out a bottle, he said, "Yes, immediate results, you'll see," or "Not more than a sip now, it's formulated for maximum potency!"

At last Sullivan and Jinny reached the front of the line. Mistress Melville licked her finger — she had long pointed nails, painted black — and rifled through a pile of bills. She looked at Sullivan with unblinking dark eyes, making him blush.

"A young customer, I see," said Master Melville, patting Sullivan on the shoulder. "And how many bottles would you like?"

"I'm sorry. I don't have any money."

"No money? This is not a charity, young man. There are real customers waiting. Get along with you."

"Give the boy a moment," said the woman.

Master Melville glanced at his wife. "A moment? Certainly, my dear." And he looked back at Sullivan.

"I can . . . I can juggle," Sullivan stuttered.

"But you never show anyone," Jinny whispered.

"Can you, now?" said Master Melville. "How delightful. Perhaps you also make bird sounds and do yo-yo tricks."

But Sullivan was not deterred. From the pocket on one side of his jacket he brought out two balls. From the pocket on the other side he brought out two more.

"You're a bit young to juggle four balls, don't you think?" Master Melville said, not unkindly. "I salute your ambition, I really do, but I have sales to make —"

What Sullivan did next was so totally unlike him that he hardly felt he knew himself at that moment. He began to juggle. He tossed the balls up in succession and began a shower pattern, throwing a little higher each time. He had never successfully done a full 360-degree spin with four balls. What's more, he was standing on uneven ground and it was too dark to see well. But he tried it now, turning on his heel so fast he felt dizzy, returning just in time to catch and toss the balls again.

"Wow!" gasped Jinny.

One . . . two . . . three . . . four — he caught the balls and stashed them back into his pockets.

Master Melville frowned as he watched. But then he broke into a smile. "Well, well! I didn't expect that. A talented boy. Don't you agree, Eudora?"

The woman, too, was studying him. What he had just done began to sink in, and Sullivan felt so faint that he thought he might keel over. Mistress Melville looked him up and down as if he were something for sale in a shop window.

"Some little talent," she said at last. "But see how pale he's gone."

"Young man," said Master Melville, clasping Sullivan's shoulder with his hand. "Do me the favor of returning tomorrow evening. We don't usually stay three nights, but we can make an exception. I have something for you. Something that will be of great use to you."

Sullivan, finding himself unable to speak, nodded. Then he took Jinny's hand and they turned around and began to hurry home.

❋

Fortunately for Sullivan, his parents had been too busy dealing with a minor crisis at the Stardust Home to realize that he and Jinny had gone out. One of the residents, Thackery Muldoon, had a pet mouse, which had escaped and slipped under Emily Potterfield's door. There had been a great deal of screaming, and the mouse had almost been flattened by a silver tea

tray before Sullivan's father had managed to rescue it. By the time everyone was settled down again, Sullivan and Jinny were at home in their pajamas.

Sullivan got Jinny into bed, a nightlight glowing in the corner, and sat down beside her.

"Sullivan," she said, turning under the covers, "why can't I tell Mom and Dad about the medicine show?"

"Because . . . because I want to surprise them with a bottle of Hop-Hop Drops. That's why I'm going to go back tomorrow, to buy it. So you can't tell them about that, either."

"Okay."

"You pinky swear?" Sullivan held out his finger.

"I pinky swear," she said, hooking her little finger around his.

Sullivan went back to his own room. In truth, he wasn't sure why he had asked Jinny to keep the medicine show a secret. Maybe it was because he didn't think his parents would let him go back again tomorrow if he told them about it. Maybe it was because he didn't know what Master Melville wanted to show him. Sullivan couldn't imagine what it might be, but he had a feeling it was something great and important, something that might even change his life.

He tried to read for a while, but he couldn't concentrate, so he went to say good night to his parents.

They were back in the upstairs sitting room, just as they'd been when he had last seen them. While his father worked at his knitting, his mother read aloud a new poem that she had written.

> In all the world, the thing I hate
> Is when I find only one ice skate.
> Or my kite has got stuck up in a tree
> Or my book has no page fifty-three.
>
> I like to finish what I start
> Whether it's playing a tune or cooking a tart.
> But a guitar's no good with a broken string
> And a tart's no tart if it's got no filling.
>
> The answer, I guess, is to take more care
> Of the things I play, and make, and wear.
> But it's not my fault, you can't blame me
> If my book has no page fifty-three.

"That's absolutely gorgeous, my dear," said Sullivan's dad. "I think that's your best poem in the last two weeks."

"Do you really?" said his mom. "I'm not so sure about the 'filling' line. It doesn't scan very well."

"You are too much the perfectionist, Loretta."

Sullivan said, "I've just come to say good night."

"Did you lay out the dishes for the morning?" asked his dad.

"I never forget, do I?" Sullivan hadn't meant it to sound angry.

"That's true. I'm sorry."

"Are you all right?" asked his mom, getting up. "I know we ask a lot of you. Do you want me to come and sit with you for a bit?"

"No, that's okay."

"Is something else bothering you, Sullivan?"

Sullivan hesitated. *Was* something bothering him? Not telling his parents where they had gone tonight — that bothered him. Samuel Patinsky's taunts — that bothered him, too. That it was okay for his mom to write poetry and his dad to always want to run his own business but not for them to take his juggling seriously — that definitely bothered him. That he was planning to lie to them tomorrow night, too . . .

"No," he said at last. "Nothing's bothering me." And he went back to bed.

* 7 *

THE SOFT CLICK

THE kids of Beanfield Middle School thought that their school was better than the ones in nearby Pittsville, Greenhaven, and Halliwell. And they liked to tell each other why.

"Our gym doesn't smell as bad as Pittsville's."

"The kids at Greenhaven wear the ugliest shoes in the world."

"At Halliwell the science teacher is missing a finger."

Unlike most of the other kids, Sullivan had actually been to other schools. He knew that the Pittsville

gym didn't smell any worse than theirs and that the kids at Greenhaven wore the same shoes as everyone else. It *was* true that the Halliwell science teacher was missing his finger—Sullivan had gone to Halliwell. Sometimes he told the kids that he lost it to a tiger at the zoo, sometimes that he suffered frostbite while climbing Mount Kilimanjaro, and sometimes that he had simply forgotten where he put it. Actually, he was a pretty good teacher.

Sullivan was having these thoughts when he should have been concentrating on the dodgeball game they were playing in gym class. Which was why it was so easy for Samuel Patinsky to nail him with a terrifically hard shot. The ball smacked into Sullivan's stomach, and he yelped as he crumpled to the floor.

"Hey, Mintz," Samuel called out. "Try not to make it so easy for me. It just isn't as satisfying."

"That throw was overhand," said Norval, helping Sullivan up. "It should be disqualified."

"That's my call," said Mr. Luria, the gym teacher. "And I say it was a fair throw." Sullivan thought that Mr. Luria must have once been the Samuel Patinsky of *his* school.

"You going to be okay?" Norval said to Sullivan.

"I . . . think . . . so," Sullivan gasped. "Soon as . . . I can . . . breathe again."

The rest of the day did not go much better. It didn't help that all Sullivan could think about was going to see the medicine show that night. During math, when the teacher asked him to go up to the board, he had no idea what the question was. At lunchtime, he dropped half of his sandwich (leftover pancakes between two pieces of bread) on the floor and spilled his juice. And he tried to hide behind a book when, for English, his teacher wrote one of his mom's poems from the newspaper on the board and asked them to write a paragraph analyzing it.

I wish that I was two feet taller
And my eyes were sparkling blue.
I wish I could win a Nobel Prize
For inventing a kind of glue.

I wish I played in a punk rock band
And was friends with a movie star.
I wish that I could wave my hand
And bring an end to war.

But if I don't win a prize one day
Or travel the world so far,
I guess it'll really be okay —
As long as I'm friends with a movie star.

Maybe the teacher thought he was being nice to Sullivan, but the truth was that Sullivan felt only mortification. He didn't like how nobody ever noticed him in school, but that didn't mean he wanted to be known as the son of the Bard of Beanfield. He didn't want to analyze his own mother's poem either; it felt icky, like having to watch your parents dance at a wedding. And when he looked up from his paper, he saw Samuel Patinsky shooting him resentful glances, as if the assignment was Sullivan's fault.

At last, the final bell of the day rang and Sullivan rushed down to the first floor. At the door of the grade one class he met Jinny's teacher, a hugely tall woman with frizzy hair named Ms. Compton. "You're such a good big brother, taking care of your sister," Ms. Compton said. Sullivan took Jinny's hand, and as soon as they were outside he started to run.

"Hey," Jinny protested. "You're going to pull my arm off!"

"Okay, okay, but hurry up."

"It's such a nice day, I think I'll walk slow."

"I hate you!" Sullivan growled.

"I'm going to tell Mom and Dad you hate me."

"Go ahead. Tell the world for all I care."

"Anyway, I hate you worstest."

At home, Sullivan rushed through his chores and

then went up to his room to get his homework more or less done. He took his juggling equipment out of the drawer and laid it on his bed—his two sets of balls, his rings, and his clubs. He had already decided that he would bring them all in case Master Melville asked to see his juggling again. The very thought made him tremble, but he was determined not to freeze up. Master Melville was in show business. He could give Sullivan all kinds of tips and hints for performing better. And maybe, well, just maybe . . . Sullivan's face grew hot.

For the truth was that Sullivan had spent half of last night in a glorious fantasy. He imagined Master Melville, standing in front of the curtains, saying, "Ladies and gentlemen, tonight there is a special person in the crowd. A young person of amazing ability. And if we applaud very loudly perhaps we can convince him to come up and show us his juggling skills. Ladies and gentlemen, I give you . . . *Sullivan!*" And Sullivan would climb onto the stage without the slightest fear and juggle better than he had ever juggled in his life.

All right, he knew that wasn't going to actually happen. Still, he wanted to be prepared for whatever opportunity might arise, which meant that he had to practice. So he picked up three balls, got in his proper stance, began to throw . . . and dropped the balls.

"No, no, no!" Sullivan growled at himself. He picked them up and tried again. He managed five throws before tossing one so wildly that he had to lunge for it, causing him to miss his next throw. *Calm down, calm down!* he told himself. And slowly he did, even if he still made mistakes. He practiced with three balls, then four (hopeless), then rings. It was when he picked up his clubs that he heard a voice at his door.

"Looks like you're having quite a workout."

It was Manny Morgenstern. Somehow Manny always knew when Sullivan was practicing. He had already decided not to tell anyone about the medicine show, not even Manny, although he still hadn't been able to come up with a very clear reason why. Perhaps he simply wanted to keep what he knew, at least for a little while, just for himself.

"You know, just staying out of trouble," Sullivan said, using one of Manny's expressions.

"That's what I used to say whenever I was getting *into* trouble."

"Manny, was there something you really wanted to do when you were a kid? Something that your parents maybe didn't take seriously? That made you really frustrated because you felt they didn't understand you or really even notice you? So that maybe you felt like you were going to explode?"

"Well," Manny said. "I had this idea of becoming a frog farmer."

"Because," Sullivan went on, "I really want—"

But Manny, thinking back to his own childhood, kept talking. "You see, I had this idea of raising frogs in the backyard. In buckets. I figured that I could raise about a thousand frogs a month. Of course I hadn't quite figured out what to do with them all."

Just then the dinner bell rang. "As soon as I hear that bell my mouth starts to water," Manny said. "I hear your father made lasagna tonight. He does make a swell lasagna."

Much later, Manny would remember this conversation with considerable pain. He would hear again Sullivan's words and realize too late that the boy had needed to talk. If only he had listened properly, Manny thought, he might have heard what Sullivan was really thinking that day. And he might have been able to offer Sullivan a few words of wisdom that would have changed everything.

❧

As always, Sullivan helped serve dinner. He didn't like how quiet it was in the dining room today, the old people concentrating on their food. It was like a restaurant in a silent movie. So he chatted with Mrs. Demopoulos, who showed him a new batch of photographs of her

latest grandchild. He let Mr. Orne complain to him about Richard Nixon, even though Richard Nixon hadn't been president for about a million years. When everyone was served, Sullivan sat with Jinny and his parents at their own table.

"And how was everybody's day?" his dad asked.

"Mine was *super* good," said Jinny. "You know what I did all day? I walked on a piperope. On my tippy-toes."

"You mean a *tightrope*," said Sullivan, glaring at his sister.

"Why are you looking at me like that? I didn't say anything about you-know-what."

"What about you-know-what?" asked his mom.

"Oh, that," said Sullivan. "Just Jinny and me playing, that's all."

"I think it's very nice of you to play with your younger sister."

"And it's nice of me to play with my older brother, isn't it?" Jinny said.

"It certainly is," his dad agreed.

"By the way," Sullivan said. "I'm going out for a bit after dinner."

"Out? Where?" asked his dad.

"To a friend's house."

"What friend?"

"Norval. We have a school project to do."

"I'm glad to see you going to another boy's house. What's the project on?"

Sullivan hesitated—he hadn't thought that far ahead. But Jinny blurted out, "Bananas! His project is on bananas."

"Bananas?" asked his dad.

"Sure," Sullivan said. "They're a pretty interesting fruit, when you really think about them."

"I'm sure that's very true," said his dad. "And you're just the person to peel back the skin and get to the truth about them. Get it? *Peel?*"

"I got it, Dad."

"Just make sure you don't *slip up.*"

"Okay, Dad."

"And no *monkeying around* at Norval's. As soon as you're done, you better *banana split* right out of there."

Sullivan's mom patted his dad on the hand. "Just stop it, dear."

❋

There are moments in life when, even as you are determined to do something, you know that it is wrong. You may not know why and so you dismiss the feeling as cowardice or laziness or some other personal failing, rather than for what it is—a warning from some deep part of the brain.

That was what Sullivan felt, packing his juggling

equipment into his backpack. It was an unpleasant, almost sick feeling, but he pushed it back down from wherever it came, went to the front hall, put on his jacket, and headed out. Walking alone, he regretted not having found a way to take Jinny with him. The streets felt very empty and the light was already dimming. He got to the corner where he would have turned for Norval's house, hesitated, and kept going. He walked faster and faster until finally he broke into a run. He went past the store, and then the first farm, to Reingold's Field. Approaching the stand of trees, he could see that the show had already started.

Sullivan joined the audience at the back and saw that the arrogant young magician was performing. He edged up through the crowd and managed to get to the front but was pushed to one side by some teenage boys. The magician had laid a wooden board over two sawhorses and was now helping the girl with red hair lie down on it. He passed his hand over her face and her eyes closed, as if she had fallen asleep. He covered her with a sheet and then, very slowly, pulled one of the sawhorses out from under the board. Even though the girl was now supported at only one end, she didn't fall.

Slowly he pulled away the other sawhorse. The board with the red-haired girl on it remained in the air,

floating. Sullivan thought he knew how the trick was done, but when the magician moved a hoop so that she passed through it, his theory was pretty much shot.

The crowd clapped and the magician put the sawhorses back, pulled off the sheet, and woke the girl before helping her down.

Master Melville came out and talked about Hop-Hop Drops. He used almost exactly the same words as yesterday, only this time he looked over at Sullivan and winked. Sullivan smiled. He felt rather important, being recognized by Master Melville, as if he wasn't a regular part of the audience but someone on the "inside." Next, the automaton Napoleon was brought out and a woman in office clothes volunteered. The game took longer than the night before, but the woman lost.

The two small dogs, Snit and Snoot, took the stage with the small boy. Sullivan realized with a shock that the whole performance was an act. The dogs disobeyed the boy because they were supposed to. In fact, Sullivan could see that by using little hand movements and nods, the boy was actually signaling to them. Every so often he slipped them a little treat as a reward. But it was all done so cleverly that Sullivan admired the act even more.

The last to come on was the girl with red hair. This time he saw something in her face that he hadn't seen

before, a quiet sadness. But what could she be sad about, he wondered, when she got to perform on a real stage? He wondered if it was part of her act, like the boy's bumbling.

And then she looked at him.

The girl was just about to jump off the end of her tightrope when she stared directly at him. Not for a fleeting moment, but for several seconds. She couldn't have been looking at anyone else, he was sure of it. Her eyes were clear, and slowly she shook her head. Just a little. Did she mean "no"? Did she mean "don't"? The curtain closed. He was flattered that she would notice him, and pushed away the unsettling feeling that her expression had given him.

"Ladies and gentlemen," called Master Melville, stepping out in front again. "Usually this is the end of our entertainment. But tonight we have a special treat for you, something rarely presented due to its tremendous degree of difficulty. A magical illusion called *The Vanishing Box*. I will ask our brilliant young magician, the Great Frederick, back onto our stage."

The curtains drew back and the magician wheeled out a large, rectangular wooden box about the size of a small coffin. He turned it in a circle, knocking hard on each side. He opened the lid and tipped it to show the bottom. Then he put the lid down again.

"I need a volunteer," said the magician. "That is, if anyone is brave enough. One person willing to have the molecules of his body dissolved to their individual parts so that they might travel through space and reassemble elsewhere. I can promise you that not one hair on your head will go missing. Of course, I can't guarantee that you will be reassembled in exactly the right order."

The magician gave an artificial laugh. He gestured out to the audience. "Do we have a volunteer?"

Three or four kids in the audience, boys and girls both, eagerly put up their hands. A couple of them even called out, "Pick me!" Sullivan watched curiously, interested to see if it mattered to the magician which volunteer he actually chose. Most likely, he would select somebody who was the right size to make the trick work, or someone who looked cooperative. Frowning, the magician held his hand to his brow and scanned the crowd from one end to another. His face changed, as if recognizing the perfect volunteer, and then he pointed his finger directly at . . . Sullivan.

"You! Yes, you. Thank you for volunteering. If you would just come up onto the stage."

Sullivan hadn't even put his hand up, but he did as he was told. Perhaps the magician preferred someone who wasn't eager. Or perhaps Master Melville had

singled him out as a fellow performer of sorts, someone who wouldn't give away any secrets.

The Great Frederick didn't hold out his hand, so Sullivan had to climb up himself. Without asking, the magician pulled Sullivan's backpack off and tossed it to the side. It was Sullivan's first time on a stage, and even though he didn't have to perform, he still felt his stomach somersault. The light of the kerosene lamps in his eyes turned the audience into nothing more than dark forms beyond the first few upturned faces. He realized with disappointment that the magician had likely pointed to him merely by chance.

Frederick opened the lid of the box. Mistress Melville began to play eerie music on a little accordion. "Look inside," Frederick commanded. "Tell the audience what you see."

Sullivan looked inside. He saw a sheet of paper with words on it:

Say, "I can see the moon and the stars. I can see the whole universe."

Sullivan obeyed the instruction. "I can, ah, see the moon and the stars. I can see the whole universe."

The magician said, "Please, step into the box. Step into the universe and join the moon and the stars."

Sullivan did as he was told. He stepped in with one foot and then the other. He felt the magician's hand on his shoulder begin to push him downward. Sullivan went along, bending at the knees, then leaning forward and putting his hands onto the bottom of the box.

"And where will the boy next appear?" said the magician. "London? New York? Ancient Rome? Or perhaps the future. That, I cannot predict . . ." As he spoke, he slowly closed the lid of the box. The light began to disappear and then, with a thud, the lid was down and Sullivan was in pitch darkness.

He remained uncomfortably on his hands and knees. The darkness was a little freaky. He couldn't hear anything, either — the box muffled sound. He wondered what the magician was saying. He wondered what he, Sullivan, was supposed to *do*. Would a mirror make it look as if he were no longer in the box when he really was?

And then he heard a soft click. There was something about the sound of that click that made his heart flutter. He felt a jolt, the bottom of the box tilted, and he was sliding down. He tried to grab hold of something, to stop himself, but there was nothing to hold on to.

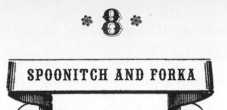

SPOONITCH AND FORKA

PARENTS have what might be called an internal alarm system. When a parent hasn't seen a child for a certain length of time, depending on where that child is supposed to be, an alarm begins to sound. It starts quietly but quicky grows louder until it can't be ignored.

Loretta Mintz was taking a load of sheets out of the dryer in the basement when she realized she hadn't seen Sullivan return from Norval's house. Mind you, she knew that son of hers could lose track of time worse than his father. She was glad he had gone to

Norval's and hoped that he was having such a good time he didn't want to come home yet. Sullivan didn't spend enough time with friends — didn't have enough friends, period. Of course, he had a lot of responsibilities, more than most kids. And having moved so much hadn't helped. Loretta felt guilty about both those things. But she also knew that Sullivan was shy and sometimes had trouble getting up the nerve to talk to other kids. He was definitely like her, not like his father, who would make friends with a chicken thief given half a chance.

She came upstairs to find Mrs. Breeze wandering down the hall in her nightgown, calling, "Ginger, come here, Ginger." Ginger was the name of her cat, who had died of old age last year. Sometimes Mrs. Breeze forgot that Ginger was gone. Maybe, Loretta thought, she didn't really want to believe it. She took Mrs. Breeze by the arm and told her that she would ask that nice man who brought his cat to visit the residents to come back again.

Up on the third floor, Jinny was already tucked in bed and Gilbert was reading to her.

"And then Red Riding Hood decided she wanted to become a professional forklift driver."

"It doesn't say that!" Jinny said. "You're making it up."

"I'm not. And look, the Big Bad Wolf wants to buy a guitar and howl his songs in coffeehouses."

"Gilbert," said Loretta. "Sullivan hasn't come home yet."

"Are you sure?" he asked, his eyes still on the book.

"I've looked through the whole house."

"I suppose we should call Norval. It's too dark now for Sullivan to walk home. I'll have to pick him up."

The telephone was in the sitting room. Jinny followed her parents, her blanket wrapped around her and dragging behind. Loretta watched as Gilbert looked through the phone book and then waited for someone to pick up.

"Hello, Mr. Simick? It's Gilbert Mintz. Sullivan's father. Can I talk to Sullivan, please? What's that? No, he told us that he and Norval had a project. Yes, would you mind? Thanks a lot."

Gilbert put his hand over the receiver. "There's a fellow who doesn't know what's going on in his own house. He thinks Sullivan wasn't over tonight."

Loretta felt a little jump in her heart. She panicked easily about her children, and now she waited anxiously for Norval's father to come back on the line. Gilbert began speaking again.

"Yes? Are you sure that's what Norval said? Well, maybe he's not quite telling the truth . . . No, I'm not

suggesting that your son is a liar. It's just that . . . All right. Well, thank you."

Loretta stepped toward him. "What is it?" she said.

"Norval says that Sullivan was never there."

"But then where did he go?"

At that moment both parents turned toward their daughter.

"Jinny?" said Loretta.

"Yes?"

"Do you know where Sullivan went?"

"He didn't tell me anything," Jinny said, and started to cry. Her parents thought she was crying because she was worrying about her brother. But actually Jinny was crying because she was telling a lie. She did know where Sullivan had gone. But Sullivan always complained that she told on him whenever he spilled something or didn't finish his homework. So she wasn't going to tell on him now. And as soon as he came home, she was going to let him know what a great sister she was.

"That's okay, sweetie," Loretta said, putting her arm around Jinny. "We'll find your brother."

"Let's phone his other friends," said Gilbert.

"Who?" asked Loretta. "He doesn't have any other friends."

"I'm sure he'll be back any minute. He probably took a walk. Maybe he met a girl he likes."

"Gilbert, he's too young."

"Of course he's not too young. When I was his age I fell madly in love with Melissa Frimp. She had a gap between her two front teeth. I thought it was adorable."

"This isn't the time, Gilbert. We need to find Sullivan."

"All right. I'll drive around the neighborhood. I'll check the school and the park. You phone every person we know. He'll show up."

The Mintzes didn't own a car, so Gilbert went next door and borrowed the neighbors', after they made him promise to be careful not to scratch it. He drove slowly up and down the streets with the windows open, calling out, *"Sullivan! Sullivan! Are you there?"* He pulled up by the school and walked to the middle of the field. He called again. He did the same at the park and in the parking lot of the supermarket. He asked a man walking his dog if he had seen a boy. He asked a woman getting out of a taxi. When he saw a pay phone, he stopped to call home.

"Hello?" Loretta said. "Sullivan?"

"No, it's me. There's no sign of him."

"I'm calling the police."

"Right. I'll drive straight home."

In all this rushing about, Jinny's parents forgot to put her to bed. She waited for the police to arrive, her

blanket still wrapped around her. Manny Morgenstern had come upstairs to wait, too. He had been having trouble sleeping and heard their footsteps overhead. When the doorbell rang, Gilbert hurried down and then ushered two police officers in uniform into the sitting room.

The man was short, stout, balding, and had a little mustache. "I'm Officer Spoonitch," he said.

"And I'm Officer Forka," said the woman, who was tall and skinny and had large teeth.

"You're kidding," said Gilbert. "Spoonitch and Forka?"

"Please, no jokes," said the woman officer. "We've heard them all."

"Of course not," Loretta said. "This is a serious matter. Our son is missing."

"Surely not missing, ma'am," said Officer Spoonitch. "Just late. Happens all the time. Has he ever run away?"

"Never," Gilbert said. "And our son is never late. We don't even know where he's gone."

"If I might say something," offered Manny Morgenstern.

"Are you a relation?" asked Officer Forka.

"No, a family friend. I know this boy, Sullivan, very well. He wouldn't run away. He's very responsible. If he hasn't come home it's because he can't."

"Oh, my!" Loretta gasped.

"I'm sorry, I didn't mean to upset you," Manny said. "But wherever Sullivan is, he needs our help."

As each of the adults spoke in turn, Jinny watched them from behind the sofa. When she was a baby she had sucked her thumb, and although she had stopped more than a year ago, she now put her fist to her face, rubbing the side of her nose with her finger just as she used to. Jinny had listened with increasing alarm and a terrible feeling that somehow Sullivan going missing was all her fault. She had lied and now the police were here and still Sullivan hadn't come home. She wanted to speak, but no words came out of her mouth. Jinny took a deep breath and tried once more, and this time the words poured out so quickly that they tripped over one another.

"Sullivan and I went to see this show, it was about doctors, and it was in the field, and there was a magician who grabbed cards out of the air and this funny kind of robot that played chess and two dogs who were so naughty and a girl on a piperope and this man who sold these drops in little bottles, and then after, Sullivan went up to the man and told him he could juggle and I think he was going back but he didn't actually tell me and also there was this beautiful woman with skin so white and long black hair and she played a big drum and—"

The doorbell rang and everyone jumped up. Jinny stopped talking. "Perhaps I'd better get it," said Officer Spoonitch, and he went downstairs while the rest waited. No one spoke, and finally Officer Spoonitch returned with a very young policeman carrying an ordinary plastic shopping bag. Officer Forka went over and the three whispered together a moment.

"Mr. and Mrs. Mintz, does your son have a green jacket?" asked Officer Forka.

"Yes," said Loretta. "Why do you ask?"

Officer Spoonitch took the plastic bag from the young policeman. From it he carefully pulled a jacket, holding the bag under it, for the jacket was sopping wet.

"Let me see," Gilbert said, hurrying over to take it. "Yes, yes, this is Sullivan's. Does that mean you've found him?"

"No, we only found the jacket," said Officer Forka.

"But where? Where did you find it?" cried Loretta.

"In the river. Caught on a branch that was bent down into the water. I'm afraid it looks bad. It looks very bad."

Sullivan's mother collapsed on the floor. Gilbert's father, standing frozen with the wet jacket in his hands, was too stunned to try to catch her.

✻ 9 ✻

A SUITABLE NAME

Dark.

He felt himself moving. Or inside something that was moving. It rocked and jostled whatever it was he was lying on. Not something hard—not the bottom of the black box anymore. Something soft, if lumpy and uneven.

A bed. He was on a bed, with a thin mattress, a rough blanket, a pillow.

He heard voices. Whisperings. But he couldn't make out any of it.

What had happened? He tried to remember, but his head hurt. The Stardust Home. His mother and father. Jinny. The lid of the wooden box closing.

He lay there, waiting for the dizziness to ease. Slowly he found he could see, if just a little. A crack here and there let gray light into a narrow, shaking room. He began to make out other beds, or bunks, against both walls. And bodies on them. He started to understand some of the whisperings.

" . . . and I was sure it wouldn't work. The hinge was jammed . . ."

" . . . anything for a nice hot bath . . ."

" . . . well, I feel sorry for him . . ."

The last was a girl's voice. Somehow he knew who it was — the girl with the red hair. He felt something rise up his throat, burning. He choked it back down again.

"Why feel sorry for someone that stupid?"

"You were that stupid once too, you know."

"He's no worse off than the rest of us."

"But he's new. It's the hardest period."

"I just hope he's good. That he can pull his weight. I'm tired of filling in the extra time."

"All you think about is yourself."

"Hey, you guys, keep your voices down. You want the Black Death to hear? I'll tell you what I hope. I hope his family comes looking."

"Not a chance. You know old Melville. He's a master at leaving a cold trail. Nobody ever finds us."

The voices stopped. Someone turned in his bed. Sullivan felt woozy again and closed his eyes. He tried to stay awake, but sleep pulled him under.

❀

When he opened his eyes again, the brightness hurt. He saw sky, branches, figures moving—but vaguely and out of focus. It took a few minutes for everything to become clear.

He was lying on the grass, propped up against the trunk of a tree. There were other trees, spaced evenly apart. It looked like an abandoned orchard, the trees grown wild, dried-up apples on the ground. The caravan with the words *Master Melville's Medicine Show* on its side stood in a clearing. Nearby, the gray horse swished its tail and ate from a bucket.

Sullivan smelled something delicious. Eggs. Sausages. His stomach knotted up and he realized that he was ravenously hungry. Blinking, he watched people moving about. Frederick the magician was standing by a camping stove, stirring the eggs in a heavy cast-iron pan. The girl with the red hair was setting dishes on a table set with a cloth, glasses, silverware. The two small dogs were playing tug-of-war with a bone while the boy who performed with them was sitting on an overturned

• 100 •

box, using a small paintbrush to touch up the side of the caravan. They didn't have their costumes on but wore jeans and running shoes. The girl had her hair tied back. The magician wore a Rolling Stones T-shirt. They looked like ordinary kids.

Sullivan pulled himself to his feet. He felt stiff, as if he'd been asleep for ages, but otherwise all right. Frederick glanced over at him and then, flipping something in another pan, said aloud, "The new boy's up."

The door of the caravan opened. Master Melville stepped out, sniffing the air and looking about, as if to judge the quality of the day. It was somehow a bigger shock to see him in regular clothes—an old plaid work shirt, overalls, scuffed shoes. He scratched the back of his head and yawned as he walked to the table. He looked directly at Sullivan and smiled.

"Let's all have some breakfast," he said.

Everyone stopped what they were doing and came to the table. The magician brought the two pans while the girl brought a tin coffeepot. They sat down, Master Melville taking the place at one end. He motioned to Sullivan.

"Come, take your place," he said, not unkindly. Sullivan came over. There were two empty chairs, one on the end and one beside the small boy. He sat beside the boy. He noticed the other kids looking at him,

but when he caught their glances, they turned away. Master Melville served everyone generous helpings, including the plate at the empty endseat, and then said, "Wait."

The caravan door opened and the woman came out. Mistress Melville. She was dressed in a shirt and pants but, as on stage, everything was black. Sullivan realized that she was the person they had been whispering about, the one they called the Black Death. Without a glance in his direction, she took her place at the table, picked up her fork, and began to eat.

"Pour me coffee," she said.

"Of course, sunshine of my life, immediately," said Master Melville, jumping up. Hunger almost overwhelmed Sullivan. He took a forkful of eggs. They were the most delicious he had ever tasted.

"It's the braised onions and the hint of Asiago cheese," said Master Melville, as if reading his mind. "The bread is a crusty pumpernickel, and the sausages—well, those you just have to try. My dearest," he said, addressing his wife, "here is the new addition to our little crew."

"I can see that. I'm not an idiot."

"You are the opposite of an idiot, my sugar plum."

"He juggles."

"You spotted him, my darling one. Just by the look in his eye."

"Well, he'd better be good. And more than good. He'd better have an *act*."

"I don't expect he does, dearest. But he will. Trust me, he will."

"And does he have a name?"

It was extremely disconcerting for Sullivan to be listening to this conversation about him as if he were not at the table. Now, at the mention of his name, he began to speak. "My name is——" But Master Melville thrust his hand toward Sullivan's mouth, motioning for him to stop.

"No, no. Not your *old* name. We don't want to hear that. Not now. Not ever. We need a new name for you. A theatrical name. How about Santiago? No, that's no good. Perhaps Mordechai. Or Valentine or Florentino."

"Look at the boy!" Mistress Melville growled. "He can't carry a name like that. Something more suitable for such an ordinary child."

"You're right as always, my dewdrop. What name, then? I know. Dexter."

"Dexter!" Sullivan couldn't help exclaiming. "That's an awful name."

They ignored him. "Yes, it suits him," said Mistress.

"Now let's not talk about it anymore. In fact, let's have silence. I hate mindless chatter during meals."

"And I enjoy a conversation. It is one of the few very small differences between us, my glazed donut. But I obey your wishes. Not another peep!"

Master Melville kept to his word. Neither he nor anyone else spoke again. Sullivan took one more bite and found that his appetite had disappeared. He sat, listening to the others chew their food, to the clatter of forks and knives. He wondered how far they had traveled from Beanfield and what direction they had gone. He wished that he was in the dining room at home, helping to serve the residents. He wished that he was sitting at his own table, with his mother talking about her latest poem and his father making bad jokes and his sister kicking him under the table.

He heard a noise and looked up to see a crow passing overhead. Then he looked at the still leafless trees and the gray sky. And he tried—tried as hard as he could—not to cry.

When breakfast was over, the girl—Esmeralda—and the small boy—Clarence—began to clean up without being told. Sullivan didn't know what to do, so he just stood up and stepped away from the table. He thought about starting to run, in any direction at all, running as fast and as far as he could just to get away

from the caravan and these people. But there are many powerful and conflicting forces that prevent a person from taking action. Fear of making the wrong decision. Fear of being lost, alone, cold, hungry. Perhaps Sullivan's parents were, right now, looking for the caravan. If he ran away, he wouldn't be here when they arrived. And so Sullivan, pulled one way and tugged another by his hammering thoughts, did not run.

Mistress Melville said, "Talk to the boy." Then she got up, sniffed loudly, and began walking toward the caravan. Master Melville watched her until she stepped up through the caravan's door and inside.

"She isn't easy," he sighed. "No, I can't say that. But she's worth it. Let me give you a piece of advice, Dexter. It's best to get on her good side. If you're not, life is only going to be a misery. And it shouldn't be that. It should be good — why, it should be more than good, or what's the point of living at all? Shall we go for a little stroll? There are a few things you need to know."

Sullivan fell in step with Master Melville and they walked between the gnarled trees. His voice was quiet and even gentle. "It's a shock, I'm sure, finding yourself here. A terrible shock. You must be very upset. And no doubt thinking of your loved ones back home. But life can be very surprising. And really, we are all on a

sort of journey, aren't we? A journey with unexpected twists and turns."

"I have to go home," Sullivan said. "My parents will be frantic. They must be looking all over for me. I lied to them. I need to let them know I'm safe and that I'm coming home or they can pick me up."

"Ah, but that's the thing, dear boy. You can't go back. Not just yet."

Sullivan stopped, and Master Melville did, too. They stood under a tree with branches that looked to Sullivan as if they were reaching down to grab him. "Why can't I go back?"

"For one thing, if we let you go back, the police will think — well, they'll think we tried to kidnap you. Which of course is not the case at all. Your falling through that false bottom — it was an accident, a faulty latch. We had no idea you were still in there. But the police assume that people like us, traveling performers, are thieves and cheats. People of the lowest morals. It's a terrible prejudice. They'd go very hard on us if we took you back now."

"But I'll tell them that you didn't kidnap me. I'll tell them it was like you said — an accident."

"I'm sure you would, dear boy. I've absolutely no doubt of your sincerity. But the authorities aren't very

keen on believing children, either. They think little more of them than they do of us. What we need is a little time for the emotions to calm down. That's all."

"If you just let me off somewhere, in some town, I could telephone. I wouldn't tell them anything about you. I'd say that I ran away. And jumped on a train or got a lift with a truck driver."

Master Melville smiled. He patted Sullivan on the shoulder and then left his hand there. "I can see you're clever. And there's nothing more appealing than a clever boy. We're going to get along splendidly. We're going to be real friends. But you see, there is another reason you can't go back. A reason that has nothing to do with us and everything to do with you."

"I don't get it."

Master Melville took a deep breath. "I wish that I didn't have to show you this. I wanted to avoid doing so. It will upset you. But I see that I have no choice."

From the big pocket of his overalls he drew a folded sheet torn from a newspaper. He unfolded it, looked at it a moment, and then reluctantly handed it to Sullivan.

"Here, poor child. Read about your fate."

Sullivan took the paper. Near the bottom, a small article had been circled in black ink.

LOCAL BOY MISSING, BELIEVED DROWNED
Special to the Beanfield Gazette

A tragic event yesterday has left one local family and the residents of a retirement home in grief. Eleven-year-old Sullivan Mintz, son of Gilbert and Loretta Mintz, went out last night and did not return. Shortly after the Mintzes, who operate the Stardust Home for Old People, called the police, the boy's jacket was found floating in the Hasberg River. The police have concluded that the boy drowned while playing on the riverbank. It is believed that the current carried his body into the deepest part of Lake Serenita.

News of the tragedy spread quickly through Beanfield Middle School. "He was like my best friend," said Samuel Patinsky. "I mean, this is going to be hard on me. I might even need to stay home from school."

A memorial service will be held at the Stardust Home tomorrow evening.

"But I'm not dead!" Sullivan cried. "I'm alive! I'm right here! We've got to tell them. My parents and my sister, they'll be so sad. We've got to hurry!"

In his excitement, Sullivan had grabbed hold of Master Melville's sleeve, pulling on him, as if to get

him to take Sullivan home right this moment. Master Melville looked down at Sullivan's hand and for a moment his face grew dark. But then he smiled again, gently removing the boy's hand. "Yes, I'm sure this is very hard on them. But you know, they have already begun to get used to it. They are coming to terms with your death."

"But I don't want them to come to terms with it! I want them to wish I were still alive."

"But there is something else you don't know. Something the newspaper didn't report. Your father had to go to the hospital."

"The hospital? Why?"

"Because he has, well, a weak heart. I suppose he never said anything, not wanting to worry you. But you must have noticed something. Weary sighs. Fatigue."

"I did see him asleep in his chair the other day."

"Exactly," Master Melville said, gravely shaking his head. "Now it's imperative that he be very careful. His recovery depends on it. The shock of losing you was a terrible blow, but finding out that you're actually alive — that could put him over the edge. It could be fatal."

"You mean, if my father found out I was alive, it could kill him?"

"Later, when he's had a full recovery, you can

certainly go back. As long as your parents' other problems are sorted out."

"You mean their financial problems?" Sullivan asked, with increasing despair.

"Yes, their financial problems. That's just what I mean. I expect you have noticed that your parents are always short of money."

"Sure, but that happens to people. They have to be careful about spending."

"That's nothing compared to the crisis your parents are in. To be blunt, they are on the verge of losing everything. The house, the business, even the furniture. They will be on the street with nothing but the clothes they wear. So you see, your disappearance is a lucky break for them. Children are very expensive, you know. They eat a good deal. They need clothes and shoes and books and all sorts of things. Without you there, your parents might just manage to keep going. So your ending up here is rather a blessing. It is saving your family. Of course, it means that Mistress and I will have to take on the expense of clothing and feeding you for a while. And we are not rich people, oh, no. But we are very *giving* people. As you see, we have taken in others. And we won't abandon you."

Master Melville began walking again. Sullivan caught up to him. All this terrible new information

was hard to take in. He said, "But it's only for a little while?"

"Just until your father is well and your parents get back on their feet. Then you can go back. And just imagine what a celebration it will be! What happiness for you all! That is something for you to hang on to, dear boy. The expectation of that moment. And in the meantime, Mistress and I will treat you like our very own child. Just as we do for these other poor, wayward children. Now come and walk back with me. I can see you shivering there without a jacket. I'm sure I have one that will fit very nicely. And I'm sure for the show tonight I can find you some small, useful job. You would like that, wouldn't you?"

Sullivan tried to calm his own breathing. He said, "If I'm going to be here, then I'd like to be useful. Like the other kids."

"That's the spirit. I could see just what sort of boy you were the minute I laid eyes on you."

Master Melville put his arm around Sullivan's shoulder. Deeply upset by all he had heard, Sullivan found the press of the man's arm comforting and un-nerving at the same time. Together, they walked to-ward the caravan.

MISHAPS REMEMBERED

DESPITE what he had said about finding something useful for Sullivan to do, Master Melville simply left him alone. Everyone else, on the other hand, seemed to have loads to do. And when they didn't, they were quite content to lie on the grass and go to sleep, or climb an apple tree, or brush down the gray horse, or read an old book with the covers torn off.

In the middle of the afternoon, Sullivan watched Frederick lay out his magician's equipment on the ground. He took out a tackle box like the ones used for

fishing gear, and when he opened it Sullivan saw that the little drawers were filled with needles and thread, tiny hinges and almost invisibly thin wire, hooks, clips, elastic bands, thimbles, small mirrors, and various glues and adhesive tapes. The magician began to go over all his equipment, touching up scuff marks, replacing bits and pieces. Sullivan watched, admiring the way Frederick wore his hair (long in front so that he had to keep flicking it out of his eyes) and how quick and precise the movements of his narrow fingers were.

At last Frederick looked over his shoulder at Sullivan. "Are you spying on me?"

"No." Sullivan took a step back. "I'm not a spy."

"Well, you look like a spy. What do you want?"

"Nothing, really. I'm just trying to learn whatever I can."

"Not from me you don't."

"I could help."

Frederick stood up. He stepped toward Sullivan, stopping only inches away. He was thin but tall, and Sullivan had to look up. "Nobody touches my gear except for me. Understand? If you go near my things, if I see you even look at them, I'm going to tear your head off. Get it?"

"I didn't mean anything. I was just trying to be nice."

"And what are you, anyway? A kid who does a little juggling? A rank amateur. The Melvilles know I'm what makes this show special. You'd better just watch yourself, ball boy. Stay out of my way."

"Why don't you pick on someone your own size, Freddy?"

Sullivan took a step away from Frederick and turned to see the small boy, Clarence, standing with his hands on his hips. Clarence was even smaller than Sullivan. But Clarence didn't look afraid. He said, "This tough guy act of yours is a real bore, Freddy. Why don't you go fix your hair? So you can pretend you're a rock star and not just a guy who plays with cards."

"Don't call me Freddy, you shrimp. And what business is it of yours anyway? I'm the headline act. You're a mere time-filler."

"Yeah, well, the audiences like me better than you. Besides, if you're the headline, why is it that Essy closes the show?"

Sullivan watched as Frederick's anger grew, his eyes blazing. "You've gone too far, Tiny. I'm going to hang you upside down by your ankles and shake you until your little brain rattles."

He lunged at Clarence. But his hand swiped through empty air, for the boy had already dodged

away. "Come on," Clarence called to Sullivan, running around the caravan. Sullivan hurried after him. They stopped as soon as they got to the other side, where the two dogs were lying under a tree.

"Thanks," Sullivan said. "I guess his bark is worse than his bite."

"No, he'll bite, all right. Kick you too, if he gets a chance. He's nasty. We haven't formally met. I'm Clarence."

The boy held out his hand. Sullivan had never shaken another kid's hand before, but he did now. "And I'm Sull—"

"Don't!" Clarence exclaimed, holding up his palm like a stop sign. "The Melvilles might hear you. They have ears like elephants. I know your name—it's Dexter. Do you want to meet my dogs? Come here, you two, and say hello to Dexter."

Immediately the two little dogs bounced up and hurried over to Sullivan. They licked his face, making him laugh as he patted them.

"They're not usually so friendly right off, so they must like you," Clarence said. "Of course, they won't go near Frederick. He once kicked Snoot and made her yelp. How old are you?"

"I'm eleven," Sullivan said. "And you?"

"I'm ten. Had my birthday last week. But I'm small for my age, so I look younger. Monty likes that. It impresses the crowd."

"Monty?"

"Montague Melville. Monty's what Mistress calls him, so we do, too—when they're not around. I've been trying to teach the dogs a new trick. Want to see?"

"Sure."

"Okay, Snit. Okay, Snoot. I'm going out now. Don't be too sad."

As soon as Clarence said the word "sad," the dogs stood up on their hind legs. They faced each other, touched paws, and started dancing in a circle. But then they both lost their balance and fell backwards, twisting their little bodies so as to land on all fours.

Clarence shrugged and gave them each a treat and a scratch behind the ears. "They can't stay up for long enough yet."

"Are they your dogs? I mean, were they yours before you joined the medicine show?"

"Sure. That's why Mistress Melville spotted me. She saw me playing with them and teaching them tricks in my front yard while the caravan was passing by. Then Monty came back and left a handbill in the spokes of my bike. The dogs couldn't do nearly as much as they can now. We were just fooling around."

At any other time, Sullivan would have connected the dots, would have come to some logical conclusions based on what Clarence had told him. If the Melvilles had deliberately sought out Clarence, then surely they had deliberately chosen Sullivan, too. Which meant that Master Melville had lied to him. And if he had lied about that, maybe he had lied about everything else. But Sullivan was too upset and confused, and his thoughts were too jumbled, to make those connections. He still believed that his getting trapped in the false bottom of the box had been an accident. He still believed everything that Master Melville had told him. His father had a weak heart. His parents barely had enough money to feed themselves and Jinny and the residents. Sullivan couldn't go home. Not until his father was better and he could find a way not to be a burden to them.

There was no lunch that afternoon (now Sullivan understood why everyone else had eaten such large portions at breakfast), but at dinnertime the table was set again. It must have been Esmeralda's turn to cook, for she brought out a very large pot of pasta in a red-pepper cream sauce. There was also garlic bread and green beans with almonds glazed with honeyed spices. Sullivan couldn't help comparing the amazing flavors with the soft, tasteless food that his father cooked at

the Stardust Home. Eating seemed to put everyone in a good mood. There was also, Sullivan detected, a certain rise of energy in anticipation of the evening's show. The performers and Master Melville began to recall and even laugh at themselves for their various stage mishaps. Once, Esmeralda's rope had not been secured properly at one end and, giving way, had caused her to fall onto her rear. Snit had lifted his leg and peed on the curtain. A stream of hidden cards had fallen out of Frederick's sleeve. And one time, Master Melville had taken a dose of Hop-Hop Drops on the stage only to start sputtering and coughing, his face turning purple.

"Not one sale!" he cried, laughing the loudest of anyone. "I didn't make one sale that night."

Only Mistress Melville didn't laugh, or even smile. When her husband finally stopped chuckling, she said, "Sloppy. All signs of unprofessionalism. And nothing to joke about."

"But they are a wee bit funny, my sweet potato," said Master Melville.

"A sense of humor is one thing, I am glad to say, that I was born without."

No one said a word after that until Master Melville, snapping open his pocket watch, declared that it was time.

The table was quickly cleared, the dishes and pots washed in an old tub, and then the caravan was readied. Sullivan guessed that the chores rotated each night. This evening it was Frederick and Clarence who had the task of washing up, and much as they disliked each other, they were able to work together smoothly, without showing any sign of their feelings. Sullivan watched them fold up all the beds and put away any loose objects. Then certain bolts, clasps, and locks were unfastened, and with a crank they lowered the side of the caravan, which became the floor of the stage. The scenery was rolled down and the curtain put up, Clarence making sure it opened and closed properly. Frederick filled the kerosene lamps and hung them. Two tall painted boards were set up, one at either side of the caravan, to act as "wings," behind which the performers could stay out of sight until their entrances.

After that, each person had to prepare for his or her own act. Sullivan watched as props and effects were checked over and put in place. Costumes were pulled on, makeup applied. Frederick loaded his coat with hidden cards, balls, and silks. Clarence checked his pockets for dog treats. Esmeralda powdered her bare feet so they wouldn't slip on the rope. While Master Melville brushed the lint off his jacket and vest, he performed vocal exercises, making weird sounds and

exaggerating his lip and tongue movements: "*Oooh . . . aaah . . . eeee.*" And Mistress Melville, having given her raven hair a hundred strokes, strapped on her washboard and cowbells and hauled her big bass drum onto her back. She put the metal contraption holding the harmonica, kazoo, and whistle around her neck. She hung instruments on her belt. She tuned up her banjo-ukulele.

And then there was Napoleon, the chess-playing automaton. Since it couldn't look itself over, Clarence did, opening and closing the little doors. Just as he was latching the last one, Frederick called out, "I see the first marks!" Sullivan didn't understand what he meant until he stepped away from the wings and gazed out across the darkening orchard. Three figures walked toward them. So a mark was a member of the audience, the word part of the secret language of performers.

Suddenly everyone was hurrying past Sullivan. Master Melville pulled the curtains closed, picked a fallen leaf from the stage, and then bowed to his wife on the ground below. She made three loud thumps on the bass drum and then launched into a quick, jaunty number, strumming the banjo-ukulele and blowing into the kazoo, crashing the cymbal and shaking the tambourine. Sullivan felt a hand grab him and pull

him behind a wing. It was Clarence. "You can watch from here," he said.

Those three people became five people and then ten people and then more, until there was a good-size crowd, those near the front sitting on the grass and those behind standing. Sullivan stood in the wing, hoping that he would recognize someone, but there was not one familiar face. So he shifted his attention and, for the first time in his life, saw a show from the perspective of a stagehand rather than the audience.

There is a moment, just before curtain, when a transformation takes place, when players leave behind their ordinary beings and become their larger, dramatic selves. It happens whether the stage is large or small, the audience a handful or in the thousands. It happens whether the actors are famous or unknown. And although he could not have described it in words, Sullivan felt it happen. He even saw it in Master Melville's face just before going on—he became eager, smiling, and confident.

He heard the crowd's expectant whisperings and realized that the people out there had changed somehow, too. And then he felt a sharp elbow in his back. "Get out of my way, ball boy!" Frederick almost knocked him over as he went by, leaping onto the stage.

But even though Frederick was nasty to him, Sullivan couldn't help admiring his skill as a magician. Seeing his act from behind revealed many of the secrets of his tricks. He saw, for example, that the cards Frederick was about to pull from the air were hidden against the back of his hand, the corners clipped between his fingers. But his ability to somehow draw a card to the tips of his fingers with a snap made Sullivan appreciate his talent all the more.

He also discovered the secret of the Haunted House. It was ingeniously simple. As Frederick brought out the cardboard sides of the house, Esmeralda crawled behind them, hidden from the audience and already in her identical ghost sheet. And at the moment that Frederick held up the roof of the house in such a way as to block himself from the audience's view for two or three seconds, he and Esmeralda switched positions. Yet to the awed crowd, it was as if the one had transformed into the other.

As Frederick came off the stage, Sullivan wanted to say something about how good he was. Maybe that would soften his attitude toward Sullivan. But he didn't get a chance because Frederick immediately grabbed the collar of the corduroy jacket that Master Melville had given him, lifting him onto his toes.

"If you ever get in my way again I'll beat you until you cry for your mother, who'll never come."

"I'm . . . I'm sorry."

"My act is perfect every time. Get it? And I won't have some little kid who juggles as a hobby mess it up."

"That's enough, Frederick. Let go of him."

Esmeralda had come up from behind Sullivan and laid her small hands over Frederick's much larger ones. Slowly, he let go. "Now go on, Freddy. You've got other chores to do."

Frederick grumbled, but he did as Esmeralda said, walking out past the wing and to the back of the caravan.

"Are you all right?" she asked Sullivan.

"Oh, sure. It was nothing. I wasn't really scared."

"No, I knew you weren't. It's just, well, not everyone understands Frederick." She straightened Sullivan's collar and smiled. "That looks better. I don't think we've properly met. I'm Esmeralda. But offstage everyone calls me Essy. And you're Dexter. It's hard, getting used to a new name, I know. Can I call you Dex?"

"Sure."

"Good. I'd better hurry and get ready for my own act. See you later, Dex."

Sullivan watched Esmeralda — Essy — run around to the back of the caravan, where she would no doubt

go into the little tent that had been set up and change into her leotard and skirt. His gaze lingered a moment longer on where she had been and then he turned around again to watch Clarence with Snit and Snoot. He saw how Clarence slipped them little treats after each trick and how, even when he was pretending to scold them, he would nod or give them a quick pat. When they came off stage, the little dogs both jumped up to say hello to Sullivan.

"If you always feel fully and completely happy, my friends, then you do not need my drops and I will not sell them to you for any amount of money."

As Sullivan listened, something occurred to him, something that seemed so totally obvious now that he thought of it. The entire show — the magic, the dogs, the tightrope, everything — had one purpose only. To sell Master Melville's Hop-Hop Drops. Exactly how the show made people want to buy the drops, Sullivan wasn't sure, but he saw that every act led up to the moment when the Melvilles would go to their little table. It was all for the purpose of getting the people to line up at the table. And the people didn't even seem to realize it.

"Are there any chess players in the audience tonight? You, sir? Yes, I'm sure you're very good. Good enough, no doubt, to win against a pile of nuts and bolts . . ."

For the third time Sullivan watched Napoleon play chess, and for the third time he saw its human opponent go down in defeat. It took Napoleon only twelve moves, so fast that the audience didn't have a chance to become deeply involved in the progress of the game. The applause was a mere smattering as the curtain closed.

Master Melville, with Frederick's help, wheeled Napoleon off the stage and down a board to the ground. Sullivan felt it was his chance to speak up, if he was ever going to, so he screwed up his courage and said, "Master Melville? You said there was something useful I could do tonight?"

"Yes, yes, of course," Master Melville said, puffing for breath. "In fact, you can wheel this thing behind the stage with Frederick. It's hard on my old back. That would be most useful, Dexter."

"Sure, I'll help," Sullivan said gladly. Master Melville straightened up, wincing, and Sullivan took his place. As soon as he and Frederick began pushing Napoleon over the trampled grass of the orchard, he felt how heavy it was.

"Watch it! You almost ran over my foot," cried Frederick.

"I'm so sorry."

"You'll be really sorry if you aren't more careful."

They kept pushing until finally they got Napoleon behind the caravan. Frederick stood up and wiped his hands together. "You can take care of the rest," he said, striding away.

"The rest of what?" asked Sullivan, but Frederick was gone. As he stood there wondering what he was supposed to do, he heard a rattling come from inside Napoleon. Surprised, he looked down to see that the entire contraption was shaking.

"Let me out!" came a muffled voice.

"Napoleon?"

"Of course it's not Napoleon! Open the door!"

Sullivan bent down and opened the small front door. "Not that one! In the back!" He fumbled with the latch and got it open, only to see half of Clarence's face! He was breathing quickly, his face red. "There's a button on top. Press it while holding on to its shoulders. Then tilt the whole top backwards. And hurry!"

At first Sullivan couldn't find the button, as it was hidden under a flap of cloth that matched Napoleon's uniform. But finally he pressed it and pushed on the shoulders, and the whole top half of the contraption tilted backwards. He grabbed Clarence's hand and helped pull him out.

"I can't believe it," Sullivan said. "It's a fake! It seemed like a real machine."

"To you and everybody else," Clarence said, stepping out. "Although if you think about it, how could a bunch of cogs and gears be able to see the board, understand the game, and decide on a move? It's pretty silly, really."

"But it doesn't look like a person could fit in there. And I couldn't see you when Master Melville opened the little doors."

"I pull up my knees when one door opens and then lie flat for another. And there are a couple of mirrors, too. Of course, when I started I wasn't much of a chess player. But with all this practice I've gotten pretty good. Being inside there used to be easier, but I've grown. It's hot as anything and I can hardly breathe. Would you mind helping me out next time, too? I hate to rely on Frederick. He pretends to forget and walks away."

"Sure, I'll help. For as long as I'm here, anyway."

"Yes, that's what I mean, of course. Want to go see the rest of the show?"

Clarence and Sullivan went around to watch from the wing, where Master Melville was already standing. He whispered to Clarence, "The game was too quick. Next time you have to string him along."

"I tried. I gave him all kinds of chances. But he was such a bad player, he didn't see them."

On stage, Esmeralda was on the tightrope. Tonight

she did something that Sullivan hadn't seen before—she stood with two feet on the rope, facing the audience, swung her arms wildly, and somersaulted to the floor. Now that he had spoken to Essy, it was even more fun watching her, and he clapped as loudly as anyone in the audience when she curtsied. When he looked across to the opposite wing, he saw Frederick gazing at her adoringly as he clapped, too.

Master Melville made his final pitch, again inviting the audience to buy a bottle of Hop-Hop Drops, then slipped behind the curtain. Everyone gathered on the stage, hidden from the crowd, and in their faces Sullivan saw a glow of energy and pleasure that came from just having performed. They whispered and joked and Master Melville praised each of them, which, perhaps despite themselves, made them happy. Sullivan stayed in the wing, for he knew that he wasn't a part of this feeling—this relief at the end of the show that joined them together.

Mistress Melville removed her instruments, and once more they set up the table next to the caravan. "Dexter," Master Melville called. "Stand by my side and hand the bottles to me." Sullivan obeyed, coming up beside them. The bottles were nestled in straw inside a wooden box, and with each sale he took one out and handed it to the man or woman. Sullivan had a

chance to examine the bottles as he did so. They were narrow and strangely nice to hold, with slightly long necks and little corks. The labels were cut out with quite elaborate borders, and the words were printed in old-fashioned type. The liquid itself, when Sullivan held it up, was translucent but colored—a vibrant purple if held one way, a deep red if held another.

A man in a cardigan handed over his ten dollars and asked, "What's in those drops, anyway?"

"A proprietary secret, my friend," Master Melville said, handing the money to his wife. "Known only to myself and the great pioneer medicine men of old. And if you want to ask one of them, just go to the third gravestone in the cemetery. He'll tell you before I will!"

When the last bottle was sold and the last audience member had wandered off, the performers had to clean up, for the crowd had left behind food wrappers and plastic bottles and paper cups on the grass. The glow had already begun to fade, leaving behind simple fatigue. And there was something else that Sullivan sensed, almost a feeling of loss, or emptiness. The wings were taken down, as well as the backdrop and curtain and changing tent, and then Frederick turned the crank to pull the stage up while Master Melville hitched up the gray horse. Inside the caravan,

Clarence and Esmeralda set up the four low bunks, which folded down from the walls. Behind the wall opposite the door, Sullivan realized, was a smaller space where the Melvilles must also have had a bed. It wasn't exactly a life of luxury, even for them.

Inside the caravan the children ate a snack of dry biscuits and milk in the glow of a candle, and then Master Melville, knocking on the plywood wall, sent them to bed. They used a basin to wash up and brush their teeth, and they changed into pajamas under their covers. There was a set laid out for Sullivan, just as there had been a toothbrush and a small towel. The pajamas were for a younger kid—they had cowboys and horses on them, and they weren't new. Clarence whispered, "Monty must have snatched them off a clothesline somewhere."

Then there was a sudden jolt, a whinny from the horse, and the caravan began to move. Frederick blew out the candle. No one talked. Sullivan could hear Clarence, who had allergies, wheezing a little. He couldn't sleep. When he closed his eyes he saw his parents' faces, their eyes dark and their cheeks stained with tears. He thought about his father's weak heart and wondered when he might be strong enough again to find out that his son was alive. He thought about their money problems and wished that he could find

a way to help rather than be a burden. And when he shook his head to dispel their faces, his sister Jinny's appeared in their place. Poor Jinny—had there ever been a cuter, more lovable sister? Why hadn't he been nicer to her, more kind and helpful? Why had he always been impatient with her? Why did he have to tell her that he hated her, the last time they saw each other? Whenever he got back, he vowed to be the best big brother ever.

He didn't even realize that he was crying. Not until he felt a gentle hand on his arm and heard Esmeralda's voice in his ear. "Shhh, it's okay," she said. "We all feel like that sometimes. Sleep is a real gift for the unhappy, you know. I'll stay right here until you're asleep."

He wanted to tell her that he was glad she was there, but no words came out. Instead, he just closed his eyes.

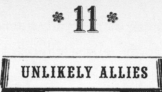

UNLIKELY ALLIES

NORVAL Simick had never been to Sullivan Mintz's house or vice versa. They had never hung out at the mall outside of town or become Facebook friends. About the only thing they had done together regularly was have lunch in the school cafeteria.

But when the newspaper published the article stating that Sullivan had drowned, Norval went into his room and refused to go to school. He did go the following day, but he was silent and withdrawn and sad. Mr. and Mrs. Simick knew their son was a sensitive

boy, but when a few days later he wasn't any better, they began to consider taking Norval to a doctor.

There is someone else who would have been surprised by Norval's reaction — Sullivan. He didn't believe that he'd made much of an impression on anyone in Beanfield, especially at school. He had no idea that Norval, who had always eaten his lunch alone until Sullivan's arrival, had been grateful for his friendship and had begun to enjoy school more as a result. Norval had seen Sullivan in a way that Sullivan had never seen himself: as smart, sometimes funny, and totally unpretentious.

"This Sullivan must have been a special person," Norval's father said to him. "What was it about Sullivan that you liked so much?"

"He was just a nice guy," Norval answered. "A really nice guy."

The news that Sullivan had drowned — well, that was a genuine blow for Norval. He had experienced one death in his family, his grandfather, when he was a hundred and one. That had been sad too, but the man had experienced a long and full life and, as he'd told Norval on one of his last visits, he felt ready to go. But Sullivan was just a kid. He hadn't really had a chance to do anything yet. He hadn't had a job, or gone to college, or learned to drive, or visited France

or China, or had a girlfriend, or performed his juggling for anybody, or done a million other things. It seemed so mean and unfair. And why a nice guy like Sullivan? Why not a stupid bully like Samuel Patinsky?

As it became an accepted fact that Sullivan had drowned, Beanfield Middle School lowered its flag to half-mast. An assembly was called, and all the students shuffled into the auditorium. Beanfield's principal, Mr. Washburb, talked about the importance of safety and the danger of "daredevil activities just to impress your friends," which didn't seem to have anything to do with Sullivan. Pushing his glasses up his nose, the principal said, "I must admit, I don't personally remember Sullivan Mintz. I only know the kids who get sent to the office when they're in trouble. But I've talked to his teachers, and they all liked him. They said he never disrupted class and always got his homework done."

Norval found the assembly highly unsatisfying. There was nothing about the sort of person Sullivan had been. Nobody who actually knew him spoke. And after the assembly, the janitor raised the flag back to the top of the pole.

For the rest of the day, Norval couldn't shake his unsatisfied feeling. He felt so crummy about it that he hardly took in what his teachers said. He wanted to talk to somebody else, somebody who had known

Sullivan, too. But who? It wasn't until near the end of the day that Norval realized something that shocked him. There was only one other person at the school who he was certain had known Sullivan. And that person was Samuel Patinsky.

Samuel had come up to their lunch table almost every day. He had said something mean or sarcastic, and sometimes he had done something mean, too. He'd picked on Sullivan in gym class and had cracked jokes about him in shop. He'd knocked his books out of his hand and tripped him in the hallway. Yes, these were awful things, but at least Samuel had known Sullivan, in a way.

And there was something else that Norval realized. Samuel hadn't been at the assembly. In fact, he hadn't been in school at all that day. Maybe he had a cold. Maybe his parents had taken him on a vacation. Or was there another reason?

Norval just couldn't let go of the thought. He decided that after school he would walk to the Patinsky house and knock on the door.

Samuel Patinsky lived in the opposite direction from the school, at the end of a dead-end road. Norval expected it to be a shabby place, with maybe a broken-down car in the driveway and a mean-looking dog tied on a rope to a tree stump. But instead it was a small

yet neat house with a freshly mowed lawn and pink begonias in the planters. Still, it took all Norval's courage to get himself to walk up to the front door, and an extra dose for him not to run away and to ring the bell.

The door opened and a woman that Norval recognized answered. "Mrs P.?" he said in surprise. Mrs. P.—he had never heard her full name—worked as a playground monitor at Beanfield Middle School, making sure kids didn't litter or hurt themselves doing something stupid.

"Why, hello there, Norval. Are you selling popcorn for the Boy Scouts?"

"No, I'm not. Do you live here?"

"For about fifteen years."

"Are you by any chance Samuel's mother?"

"Of course I am. Has Samuel never mentioned it?"

"I guess I forgot," Norval said, although he was sure that Samuel never had. All he ever called her was *the fun police* because she once stopped him from going headfirst down the slide with two little kids that he had forced to sit on top of him. "Is Samuel in?"

"Yes, he's in his room. I hope he hasn't done something to you."

"No, he hasn't."

"Actually, he's been pretty down in the dumps.

What happened to that unfortunate child, Sullivan Mintz, has really upset him. But then, he's a sensitive boy."

"He is?" Norval's voice rose.

"I'm sure it would do him a world of good to see a friend. Come on in."

"I'm not exactly—" Norval started to say, but then he stopped and just followed Mrs. P. through the front vestibule and down a hall. Mrs. P. knocked lightly on a door. "Samaleh? You have a visitor, a friend from school."

Samaleh? Samuel Patinsky actually had a mother who loved him! She opened the door and gently ushered Norval in. Looking around, Norval saw a normal kid's room—model airplanes hanging from the ceiling, piles of comics, an MP3 player on the desk. Even more surprising, Samuel was lying on his bed in bunny-decorated pajamas, with his hands behind his head, staring up at the ceiling.

"Sweetie, it's Norval Simick to see you."

Immediately Samuel sat up with a frown. "Who? Oh, it's you."

"Well, I'll leave you two alone. Norval, see if you can cheer Sammy up."

Norval didn't want Mrs. P. to leave, but she did,

closing the door behind her. As soon as she was gone, Samuel's face took on its usual mean scowl. "Who said you could come to my house?" he said. "I might bash you right now."

"I'll leave," Norval said, reaching for the doorknob.

"No, don't. My mom will just ask me why. You have to stay at least ten minutes. Did some teacher send you because I haven't handed in my homework?"

"Nobody sent me," Norval said. "I just—it's only—oh, it's hard to explain. The truth is, I don't know who else to talk to. You're the only other person who knew Sullivan."

At the sound of Sullivan's name, the most astonishing thing yet happened. Samuel began to cry. It was about the ugliest sight Norval had ever witnessed, and it was painful, too.

"Are you okay?"

"Sullivan . . . is . . . dead. And I was so mean to him."

"If you don't mind my asking, why?"

"I don't know."

"Really?"

"I mean, my big brother was always mean to me. He took my stuff. He called me names. He tripped me and pushed me. Then he went off to college. I thought I'd be glad, and in a way I was, but I was also lonely.

And then I saw this new kid, Sullivan. He looked at me like he was afraid, I guess because I'm kind of big. It made me mad, so I shoved him into a locker. It made me feel like my brother. And it just went on from there. I didn't even enjoy it. And now I wish I'd been his friend. But it's too late."

Norval went over and sat on the bed. Gingerly he reached out, gulped, and put his hand on Samuel's shoulder. He wasn't sure what to say; after all, Samuel really had been mean to Sullivan.

Samuel said, "Did you go to the assembly? I just couldn't. How was it?"

"Honestly? It sucked. Principal Washburb didn't say anything real. Sullivan's going to be forgotten at school in like two seconds."

"But he can't—we can't let him be forgotten!" Samuel said with determination. "Listen to me, Norval—"

"Hey, that's the first time you've ever used my name."

"We can't let Sullivan be forgotten at Beanfield Middle School. I can't take away what I did to him, but at least I can do something. It's up to us to make sure he's remembered."

"Sure, but how?"

"I don't know. Wait, I do know! A day. A special day." Samuel stood up. "You and I have to make, or start, or establish or whatever you call it, a Sullivan Mintz Day. What do you say, Norval? Are you with me on this?"

"Uh, I guess so," Norval said. "Yes. Yes, I'm definitely with you."

"All right!"

Samuel jumped up, and for a moment Norval thought he was going to slug him, but Samuel only patted him on the back.

* 12 *

OVER the next week, Sullivan learned the routine of Master Melville's Medicine Show. The caravan traveled during the night so that if it passed through any towns or villages it would be less likely to draw attention. Occasionally a person, unable to sleep, might glance out a window, or a worker sweeping the sidewalk or closing up a tavern or baking the next day's bread might look up and see this strange apparition of horse and caravan passing by. But the next day, it would seem like a dream.

Shortly after dawn the caravan would stop by a clump of trees between two fields, or an empty lot — some unattended place not too far from where people clung to the outskirts of a town. Master Melville would rouse the players out of bed, breakfast would be made and served, and then Master Melville and Frederick would take bundles of handbills and set out in opposite directions, placing them at people's doors. The others would work on their routines, or lie under a tree day-dreaming, or find another way to pass the time.

Esmeralda had some old schoolbooks — arithmetic, history, science — and she would give lessons to Clarence. And when she was done she would spend time with the gray horse, brushing it, checking its hooves for stones. The Melvilles had no name for it, but the kids called it Soggy, short for Soggy Biscuit, after the famous racehorse named Seabiscuit. The gray was no racehorse, but all of them, even Frederick, liked to pat his nose and talk to him and offer him treats. Esmeralda paid him the most attention, though, and Soggy always raised and then lowered his big head when she came near, wanting her to talk into his ear. The horse tolerated Master Melville, understanding that he was, indeed, his master. He did not like Mistress Melville and whinnied nervously when she came near. But he loved Esmeralda — that, Sullivan could see.

Slowly Sullivan came to believe that Master Melville had lied to him and that he had been deliberately entrapped. He, like the others, was being held against his will. But surely *some* of the things Master Melville had told him were true, and so Sullivan spent his time scheming how to get away when he felt that the time was right—that is, when enough time had passed for his father to recover from the shock of his disappearance and supposed drowning. And also when he had figured out how not to be a financial burden on his parents. But getting away . . . that was the main thing.

First, he considered jumping on the horse and riding off. Only he didn't know how to ride a horse and would probably get thrown and break his neck. Next, he considered sneaking a note to somebody in the crowd that said: *Help! I've been kidnapped! Take me with you!* But wouldn't people think it was part of the act? They might even show it to Master Melville. Or what if they weren't nice people and decided to keep him to plow their fields or wash their floors?

He considered many other plans, too—writing a message on the roof of the caravan that might be seen by a passing airplane, dressing up in some of Esmeralda's clothes and pretending to be a girl. But in the end the one that made the most sense to him

was slipping out of the caravan at night. That way the Melvilles wouldn't even know he was gone until morning. The only problem was that Master Melville always locked the back door of the caravan from the outside. With a padlock. A heavy steel padlock.

Sullivan soon realized he couldn't spend the entire day thinking about his escape plan. He had to do something else with his time. The logical thing, he decided, was to practice his juggling. After all, he had brought his equipment in his backpack. (How long ago that seemed! How naive he'd been, expecting to be showered by Master Melville's compliments.)

And so, on the third day of his "captivity," as Sullivan thought of it, he took his backpack from under his bunk in the caravan, found a clear space of grass, and began to juggle. He started with a basic three-ball half-cascade and found himself rusty, or just off somehow, because he kept throwing too high, or too late, or he missed a ball as it came down. One ball even hit him on the head—just as Frederick was walking by with his magician's suit, an ironing board, and one of those old-fashioned irons that you heat over the fire.

"That's a move I've never seen," he said. "Did you invent that all by yourself? What do you call it, the Concussion?"

"I'm a little out of practice."

"Even if you were in practice, you'd stink. But keep it up. I'm sure if you work really hard you'll be merely lousy one day."

And with a snort of laughter he passed by. Sullivan narrowed his eyes at Frederick's receding back. He wanted to say something clever, but all that came out was "Yeah . . . so . . . and you, too." Then he picked up the balls and started again.

After a few minutes his rhythm came back to him. He added the fourth ball—cascade, under the arm, under the leg, spin. He moved on to the rings and the clubs. Juggling is a skill that, like playing a musical instrument or downhill skiing, requires a keen sense of rhythm, an ease of movement, and quick thinking that is both learned and instinctive. It can make a person feel totally occupied and totally free at the same moment. For someone feeling troubled, it can be wonderfully soothing—almost a form of therapy. As Sullivan's mind became focused, he felt lifted beyond his loneliness and worry.

He was just tossing a club when Frederick walked back again, the ironing board still under his arm.

"Oooh, I'm sure your mommy would be impressed."

Sullivan caught the clubs and turned to face him. The soothing feeling had instantly evaporated. "What's your problem, anyway?"

"My problem? You're my problem. You don't be-long here. With us. We're real performers. And what are you? Nothing."

"Well, I don't even *want* to be here. I don't want to be one of you. And I'm not nothing. And I don't care what you think——"

But Frederick had continued on with a wave of his hand. Sullivan was left shaking with anger. What did he ever do to Frederick? Did he *ask* to be kidnapped? Because that's exactly what had happened to him. This was no accident. He was kidnapped and he was a pris-oner and he hated it and wanted to go home.

Sullivan shoved his equipment into his backpack. He picked it up and strode toward the caravan. But then Clarence, who was sitting under a tree with the dogs, said, "Hey, Dexter. Sit down a minute."

"No, thanks."

"Come on. Take a load off."

Sullivan stopped. "My dad used to say that."

"Mine, too."

Sullivan walked over to him and sat on the ground. Clarence said, "You can't let Frederick get to you. He's just a jerk. And he wouldn't have said anything if you weren't good."

"I don't think so."

"I'm serious. He hates competition. He's always

judging who gets the most applause. And he sees that you're talented. Raw, sure, but talented. It gets his blood boiling."

"I hate him."

"I don't think I hate him. I feel sorry for him."

"Sorry?"

"Magic is the only thing he has." Clarence paused, a pained expression on his face. "Oh, jeez, what did these dogs eat? They're so gassy today. Maybe that should be in the act. *Clarence and His Amazing Farting Dogs.*"

Sullivan laughed. Snit and Snoot immediately jumped on him, licking his face and knocking him over.

❋

Each night the show began at dusk, the kerosene lamps illuminating the stage. And each show was a little bit different in feeling. Sometimes it was the audience, more talkative one night, more silently attentive the next. Sometimes it was a performer—Frederick glaring even more angrily than usual, or Esmeralda more comic or more elegant. On most nights somebody tried something new, to make his or her act better and, as Clarence told him, because doing the exact same thing got boring after a while. Sullivan never tired of watching, though. He didn't want to envy the others

on the stage, not when they were all here against their will; didn't want to covet the applause of the crowd, the praise of Master Melville. But he couldn't help it.

After the show — after the excitement faded away and the night grew silent — was the worst time. The time that missing his mother and father and Jinny hurt like the deepest wound. But even this he started, slowly, to become used to. The pain itself became a kind of comfort to him as he lay on his bunk and felt the rhythm of the caravan's wheels. And he learned to fall asleep this way, easily and without dreams.

One evening near the end of his second week, as Sullivan helped Clarence pick up trash after the performance, a girl came up to them and said, "I liked the show. It's the best thing I ever saw, even better than the Ice Capades."

Clarence looked around a moment, as if to see whether they were being watched. The Melvilles were still busy selling Hop-Hop Drops at the table beside the caravan. "Thank you," he said. The girl was very tiny, even smaller than Clarence, with straight bangs and large eyes and a tiny nose. She was also very talkative. "I don't know what I liked better, the magic or the dogs or the tightrope," she went on. "And the lady who plays the music! She's beautiful, isn't she? But kind of scary. She never smiled once. I wish I played

an instrument. Or had a dog. We've only got chickens and cows and a goat. But I'm really good at chess. I'm the school chess champion. My name's Lillian. Lillian Reilly. But everyone calls me Lilly. I wanted to play chess with Napoleon, but the man didn't pick me. Do you think he decided I was too young? I'm not as young as I look. I'm eleven. I'm just small. Which is strange, because my brothers and sisters are all big. I'm the runt of the litter, my dad says. He's the one who taught me to play chess but now I can beat him, too."

Lilly certainly was a talkative girl, thought Sullivan.

"Listen, Lilly," Clarence said, almost in a whisper. He glanced over his shoulder and then slipped his hand into his pocket. From it he drew out an envelope. Sullivan saw that it had an address and a stamp on it. "Could you mail this for me? It's to my parents." Lilly took it from him. "It would mean a lot to me . . ."

Clarence stopped. Sullivan had felt it, too—a narrow hand on his own shoulder. He turned to see Mistress Melville standing behind them, her long black hair framing her pale face. "Why, there's no need to bother the girl," she said, smiling coldly. "I'll be glad to mail your letter."

She released her grip on Sullivan, reached between them, and snatched the envelope from the girl's hand.

She held it to her breast, tapping her long nails against it. "Now run along, child. I'm sure your parents are waiting for you. We've got a lot of work to do here."

Then she grabbed Sullivan and Clarence by the collar and pulled them away. As they approached the caravan she hissed at Clarence, "You've been warned before. You don't talk to people. And you certainly don't write letters. But a warning wasn't good enough, I see. You need to be taught a lesson."

"I won't do it again, I won't! I was stupid. And . . . and ungrateful. I'm sorry."

"Yes," Sullivan pleaded. "He's sorry —"

"And he's going to be even more sorry in a minute. You, go and help the others," she ordered, putting her hand against Sullivan's back and giving him a hard shove.

He did as he was told. Clarence was made to sit by one of the caravan's wheels. When the caravan was packed up and the beds down, he was sent inside with Sullivan and the others without the usual evening snack. They changed under their covers, and Sullivan saw that Clarence was trembling. They lay in bed in silence and as Master Melville locked the door from the outside, Sullivan could hear him speaking to Mistress.

"Not too harsh now, my dearest. He is just a small boy. He's not that strong, you know."

"Don't be so pathetic," came Mistress Melville's voice. "It disgusts me. He must be made an example. To the others, and especially to the new boy. Now hurry up."

Sullivan listened, but there were no more voices. The horse whinnied as always and the caravan began to move.

"Maybe it won't be so bad," Sullivan whispered. "I mean, she is human, isn't she?"

But no one else said anything, not Esmeralda with soothing words or even Frederick, who might have been expected to tell Clarence how stupid he had been. The caravan rattled on, and even in the dark Sullivan knew that no one was asleep. They had traveled for nearly an hour when the caravan slowed. The wheels ground against gravel and stopped. A moment later came the key in the lock, and the door opened.

"You!" Mistress Melville said, pointing at Clarence. "Out."

Clarence slipped out of bed. He stood in his pajamas, his feet bare. A damp gust of wind swirled in. Clarence walked slowly to the door and stepped down beside her. Mistress Melville held a chain, which she wound around one of his wrists and locked. Then they began to walk away, Clarence with his head down. Through the open door, Sullivan and the others watched them go.

And then Sullivan saw what they were walking toward.

A cemetery.

The caravan had pulled up to a small, old cemetery. Behind a rusting fence were gravestones, their corners worn by decades of rain and wind, leaning this way and that. A cemetery in the middle of nowhere, surrounded by trees that must have died from some blight, for they had no spring leaves. Sullivan could see the two figures step over the broken gate. He saw Mistress point and Clarence hesitate a moment before he lay down on a gravestone that had fallen over. Mistress attached the other end of the chain to something—a broken piece of the iron fence, perhaps. Then she walked back, looked through the doorway at the rest of them, and shut the door. They heard the sound of the lock. Then they were moving again.

"We can't be leaving him there," Sullivan whispered. "In a cemetery! And do you hear that? It's starting to rain. We can't leave Clarence."

"There isn't anything we can do," Frederick said glumly. Esmeralda just lowered her head.

At Halloween, children like dressing as ghosts and goblins. They like putting Styrofoam gravestones on their lawns, plastic ghouls on their porches. But a real cemetery at night, with dead people moldering in the

ground or already reduced to a pile of bones, and the cold, clammy feel of the stones, was nothing like Halloween. Sullivan couldn't sleep. Not with the image of Clarence lying there. What if he was found by wild animals? Or a grave robber? And while Sullivan didn't exactly believe in ghosts, he didn't have any proof to the contrary, either. What if the spirits of the dead really did come out at night? What if Clarence was so frightened that it made his heart stop?

It was clear from the turning and sighs in the other bunks that nobody else was sleeping, either.

And the caravan rolled on.

It was many long hours before the faintest light could be seen through the cracks in the walls. And another hour still before the caravan came to a halt. Some time after that, Sullivan heard the key in the padlock and then squinted against the sudden light as the back door was flung open.

"All right, my dears. Rise and shine," said Master Melville, a little less energetically than usual. "No dawdling, now. Time to make breakfast."

They all got up, dressed under their covers (Sullivan was becoming quite good at it), and stumbled out into the morning. Master Melville whistled as he set up the camping stove, but Sullivan thought that he was covering up his own worry about Clarence.

He had dark circles under his eyes, and when he said, "Why don't we have pancakes, eh?" Sullivan could see that his smile was forced.

"Hey," Frederick said under his breath as he walked past the others. "Soggy's gone."

Indeed, the horse was not in his harness or any-where nearby. And when the pancakes were ready and they all gathered at the table, Mistress Melville did not come out of the caravan to sit at the head of the table.

"She's gone to get him," Frederick whispered.

"What's that?" said Master Melville testily. "No whispering, now. Eat up."

But Master Melville himself did not touch his break-fast. He looked off into the distance, his jaw grinding as if he were chewing invisible gum. At last he said, "Perhaps I should say a word or two." He looked at them now, from one to another. "Rules are there for a reason. They pro-tect us, you see? All of us. Discipline is also there for a reason. We are a company of performers. Members of an honorable profession. We hold on to something of value, great value. We exist out of time, far from the noise of the contemporary world. This is why we delight our au-diences. This is why we bring—I am not ashamed to say it—a little happiness. But what we have, what we *do*, is fragile. Make no mistake, it is easily broken. Any

one of you can destroy what we have made. I know that. Mistress Melville knows that. Perhaps Mistress and I have different ways sometimes, but our goals are identical. And we do not waver in them. Or in our deep concern for each and every one of you. You are our family. That's right, our family. And now, finish eating. Dexter, you haven't touched your pancakes. Go on, you all need your strength."

But Sullivan couldn't eat. When breakfast was done, they began cleaning up. Sullivan still did not quite understand the rotation of jobs, and someone always had to tell him what to do. Today he was drying dishes while Esmeralda washed. He tried to ask her about Clarence, but she just held up her hand, as if to say, *No, please, I just can't speak.*

In fact, nobody spoke at all. Not all morning, or into the afternoon. And nobody did much of anything else, either; no practicing or cleaning equipment or even reading a book. Esmeralda sat on a tree stump and stared. Frederick leaned against the back of the caravan, switching a tree branch against the ground. Even Master Melville didn't do anything except sit in a folding chair under a tree with his hat on and his eyes closed.

And then, in the middle of the afternoon, Sullivan heard it. So did the others. Hoofbeats. Esmeralda

stood up. Frederick dropped his branch. Master Melville put the folding chair by the caravan. And all of them stood and waited.

The horse appeared at the top of a low, distant hill. It was moving at a gallop but it still took some time before the figure really grew larger; before Sullivan could make out Soggy's ears and nose. And Mistress Melville, leaning forward, her arm snapping a riding crop against Soggy's side.

At last the horse was upon them and Mistress Melville pulled up on the reins. Her black attire was covered in a fine dust, as was her face. Only when the horse swung around did Sullivan see Clarence clinging to her from behind, his face in a grimace, his eyes closed as if he was somehow able to hold on while asleep or unconscious.

"Easy now — let's help the boy off," said Master Melville. He had to pry Clarence's fingers from Mistress Melville's waist, but as soon as he did, Clarence slumped backwards and would have fallen to the ground if Frederick hadn't caught him. Then Master Melville picked him up and carried him into the back of the caravan. Mistress Melville snapped, "Take care of the horse," then dropped the reins and retreated into the front part of the caravan.

"Water!" Master Melville called through the open

back door. "And then some soup broth. Warm, not hot."

Esmeralda ran to get the plastic water jug and hurried back with a tin cup of water. She came out sniffling and went to the stove that Frederick had already brought out. "He's very weak," she began. "But he opened his eyes. And do you know what he said? He said, 'I didn't see a single ghost.' And then he tried to laugh, but he couldn't."

Sullivan took care of Soggy. He brought him a bucket of water, which the horse noisily slurped up, and then an armful of hay. While Soggy ate, Sullivan wiped down his steaming flanks. When the soup was warm, Esmeralda carried it into the caravan while Sullivan waited outside, standing beside Frederick. It didn't matter that they didn't like each other, not now.

"The Mistress, she's gone too far," Frederick said.

Esmeralda came out and took the brush from Sullivan, then went to speak quietly to the horse. At last Master Melville came out, rubbing the side of his face with his hand.

He spoke to them, although he did not look directly at any of them. "The boy is all right. He needs to sleep. Let . . . let that be a lesson to everyone."

He said the words as if his heart wasn't in them.

* 13 *

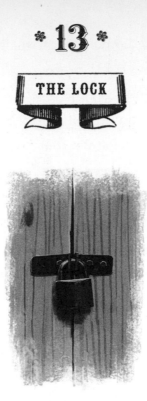

THE LOCK

CLARENCE was allowed to lie in bed for the rest of the day and sit quietly behind the caravan during the evening performance, but the following evening he was back in the show again. Sullivan was so shaken up by what Mistress had done, and so frightened that something similar might happen to him, he became even more determined to get away. If all that was stopping him was the padlock on the door of the caravan, then he would find a way to break it.

His first thought was to disable the lock somehow,

maybe by sticking mud into it when it was open. But Master Melville would see the blockage as soon as he tried to lock it. Then Mistress would demand to know who did it, and Sullivan didn't know if he'd be able to prevent himself from looking guilty.

Was there some way to get a duplicate key? he wondered. But no, that wouldn't work. The lock was on the *outside* of the door.

For an entire day Sullivan pondered the question. And then, as he passed the back of the caravan late the next afternoon, he realized that it wasn't just the padlock that kept the door secure. Because the lock had to, well, lock onto something. And that something was a loop of metal — or rather two of them, each welded to a flat piece, one of which was screwed to the back of the caravan, the other to the frame of the door. When the door was closed the two loops lined up and Master Melville slipped the lock through them.

And if one of those pieces of metal came off? The door would open!

As soon as the idea came to him, he had to set the table for dinner. By the time he got another chance to examine the loops, it was too dark to see well enough. He had to wait until the next day, and a time when neither of the Melvilles might be looking to see what he was up to. He didn't want any of the other kids to

see, either. Frederick might tell on him, and Essy and Clarence might try to stop him, thinking that trying to escape was too dangerous.

When he did, finally, get to look closely, he saw that the flat plate welded onto each loop was attached by two screws. Except that the plate on the door was already missing one screw. Which meant he only had to remove the other screw.

Which meant he needed a screwdriver.

Master Melville had a toolbox, but he kept it on his side of the caravan and there was no way Sullivan could get to it. So he kept his eyes on the ground for something that he might be able to use. Over the next few days he found a nail, a bit of twisted wire, and part of a broken zipper, but none of them worked as a screwdriver. And then, cleaning up after a show, he saw something glint between blades of brown grass. It was a pair of nail clippers, one of those little silvery contraptions with a chain on it and also a tiny nail file that swiveled out. The file felt thin enough, and strong enough, too. He slipped it into his pocket, but he didn't get a chance to try it out for the rest of that day. The next day he kept it hidden in his hand and then paused behind the caravan to try the screw.

It turned!

"Why are you dawdling about?" cried Master Melville. "Help with the curtain, will you?"

Every time he passed, Sullivan turned the screw a rotation or two. And slowly it came out of the door. But then he turned it one too many times and the screw and the piece of metal both fell from the door to the ground!

Sullivan searched frantically through the grass. He found the metal loop but he couldn't find the screw. When he saw Mistress out of the corner of his eye, he stood up quickly and shoved the loop into his pocket. Master Melville would see it was gone as soon as he went to lock the door that night. Sullivan felt the blood drain from his face. He didn't want to be left in a cemetery or have some other awful thing happen to him! He had to think, he had to think!

But he couldn't think, not of a single thing. The stage was ready, the lanterns lit. Sullivan saw the first mark approaching in the distance. His heart beat wildly in his chest. He would have to stick the metal piece on with something. With glue? But he had no glue. With chewing gum? He had no chewing gum, either.

But he knew where there was a piece.

A very old piece. An old, already chewed, dried-up

piece. It was stuck to the side of his fold-down bed; he had felt it once with his hand. Who knows what other kid had put it there. All Sullivan had to do was pull it off, chew it to make it soft (hoping that he didn't catch the bubonic plague or some other disease), and stick it on the back of the metal piece. The only problem was that he couldn't get to his bed — it had been folded up to allow the stage to come down. He would have to wait for the stage to go up again — in other words, until the very last moment.

Sullivan did not enjoy watching the show that night. He kept putting his hand in his pocket and feeling the metal piece and imagining what the Melvilles would do if they found it missing. When the show was finally over he made so many mistakes as he helped to take down the stage that Frederick and Master Melville both snapped at him in irritation.

And then at last they were in the caravan and changing under their covers. Sullivan only pretended to get out of his clothes. Then he reached over to the side of his bed, feeling along the edge until he touched the hardened lump of gum. He needed to use the nail file to pry it off. He grimaced in the dark and put it in his mouth. It tasted musty and cobwebby and without a hint of whatever flavor it had once been. It hurt his

teeth to try and chew it, but after a minute or two it finally began to soften. He chewed and chewed until it was ready and then he plastered it on the bottom of the metal piece, as flat as he could make it. He threw off his covers and hurried up the aisle between the beds.

"Where are you going?" Clarence asked.

But Sullivan didn't answer. Instead, he stepped outside and peered closely at the door to see the mark in the paint where the metal piece had been before. He stuck it on, pushing hard. Then slowly he drew away his fingers.

The gum held.

"And just exactly what are you doing?" Master Melville asked.

Sullivan jumped. "I'm sorry. I just really have to, ah, pee one last time."

"You know that you're allowed to go before you change and not again."

"I know. I'm sorry."

"All right. But don't go too far. I want to be able to see you. Just turn your back, please."

"Yes, Master Melville."

Sullivan walked away from the caravan until he reached the trees. He turned his back and tried to

go, but the truth was he was too scared. So he just pre-tended and then came back.

"Hurry up. To bed with you. And what are you do-ing still in your clothes? Get changed."

Sullivan scampered into bed, pulling the covers over himself. He held his breath and listened, afraid the metal piece would fall off. But sure enough, he heard the sliding of the key and then the click of the lock. It held! A moment later the caravan began to move. He knew that the others would be asleep in moments — they were always tired from the show, and the turning of the caravan's wheels was like the hypnotizing tick of a clock to them. Esmeralda was right — sleep was a gift.

Sullivan waited a while longer, just to be sure, until at last he could wait no more and slipped his feet out of bed and into his running shoes. He heard Clarence's wheezy breathing and a snore from Frederick. Snit and Snoot, lying on the end of Clarence's bunk, looked up at him and he patted their heads to settle them. Then he stood at the back of the caravan, took a breath, and pushed on the door. Immediately the metal piece pulled off and the door swung open.

Sullivan felt the cold air on his face as he looked down at the moving dirt road. A line of evergreens on either side of the road receded behind them. He

set his jaw, grabbed the edge of the door frame, and
pushed himself out.

The ground came up and hit him hard. He rolled
over and over in the dust, and when he stopped he was
on his back. He opened his eyes and saw the moon.

YELLOW EYES

FOR someone who has been deprived even for a short time, the sudden experience of freedom can feel strange and even disconcerting. First, there is disbelief. Are the shackles really off? Am I no longer being watched? Then, a delirious joy. But after that comes fear. Of being alone. And unprotected. Of having to make decisions that could turn out disastrously.

The landing stunned Sullivan. He sat up in the dirt road, catching his breath and listening as the sound of the caravan's wheels grew fainter and fainter. He

could not believe his plan had really worked. Surely the Melvilles would swoop down on him at any moment. But nothing happened and slowly a sensation of wonder came over him. He could feel himself grinning in the dark. He was free; he could go home again. He would see his mother, his father, his sister. But after that came another, more unnerving sensation. He was in a strange place, in the dark. A moment ago he had at least had Clarence and Esmeralda and even Frederick for company, and all of them were in the same situation. But now he was as alone as he'd ever been in his life.

He got up, dusted himself off, and rubbed his shoulder where he had first hit the ground. He looked around and decided on another dirt road that branched off to the left. Maybe he would see a house or a farm —some lighted window he could walk toward.

But as he started out he saw nothing, only the dark shapes of trees. An owl hooted. He walked for fifteen minutes, a half hour, an hour, and after that he lost all sense of time. He was plodding along, not even trying to see anymore, when a swarm of small insects encircled him, fluttering against his face.

"Get away, get off!" he cried, waving his hands at them, hurrying forward. But they followed him like a cloud, one of them stinging him on the neck. Another

pushed its way into his mouth and he struggled to spit it out. And then there was something else—larger, black things flittering close by but not quite touching him. Bats. They were feeding on the insects around his head.

"Ahhhhhh!"

Sullivan covered his face with his hands and started to run. He might still have been screaming, he wasn't sure; he knew only that he had to get away from these awful things. He ran flat out with his hands over his eyes, not caring where he was going.

Until he hit something. *Smack!*

Sullivan collapsed to his knees, moaning. He had gone forehead-first into a large object—not a tree. It was harder than a tree. His head rang. He couldn't breathe. He stayed on his knees until he could finally suck in a little air. The pain lessened to an awful throb and then he felt something warm and wet on his face. He touched his forehead with his hand. It was sticky. He put his finger to his tongue and tasted his own salty blood. He lay down in the dirt.

He knew he couldn't stay there and so he made himself stand up. He felt shaky, but he didn't go down again. He stepped toward whatever he had run into, slowly this time, with his hands outstretched. And touched rock. A sheer rockface, rising straight up from

the ground. The road, he could just barely see, veered to the right. He wished that he could have a drink of water; his mouth was so dry. He took some slow, deep breaths and began walking again.

He didn't know how long he trudged on. It was still dark. His feet hurt and he had pains in the backs of his legs and he had a terrible thirst.

Listening carefully, he thought that he heard a trickling sound.

Water. To get closer to it, he went off the road, through sharp bushes that scratched his hands and face. But there it was, a small brook. The sound he had heard was the water running over rocks. It was the most beautiful music in the world. Sullivan leaned down and put his face to the water and sucked it up noisily. He'd never tasted anything better. He put his whole face and then his head in the water, and when he sat up again he let it drip down his back. He drank again. And then he looked up and saw two yellow eyes staring at him.

"Hello?" Sullivan said.

The eyes growled. Sullivan's heart pounded. The first thing he thought was: Wolf. But then he remembered that there weren't a lot of wolves left except in uninhabited places, so maybe it was a dog. A dog that had no home and had gone wild. The eyes came

closer, and then he could just see the outline of a snout and the glint of teeth as it gave a low snarl. Backing up, Sullivan felt the scratchy bushes behind him. To push his way through them he would have to turn around.

"Please, please leave me alone," Sullivan pleaded softly. "Just go away, doggy."

The animal leaped. Its heavy paws came down on Sullivan's shoulders, knocking him backwards into the bushes. It snapped its jaws, grazing his neck. Sullivan felt its hot breath even as he reached out to push at its thick neck, trying to hold it off. But it was far too heavy and too strong and Sullivan shut his eyes, not wanting to see its teeth sink into him.

There was a yelp and squeal and then the animal was being pulled off him. He heard a thump and growl and then the pounding of the dog's running feet. Sullivan lay in the bushes, his cheek searing from a tear in the skin. He couldn't move, too exhausted from the fear draining away. Then he felt a hand. A woman's long, narrow fingers holding his own and then pulling him onto his feet.

"There, there, it's all over. No need to worry anymore. I have saved you. Yes, I've saved your life."

Mistress Melville. Sullivan could not stop himself from grabbing her around the waist as he began to sob.

She patted him lightly on the head. "There, there," she said again. "That's enough." She pried him off.

The caravan wasn't far away; they must have turned back to find him. Mistress led him by the hand and at the caravan door she used a damp towel to wash away the blood. She put a bandage on his head. She took him inside and tucked him into his bunk, leaning over so that her lips almost touched his ear. "We're your family now. Let us take care of you." Then she was gone and he felt the caravan's wheels turn.

He couldn't keep his eyes open.

❊

It took him a long time to wake in the morning. He heard whispering but only gradually could he make out the words.

"You're a traitor, Frederick, that's what you are."

"You think you know everything. And if I hadn't said anything? What would have happened to him, Clarence? He'd have been torn apart, that's what."

"But you didn't know that. For all you knew, he was already in contact with his parents."

"Of course he wasn't. Besides, what do you think would have happened to the rest of us if he had gotten away? What would they have done to us, eh? Worse than lying in some old cemetery, I'll tell you that. Do you think he worried about us before taking off? No,

he only cared about himself. You should be thanking me."

"Thanking you? That's a joke. Admit it: you actually want to be here. You look up to them. And Mistress has you wrapped around her little finger. All she has to do is speak to you in a certain tone of voice."

"I don't know what you're talking about, but if you know what's good for you, you will shut right up—"

"That's enough from the both of you! We've all got to help each other the best we can. Now hush up and let him sleep."

"I'm not sleeping," Sullivan said, turning over. "I'm awake now."

Esmeralda slipped out of bed and came to his side. She ran her hand through Sullivan's hair. "Are you all right, Dex? There's a spot of blood coming through your bandage. You had a pretty rough time."

"I'm all right. I'm sorry if I made things harder. I was going to tell the police about all of you."

"Of course you were," Clarence said. "We're not worried about ourselves. It's you we're concerned about."

"I sure wouldn't like to be you right now," Frederick said. "None of us has actually tried to run. They must be thinking up some pretty severe punishment."

"Don't scare him," scolded Esmeralda. She turned

back to Sullivan. "Whatever happens, we'll help you. You'll get through it."

"That's right," Clarence said. "You'll get through it."

But he sounded doubtful. Sullivan hadn't wanted to consider the consequences of getting caught. What exactly were they going to do to him?

At that moment he heard the key in the lock — the door must have been fixed. When it opened, bright daylight filled the interior.

"Morning, dear children," said Master Melville. "Rise and shine. Today is a special day." He stepped up and into the caravan.

"Why?" Esmeralda asked. She had still been kneeling by Sullivan's bunk, but now she stood up. Master Melville came over and looked down at Sullivan. He said slowly, "Because of our Dexter."

"What are you going to do to him?" Clarence blurted out.

"Do? I'm going to let him begin his training. You see," he said, looking into Sullivan's eyes, "you must have a proper juggling routine, something really good, if you're going to join the show."

"I'm . . . I'm going to perform?" Sullivan said.

"Of course, dear boy. Isn't that, in your heart of hearts, what you really want?"

✳ 15 ✳

No matter what Gilbert and Loretta Mintz felt, no matter how they suffered because of the loss of their son, they still had to keep running the Stardust Home for Old People. They had to get three meals a day in front of the forty-eight residents, had to wash dozens of bags of laundry, had to arrange for doctor visits and medication, for Scrabble tournaments and movie nights.

Not that anyone ate very much. Two weeks went by and still no one wanted to play Scrabble or watch a movie. For it wasn't just Sullivan's parents who grieved

over his drowning. Every resident had known Sullivan well, had shared a joke with him, or had told him a story about the old days. Most kids think of old people as if they had always been old—as if they had been *born* old. But the truth is, their young selves still live inside them. Sullivan had been a rare boy, genuinely interested in hearing about their pasts, and for that they had all loved him. Seeing Sullivan had made them feel as if they were still a part of the world. As if they still mattered.

And now he was gone. Gilbert made fried chicken, almost everyone's favorite, and most of it remained on their plates. Loretta organized a Cary Grant movie night with decorations and popcorn (and softer treats for those with false teeth), and nobody came. It wasn't good for the health of the residents to be so depressed, but it was hard for Gilbert and Loretta to do much about it, given that they felt even worse.

And then there was Jinny. Sullivan's sister had reacted in a most alarming way. She pretended that Sullivan was still alive. She would say, "Let's make brownies. They're Sullivan's favorite." Or "We can't touch anything in Sullivan's room. It has to look just the same when he comes back." Or "I hope Sullivan comes home in time for my dance recital." Sullivan was almost all she ever talked about.

Hearing Sullivan's name so much was hard on his parents. But it was even worse to see Jinny living in a fantasy world. They let it go on for a while, for the thought of insisting on the truth was too painful, but soon it began to seem that this illusion might actually be harmful to her. Jinny had to come to terms with the way things really were. She had to accept that her brother was dead. And so one evening when she was ready for bed, they sat her on the sofa for a talk.

"We understand how hard it is to let go," said Loretta, holding her daughter's hand. "But we all have to face the sad, sad truth. Your brother is gone. He isn't coming back. And it's going to take a long time for the hurting to go away."

"But we'll always remember him," Gilbert said, taking her other hand. "We can talk about him whenever you want. Just not this way. You're so young. You've got your whole life ahead of you, Jinny. We want you to learn to be happy again. You have to try. We all have to try."

Jinny shook them off, stood up, and stamped her feet. "I won't try! I won't try!" Then she ran into her room and pulled her blanket over her head and cried. She wouldn't speak to either of them, and so they just stood in her doorway until, exhausted from crying, she finally fell asleep.

In the morning, Gilbert and Loretta went to Manny

Morgenstern's room to talk to him about Jinny. Even at eighty-one, Manny was the most active resident at the Stardust Home, although lately he had taken to staying in his room. He would stand at the window and look out on the street for hours. And that was how they found him when they knocked on his door.

"Jinny adores you," Loretta said. "And she knows that you were close to Sullivan. Maybe you could talk to her."

"We think she needs to hear it from somebody else," Gilbert said. "That Sullivan isn't coming back."

Manny looked at them. He ran his gnarled fingers through his sparse white hair. He stroked his bearded chin. "Yes," he said at last, "I'll talk to her."

❋

Life, thought Norval Simick, could sure be strange. Not long ago he had considered Samuel Patinsky his worst enemy. Maybe Samuel hadn't picked on him as much as he had Sullivan, but he had still insulted him, or pulled his chair out from under him, or tore his homework into bits.

And now Samuel wasn't doing any of that, not to Norval or anyone else. Well, Norval did see him pull a chair out from under a kid in History class, but then he helped the kid up and even apologized. It was as if he couldn't keep himself from doing it — like it was

an old habit—but then was sorry he had. And since then, he hadn't been mean to anybody.

And here they were now, sitting in the lunchroom across from one another. Samuel was eating a salami sandwich and talking seriously about organizing a Sullivan Mintz Day.

"The thing is," Samuel was saying, "it can't be a downer. You know, all depressing because of what happened to Sullivan. It has to be a real celebration. Don't you think?"

"I agree," Norval said. "In fact, that's what we should call it. Not a memorial or anything like that. We should call it the Sullivan Mintz Celebration Day."

"That's genius," Samuel said. He chewed some more on his sandwich. "We have to take this to the principal."

"Samuel, can I ask you something?"

"Shoot."

"What's it feel like? Not, you know . . ."

"Not being a jerk?"

"Basically, yes."

"It feels weird, actually. I mean, okay, it's wrong to be a bully. But people knew who I was. I had a certain stature. If I'm not this guy everybody is afraid of, then who am I?"

"Wow." Norval nodded sagely. "You're having an identity crisis."

"You're right! I *am* having an identity crisis."

"I've heard about them, but I've never known anyone who actually had one."

"Neither have I," said Samuel. "I might even be the first in all of Beanfield. Pretty cool. Hey, but let's not get sidetracked here. We're talking about the Sullivan Mintz Celebration Day."

"Right. Maybe we should prepare a little more. Actually, a lot more. We have to make sure he doesn't turn us down."

Samuel was already getting up. "Then what are we waiting for? Let's get to work."

❈

Manny waited until he found Jinny alone in her room, sitting with her various dolls and stuffed animals in a circle, each with a toy teacup in front of it. There was one space open in the circle. Manny knew who the space had been left for.

"Hey there, Jinny," he said. "Mind if I join your tea party?"

"Okay," Jinny said. "But don't take Sullivan's spot. You can push Hoppy closer to Teddy-Poo. Just don't let them poke each other."

"Sure thing." He lowered himself with a groan. "Boy, it was easier sitting on the ground when I was just seventy," he said, trying to cross his legs. "You know, Jinny, I sure miss Sullivan."

"Me, too," said Jinny.

"I hear you think he's coming back."

"Yup. He went to see the doctor show."

"Yes, I heard about you telling that to your parents. They think you have a good imagination."

"I know what that means. They think I made it up. I didn't. There was a lady in black who played a big drum. And a man who sold bottles. And a girl who walked on the piperope. I saw it with Sullivan. He went to see them again, I know he did. That's where he is."

"Jinny, do you mean a medicine show?"

"That's what I said."

"I seem to remember Sullivan asking me something about medicine shows." Manny rubbed his goatee. "That's a bit odd."

"I can show you something," Jinny said.

"All right, then. Show me."

"You have to get up."

"You have to help me."

So Jinny helped Manny up from the floor, which wasn't too difficult as Manny was so thin that he

weighed about as much as a stack of paper. Then she took his hand and walked him out of her room and into the hall.

"Where are we going?" Manny asked.

"Sullivan's room."

It was right beside Jinny's. The door was closed— it was always closed now—and Jinny opened it and then closed it again after she and Manny were inside. "I'm not supposed to come in here," she said, "because they think it will make me sad. But I like it in here."

Manny and Jinny looked around. They looked at the shelf of Peanuts comic books over the small desk. At the bulletin board crowded with photographs, funny drawings, and a ribbon with the word *Participant* on it that Sullivan had gotten for finishing second to last in a race. At the posters of famous jugglers. At some laundered clothes folded neatly on the dresser.

"I like it here, too," said Manny. "But what did you want to show me?"

"Oh, I almost forgot," Jinny said. "I want to show you this."

Jinny went over to the dresser and pulled out the bottom drawer.

Manny looked into it. "It's empty. It's an empty drawer."

"Exaply."

"But I don't see——"

Manny stopped. His heavy eyebrows knitted together. He looked from side to side and then back down. He said very quietly. "Jinny, quick now, go get your parents."

Manny stood and waited. He could hear Jinny calling and then Gilbert asking what was wrong and Loretta saying hold on a minute, her hands were covered in sugar, and a few moments after that the three of them came into Sullivan's bedroom. Jinny went right in, but her parents stopped in the doorway.

"Now, Jinny," said Gilbert. "We already told you that it's not a good idea to play in here."

"Come and see this," said Manny.

Gilbert and Loretta looked at each other. Loretta wiped her hands on her apron and the two approached, standing on either side of Manny. Jinny came up alongside her father so that the four of them were staring down.

"It's an empty drawer," said Gilbert.

"Yes," said Manny. "But what did Sullivan keep in there?"

"His juggling things," said Loretta.

"Right. And where are they now?"

"I don't know," said Loretta.

"They're with Sullivan! They're with Sullivan!" Jinny jumped up and down.

Manny said, "Why would he take all his juggling equipment? Even the instruction books."

"That's a good question," said Gilbert. "But what's the answer?"

"Because he must have thought he needed them," said Loretta.

"For the medicine show!" said Jinny. "That's what I said before."

Loretta put her hand to her mouth. "Gilbert," she said. "We have to call the police."

❄

It was nearly three hours before Officer Spoonitch and Officer Forka arrived at the Stardust Home. "We're very sorry," said Officer Spoonitch, wiping his feet on the mat, "but we were on another case. We're very short-staffed at the moment. A lot of our officers are home sick with the flu."

"I just got over it," said Officer Forka.

"We're glad you're here," said Gilbert. "We would like to show you something."

Soon there were six of them in Sullivan's room, all staring down.

"An empty drawer," said Officer Spoonitch, "isn't a very solid piece of evidence."

"But it's something," said Loretta. "It's a lead, isn't it?"

"A lead usually points us in a certain direction," said Officer Forka. "But this doesn't point anywhere."

"It points to Jinny telling the truth about the doctor—I mean the medicine show," Manny explained. "They just might have something to do with it. What did you say the full name was, Jinny?"

"I'm not sure. Master Marvel's Medicine Show. Or maybe Master Moorville. Or Mellrose."

Officer Spoonitch coughed. "I think I might be coming down with something now." He swallowed and felt his throat. "The case isn't officially closed since no body—since your son wasn't actually found. We'll see if these names turn up anything."

"Thank you," said Loretta.

Officer Spoonitch put his hand on his forehead. "I think I need to lie down."

❉

For four days Gilbert and Loretta waited to hear from the officers. At last, just after dinner, Officer Forka arrived at the door. While Gilbert, Loretta, Jinny, and Manny sat and listened, she apologized for the delay, saying that Officer Spoonitch was down with the flu and the police force was even more short-staffed. She had finally been able to search the police records and other

directories but found no record of a Master Marvel, Moorville, or Mellrose. And there were no businesses anywhere listed as a medicine show. She had reached another dead end.

Officer Forka was not uncaring, and neither was she incompetent. Through long experience, she had learned that the great majority of crimes and accidents are not unusual or strange or even difficult to understand. If a boy goes missing and his jacket is found in the river, then it is almost certain that the boy has drowned. And while weird clues turn up in almost every case, in the end those clues usually don't matter. Officer Forka did not want to give the Mintzes bad news, but it was her duty to be honest with the family of a victim. It was also her duty to move on to cases that really did need solving. So Officer Forka said she was sorry and then got up and put on her cap and left.

For a long moment, none of them spoke. At last Gilbert said, "It was worth trying. Everything is worth trying." But he didn't sound as if he meant it.

"But what about the medicine show?" Manny asked.

"Sullivan loved to read about all those old entertainments. Circuses, vaudeville. I'm sure he liked to tell Jinny about them. But medicine shows don't exist anymore."

"You don't believe me?" Jinny protested.

Loretta turned and took Jinny's hand. "I believe absolutely that you wish your brother was still here."

Jinny pulled away. "I'm going to find my brother. That's all. I'm going out to find him."

She stood up and marched to her room. Her parents followed and watched as she packed a pair of socks, a sticker book, and a Kit Kat into a pillowcase. Then she marched downstairs, put on her pink fuzzy hat with pussycat ears, and went out the door.

They found her on the sidewalk. They made her come back inside.

The next day they found her three doors down.

The day after that they found her at the corner.

Gilbert said, "This isn't a game, Jinny."

"I know it isn't a game. I'm not playing piddly-binks, you know."

"I think we'd better have a family meeting," Loretta said.

"Yes, we better," Jinny agreed, folding her arms with determination. "Because I'm going to look for my brother and you can't stop me."

The meeting was held that evening after dinner. Jinny's parents asked Manny to come, too. Now that Sullivan was gone, he had become even more a part of their family.

"So here we are," Gilbert said. "And you know why, Jinny."

"Yes, I do. Because I am going to look for Sullivan."

"You're six years old, honey," said Loretta. "You can't leave on your own. You'll get lost. It isn't safe. There's really no room to negotiate on this point."

"Okay," Jinny said.

"Good," said Gilbert.

"Manny can go with me."

Loretta sighed. "Jinny, dear, Manny can't go with you. He's eighty-one years old. A very spry eighty-one, but still, that is really quite old. Forgive me for saying it, Manny."

"That's all right. I'm definitely old," Manny said.

"Please tell Jinny that you can't go with her. That we're all very sad, but it won't help if she runs away. Tell her she has to stop."

Manny considered a moment. He rubbed his chin. "I'll go," he said.

"What?" exclaimed Gilbert.

"Jinny and I will go look for Sullivan. You see, Gilbert, Loretta, I think she needs to. I think she'll never get over it if she doesn't."

"That's right, I'll never get over it," said Jinny.

"What are you saying, Manny?" Loretta cried. "This is crazy. This is irresponsible."

Manny said, "I feel very well these days. I've got my pension money to keep us going if we're careful. I can even give Jinny some lessons while she's away from school, teach her how to read. Give us two weeks. If we don't find something definite in that time, we'll come home."

"That's right," Jinny said. "After two weeks. I'll even spit-shake on it."

Jinny spit on her hand and held it out to shake. Loretta began to cry quietly.

"Hooray!" said Jinny. "I'm going to look for my brother!"

* 16 *

THE DIRECTOR

SULLIVAN stood watching Frederick on the open grass. Behind Frederick ran a fence, and behind the fence stood four goats. The goats were watching Frederick too, and every so often one would *maa* in approval.

The older boy was talking aloud and gesturing while holding a length of rope in one hand and a large pair of scissors in the other. Sullivan had decided to approach him for help in creating his own act, since he seemed the most professional and polished of the

performers. He was constantly rehearsing, learning new effects, even changing his patter.

Unfortunately, he was also Frederick. Cold, unfriendly, and mean. As Sullivan watched, he tried to work up his courage to approach him. Master Melville had told Sullivan again that it was time to create an act for himself and then had gone into town to get food and supplies. After his attempt to run off, Sullivan had been surprised and relieved not to be given some awful punishment, and he didn't want to anger Mistress Melville — who had, after all, rescued him — by refusing to perform. Going along with developing an act would encourage the Melvilles to believe that he had accepted his fate. They would stop watching him so closely and he could then find a better way to get free. And in the meantime, practicing would give him something to do. That he might actually *want* to create an act — that, he refused to believe.

But he just wasn't sure how to approach Frederick. At last Sullivan made himself walk toward him.

"Frederick, I was really hoping —"

"Ah, look what you made me do! I cut the wrong loop. You're a pest, Dexter."

"Yes, I'm sure I am, and I'm sorry about that. But I was really hoping, if it isn't too much trouble, that you

might help me put my juggling act together. I mean, your own act is so great. It's really slick."

Frederick looked down at Sullivan. He narrowed his eyes. "Your compliments don't mean a thing to me. Do you think I would waste my time helping a hack like you? A total amateur? What do I care if you fall flat on your face? I'll enjoy hearing the audience boo you off the stage. Get lost."

He made a shooing motion with his hand. Sullivan backed away. It was hopeless. He turned around and saw Esmeralda. She was hanging some wash on a line strung from the door of the caravan to a rusting tractor. She wore a linen top and a peasant skirt and her hair fanned over her shoulders. Each of them was responsible for his own washing, something that Sullivan had never had to do before, and Esmeralda had patiently shown him how to get all the soap out of his clothes. Why hadn't he thought of asking her to help him?

"Hey, Essy," he said, walking over. "I was wondering if you could do me an awfully big favor."

Esmeralda turned around. "Sure, what is it?"

"I'm wondering if you could help me develop my juggling act. I don't have a clue what to do."

She nodded. "I remember that feeling. I'd love to,

Dex. There's only one problem. I wouldn't be very good at it. I needed help to figure out my own. I think I'd be a terrible director for somebody else."

"Who helped you?" Sullivan asked.

"The same person who helped Frederick. Clarence."

"Clarence? *Clarence* helped *Frederick?*"

"Not that Frederick would ever admit it. In fact, he pretends that Clarence only gave him a pointer or two. But it's not true. Clarence figured out all the important things—the tone, the feeling, the presentation. He's terrific. You should ask him."

"Okay." He watched her get back to hanging up her wash.

Sullivan walked past a pile of big rocks that had been pulled out of the field by some farmer a long time ago. He went to find Clarence on the other side of the caravan. Clarence was washing, too—only he was washing Snit and Snoot. He had a basin of soapy water and was scolding the two little dogs for jumping into the tub and then onto him, covering him with soapsuds.

"That looks like fun," Sullivan said.

"It isn't after you've done it a few hundred times. They rolled in something by the creek and came back stinking. There's nothing these two like better than to

smell disgusting. Maybe I should try washing them as part of the act."

"I bet you could make it work," Sullivan agreed. "You've already done a lot for me, Clarence. I really appreciate it. But I need somebody to help me with my act. I don't even know how to start. Or what to say. What sort of person to be on stage. Essy told me how you helped her and Frederick. I know I don't have a lot of talent and I'm just an amateur, but if I don't try, the Melvilles are going to make things worse for me."

Clarence wiped some soapsuds from his face. "Let me check my schedule," he said. "I've got a business meeting at ten. Then a massage. After that I've got to meet with a television producer. But I might have some time after that."

"Oh, sure."

"Dexter, I'm kidding. Of course I'll help you. Anyway, I like doing it—it's something I'm good at. Could you grab that other towel and dry Snoot? Then we can get started."

Drying Snoot, it turned out, was like trying to gift-wrap a seal. Sullivan got wetter as the dog got drier, but at last it was done. He went into the caravan, picked up his backpack, and brought it over to Clarence and laid out the equipment: two sets of balls, three clubs, and the rings. He remembered exactly where and when

he'd bought them, how he had saved his allowance. He remembered his hours of practicing in his room and how Manny would stand in the door and watch him. All of that seemed like a long time ago. The terrible taste of homesickness swelled in his throat, but he swallowed it down and asked Clarence how they should start.

The first thing that Clarence asked was to simply see what Sullivan could do. He started with three balls, moving from the basic cascade to the more complicated moves and finally adding the fourth ball. After that he used the rings and clubs, although his routines with each of them were more limited. He never fully got in the groove, but he didn't mess up too much. He did well enough to give Clarence a good idea of his abilities.

"I need a few minutes to think," Clarence said. He began to pace back and forth, head bent down, scratching at his nose. Just when Sullivan thought he couldn't take the waiting any more, Clarence sat on the grass. Sullivan joined him.

"Okay," Clarence said. "Let's take stock of what we've got here. Your skills are pretty decent for an amateur. You've got pretty much the standard set of juggling moves, maybe a bit extra, but nothing really fancy. There's a lot of repetition—the same moves,

just with different objects. There's nothing that could be a climax to the show. But there's a good base to work from. First, we'll want to get your throws higher to make them more dramatic. Also cleaner and crisper. Then we'll need to add some showier stuff, which will take practice. And we'll have to find a way to get each routine to connect to the next, like scenes in a story."

Sullivan listened. It seemed like an awful lot to do. Maybe more than he was capable of. But he said, "Okay, I'm willing to try."

"Oh, and of course there's the most crucial thing," Clarence said.

"What?"

"Your personality."

"I need a personality?"

"Definitely. Frederick wouldn't be half as mesmerizing if he didn't have that snooty, ain't-I-better-than-you attitude. It makes him seem larger than life, kind of like royalty. When he started, he was trying to be friendly with the audience, trying to be funny — man, is he terrible at telling jokes. And Essy, she was doing straight ballet stuff. Elegant, but also pretty boring. But when she wasn't rehearsing for the show she'd goof around, do all these weird jumps and moves and twirls that she made up. I just suggested that she put them in the act. You see, your stage personality has to be

something authentic, something that comes from who you are."

Snit and Snoot rambled over, Snoot nudging Sullivan under the arm to be patted. Sullivan rubbed her ears. He could see that Clarence was right. The only problem was, he had no idea what sort of stage personality he ought to have. What sort of personality did he have now? Did he have any personality at all?

Sullivan said, "I'm not funny. And I'm not snooty. And I'm not mysterious, either. I don't think there's anything special about me."

"Of course there is," Clarence said. "It just isn't as obvious as for someone like Frederick. We'll figure it out. Tell you what, Dex: We'll just start with the routines. Work on them and let the personality come after. I think we should begin with balls because you're best at them. We'll work your different moves into a flowing routine with some highlights so people can clap, and come up with an exciting finish. And then we can move on from there. Sound all right?"

"Sounds good," Sullivan agreed, although he felt doubtful. Doubtful about everything.

❊

They worked every day. First Clarence would help Sullivan figure out a series of moves. A sequence might begin modestly and then grow and grow until

it *seemed* as if Sullivan was going to lose control (but he actually had to be fully *in* control), and then climax in a shower of high throws followed by dramatic catches. Or it might grow quickly, quiet down again, then grow, back and forth, ending in a totally unexpected move like a series of spins or over-the-shoulder, under-the-leg throws. The point, Clarence said, wasn't just to juggle well but to create a drama, with rises and falls, moments that were like whispers and others that were full of excitement. "I want the audience to worry about you," he said. "To think you're going to drop everything or get bonked on the head. I want them to feel as if their concentration is somehow helping you. I want them to be *involved*. I want them to be committed."

Sullivan had certainly never thought of such things when he was learning to juggle. He had thought it was enough just to keep the objects in the air without dropping them. But Clarence even choreographed a moment where Sullivan dropped a ball as if by mistake. And then, while keeping the other two in the air, he had to struggle to pick it up with his foot. Dropping one, Clarence said, would show the audience that he wasn't perfect, that he might fail at any time. That would make them root for him. And picking it up again would give them a chance to cheer encouragement.

Once the routines were set, Sullivan had to practice them over and over. If one part gave him trouble, then he had to practice just that for a stretch. It was hard and tiring work. He was only too glad when dinner came, for all that practice gave him a ravenous appetite. And each night, watching the others perform from the wing, he had a new appreciation for their skills and talents. He saw now that they were also actors, each playing a character that the audience believed in. He was amazed at how they could make the audience hush with expectation or gasp in fear, or clap in relief and appreciation.

"Watch them, watch them, dear boy!" Master Melville whispered to him one evening. "Let them all be your teachers. Each has learned from experience. By *feeling* the reaction out there. Now they play the crowd like a fish on a line. Watch, and you'll see!"

* 17 *

ONE morning Sullivan woke up to find that the caravan had stopped beside a burned-out house. The shell of the house still stood but all the window and door frames were charred and the roof had collapsed. Through the broken windows he could see curling wallpaper and even a blackened table and chair. There was something sad and forlorn about the sight. He wondered what had happened to the family that used to live there.

Distracted by the house, Sullivan at first didn't

notice a tent he'd never seen before erected behind the caravan. It was an old canvas tent, the size of a large shed, with painted images, chipped and faded, of horses and clowns and trapeze artists on it. Sullivan could just make out the ghostly words on the side: *Mandoni's Miniature Circus—Half the Size, Twice the Fun.*

No one else seemed to take notice of it; they all just went about their business getting breakfast ready. It was only when they were seated and had begun to eat, without Master Melville joining them, that Sullivan finally said something.

"Why is that tent up?" he asked.

Mistress looked sideways across the table at him. "Somebody tell the boy." She sighed. "I certainly can't be bothered."

Clarence said, "It's B and B Day."

"B and B Day?"

"Brewing and Bottling. Master Melville is making up a new batch of Hop-Hop Drops. We must be almost out."

"He makes it himself?" Sullivan asked.

"Enough questions," Mistress said. "All this talk hurts my head."

The rest of the meal passed in silence, but Sullivan couldn't suppress his curiosity about the making of

Hop-Hop Drops. He had often wondered about them
—what the ingredients were, how they were made,
whether or not they actually worked. From a small hole
cut near the top of the tent, smoke rose steadily into
the pale sky. Every so often there was an odd sound
of grinding or whirring, and once in a while Master
Melville could be heard cursing to himself or suddenly
crying out.

Clarence had assigned Sullivan the task of improving several moves in his club routine, moves that two
weeks ago he hadn't been able to do at all. In one he
had to lean his head back and balance a club on his
nose. After ten seconds or so he had to drop his head
forward, catch it, and begin juggling again. First he'd
had to learn to get it onto his nose and balance it.
Then he'd had to learn how to tip it off without losing
control. And *then* he'd had to learn how to catch it and
start throwing again. He could do each move by itself,
but doing all of them in succession was really hard.
Right now he could manage it maybe one out of three
times. He had to be able to do it every time.

Sullivan fetched his backpack and chose a spot not
far from the flap of the tent. He started to practice
but he couldn't help listening to the sounds coming
from the other side of the canvas. At this distance, he
could hear a bubbling sound. Also mutterings. And

then Master Melville stuck his head out the flap and began to shout:

"Capsicum! I need capsicum!"

"There's no need to shout," Mistress answered from under an elm tree where she had gone to brush her long black hair. "There's some in the caravan. I'll get it."

"No need to shout? Do you know what it's like in here? Do you understand the necessity of precise timing? Do you comprehend at all the danger of ignition, combustion, and conflagration? You do not, no, you do not!"

Sullivan had never heard Master Melville dare talk to his wife this way. He was always trying to appease and flatter her. And when he neglected to, Mistress Melville let him know it. But now all she did was go into the caravan, fetch an unmarked aluminum can, and put it into his hands.

"There now, don't get your knickers in a knot," she said mildly.

He didn't answer, but pulled himself quickly inside again. Mistress gave Sullivan a dark look and walked back to her place under the elm tree. Immediately he began to throw his clubs, wanting to look busy. He tried the balancing move, and bonked himself just above his eye.

It was a good half hour before Master Melville stepped out of the tent again, rubbing his hands on a cracked leather apron tied around his waist. "Ah, Dexter," he said, his voice sounding far more cheerful. "Bit tense in there sometimes. Bit agitating. Have a short break now, during the first brewing stage. It's really quite a process, I must say. A little of this, a pinch of that. Stir, heat, boil, cool, shake, boil again. And when the stuff is done it needs to age three weeks in the bottle. Tastes quite awful. Bitter. Acrid. Sour. Burning. And an aftertaste of sickly sweet. But if it didn't taste that way, it wouldn't do any good, would it?"

Sullivan nodded in agreement and asked, "Do you take it too, Master Melville?"

Master Melville frowned. "Do I look as if I need it? Do I appear to you anything but the picture of happiness? Could I be in anything but a state of bliss, married to such a woman as I am? Really, I'm offended at the very thought of it. Now get along with you — I've got much more work to do."

And he went back into the tent, pulling the flap closed behind him.

❊

Clarence still hadn't come up with a personality for him, but Sullivan kept practicing. He worked on juggling with crossed arms, and then uncrossing and cross-

ing them again while keeping the balls in the air. His moves became sharper, more precise.

One day after breakfast Sullivan said, "What should we start with today? Rings?"

"No, none of the usual," Clarence replied, holding a burlap sack at his side. "You need something else. Something unusual and unexpected."

"Like what?"

"Like this."

From inside the sack, Clarence drew out . . . a toaster.

"Excuse me? I'm supposed to throw *that* in the air?"

"And this," Clarence said. He brought out a rubber boot.

"Yeah, right." Sullivan laughed nervously.

"Oh, and also this."

A piggy bank.

"Is that porcelain?" asked Sullivan. "Isn't it breakable?"

"Very breakable." Clarence smiled. "The crowd is going to love it."

"I can't juggle a toaster, a boot, and a piggy bank. The toaster will land on my head! You're crazy, Clarence. I won't do it."

Clarence tossed the toaster at him. Sullivan caught it clumsily against his stomach. "Shall we get started?"

It was almost like learning to juggle all over again. First, he started with just the toaster. Clarence took out the insides to make it lighter, and Sullivan tossed it from one hand to the other, getting used to the way it felt, how to wrap his fingers around it. Then he did the same with the boot, after Clarence stuffed it with rags to make it stiff and sewed it shut at the top. Finally, Sullivan tried the porcelain pig. Clarence brought out a mattress from the caravan for Sullivan to stand on so that if the pig fell it wouldn't break.

Sullivan threw it . . . and missed. It bounced off the mattress. The curly tail broke off.

Clarence looked at it lying there. "The tail would have just gotten in the way," he said.

Next came throwing two of the objects — first the toaster and the boot, then the boot and the pig, then the toaster and the pig. Only when he could do that easily did he try all three. And then try again. And then again. The hardest part was adjusting for the different weight and shape of each object, both when catching and throwing, first deliberately and then, in time, without having to think. But he did it. He learned to juggle a toaster, a boot, and a piggy bank.

"This is fun," Sullivan said, throwing and catching, throwing and catching. "But there's no way I'm going to try a spin."

"I didn't even ask you to," Clarence said.

"Fine. I'll try one. But if I don't make it the first time I'm not trying again."

"Whatever."

Sullivan threw the objects. He spun on his heel, 360 degrees. He caught them.

"Showoff," said Clarence.

❋

Lying in his bunk that night, even before the caravan began to move, Sullivan felt himself falling asleep. He started awake at the sound of the lock opening again.

The back door swung wide and Mistress Melville stepped in, holding a lantern that illuminated her face in a ghoulish way. "Never use a boy to do a woman's job," she said. "You, the one who juggles."

"Yes?" Sullivan said, sitting up. The others were all up too, and watching silently from their bunks.

"I've got it."

"Got what?" Sullivan asked.

"Your personality. For your act."

"You do? What is it?"

"I'll tell you tomorrow."

She stepped backwards out of the caravan and closed the door again, leaving Sullivan and the others in darkness.

✳ 18 ✳

THREE LEGS

 ANNY Morgenstern told Jinny an old riddle. What creature begins its life walking on four legs, then uses two legs, and finally three legs? Jinny made a lot of guesses — a weird spider? A robot? But finally Manny had to tell her the answer: a human. First it crawls on all fours, then it learns to walk on two, and finally, growing old, it uses a cane. And then he took his own rather splendidly carved cane from his closet. It was the last thing he needed before he and Jinny set out to look for Sullivan.

"I need one, too!" Jinny cried, and ran to her room. She came back with a plastic red and white striped cane, like a big candy cane, with a squeaker on the end that made a noise whenever she set it down.

"Ready?" Manny asked, putting on his fedora.

"Ready!" said Jinny.

But Jinny's parents, Gilbert and Loretta, weren't ready. First, Loretta insisted that the two have an enormous breakfast of eggs and sausages and toast. In the morning edition of the *Beanfield Gazette* there was a new poem by the Bard of Beanfield. Jinny's dad insisted on reading it out loud.

> *To lose one kid is bad enough.*
> *In fact, there's nothing worse.*
> *But to have to watch a second leave*
> *Is truly a parent's curse.*

"Well, Mom," Jinny said brightly, "it's your shortest, but it's not your bestest."

Gilbert wanted to check that Manny had enough money in his money belt, and that Jinny, too, had money in a little pouch on a string around her neck. Also that Manny had the maps and the first-aid kit and the phone number of the police station. Loretta wished that they could afford a cell phone for the pair,

but Manny assured her they would find pay phones and check in regularly. At last, Jinny's parents agreed that the two were ready to go. But not without a farewell first.

Outside the Stardust Home, forty-seven old people lined up: a row of wheelchairs in front and another row of people leaning on them behind. Jinny stood with her Kooky Kitty backpack and her toy walking stick and her straw hat. Manny had his own canvas army backpack with leather straps. In the doorway Gilbert and Loretta held on to each other, Gilbert sniffling and Loretta flat-out crying.

Manny raised his cane and turned to face the crowd. "Dear friends," he said. "We embark on this journey for one purpose and one purpose only. And that is to find our own wonderful boy, Sullivan. And if we don't find him, then to find out what happened to him. But Jinny here believes that Sullivan is out there somewhere, and I believe Jinny. Don't worry about us. We'll take care of each other, won't we, Jinny? And we'll keep in touch. Please don't be glum," Manny added, for to his dismay, people were beginning to cry all up and down the rows. "We've had our sad days. This is the beginning of happier times!"

"Hooray for us!" Jinny cried. "Hip hip, hooray!"

Lorretta stepped toward them and put her hands

on Jinny's shoulders. "Remember, you can come home anytime. And if it looks like you won't find Sullivan, don't be afraid to tell us. Just come back. You need to eat properly, and drink three glasses of milk a day. You too, Manny—you need the milk for those old bones of yours. Oh, I can't believe we've agreed to this."

"Now, now, Loretta," Manny said. "You act as if I've lived my whole life in the Stardust Home. I was an adventurous lad in my day. I traveled from here to there and back again, with hardly two pennies to rub together. I may be old, but I'm resourceful. We'll be just fine. Now, we'd better get going. Goodbye, Loretta, Gilbert. Goodbye, forty-seven! See you all soon!"

"Goodbye!" yelled the people gathered in front of the Home. "Good luck!"

Jinny hugged her parents hard. For the first time she, too, felt tears in her eyes. Wiping them away, she said, "Aw, Mom, you sure do a lot of cry-babbling."

"Yes, I do," Loretta agreed. Then she hugged Manny. Gilbert hugged Manny, too.

"Down the belly brick road!" cried Jinny. She hooked her arm with Manny's. And the two began marching forward, Jinny's cane squeaking each time it hit the ground.

❋

They walked and walked and Jinny did not look back until they were quite far away. When she did, she could still see them all, very small, lined up along the sidewalk. The sight made her heart hurt, and for the first time she felt scared. Where were she and Manny going? How long would they be gone? She believed that her brother was alive, but that didn't mean she knew where he was or how to look for him.

"Where are we going first?" she asked Manny.

"Well, I thought we'd better take a look at the river. I hope that won't be too hard for you, Jinny. It's where the last piece of evidence—Sullivan's jacket—was found. I don't know what we might learn there, but you never know."

"Okay." Jinny nodded. Ever since Sullivan had disappeared, she hadn't wanted to see the river. She hadn't wanted to go near it. But now she had to. The two of them walked on and on—it took them a good hour to reach the part of the river that flowed through Beanfield Park.

Here, it was calm and quiet, the grass trimmed neatly along the banks and pretty willow trees planted along the shore. But the spot where the police had found the jacket was farther along, after the park ended and a stretch of wild scrub began. Manny and

Jinny kept going, pushing through branches and brambles with their canes, getting scratched and poked at every step.

It took them a while to get to a small incline, where the ground was soft and moss-covered. They found the tree where, caught on a slender branch, Sullivan's jacket had been discovered. They knew it was the right tree because the police had said it had been hit by lightning. Just being there made Manny tear up. "Careful now," he said, using his cane as he made his way down. The moss felt spongy underfoot.

"What do we look for?" Jinny asked. Her voice trembled.

"I don't know," Manny admitted.

Just then Jinny felt a drop on her nose. Then another on her cheek. "It's starting to rain," she said.

There was nothing to do but move on. They walked for a good half hour along the road before the rain slowly began to stop. When they came to a picnic table in a small playground, they stopped and took out the chicken salad sandwiches, carrot sticks, and squares of chocolate that Gilbert had packed for them. They ate without speaking, and it was only when they were done that Jinny said, "Where do we go now, Manny?"

The truth was, Jinny had believed that if she went looking for Sullivan she would find him right away, the

way she found him when they were playing hide-and-seek. It was only now that they had been out for a few hours that she realized it would not be as easy as she had imagined. They would not simply see him standing on a street corner or sitting on the curb having an ice cream. Finding him was going to be much harder than that.

Manny, of course, knew that finding Sullivan would be difficult. In fact, he knew that it was probably impossible. Despite what he had told the residents of the Stardust Home, he did not absolutely believe that Sullivan was alive. Manny had not really agreed to go looking in order to find Sullivan. He had agreed because he thought that Jinny *needed* to go looking. That she would never get over the loss of her brother if she didn't look. He was doing this for Jinny, not Sullivan.

But since they were looking, they might as well try their best. Manny said, "I'd like you to show me the spot where you and Sullivan watched that performance. That medicine show, as you called it. Maybe we'll learn something. Do you know where it was?"

"Runny Cold's Field," she said.

"Pardon?"

"That's what Sullivan called the place. Runny Cold's Field."

"Do you think you can find it?"

Jinny looked around. "Not from here," she said. "But if you take us to the store, the one where Sullivan and I go for candy, I think I can find it from there."

"All right, then." Manny got up, slinging his pack back on. He banged his cane on the ground, trying to show some enthusiasm that might raise Jinny's spirits as well as his own. "Let's go."

Jinny slung on her own backpack and banged her own cane, making it squeak. "Forward march!" she said, and began marching like a soldier.

"It's the other way, Jinny," Manny said.

"Backwards march!" she cried, doing just that.

By the time they reached the store, it was late afternoon. Both Manny's and Jinny's feet hurt from walking, but neither of them complained. They went on, past one farm and the next, past the stream and the billboard for condominiums. "Down there," Jinny said, pointing to the line of trees.

"Ah," Manny said. "You don't mean Runny Cold's Field. You mean *Reingold's* Field."

"That's what I said."

They used their canes as they moved down the slope. "It was right here," Jinny said. Manny looked at the ground. The dry grass was pressed flat here and there, but it was impossible to tell from what. There was an indentation that might have been from a wagon

wheel, but then again it might have been from a million other things. Manny looked up and surveyed the area. He didn't see anything that might help them.

Jinny used her cane to search through the grass and the few low bushes nearby. The place brought back vivid memories of the two evenings — the strange music, the crowd, Sullivan's excitement as she clutched his hand. She pushed aside a clump of longer grass and saw something, a bit of paper, lying there. She picked it up and scrutinized it. Although she knew her letters, she still couldn't read. But she *did* recognize it.

"Manny, look," she said.

He came over and peered at the paper. "It's just a torn scrap," he said. "Most of it's missing. I can make out a few words. *Show*. And *Wonder*. And *Snoot*. And *Drops*. But what does it mean?"

"It's the flyer from the medicine show. Like the one we found. Snoot is the name of one of the dogs — I remember that. And drops, that's what the man was selling, little bottles of drops."

"Well, I'll be," Manny exclaimed. "Just like you said, Jinny. And if I know Sullivan, he would have wanted to see it again. Also like you said. This is indeed something. This is a start."

"Woohoo!" Jinny shouted, banging her squeaker cane on the ground. "Now what do we do?" she asked.

Manny looked at the sky. "The sun's going down. We can try one more thing. And then we'll have to find a place to stay for the night."

※

They started walking again, but it was some time before they came to the next farm. It was not abandoned, or about to be turned into condominiums, but a real working farm, with fields of hay and cows being herded into the barn for the evening milking. Manny and Jinny watched from the fence, Manny saying that the farmer would be too busy to talk to them right now. So they waited until he came out of the barn again and walked to the house and took off his rubber boots and went inside. Then they went around to the gate and down the front path. It was an old red-brick house with painted wooden gables but also a satellite TV dish attached to the roof. Manny knocked on the front door and they waited until a woman in an apron appeared.

"I'm sorry, but we don't want to buy anything today."

"Oh, we don't wish to sell you anything at all," Manny said, taking off his hat.

"Or religion, either," the woman said. "We've got our own."

"No, no. We're looking for a boy, a family member who is lost. We're just wondering if by any chance you saw this."

Manny held out the scrap of paper. It only had the three words on it, but the woman's face changed, as if she recognized it. "Yes, we went to see them," she said. "You say a boy is lost? How awful. Let me call my husband. He was there, too."

Her husband, the man who had taken in the cows, was very big. He almost filled the entire front door, with his wife edged in beside him.

"These people are asking about the wagon show that came by."

"Yes, we saw it," the man confirmed. "Good, old-fashioned entertainment. A lot better than anything on television, even with all those new channels."

"By any chance did you see a boy there? About this high. Sandy hair. With a backpack."

"Not that I recall. But there was a good crowd, and I was watching the stage. What about you, Ellen?"

"I'm afraid I don't recall, either."

"Do you have any idea where they were going next?"

"No, I don't," the man said. "They were gone when I went by the field the next morning."

"I saw them leave," the woman said. "In the night. I couldn't sleep and I was in the kitchen having a cup of tea. I saw the wagon go by. It passed the house heading west. That way. And then it turned north at the tree stump there. There's a road going off, but you can't see it from here."

"That's a big help," Manny said. "We won't bother you anymore. Thank you."

But Jinny said, "Something sure smells goody-good in there."

The woman looked at her a moment. "Supper's almost ready. Are you hungry?"

"Starving," Jinny said.

"Then you'd better come in and join us. Is this boy related to you, young lady?"

"He's my brother. We're going to find him."

"I bet you are. And where you staying tonight?"

"Oh, probably under a barrel somewhere."

The man said, "We've got a guest room with two beds. You're welcome to it."

"That is very, very kind of you," Manny said. "We accept gladly. Perhaps over dinner you might describe the show that you saw. The acts, what the people looked like."

"Sure," agreed the man. "You think your boy ran off and joined them?"

"We don't know what to think." Manny shook his head.

"A good supper and a night's sleep are bound to help," said the woman, ushering them in. "I'll just put two more plates on the table."

* 19 *

HOW TO CLIMB AN INVISIBLE LADDER

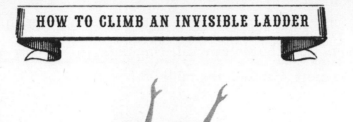

SULLIVAN awoke to a changed landscape. The caravan was set up against a rise of hills, behind which rose even higher hills that were bare rock along their upper ridges. Small wildflowers grew, yellow and blue and white. The water from the nearby stream was cool and clear. Stumbling into the light and the fresh air, still groggy from sleep, Sullivan had felt with a pang how they were moving farther and farther away from Beanfield. Farther away from his family, from the Stardust Home, from anyone who knew him.

Now he stood on the dry ground covered in scraggly grass with his juggling equipment placed around him. He waited for Mistress Melville to come out of the caravan and tell him what his personality was going to be. But Mistress was taking her time. Clarence came around from behind the caravan, Snit and Snoot trotting behind him. He sauntered over to Sullivan, whistling, his hands in his pockets.

"I guess you don't have any reason to be nervous," Sullivan said.

"Well, I am. I've put a lot into your act. Actually, I always whistle when I'm nervous. But the Black Death has a good eye for talent and how to use it."

At that moment, Mistress Melville emerged from the caravan, and Clarence stopped talking. She wore a black bathrobe and black slippers and even a black hairnet. She walked directly over to them, looked sourly at Sullivan, and said, "You're the *accidental juggler*."

"Accidental? What do you mean?"

"It means that you don't intend to juggle things. You're just an ordinary kid. With no special talent at all. Juggling just happens to you, by accident. Here's an example. You're walking across the stage, perhaps whistling in that annoying way that this little dog-keeper has. Walking down the street without a care in

the world. You look down and notice three balls on the ground."

"How did they get there?"

Mistress Melville shook her head impatiently. "It doesn't matter how they got there. They just *are* there. So you pick up a ball and look at it. Then you pick up the other two. You shrug and pretend to throw them away but instead they come back down to you. Surprised, you catch them and throw them again. The whole time you're juggling—walking around, suddenly doing an under-the-leg move—you're totally surprised. Sometimes you're delighted by it—I mean, really amazed. And then other times, such as when you suddenly speed up and the balls look like they're going out of control, you're shocked and even scared. You see, it's all by accident. The crowd will laugh, but they'll be on your side, too."

Sullivan frowned as he listened. He thought about the idea. "You thought of this because I look so ordinary. Because it seems like there's nothing special at all about me."

"I thought of it because I know the audience will *like* you. Now get to work."

She turned around and walked back to the caravan. Only when she was gone did Sullivan speak to Clarence. "Juggling is hard enough," Sullivan said. "But

trying to make it look like an accident? That'll be even harder."

"That's true. It'll take really good balancing skills. And control of your body so that you don't give away the moves, don't prepare yourself as if you expect to be juggling. And you have to really act. But all good performers do. It's brilliant. It'll be great, you'll see. I know you can do it."

Sullivan looked down. He kicked at one of his juggling balls with the toe of his shoe. "Okay," he said. "I'll try."

"Excellent. Let's get started."

❋

Becoming the accidental juggler turned out to be even more difficult than Sullivan expected. Acting as if he didn't mean to juggle meant that he couldn't stand in his usual way. He had to juggle while half turned, or with one foot behind the other, or even as he walked, or leaned over backwards, or pretended to stumble. Not only did it look totally fake at first, but he kept dropping the balls or the rings or whatever he was using. It felt as if all the improvements in juggling that he had made in the last weeks had suddenly vanished.

And then there was the acting part. Looking surprised when he knew just what was coming. Or afraid. Or gleeful. Or confused. He was even worse at all of

that. Clarence called in Esmeralda to help. Esmeralda, Clarence told him, had taken acting classes. Glad to be of assistance, she began a crash course in acting that very afternoon that lasted a whole week. She began with exercises, like trying to move one part of his body without moving any other part—his big toe, his stomach, his right ear. He had to pretend he was a creature from another planet and find a new way to move himself across the ground. Then he was an explorer trying to communicate with people who spoke a language he had never heard before. Then came miming—climbing an invisible ladder, baking an invisible cake, drinking an invisible glass of water. When Clarence chuckled at him, Sullivan emptied an invisible glass over his head.

After that came more involved improvisations, like having to stand before a firing squad or jump out of an airplane. It was strange and disconcerting work, and the only part that Sullivan enjoyed was getting to spend time with Esmeralda. She was remarkably patient, and unlike Clarence, she never laughed at him. "I know you can do it, Dex," she said quietly when he got discouraged. Then she would put her arm around his shoulder and whisper suggestions into his ear, her red hair brushing against his cheek. And when he did something well, she would jump up and give him a hug,

making him blush. The only thing he didn't like was catching sight of Frederick pretending not to watch them.

In the mornings, Sullivan continued to practice his juggling. At night, he found it hard to sleep. He couldn't stop going through the routines in his mind, his hands twitching as if they were catching and throwing objects. And when he did finally fall asleep, he would have weird and vivid dreams about jumping out of airplanes or running through fire. He would wake with a start only to find that it was dark and the caravan was still rolling on.

20

THE OLD LIFE PARTY

A TREMOR of excitement spread as they passed the news from one to another. Sullivan could see it move from Frederick to Esmeralda to Clarence, and at last it reached him, too. It had been four weeks since Sullivan arrived, and for the first time the Melvilles were going out. That meant that tonight the young performers were going to have an old life party, the first one in months.

Every so often, Clarence explained to Sullivan as he washed dishes in the basin while Clarence dried,

instead of moving on right after dark, Master and Mistress Melville would go out. They would dress in their ghoulishly best clothes, lock the kids into the caravan, and set out for a night on the nearby town. What they did, nobody was exactly sure. A restaurant, a movie, or dancing, perhaps. All the kids knew was that they would not be back for hours.

And what was an old life party? Sullivan wanted to know. An old life party, Clarence said, was exactly what it sounded like. A party to remember the life each of them had before joining the medicine show. Family, friends, school—all that stuff. They would even use their real names, not the ones that the Melvilles had given them. They would say all the things that they could never say at any other time.

But a party wasn't a party without food, drink, decorations, and music. So each of them was assigned a task. Clarence was on dinner duty that day, so he had to snatch the food. Frederick would handle the drink —he was famous for his "mystery fruit punch." Esmeralda would make the decorations. That left Sullivan with the job of supplying the music.

"How can I get music?" Sullivan asked. "I mean, it's not like I can go out and hire a band. And we don't have an MP3 player or anything like that. It's impossible."

"Nothing is impossible," Clarence said with a shrug.

"That's right, ball boy," Frederick growled as he passed by. "You're not going to let us down, are you?"

"Don't you worry. I'll get us music," Sullivan spat back. He hated the way Frederick talked to him, as if he didn't belong there, as if he wasn't as good as the rest of them. He would show Frederick. He'd get music. Great music. He just didn't know how.

Over the course of the day, Clarence managed to hide a bag of carrots, a block of cheddar cheese, a half-jar of pickles and another of peanut butter, some crackers, a container of strawberries, and a bar of chocolate. "Just wait and see what I do with these!" he said happily.

For decorations, Esmeralda decided on an underwater theme. When the Melvilles weren't watching, she took some old newspapers, cut them into strips, and began to color them blue and green with sticks of stage makeup. Frederick, meanwhile, worked inside the caravan, mixing up his famous punch, the recipe for which he kept as secret as Master Melville's recipe for Hop-Hop Drops.

The only one who didn't know what to do was Sullivan. He thought of trying to swipe Mistress Melville's musical instruments — her drum, her banjo-ukulele, her kazoo. But Mistress was very fond of her

instruments and spent a lot of time cleaning and polishing them. She didn't even let Master Melville touch them, and Sullivan didn't want to imagine what she would do if she found out he had. Besides, none of them could play. He thought of singing, only he could never remember the words to songs, and besides, he had a hard time keeping a tune. By late afternoon, when the others were starting to get ready for the evening performance, he still had nothing. He was going to let them down.

Sullivan was sitting on a tree stump feeling depressed when Master Melville came by, using a brush on his black top hat. "Why the long face, dear boy?" he asked. "You must make the best of it, whatever the circumstances. I learned that early in life."

"Yes, sir."

Master Melville crouched down. "Don't tell me. You've got something to do and you don't know how to do it. Something for a certain event."

Sullivan looked at Master Melville in surprise. He almost blurted out, *You know about the party?* but managed to stop himself. Maybe Master Melville suspected something and was trying to trick him.

"Do not worry, dear boy, I have no nefarious designs. Between you and me, I know about these little shindigs. Personally, I think it's good for you all to

blow off a little steam. Get your feelings out. Mistress Melville, well, she might have a different attitude. But why worry her, eh? It's hardly important enough, I'd say. So if I find a little food missing, or something else is amiss, I take care of it myself. You see? I've got your best interests at heart. Now I wonder what your task is."

Sullivan hesitated. If this was a trick and he gave the party away, he would be betraying all of them. But something made him believe that Master Melville was being sincere. Maybe Sullivan could respond in a way that didn't incriminate them.

"It's always nice to have a little music," he ventured.

"Of course. What is a social occasion without the sweet strains of melody? I understand. But it is a tricky request to fulfill."

"It's impossible," said Sullivan, and then immediately realized that he had forgotten to be careful.

"Well, it just so happens that I have an old wind-up gramophone and a box of records. A little temperamental, but it works. Mistress and I sometimes listen on the road while the rest of you are all fast asleep."

"Yes, I've heard it," Sullivan said. "I thought I was dreaming."

"Mind you, it could use a good dusting. And since

you've got nothing to do, I don't see why I shouldn't put you to work."

"Put me to work," Sullivan said. "Please put me to work."

"I will, then. Dexter," he said in a louder voice, "I see you've got nothing useful to do. In that case, you can clean and polish my gramophone. And the records, too. I expect to have it all back first thing tomorrow morning. Or there will be trouble. Do you understand?"

"Yes, Master Melville. Thank you."

"Thank me? For giving you extra work? You are a strange boy. Now come along and I'll give it to you. And be careful with it! If you damage it there will be severe consequences, I promise you that."

Master Melville turned on his heel and strode toward the caravan. "Yes!" Sullivan whispered under his breath, and he ran to catch up.

❄

The show that night could not have been called anyone's best performance, Sullivan thought. Everyone was too excited about the old life party to concentrate properly. Frederick dropped a handful of cards that were hidden behind his hand. Napoleon the chess-playing automaton lost to a boy in high school. Master

Melville hissed at them as they came offstage, but he didn't seem to mean it. The truth was that he, too, must have been looking forward to the evening out with Mistress, because his pitches for the Hop-Hop Drops lacked their usual spark.

When the show was over and the last bottle sold, everyone rushed to clean up. The stage became the side of the caravan again, the props got put away, the horse was given his nightly oats. "Hurry up and get to bed!" grumbled Master Melville unnecessarily, for they were all in their pajamas and tucked into their bunks in record time.

The person who *did* take a long time was Mistress Melville. Sullivan could hear her husband pleading for her to hurry. But at last Sullivan heard her come out of the Melvilles' side of the caravan and step down. A moment later the back door swung open, and in the light cast from a small lamp held in Master Melville's hand, Sullivan could see both of them peering in, framed in the doorway. Mistress wore a tight black bodice, cut low and with a small diamond pendant dangling against her pale skin. Her lips were painted blood red, and dark makeup lined her eyes. Her black leather gloves went up to her elbows.

"Hurry up, Monty," said Mistress. "Lock them in."

"You get up on the horse, love of my life. I'll be there in a moment."

"You will if you know what's good for you."

She moved away. Master Melville took his ring of keys from his pocket. "Night-night, dear boys and dear girl," he said. When he smiled, a gold tooth glinted. "Do enjoy yourselves." He shut the door and fastened the padlock.

Silence. No one so much as stirred. Sullivan lay in the dark, listening to the fading clip-clop of Soggy Biscuit's hooves. They waited, but for what?

A match flared and then a candle was lit.

"All right, everyone," said Clarence. "It's party time!"

They threw off their covers. Clarence lit more candles standing in blue or yellow or red jars, casting colored streaks of light. Esmeralda pulled at paper tabs here and there, releasing her decorations, which dangled from the ceiling. Frederick slid the big bowl of his mystery punch from under his bunk, and Clarence brought out the trays of food. He had turned the various items he had snatched into hors d'oeuvres —cheese and pickle on crackers, carrot sticks spread with peanut butter, strawberries covered in chocolate.

Now it was Sullivan's turn. The gramophone was covered by an extra blanket at the end of his bed. He

pulled it off to reveal the small oak box with a crank at one end and a flat, circular table and arm on top. From the foot of his bunk he drew out a brass horn, with a wide mouth that tapered down to a narrow end, which Sullivan attached to the box. It was a good thing that Master Melville had left instructions tucked inside the horn. From under the bed he produced a stack of small records in paper sleeves. He pulled one out, put it on the circular table, turned the crank, and lowered the arm. He looked up to see the others watching him as the scratchy, faraway sounds of a long-dead orchestra began to play. A woman sang:

> *I've been to Argentina*
> *And the Smoky Mountains too,*
> *I've seen the view of Naples*
> *But it means nothing without you . . .*

Clarence smiled. Swaying to the music, Frederick began scooping soup-spoons of punch into mugs. Esmeralda got up again, standing in the candlelight in her nightgown. She walked to Sullivan's bunk and said, "May I have this dance?"

"But I don't—"

Esmeralda pulled him up. She put one of his hands on her waist, held his other with her own, and began

to waltz up the narrow aisle. Her touch was soft and warm, and she smelled like lemons.

"Divine," Esmeralda said. "It's too, too divine."

It was the best party Sullivan had ever been to. They ate and they drank and they danced and they laughed. Even Frederick. Sullivan finally heard, for the first time, what Clarence and Frederick and Esmeralda's real names were. And when someone, instead of calling him Dexter, said, "Care for another mug of punch, Sullivan?" or "Stop making me laugh, Sullivan!" he felt tears sting his eyes and he had to quickly wipe them away.

When finally they became tired from dancing and the lateness of the hour, they sat on their bunks and talked quietly by the light of a single remaining candle. They had heard all of the records many times, but it was that first song they liked best, and they asked Sullivan to put it on the gramophone again.

I've seen lions on safari
And the top of Katmandu,
I've drunk champagne in Paris
And thought only about you . . .

And when it was over and there was only the soft hissing sound of the needle on the cylinder going round

and round, Clarence — whose real name was Matt — said, "I'll go first."

"First?" Sullivan asked.

But Clarence just went on. He said, "Pancakes. My dad made pancakes every Sunday morning. With blueberries, in the summer. And lots of maple syrup. He would sing opera in a really off-key voice while he flipped the pancakes in the pan. And my brothers and I would argue about who got the next one. When I close my eyes I can taste those sweet pancakes. And I can hear my dad singing."

The others raised their mugs of punch and drank, so Sullivan followed suit.

Esmeralda — whose real name was Louise, even though she didn't look at all like a Louise to Sullivan — said, "One time I had this nightmare. I was really little, only five or six. I dreamed that these ghosts in bowler hats and glasses were chasing me."

"Bowler hats aren't exactly scary," said Frederick. (In real life, he was Oscar.)

"Well, they were scary to me. I was screaming, but no sound came out of my mouth, and then they were about to grab me and I woke up. My parents let me keep a flashlight by my bed, and I turned it on and walked down the hall to their room. They were still up, watching an old black-and-white movie on TV. I still

remember what it was called. *The Philadelphia Story.* They let me snuggle in between them and watch with them. Only I fell asleep before it was over."

Again, the kids raised their mugs and drank. "Sweet," Clarence said at last. "Very sweet. We know to skip Oscar, so it's Sullivan's turn."

"Why do we skip Frederick—I mean, Oscar?" Sullivan asked.

"Because he won't do it."

"That's right," said Frederick. "So go ahead."

"I don't know what to say," Sullivan said. "I haven't had time to think about it."

"You don't have to think," said Clarence. "Just tell us the first memory that comes to mind."

"Okay . . . I guess my birthday, two years ago. My little sister, Jinny, insisted on singing 'Happy Birthday' to me all by herself. Standing on a chair. Wearing a paper crown. Holding a fork. Only she used to get words wrong all the time—she still does, sometimes—and she sang, 'Hopping Bird Day to You.' It was so funny, but me and my mom and dad were trying not to laugh and hurt her feelings. And ever since then we've always sung 'Hopping Bird Day' on our birthdays."

There was a silence as they all drank their punch. Then Esmeralda said, "That was a good one."

"Yeah, really good," Clarence agreed.

And at that moment, they heard something. It was the squeak of a foot on the step up to the front bench of the caravan. Then came the sound of Soggy Biscuit being hitched to the caravan. The horse whinnied and a moment later the wheels began to turn.

"Party's over," said Frederick, yawning.

"Good night, everybody," said Esmeralda.

Clarence blew out the candle. Sullivan put away the gramophone and lay down in his bunk, pulling up the blanket. During the party he had been truly happy for the first time since being locked inside that trunk. But talking about his old life had brought it all back to him, so that the pain of homesickness, which had subsided to a dull throb, grew sharp again. He missed his sister, Jinny. He missed his mother and his father. He missed Manny Morgenstern and the Stardust Home. But at the same time, he realized that he had never had such close friends as he did now in the caravan. It was a strange thought, but it was true.

* 21 *

JUST as a book does not truly come alive until someone opens it and begins to read, so a performer needs an audience. A few days after the old life party, they found themselves camped beside an abandoned miniature golf course. It still had its worn plastic grass, a little bridge, even a windmill, although two of the wooden blades were broken off. There were some clubs and balls lying about and Frederick and Esmeralda immediately began to play. Master Melville didn't seem

very happy to see the golf course and cursed under his breath. Sullivan had noticed that he never liked anything that looked as if it had been built in the last fifty years.

The land around the course was flat and boring. Sullivan watched Esmeralda miss the ball, laugh at herself, and then ask Frederick to show her how to hold the club. "Let's play too," he said to Clarence.

"Listen, Dex," Clarence pronounced slowly, ignoring his suggestion. "I think you're ready."

"Ready? To go on stage, you mean?"

"Not quite, Dex. You're ready to show the act to the Monsters Melville. I'll go and tell them."

"This moment? Without warning me? Without practice?"

"You've been practicing for days. No point in giving you time to get nervous."

"It doesn't take me any time to get nervous. I can get nervous in a second. I'm nervous right now. My knees are shaking."

"Good. You don't want *not* to be nervous, either. I'll be back."

With a sinking stomach, Sullivan watched Clarence approach Master Melville, who listened to him, nodded, and walked over to his wife. Then Melville shooed the other performers — except for Clarence,

the "director"—into the caravan. A moment later, Master and Mistress were walking toward Sullivan, Clarence at their side.

Sullivan closed his eyes and wished that he would disappear. It was a childish wish, he knew, but he wished it anyway.

He opened his eyes. And saw them standing in front of him.

"Don't dawdle," said Mistress peevishly, not even looking at him. Sullivan always had the impression that it annoyed her immensely to have to acknowledge his existence. "I don't want to stand here all day."

"Yes, get on with it," said Master Melville.

"Right," said Clarence. "I'll just set things up on the grass as if it were the stage. Come on, Sullivan, go to your starting place offstage."

Sullivan watched as Clarence went to get the balls and other objects and arranged them on the ground.

"Monty," said Mistress. "Fetch me a chair."

"Of course, my petunia, how thoughtless of me."

They waited as he hurried to the side of the caravan, picked up a folding chair, and brought it back. Mistress Melville looked down at it a moment, as if it might not be clean enough, and finally sat. Sullivan looked with a surge of panic over to Clarence, who nodded, signaling him to begin.

And so he began. He wished Mistress Melville were playing her instruments—the afternoon felt absolutely silent as he pretended to wander onto the stage and then notice the balls lying there. He picked one up, another, then acted as if he meant to throw one away but found himself catching it again. He kicked the third ball on the ground, actually lifting it up into the air. And then he was juggling all three, his throwing a little off so that he had to lunge to catch a stray ball here and there, but fortunately, that could be seen as an intentional part of his "accidental" juggling routine.

The rest of the act went well enough, though he felt as if he were in a dream. He forgot most of what Esmeralda had taught him about acting. At last he performed his final spin, caught the toaster, rubber boot, and china pig, and took a bow.

There was a moment of total silence. And then Master Melville stood up and began to clap vigorously. "Bravo!" he said. "Well done. An excellent routine. Amusing and original. The boy comes off as very likable. I take my hat off to both of you."

Sullivan turned to Clarence, who looked visibly relieved. Clarence looked back at him and grinned.

Mistress stood up. "Drop the clubs," she said.

"What's that, my beloved?"

"The clubs. They aren't different enough. They bored me to tears. Get rid of them."

"Of course, you're right as always. Once more your keen artistic eye proves itself. But without them, the act will be too short. The boy needs something else instead."

Mistress Melville shook her head with impatience. "Torches," she said flatly.

Sullivan heard the word with alarm. "Torches? You mean, as in *fire?*"

"Of course I mean flaming torches. What good would they be if they weren't on fire? The audience always enjoys feeling a little terror on behalf of the performer. The boy can make his debut in three days."

"That might be a little soon, my sweet——"

"It isn't soon enough, in my opinion. It's about time he started to earn his keep."

At that she stood up, knocked over the chair, and walked away. Master Melville picked it up and hurried after her. Immediately, Sullivan went over to Clarence.

"Torches? There's no way I'm juggling fire."

"It's not that hard," Clarence said. "It's just like clubs. You just have to make sure you don't grab the wrong end."

❊

Sullivan did not know where Master Melville found three juggling torches, but the next day they were on Sullivan's bunk. They had obviously been used before, the ends scorched from having been lit many times. The handles were just like those on his clubs, but the rest looked kind of like a giant match, with a bulb at the end. Clarence instructed Sullivan to juggle them unlit first, to get used to their weight and feel. Luckily, they felt a lot like his clubs, and it took him only a half hour or so to feel comfortable with them. Then Clarence showed Sullivan how to dip the bulb end of each torch into a bowl of liquid fuel, carefully shaking off the excess.

"That fuel's dangerous stuff, so be careful. Now go ahead and light one."

"*You* light one," Sullivan said. "I don't want to."

"Well, I don't want to, either. You're the juggler."

Sullivan gave Clarence a dark look and picked up the box of matches. He struck one and then held it to the bulb of a torch. Immediately it whooshed into flame, causing him to hold it as far away from himself as he could. When the fire had calmed a little, he touched the first torch to the second and third, and they, too, whooshed into flame, flickering and hissing.

"Remember," Clarence said. "Stay in control. Don't

try any moves that you can't do perfectly every time. And don't worry. I've got a bucket of water to throw on you just in case."

"Very comforting," Sullivan said. He placed his feet, held the flaming torches, breathed in and out, and began.

He was juggling fire.

He could feel the heat from the torches on his face as they passed up or down. Slowly, Sullivan relaxed, falling into the rhythm of the routine.

"Hey, this is kind of fun," he said.

"Not too fun, I hope," Clarence replied. "Don't forget that you're playing with fire. *Really* playing with fire, I mean."

For two whole days, Sullivan practiced with the torches. He practiced lighting them, juggling them, and extinguishing them, over and over. If he forgot some safety measure, such as moving away from the bowl of fuel before starting to juggle, Clarence would stop him.

"Remember how you used to balance a club on your nose?" Clarence asked. "Well, a torch is really just a club."

"This is where I draw the line," Sullivan said. "I am *not* balancing a torch on my nose."

"It's your choice."

"You know I'm going to try, don't you?"

"Yes, I do," Clarence said, and smiled.

❋

On the day of his first performance on stage, Sullivan practiced all morning, running through the act over and over. Badly. He dropped balls, he dropped the toaster, he even let a flaming torch land between his feet and jumped away, yelping. Then it was time for lunch. After lunch, he went into the bushes and threw up.

Esmeralda brought him a cup of water and a towel. "It's normal," she said, putting her hand on his arm and walking him back toward the caravan. "On the day of my first show, I fainted three times."

"Maybe ball boy isn't meant for the stage," said Frederick, who was leaning against the caravan and spreading a deck of cards along the length of his arm. With a flick of his shoulder he made the first card turn over, flipping all the rest.

"He'll do great," Clarence said, patting Sullivan on the back. But Sullivan wasn't so sure. What if Clarence and Esmeralda were wrong and Frederick was right? What if he didn't have what it takes? The talent, the courage, the ambition—whatever it was that made a person a real performer. His stomach churned.

He ran for the bushes again.

Soon it was time to prepare for the performance. He and Clarence lowered the side of the caravan to make the stage, and put up the curtain and the wings. Frederick ironed his tuxedo and loaded the pockets. Esmeralda did her stretching exercises.

Clarence had to sew up a tear in Napoleon's jacket. "Some little kid poked it with a stick yesterday while I was in the middle of the game," he said. "But the worst thing is that it's just getting too tight in there. I might not be very big, but I'm still growing. I can hardly breathe."

"What's going to happen when you're too big to fit in it?" Sullivan asked.

"Good question."

Just then Frederick called out, "I see the first mark!"

Sullivan shaded his eyes against the sinking sun. The stage was set up in a meadow strewn with tiny white flowers. In the distance was a fence with a stile —a set of steps on either side for climbing over. He saw four figures wait their turn to go over the stile. As they began to cross the meadow, more people approached.

The other performers scrambled to their places. Sullivan shook himself, whispered "Help me" under his breath, and hurried to the wing.

* 22 *

AN ADVANCED IDEA

(M)ANNY Morgenstern used his cane to open the door of the telephone booth. He stepped out to where Jinny was waiting for him. She was sitting on the grass at the side of the road, hunting for four-leaf clovers. They needed luck, and finding one was the best way she could think of to get some.

The eighty-one-year-old man and the six-year-old girl had been on the road now for over four weeks. In that time, spring had turned into early summer. Manny had promised Jinny's parents that they would

come home after two weeks, but Gilbert and Loretta had reluctantly agreed to let them keep looking for a while longer. "I don't think Jinny is ready to give up," Manny had told them on the phone. "She might just run away again." But still they had found nothing. Oh, there was a rumor here and there of a wagon passing in the night, or somebody hearing from a cousin about somebody else seeing an act on a little stage — vague whispers that sent them in a westerly direction — but that was all. They had slept in cheap and not very clean motels, in rented rooms, in dusty attics and damp basements, and a few times in the homes of kindly people who fed them sorely needed home-cooked meals. Every day, Manny had given Jinny a reading and an arithmetic lesson.

The telephone booth was outside a general store called Muckricker's Feed and Supply. The store was on the edge of a town called Perlitsky, population three hundred and seventy-five. Manny had just phoned Gilbert and Loretta, letting them know that he and Jinny were all right and not to worry. Still, Jinny's parents both said that it might be time to come home. In truth, Manny wasn't so sure they were all right. They were tired, they both had blisters on their feet, Jinny was having nightmares and missed her parents, and Manny was having chest pains. After hanging up, he

had phoned the police department and had spoken to Officer Spoonitch. "It's official," the police officer had said with regret in his voice. "Drowning, no body recovered. The Mintz case is closed. I'm sorry."

Jinny didn't find any four-leaf clovers. Finally, she pulled a three-leaf clover out of the ground and split one of the leaves in two. If she couldn't find luck, she decided, then she would have to make it. She saw Manny emerge from the booth and asked, "What did the police say? Are they going to send a bunch of heli-crappers?"

"No helicopters right now," Manny said. He looked through the window of the general store and saw that it had an old-fashioned counter with stools and a soda fountain. "I think we could use a pick-me-up," he added. "How about we go inside and have ourselves a couple of vanilla milk shakes?"

"I like strawberry," Jinny said.

"Strawberry it is."

So they went through the door and up to the counter, and Manny helped Jinny get up onto a stool. The man behind the cash register came over, put on an apron, and said, "What can I get for you?" He was thin and had a crooked nose and a comb-over, his hair long on one side and so he could sweep it over to cover his bald spot.

"One vanilla milk shake and one strawberry," Manny said.

"Coming right up."

While the man made their milk shakes, they looked around. The store had shovels and rakes hanging from the ceiling, pots and pans on the shelves, batteries, snow boots, and just about anything else you could think of. By the counter was a bulletin board where people had posted notices. There were two for lost dogs, one with a pasted-on photograph of a tractor that was for sale, another offering yoga classes. Jinny sounded out some of the words that she could see from her perch on the stool.

The man put their milk shakes on the counter. They were in tall, cold glasses, with long spoons.

"Delicious," said Jinny.

"Mmm," agreed Manny.

For a while they slurped in silence. Then Jinny said, "Manny, remember I told you about the medicine show?"

"Of course," said Manny.

"And that the people on stage were kids? The boy who did magic and the smaller boy with the dogs and the girl on the piperope — I mean, tightrope."

"Sure, I remember."

"Where do you think they came from?"

"I don't know."

"They must have moms and dads too, right? And Mannys."

"I'm not sure about the Manny part, but sure, they must have parents." Manny nodded slowly. "I understand what you're saying. Maybe those kids disappeared, too. And their parents are also trying to find them. Or have given up. But those parents are out there and maybe they know something. So we should find them. That's brilliant, Jinny."

Jinny smiled. "I know," she said. "I'm very advanced for my age."

❋

At many schools these days the office is a hive of activity. Students come in to make announcements over the PA system, to help the secretaries, to plan assemblies and special events. They feel at home, as if the office, like the rest of the school, truly belongs to them.

But in some schools that have not changed with the times, the office is still a place where students go for only one of three reasons. They need a late slip, they need to leave early, or they are in trouble. Beanfield Middle School was, unfortunately, one of these schools.

Norval Simick had never gone to the office before.

And he had never wanted to. But now he sat on the hard wooden bench that faced the counter behind which the secretaries worked. He felt his knees shaking.

Beside him sat Samuel Patinsky. Samuel *had* been in the office before — nine times, in fact. Each time he'd been sent there by a teacher for not doing his homework, or for throwing pencils, or (in one instance) for dangling the guts of a dead frog in a girl's face during science class. But he'd never before gone to the office *voluntarily,* and he was more nervous this time than he had ever been.

Norval and Samuel had come prepared. In Norval's hand was a folder filled with twelve pages describing their plans for a Sullivan Mintz Celebration Day. The two of them had worked together, after school and on weekends, for hours.

One of the secretaries leaned over the counter. "All right, you two," she said without smiling. "Mr. Washburb will see you in his office. Hurry up now — he's a busy man."

Norval nodded his determination at Samuel, and Samuel nodded back. Then they got up and marched single file into the principal's office. Norval entered first and reached out to shake Principal Washburb's hand. The principal looked surprised, but he half rose

out of his chair and took Norval's hand in his own. Samuel did the same. Then they sat down.

"Well, well," said Mr. Washburb. "It's been a while since you've had to come to my office, Samuel. As for you, ah, Norval," he said, looking down at a sheet of paper, "I'm sorry to see you getting into trouble for the first time. Now tell me what you two did to get sent here. Lit a stink bomb? Wrote something nasty on the board?"

"No, you've got it wrong," Norval said, leaning forward. "Nobody sent us. We came on our own."

"That's right," Samuel said.

"I see. You want to turn yourselves in."

"No, that's not it, either," Norval insisted. "We're not in trouble. We haven't done anything wrong. We're here with a proposal."

"That's right, a proposal," Samuel concurred.

"Hmm, I see. Rather unusual. All right then, what is it that you propose?"

Norval motioned to his partner, and Samuel took a deep breath. "We'd like to hold a Sullivan Mintz Celebration Day."

"The boy who drowned?"

"Yes," Norval said. "We don't want him to be forgotten. He went to this school. He belonged here, or at least he should have. We want to hold a special day —"

"A special day, you say? You mean, a whole day?"

"That's right, Principal Washburb. A day remembering and celebrating Sullivan. Here, it's all laid out in these plans." Norval slid the folder across the desk.

Principal Washburb used two fingers to open the folder. "Hmm," he muttered as he looked over the top of his glasses. He scanned the first page, turned it, looked at the next, and so went through all twelve pages. "You've done a lot of work. A great deal of work." He closed the folder and picked it up. Then he opened a desk drawer, dropped the folder into it, closed the drawer, and locked it with a little key. "I don't know what you're trying to pull here."

"Pardon me?" Norval said.

"Obviously this is some kind of stunt to humiliate me and the school. So let me assure you, there will be no Solomon Mint Celebration Day."

"That's *Sullivan Mintz*," said Samuel. "And why not?"

"Remembering a boy who died? Even if you weren't trying to pull something, how is that going to help anybody learn their times tables or know who won the War of 1812? It's just going to upset the student body. Make people depressed. Besides, I know for a fact that almost nobody in this school even remembers him. Listen, you two. It's almost summer vacation. The school

year will be over soon. By next fall this unfortunate incident will have completely vanished from the students' thoughts, which is just the way I want it. Now the two of you had better get back to your class before I find another reason for you to be here."

And before they knew it, Norval and Samuel were back in the hallway, walking slowly to class. "We should have known Washburb would say no," Samuel said. "He doesn't care. Nobody does."

"No, that isn't true. People do care. Or, they will."

"Come on, Norval, it's over. Let's just forget about it."

Norval grabbed Samuel's hefty arm and pulled him to a stop. "No, we're not going to forget about it. This is about Sullivan. It's *for* Sullivan."

"What are we going to do?" Samuel asked.

"We're going to have Sullivan Mintz Celebration Day, that's what. With or without permission. And soon."

Frowning, Samuel looked down at Norval. But slowly his frown turned into a grin. "Oh, yeah," he said. "I like the sound of that."

❋

Gilbert and Loretta agreed to let Manny and Jinny stay out for one more week. With their help, Manny placed a classified advertisement in hundreds of small newspapers across the country.

HAVE YOU LOST YOUR CHILD?

Has your son or daughter gone missing? Did he or she like to do magic tricks, or walk on a tightrope, or perform in some other way? Did he or she vanish without a trace? If so, please contact Gilbert and Loretta Mintz at the Stardust Home for Old People in the town of Beanfield.

For the next few days, Manny and Jinny continued to look for Sullivan. They showed his picture to people in stores and on the sidewalks. They asked if anyone had seen an old-fashioned wagon or heard about a medicine show.

Then one afternoon nearly a week after the advertisements went out, as the pair walked down the main street of another small town, Manny said, "Now, listen, Jinny. You have to understand that this ad might not bring us any closer to finding Sullivan. I guess there are a lot of missing children out there because your parents have been overwhelmed with responses. But so far, none of the people's stories have matched the pattern of Sullivan's disappearance. This idea might just lead us to another dead end."

"But we still might hear from somebody whose

story does match," Jinny said. "We're not going to give up yet, right?"

"No, of course not," Manny replied, a little sadly. "And it's still early. We don't have to give up hope."

But the truth was that Manny didn't have much hope left. They had been looking for a long time, without success, and they were worn out. Jinny needed to be with her parents. She needed to go back to school and play with other kids. At this point, the most he hoped for was a way to help Jinny find some sense of peace and acceptance before they returned to Beanfield and got on with their lives.

"You know," Manny said, "just because we can't find Sullivan, doesn't mean he isn't out there somewhere. Maybe he's fine. Maybe he's thinking about us, too. Of course, there's still a chance your parents will uncover some new clues because of our advertisement. Then the case could be reopened, and the police will take over. Either way, the time has come for us to go home, Jinny. We've made some progress and done our best, and I have a feeling that, wherever he is, Sullivan would be just so proud of you."

Jinny didn't say anything, but for the first time she didn't argue against going home. Instead, she took Manny's hand and they kept walking.

* 23 *

THE FIRST TIME

THE first time for anything can have a powerful significance. A child's first step, a teenager's first kiss, an adult's first day at work. It's true that people don't remember most of their firsts, and some of them they'd rather forget. But as Sullivan stood there in the wings behind the curtain and peeked out, he knew that this was a night he would never forget as long as he lived. What it would mean to him—that, he couldn't know.

Sullivan saw a family of four approaching the stage. Then a couple of teenagers, some men by themselves

with their hands in their pockets, a young man with a young woman holding a bunch of wildflowers. Then more families, kids jostling against one another on the grass, until there were thirty or forty in the crowd pressed in front of the caravan stage.

The lanterns on either side cast their light onto the faces waiting for the show to begin. Sullivan peeked out again, although he had been told more than once by Frederick that it was unprofessional. He could feel his whole body trembling. His breathing was quick and shallow. Master Melville had scheduled him last so that he could make a point of introducing him for the first time ever, which meant that Sullivan had to watch everyone else before he could get his own act over with. If he could have thought of some way to get out of going on at all, he would have done it. But he had stopped throwing up, and even though he had felt faint once or twice, he hadn't managed to get himself to black out.

And then there was that small part of him that *wanted* to go on. That wanted to see if he really could perform in front of an audience. That wanted to see if they *liked* him.

Esmeralda came up and kissed him on the cheek. "You'll be great, I know you will. Try to relax and enjoy yourself."

"Enjoy myself?"

"That's right, Dex," said Clarence, coming up behind him. "The audience can't enjoy your act unless you do. Just keep focused. And remember, a mistake isn't the end of the world. There isn't any such thing as perfection. Just smile and keep going."

Sullivan had been warned about perfection before, but at the moment he couldn't remember when. He felt a push against his shoulder. It was Frederick. "Don't block my way when I have to go on, ball boy. Try not to be too big a disaster. I don't want to have to mop up after you."

"After me?"

"Why do you always repeat what I say? Master Melville told me that if you bomb I have to hurry onto the stage and do some more tricks so they don't go away without buying any Hop-Hop Drops. So *try* not to stink, all right?"

Oh, great, thought Sullivan. As if he wasn't feeling enough pressure. And then there was Mistress Melville, who didn't say anything but glared at him from behind her drum and washboard and banjo-ukulele as she took her position beside the stage. It felt as if her dark eyes bored right through him.

Then she began to play her introductory tune, beginning with a low rumble on the drum, then a hypnotic rhythm on the washboard, then an accompanying

strum on the banjo-ukulele, and finally the melody on the kazoo. From the opposite wing, Master Melville entered the stage with a welcoming sweep of his arms. He smiled and laughed and joked and winked, making friends with the audience, and then introduced Frederick, who, once again, shoved Sullivan's shoulder as he went by.

Maybe there wasn't such a thing as perfection, Sullivan thought, but Frederick sure looked as if he performed every illusion flawlessly. He received loud applause from the crowd. Next came the chess-playing Napoleon, who did battle against a man who said that he was a high school mathematics teacher. The game went back and forth, one moment the man winning a bishop, the next Napoleon knocking over a knight. But at last Napoleon was victorious, and as his bells rang, and his wooden hand pinched his three-corner hat and raised it up and down, the crowd whooped.

Paralyzed by the thought of having to go on soon, Sullivan momentarily forgot his job following the automaton's performance. He had to run to the back of the stage and pull out Clarence, who was half fainting from lack of oxygen. "I can't . . . I can't do it anymore," he said. "I've grown too much." But he had no time to recover, only to wipe the sweat from his face and prepare Snit and Snoot for their act.

And despite his exhaustion, Clarence's dog act went wonderfully. The audience laughed from beginning to end. Was everyone especially brilliant and talented tonight, or did it just seem so to Sullivan? He felt his heart race even faster as Esmeralda performed on the tightrope, knowing that he was next. He didn't know how someone could be so lovely and graceful *and* funny *and* silly all at the same time, but somehow Esmeralda was.

As soon as the curtain closed, Frederick took down the tightrope and Clarence began to set out Sullivan's juggling props. Master Melville came out in front of the curtain.

"Ladies and gentlemen, what a positive smorgasbord of talent you have seen tonight. Young people at the pinnacle of their peculiar art forms. And in a moment I will have the honor of offering you the effective relief of Master Melville's Hop-Hop Drops at only ten dollars a bottle. But our show is not over, no sir. First, we have for you an extraordinarily special event. An artist so fresh, so young, so inexperienced that he has never before graced this or any other stage. But an artist who I sincerely believe is destined for the greatest triumphs. You, ladies and gentlemen, are witnessing the birth of a star. May I present, for the first time ever, *Dexter, the Accidental Juggler!*"

Sullivan didn't move. He knew that he was supposed to; he just couldn't get his feet to work. He felt a hard shove against his back — he knew without thinking that it was Frederick — and found himself stumbling onto the stage. A few chuckles came from the crowd. He regained his composure and did what he had practiced, whistling as he pretended to walk down a street. He passed the three balls, kept going, stopped, backed up. He looked at the balls. Then he looked at the audience.

The audience laughed.

He could see only the first row of upturned faces in the lantern light, but the laughter made him a little less nervous. He picked up one ball, felt its weight in his hand. Suddenly it was in the air and he had to reach out and — yes — snatch it. He smiled at the audience, as if to say, *I sure never expected to catch it.* He picked up the second ball, felt the two in his hands, threw one into the air, and then, looking shocked, threw the other. A moment later, he had kicked up the third.

He did not drop a ball, did not even fear that he would. And when the audience gasped with delight or laughed or held their breath, it felt completely natural to him, as if their reaction was the only thing that had ever been missing. He finished the ball routine by toss-

ing them so high that they flew right over the caravan (where Esmeralda would gather them up).

The rings came next. And after them the toaster, the rubber boot, and the china pig. They had been set on a little table with a sign saying GARAGE SALE leaning against it. He picked up the boot first, then looked around for the other but couldn't find it. So he picked up the toaster and pushed down the lever. He put the boot and the toaster under one arm, and picked up the china pig. He shook it near his ear to hear if there was any money inside. Nope. He shrugged and was about to put the pig down again when he tripped . . . and threw the pig, the toaster, and the boot up in the air.

And kept throwing them. A look of confusion on his face, he walked about the stage. He tried to put the objects down, but somehow they kept going up. He spun around and still caught them. He threw them higher and higher, trying to get rid of them, and then — *bang, bang, bang*—one after another they came down into his arms as he fell to the ground.

And got up smiling.

All that was left were the flaming torches. Clarence had directed this part of the act as a little lesson in the danger of playing with matches. Recovering from his encounter with the household objects, Sullivan next

found a box of matches on the ground. He picked them up, looked from side to side to make sure nobody was watching him, and then lit one. He gleefully held up its little flame.

Then he noticed the three torches on the ground. If lighting a match was fun, surely lighting one of these big things would be even more fun! With a big smile on his face, Sullivan lit a torch.

Whoosh!

He reeled back from the sudden flame. By accident, he touched it to the other two torches — *whoosh* and *whoosh* again! This was a lot of fire. The expression on Sullivan's face was more than worried. He had to get rid of them somehow. How about throwing them away? But what comes up must come down . . . and a moment later, he was juggling fire.

Because he looked terrified, the audience feared for him. But Sullivan had practiced so much that he knew he would not drop a torch, just as he hadn't dropped anything else in the act, unless it was intentional. And the audience, despite its fear, somehow knew that the boy with the torches would not fail. Not even when he balanced one on his nose. And when at last he threw them all into the air, picked up a bucket of water, and caught each one in it, sizzling as it went out, they whistled and cheered and stamped their feet.

Sullivan put down the bucket. And ran off the stage.

Master Melville caught him in the wing. "Back, dear boy, back you go to take your bow. Don't you hear them? You're a hit! They want to applaud you again! Go!"

And so he walked out and, blinking rapidly as if awaking from a dream, he heard the applause and shouts and saw the smiling faces below.

He bowed three times and ran off again, not stopping until he was safely on the other side of the caravan, in the dark. A moment later Clarence and Esmeralda were congratulating him, hugging him and telling him how well he had done.

"I'm so proud of you," Esmeralda said, surprising him with a hug. "You were so totally wonderful. I couldn't take my eyes off you."

"Fantastic, Dex," Clarence said. "You really pulled it off. That was three times better than any rehearsal. The audience really pushed you to your best. That's what happens to a real performer. Tomorrow I'll give you some notes, just little things that might be improved. But really, you don't need me anymore. You're way beyond anything I know."

And then Frederick came up to him. He put out his hand and Sullivan shook it. "Good show," Frederick said, and walked away.

What Sullivan felt at that moment would have been impossible for him to describe. A great tingling excitement through his whole body. Tremendous relief that it was over. Pride and amazement. Happiness at his friends' affection for him. And, perhaps most amazing of all, a desire — no, a *need* — to do it again.

* 24 *

ROCKING, SHAKING, POINTING

IT was during the dessert course at the Stardust Home for Old People that Elsa Fargo collapsed, sending her bowl of tapioca flying across the room.

It is a simple fact that in a house full of old people there is going to be a regular need for doctors, nurses, and ambulances. While Loretta, who had taken an advanced first-aid course, rushed to Elsa's side, Gilbert was already phoning 911. Within minutes the paramedics were carrying their equipment into the dining room as the other residents looked on.

Elsa's sister, Rita, stayed by her side. The younger sister (she was only seventy-eight) held Elsa's hand while the paramedics carefully put their patient on the stretcher. "You've got to be all right," Rita said, still holding her hand. "You just have to, Elsa."

"Oh, I'll be fine," Elsa said weakly. "I'm not dying yet. Not until Sullivan comes home. You hear that, Loretta? Gilbert?"

"We hear you," Loretta said, wiping away a tear.

After the ambulance was gone, the rest of the residents shuffled back to their rooms. Nobody watched television or played cards. When the telephone rang, Gilbert answered. It was a nurse at the hospital, saying that Elsa was all right and could come home tomorrow. Gilbert went straight to Rita's room to tell her the good news.

It was another hour before Gilbert and Loretta could retire to their own apartment. Loretta opened up the account books and began to sort through a pile of bills. Gilbert picked up his knitting but just held it in his lap.

"More than two months," Gilbert said. "It's been more than two months since Sullivan disappeared."

"And Jinny and Manny have been gone for weeks," Loretta said.

"It's unbearable," said Gilbert.

"Yes."

"And now we're getting all these calls from other parents whose children have gone missing, because of the classified ad. And so far, not one of them fits the pattern," Gilbert went on.

"So many missing children. And each of their parents still hoping to find them."

"Do you—do you think he's alive, Loretta?"

His wife paused. "I don't know. I suppose there's a difference between what I believe and what I *want* to believe. I know that I want to believe he's all right."

"And if he is alive, what do you think Sullivan's doing? Right now, I mean."

"I don't know. Missing us, I suppose. I only hope he's not too lonely or too miserable. I hope there's something good for him out there."

They lapsed into silence. It was late and they were tired and ought to have gone to bed. But neither of them moved.

❋

That night, Norval didn't sleep much. Mostly, he stared up at the ceiling and thought about Sullivan. He had this strange feeling that he and Samuel and Sullivan were in this together, like the Three Musketeers. Or the Three Stooges, maybe. Which made no sense, because Sullivan was gone. And how strange

and pathetic, he thought, that it had taken Sullivan's death for him and Samuel Patinsky to become friends. If only Sullivan were around, just think what fun the three of them could have together. And how happy Sullivan would be. Instead of being picked on, he'd have another friend.

"I wish you were here, Sullivan," Norval said into the darkness.

Finally, he fell asleep. But at the sound of the alarm clock he jumped out of bed, tripped while trying to put on his pants, and tried so hard to pretend that everything was normal at breakfast that both his parents asked him if something was wrong.

He walked to school feeling as if some other personality had taken over his body. As he approached the front doors he saw Samuel waiting for him on the top step.

"Jeez," Samuel said. "You look like you're about to puke."

"I think I *am* about to puke. I've never done anything like this before."

"*Nobody* has ever done anything like this before."

"I mean, I've never gotten into trouble."

"Well, you're going to get into trouble now. Big-time. You prepared for that?"

Samuel looked hard at Norval. Norval felt drops of sweat break out on his forehead, but he said, "Yes. I'm ready."

"All right then. We meet in the caf at lunch."

"Got it."

All Norval could do that morning was watch the clock. For him, the school day had always passed quickly, but today it crept along like a melting glacier. At last, the lunch bell rang. He went to his locker, pulled out his backpack, and headed for the cafeteria. The cafeteria doubled as an auditorium and there was a stage at one end. It was already crowded with kids lining the tables, and at first he couldn't see Samuel. But there he was, standing in front of the stage.

"Let's do it," Samuel said.

Norval looked over his shoulder to check for teachers and then pulled himself up onto the stage. Luckily, he had been a member of the crew for the most recent school musical, *Beans, Beans, Beans!* He slipped behind one of the curtains and used a rope to lower one of the flies that were used to hold up scenery. Once it was on the ground, he opened his backpack and unrolled the banner.

Norval and Samuel had made the banner together. Three bed sheets stitched end to end, it was

an impressive six feet high and twenty-four feet long. Attached to its top at two-foot intervals were ties made from shoelaces, and now Norval used them to attach the banner to the fly, scrambling on his knees across the stage. Panting from both exertion and fear, he looked around for Samuel.

He was there, all right. Holding the principal's microphone in his hand. He gave Norval a thumbs-up.

"Here goes," Norval said, feeling as if he was about to seal his own fate. He went to the other side of the stage, counted to three, and then, as quickly as he could, hauled up the fly.

The banner unfolded perfectly. Next, he opened the curtains. Immediately, students began to notice it — how could they not, it was so large. They whispered, giggled, pointed. The red letters were enormous.

The unofficial, against-the-rules, fantastic SULLIVAN MINTZ CELEBRATION DAY!!!

"*Yes, ladies and gentlemen,*" Samuel shouted into the microphone as he strode to the front of the stage.

Everyone turned to look at him, and somebody called out, "Way to go, Patinsky!"

Samuel waved. "That's right. Today we're going to

celebrate the life of Beanfield student Sullivan Mintz. And we're going to start it off . . . by *dancing!* Do it, Norval!"

Norval had almost forgotten the next step! He tripped across the stage to the sound console. Samuel had already plugged in his MP3 player; all Norval had to do was press play. He turned the volume all the way up, hit the button, and the cafeteria shook with the beat of drums and the wail of electric guitars. When he turned, he saw Samuel actually starting to dance. Right on stage, by himself, rocking his big body, shaking his butt, pointing his index fingers out at the other students, all with an enormous grin on his face. Norval couldn't help laughing out loud. The lunchroom aides were laughing, too. *Man,* he thought, *if only Sullivan could see this.* More unbelievably, some of the students—girls, mostly—started swaying to the music. Then *they* started dancing! And then a few boys joined in!

"Yeah, baby, get down!" Samuel growled into the microphone. "Now, who's got a memory of Sullivan they want to share? I mean, he was a student here, right? He went to class with us, walked the halls. Some of you must have something to say. Don't be shy."

At that moment, Norval saw something that made

him freeze. Principal Washburb was moving up the aisle. Norval could see that he was shouting, but it was impossible to hear him over the music.

Washburb was having trouble getting through the dancing crowd. Somebody even elbowed him in the nose, knocking his glasses sideways. Turning again, Norval saw a girl pull herself up onto the stage. He recognized her; she was in the grade below them and always wore her hair in a ponytail. The girl took the microphone.

"At the beginning of the year," she said, "my dog died. He was old, but it was still really sad. I was crying at my locker and this boy came up and asked me if I was okay. I showed him a photograph and he said that it must have been a really great dog. He was just sweet to me, that's all. He made me feel better. I never even knew his name until I saw his picture in the paper. It was Sullivan Mintz. He was really nice. I guess I just want to say, 'Thanks, Sullivan, wherever you are.'"

The girl's eyes were shining. Quickly she gave the microphone back to Samuel and jumped down into the dancing crowd. "Yes, he was!" Samuel shouted, taking back the microphone. "Sullivan Mintz was a nice guy and we'll never forget him!"

"Sullivan Mintz forever!" somebody shouted.

"Sullivan Mintz forever!" the crowd shouted back.

Everyone danced.

Principal Washburb finally reached the stage. He hauled himself up, caught his breath, and marched over to Samuel.

"You and your buddy are in for a world of pain," he bellowed.

Samuel just kept on dancing.

* 25 *

LETTING GO

S ULLIVAN performed the following night and the one after that. Each time he grew a little more confident, of his juggling and his acting ability both. He started to sense more clearly the response from the audience — anticipation, fear, amazement. He could even tell when their attention lagged once or twice, although he hadn't yet figured out how to tighten up those moments.

Everything seemed different to Sullivan now. He wasn't just a bystander, somebody watching from the

wings while the others performed. Now he, too, was a part of the show. When he was helping to set up the stage, he was also setting it up for himself. When he was going to sleep in the caravan, he was as tired from his performance as Esmeralda, Frederick, and Clarence were from theirs. When Master Melville sat down for dinner and said, "Eat up, my dears. You'll need your strength," he was talking to Sullivan, too.

And in small, subtle ways, the others treated him differently as well. Coming off the stage, Frederick didn't insult him anymore. Instead he would say things like, "It's an easy audience tonight," or "Watch out for the heckler in the second row." Esmeralda always noticed and complimented him when he did something particularly well. And Clarence, who had been his director, now talked to him like a fellow performer. Sullivan couldn't help marveling at all the changes.

After his fourth performance, as he gathered up props, Sullivan noticed that the line to buy bottles of Hop-Hop Drops was longer than usual. Could it possibly have anything to do with his act? As he stood watching, he noticed some people in the line looking at him and whispering, as if he were some sort of celebrity. He felt himself blush with pride and turned away to help Frederick bring down the stage.

When the camp had been cleaned up and the last

bottle sold, the other kids brushed their teeth in the field with cups of water. But Sullivan didn't join in or follow them into the caravan. Instead, he remained standing outside, feeling the cool air and watching Master and Mistress count the money and lock it in the metal box. He wasn't sure why he was waiting there. Perhaps he wanted Master Melville to say something more, to tell him again what a hit he had become. But no, it wasn't that. He realized it was Mistress he really wanted to hear from.

Mistress Melville alone had not once complimented his performance. When he came off the stage, he couldn't help looking to see if she had been watching him. But she was always tuning her banjo-ukulele or wiping down her harmonica. He didn't know why it should be important to him, when she was clearly a mean and cold-hearted person. Maybe it was that she was so pale and beautiful that a single kind word from her would mean more than a hundred from someone else.

Master Melville packed up the table and chair while Mistress picked up the money box. Perhaps now was the time he might coax her to say something. Even if all she said was that he wasn't terrible, he thought he would be satisfied.

She began to walk by. Quickly he said in an unnaturally high voice, "It was a good show, wasn't it, Mistress?"

She stopped. And looked at him. "Why are you talking to me, boy?"

"No reason. I was just—"

"And why are you standing there when you should be in the caravan? You're not planning to run again, are you?"

"No, Mistress, I wasn't. I only thought—"

"You thought? Why do you believe that you have a right to think anything? *I'll* be the one to tell you what to think. You had better understand that you are now a part of this medicine show. So get yourself ready for bed. You have to perform again tomorrow. And the night after that and the night after that. This is your life now, boy."

She walked away, the money jingling in the box. Master Melville put out the last lantern, and suddenly, it was dark. Sullivan heard low voices in the caravan, the snorting of the horse, a cricket starting to chirp in the tall grass. Master Melville came up and said quietly, "You must be tired. Time for a much-deserved sleep. Go on with you now." So Sullivan went on. He found his toothbrush and walked to the edge of the

field, where he brushed his teeth. He went behind a tree to pee. He washed his hands and face in the basin that had been left out, then he tossed away the dirty water and clipped the basin to its place underneath the caravan.

He went to the back of the caravan and climbed inside. And then, as Master Melville closed the door and the room went black, and he heard the key in the lock, Sullivan remembered something. He remembered his parents, Gilbert and Loretta. He remembered his sister, Jinny. And Manny, too. He thought of Norval, his one school friend, and even, for some reason, of Samuel Patinsky. And he realized that he had not thought of them all day, not once. He had thought only of his performance on stage. Had looked forward to it, had hoped to succeed more than he had hoped for anything before, and when he had succeeded he gloried in the applause and shouts and praise. In all of that, he had forgotten the people back home. He had forgotten the family that loved him. And forgetting, even for that short time, felt like letting go. It had been a relief, he realized now, not to be missing them all the time.

The caravan began to move. Somebody turned over. Somebody else sighed in his sleep. Sullivan stared

up into the darkness. He had friends — his first real friends, who cared about him and who relied on him. He was good at something that really mattered to him, something that was valued and important and that thrilled him to do. Mistress Melville was right. He was a member of the medicine show. He would keep looking for a way to escape, of course, and eventually he had to get back to his family. But for now, he thought he could be happy here. He'd found a place where he belonged.

✳ ✳

I want to thank my two fine editors, Lynne Missen at Penguin Canada and Lynne Polvino at Clarion Books, for their hints, nudges, and explicit requests, all of which helped to make this a better book. Also thanks to Marie Campbell for shepherding the manuscript to its proper homes. And a final grateful acknowledgment to the Ontario Arts Council for a Works in Progress grant.